THE NORTH AFRICAN
AIR CAMPAIGN

THE NORTH AFRICAN
AIR CAMPAIGN

U.S. Army Air Forces from
El Alamein to Salerno

Christopher M. Rein

UNIVERSITY   PRESS   OF   KANSAS

© 2012 by the University Press of Kansas

Published by the University Press of Kansas (Lawrence, Kansas 66045), which was organized by the Kansas Board of Regents and is operated and funded by Emporia State University, Fort Hays State University, Kansas State University, Pittsburg State University, the University of Kansas, and Wichita State University

Library of Congress Cataloging-in-Publication Data
Rein, Christopher M.
The North African air campaign : U.S. Army Air forces from El Alamein to Salerno / Christopher M. Rein.
    p. cm. — (Modern war studies)
ISBN 978-0-7006-1878-1 (cloth : alk. paper)
1. World War, 1939–1945—Campaigns—Africa, North. 2. World War, 1939–1945—Aerial operations, American. 3. United States. Army Air Forces—History. 4. Africa, North—History, Military—20th century. I. Title.
D766.82.R37   2012
940.54'4973—dc23
2012024110

British Library Cataloguing-in-Publication Data is available.

Printed in the United States of America
10 9 8 7 6 5 4 3 2 1

The paper used in this publication is recycled and contains 30 percent postconsumer waste. It is acid free and meets the minimum requirements of the American National Standard for Permanence of Paper for Printed Library Materials Z39.48-1992.

For my girls:
Krista, Madeleine, Alexandra, and Jocelyn

I don't want you all to be "parrots" and just go along with what my views are on winning the war. It might be that you have different ideas and I would like to hear different ideas. It may be that I am wrong and you can show me where I am wrong.

—Henry H. Arnold, HQ, USAAF Staff Meeting,
1 December 1942

Contents

Acknowledgments   ix

Introduction   1

1. Theory and Doctrine During the Interwar Period   10

2. The Western Desert: Learning with the British, June to
    November 1942   39

3. TORCH and Twelfth Air Force: June to November 1942   67

4. The Tunisian Campaign: November 1942 to May 1943   97

5. The Sicilian Campaign: May to August 1943   135

6. Ploesti and Salerno: August to September 1943   168

Conclusion   195

Appendix 1: USAAF Aircraft in the North African
    Campaign   213

Appendix 2: Air Orders of Battle   221

Notes   239

Bibliography   271

Index   281

Acknowledgments

It is said that success has many parents but failure is an orphan. If this work is judged a success, I would like to acknowledge the many parents who had a hand in its creation.

The roots of any project grow in the intellectual milieu scholars create. Therefore, it seems appropriate to first acknowledge several scholars who have profoundly influenced my thinking about warfare in general and combat in the third dimension in particular. Mark Clodfelter and Tami Davis Biddle have both provided sound critiques of strategic bombing theory throughout the twentieth century. Their work gives airmen and scholars an opportunity for serious reflection on airpower's problems and possibilities. Thomas Hughes and David Spires demonstrated that there was much still to be learned from tactical operations in World War II. Dennis Showalter first suggested that the Mediterranean might be a useful venue for a study of air operations. David Mets and Joel S. A. Hayward, both first-rate scholars of airpower, have provided further inspiration with their own works on the period. Mets is the author of a masterful biography of Carl Spaatz, and Hayward's book is a model study of an air campaign. Robert S. Ehlers Jr. has been a thoughtful critic and avid supporter of the project as well.

Other institutions provided more tangible assistance. At the U.S. Air Force Academy in Colorado Springs, Colonel Mark Wells and Colonel John Abbatiello provided their direct support by granting me an opportunity to pursue this project. My strongest professional relationships have grown out of my many contacts at the Academy. At the University of Kansas, Adrian Lewis, as my adviser, and Ted Wilson, Jeffrey Moran, Roger Spiller, and Stephen Dickey, as committee members, made a valuable investment of their precious time to see this project through to completion. I remain grateful for their support and suggestions in making this a far better product than it ever could have been otherwise. At the University Press of Kansas, Michael Briggs and Kelly Chrisman Jacques provided expert assistance in guiding the manuscript through to publication. I am also indebted to the anonymous reviewers for their criticisms, praise, and suggestions.

Archivists at several institutions lent their time and expertise to help find and use the most important resources. At the Clark Special Collections in the Air Force Academy's McDermott Library, Mary Elizabeth Ruwell and John Beardsley provided valuable assistance with their extensive holdings of manuscript collections, including access to the microfilm copies of the Library of Congress's Henry H. Arnold Papers, which spared this scholar much expense. At the Air Force Historical Research Agency, Joe Caver and Sylvester Jackson likewise facilitated my work with their expert knowledge of that archive's many holdings and their patient explanations of its filing system. I am also grateful for the assistance provided by archivists at Utah State University, Syracuse University, the Army War College Library at Carlisle Barracks, Pennsylvania, the Eisenhower Library in Abilene, Kansas, the Library of Congress, and the Marshall Library in Lexington, Virginia. Vance and Sandy Skarstedt and Tom and Nicole Katsikides provided welcome breaks during lengthy and otherwise lonely research trips.

On a personal level, I am forever indebted to my mother, Marilyn Rein, who first encouraged an early interest in history and has nurtured and supported it ever since, and my father, Charles Rein, who taught me, above all else, the value of an education. These are gifts I hope to pass on to my own children. My wife, Beth, has sacrificed much while I was away working on this project, and I am daily inspired by her efforts and the way that she bears all that life throws at her. Krista, Maddie, and Ally gave up a substantial amount of time with their Daddy while he was away at school. I hope that I can repay them in the form of a few more sledding trips and ice cream runs. Jocelyn arrived in the midst of the writing, but her contribution in the form of many uninterrupted hours of peaceful slumber is both noted and appreciated.

THE NORTH AFRICAN
AIR CAMPAIGN

Introduction

This book has, at its core, asked the central question: "How should air forces be employed?" Or, to simplify and focus in a little, "What *should* the U.S. Air Force do?" Of course, this question rests on the underlying assumption that the United States will have an Air Force. Although there are periodic calls for disarmament, or at least some consolidation within the defense establishment, it seems likely that the country will continue to devote at least some fraction of the current $143.4 billion annual allocation to maintaining an Air Force.[1] Therefore, it seems both pertinent and relevant for both the operators of that air force and the citizens of that nation to have a clear objective for their air force. In her study of the rhetoric airmen used to claim what they could accomplish, and the reality of what they have accomplished, Tami Davis Biddle found, "How aircraft might be employed in war—and what they might accomplish—were among the most pressing military questions of the early twentieth century."[2] This is still true in the twenty-first century. Philip Meilinger has observed that "airmen, from any country, have seldom been accused of being thinkers, and precious few have taken up the pen to write down their thoughts on how airpower should be employed in war."[3] This study hopes to contribute to a remediation of that general defect.

The answer to the question, "What *should* the U.S. Air Force do?" requires us first to answer a related question, "What *can* the U.S. Air Force do?" The answer to the first question depends highly on the second, as the service's objective should clearly be attainable. If, for example, a theorist were to suggest that an air force *should* be able to win wars or resolve conflicts independently through strategic attack, then that theorist should be able to demonstrate that an air force *can* win wars or most effectively resolve conflicts by such methods. But, for many, this assertion remains unproven.

Accordingly, to answer our second question, "What *can* the U.S. Air Force do?" we ought to answer a third question, "What *has* the U.S. Air Force done?" For as long as warfare has been studied, theorists have based their observations on historical examples. The master, Carl von Clausewitz, based much of his signal work *Vom Krieg* ("On War") on historical examples from the preceding centuries of European conflict, especially the campaigns of the Napoleonic wars, in which he took part. It therefore seems important that we have a clear and relatively uncontested understanding of what air forces in general, and the United States Air Force (USAF) and its predecessor, the United States Army Air Forces (USAAF) in particular, have been able to accomplish in prior conflicts in order to find an appropriate answer to our central question.

American Airpower in North Africa, 1942–1943

In summer 1942 Axis forces controlled almost the entire southern shore of the Mediterranean Sea, seemingly fulfilling dictator Benito Mussolini's dream of turning the Mediterranean into an Italian lake. From east to west: Vichy French forces were in Morocco, Algeria, and Tunisia; Italy controlled Libya; and combined German and Italian forces had entrenched in front of British positions at El Alamein, less than sixty miles west of Cairo. Only small British forces clinging to tiny bases at Gibraltar and Malta, coupled with their meager and depleted army in Egypt protecting the lifeline to the Suez Canal and Middle East prevented the Axis from consolidating control of the entire theater.

Less than one year later, Axis forces would be expelled from the African continent, losing more than 300,000 highly trained (and thus irreplaceable) troops as well as tanks, trucks, artillery pieces, and airplanes, most in the final, disastrous defeat in Tunisia. After Allied forces landed and assembled in November 1942 and quickly pushed into Tunisia, French colonies in North Africa became so secure that British prime minister Winston Churchill and President Franklin D. Roosevelt hosted a summit conference in Casablanca in January 1943. Despite stalling within sight of their objective, Allied forces waged an attritional battle that ground down the remnants of Generalfeldmarschall Erwin Rommel's once-vaunted Afrika Korps and the bulk of the Axis air strength in the Mediterranean. Equally impressive, the British Eighth Army in the Western Desert uncoiled from its blocking position in Egypt and chased the Axis forces more than one thousand miles, liberating Libya in the process, before joining the forces in Tunisia. By the end of 1943, Allied armies had jumped across the middle sea, capturing Sicily, Sardinia, and Corsica and occupying the Italian boot to a line less than one hundred miles south of Rome, knocking Italy out of the war in the process. This remarkable reversal of fortune marked the first significant triumph—albeit over only a small portion of Hitler's Wehrmacht—by the western Allies and, as both Rick Atkinson and Douglas Porch have argued, provided a proving ground where equipment, tactics, and leaders were refined and prepared for the eventual assault on Hitler's Festung Europa (Fortress Europe).[4]

In addition to highlighting the USAAF's operational accomplishments, this book also seeks to call needed attention to the air campaign itself. In *An Army at Dawn*, the first volume of his award-winning trilogy on World War II in Europe, Atkinson largely ignores the developments within the army's air arm, despite the fact that it was experiencing many of the same growing pains, and grooming future leaders, just as the ground forces were. Likewise, Porch's comprehensive study of the war in the Mediterranean, *The Path to Victory*, although providing some excellent detail on the air forces, must balance discussion of the air campaign with other events in the theater. It is hoped that this book will correct these omissions and provide a more complete understanding of the conditions that led to the Allied victories both in North Africa and the war in general. Ideally, it will serve as an adjunct to, rather than a replacement for, those otherwise excellent studies.[5]

American aircraft, especially heavy bombers, played a significant role in the successful ground campaign in North Africa, severing naval supply lines and driving Axis aircraft from the skies. This model air campaign has been largely neglected by scholars and military professionals, who have preferred to focus on either the ground force's role in the campaign or the growing strategic bomber offensive then gathering steam in Great Britain.[6] That campaign's apparent success against targets on the European continent has led some airmen to believe that the decision to restrict the diversion of assets from the strategic air forces was correct and that the deployment of scarce heavy bomber forces to North Africa in 1942 was a misuse of assets.[7] By carefully analyzing, for the first time, the deep internal struggle over asset allocation at the highest levels of the Allied decision-making process, this book demonstrates that American aircraft in North Africa were, as directed in *Army Field Manual 100-20* (*Command and Employment of Air Power*), issued at the conclusion of the campaign, "properly and profitably employed against enemy sea power, land power and air power."[8]

In the following pages, readers will find a traditional campaign narrative.[9] It seeks to show that, from June 1942 to September 1943, the

U.S. Army Air Forces played a critical role in the effort to clear the Mediterranean of Axis forces and thereby liberate occupied territory. The story begins with the deployment of the Halverson Provisional Detachment to the Middle East in June 1942 to augment the British Royal Air Force there. But rather than immediately attack the Axis forces then threatening Egypt, the United States launched a single, ineffective, and costly raid on the oil refineries near Ploesti, Romania. The narrative ends with the second and more famous raid on that same target on 1 August 1943, which again cost the USAAF heavy casualties and failed to produce the desired results. During the intervening fourteen months, the USAAF was employed in an exclusively *tactical* (or, more correctly, *operational*) role; it also developed and demonstrated a pattern of interservice cooperation that remains at the foundation of American close air support air doctrine today. Despite learning much about how to conduct an operational campaign, the USAAF did not alter its strategic priorities.

The survivors of the first Ploesti raid in June 1942 turned their attention to the Libyan ports of Benghazi and Tobruk, where they augmented British forces seeking to strangle Rommel's army. The bombers inflicted heavy damage and, by denying the Axis forces an end run through the eastern Mediterranean away from Malta, forced Axis convoys back into range of the depleted forces operating from that beleaguered island. In supporting the battle at El Alamein, the Operation TORCH landings in Morocco and Algeria, the major victory in Tunisia, and the invasion of Sicily, American airmen helped decide the course of the campaign. To be sure, they enjoyed a material superiority over the German and Italian air forces in the theater, aided greatly by the concentration of German air assets in defense against the Britain-based bomber offensive, but economic production was not the deciding factor. The best weapons in the world are useless unless operated by trained and motivated individuals following capable leaders. Fortunately, the Allies enjoyed all three in the North African campaign. The rapid advance of the ground forces in the theater, coupled with the simultaneous Soviet successes in the Caucasus and at Stalingrad, removed any potential threat to Allied petroleum resources in the Middle East and ensured that Hitler would never acquire the oil and gasoline he needed to maintain control of Europe.

But the substantial commitment of American aircraft to North Africa was not without detractors. The theater commander, General Dwight D. Eisenhower, repeatedly requested additional heavy bomber assets for North Africa, only to be denied by the Combined Chiefs of

Staff committee, which was being lobbied heavily by air leaders. (The Combined Chiefs of Staff committee, the supreme Anglo-American military authority, comprised the U.S. Joint Chiefs of Staff and the British Chiefs of Staff.) Thus on the few occasions when assets were shifted from the United Kingdom to North Africa, they were earmarked for employment on specific missions, such as the low-level raid on Ploesti in August 1943 that decimated the attacking force.

Reflecting on the campaign years later, U.S. General Omar Bradley claimed, "In southern Tunisia, I had seen what could happen to ground forces when the airmen pursued strategic rather than tactical objectives."[10] Postwar historians picked up on Bradley's and others' complaints and accused the USAAF of neglecting ground and naval forces during the campaign. Such comments, however, betray postwar frustrations with Cold War–era defense budgets and resource allocations while ignoring the USAAF's tremendous *operational* contributions. The USAAF was definitely focused on strategic objectives—a result of theoretical and doctrinal developments during the interwar period—but this obsession did not really begin to impact *direct* support for the surface forces until after the conclusion of the North African campaign; the USAAF continued to provide *indirect* support, in the form of diversion of German assets, throughout the war. (See Chapters 5 and 6.)

The essential elements of an air campaign are conducted at the tactical level, where airmen fly the individual sorties, yet their impact is felt on the operational and strategic levels. The cumulative effects of sustained operations can win air superiority and permit ground and naval forces to exploit this freedom from attack. And in focusing primarily on the senior commanders in the theater, I do not wish to minimize the courage and competence of Allied airmen who flew the missions and manned the extensive network of support forces that kept them in the air. But few individuals had the ability to influence the target selection and resource allocation decisions that determined the course of the campaign and, eventually, the outcome of the war.

Since the end of the war in 1945, airpower scholars have discussed and debated the merits of the Combined Bomber Offensive.[11] The combined Anglo-American strategic bombing campaign against German cities and industrial targets undoubtedly hastened the end of the war, primarily by destroying the German Luftwaffe. It set up the epic invasion across the English Channel and the continued destruction of German petroleum and transportation infrastructures. In the process, Allied bombers devastated urban residential and industrial areas and inflicted massive casualties on noncombatants, causing some to accuse the Allies of surrendering the moral high ground to the Nazis.[12] Western air forces have since renounced the deliberate targeting of civilians in air campaigns and today avoid noncombatant casualties if at all possible. But the complex nature of the modern battlefield, coupled with imperfect intelligence and equipment failures, virtually guarantees that civilian deaths will still occur. This change in itself makes the question of proper employment of air forces even more important.

Yet no amount of carpet-bombing was sufficient to stop the Nazis' murder, torture, and enslavement of innocent European civilians: Many concentration camps and crematories continued to operate until they were liberated by Allied ground forces. In the postwar period, air planners and scholars have periodically asserted that air forces by themselves are capable of winning wars and halting genocide without the commitment of ground forces. This has yet to be proven.[13] What has been demonstrated conclusively is that air forces are an essential part of the joint-force team. Throughout World War II, ground forces and naval forces of all nations advanced only when air forces attained air superiority (and often failed to do so when it was not attained). In the midst of the campaign in North Africa, General Carl Spaatz, the senior American airman in the theater and later the first Chief of Staff of the United States Air Force, observed that "in order for the army to advance . . . the air battle must first be won."[14]

Control of the air has thus become a prerequisite for success in conventional warfare. But airpower cannot win wars alone. Military forces seeking to halt genocide and provide humanitarian relief can do so only by physically occupying the killing grounds. For all its many attributes, airpower's inability to take and hold physical ground makes it less useful compared to ground forces in halting genocide and ethnic cleansing. Yet by facilitating the ground advance in any way they can, even with nonlethal means (such as moving supplies, evacuating casualties, and collecting intelligence), airmen can make their most significant and useful contributions and bring conflicts to quick and successful conclusions. This is the role in which airpower is most "properly and profitably employed."

Sources

Since the end of the war, few new sources have come to light that would fundamentally change our understanding of the USAAF's role in the North African campaign. As a result, little has been written since the official histories were published shortly after the end of the war. Even the German documents captured by the Allies, as well as the publication of memoirs and studies from the Axis perspective, did little to shed any new light. Accordingly, this book uses many of the same resources that were used to compile the official and other histories, including manuscript collections in the Library of Congress and other repositories, and official USAAF/USAF records, stored at the National Archives and Records Administration facility in College Park, Maryland, and the Air Force Historical Research Agency at Maxwell Air Force Base near Montgomery, Alabama. Instead of duplicating the official histories, this book focuses on challenging many of their *conclusions* and correcting their *emphasis*, revealing much of the less-flattering discussion over the allocation and employment of air assets that significantly impacted their use.

Wesley Craven and James Lea Cate's masterful seven-volume series, *The Army Air Forces in World War II*, remains a valuable resource.[15] Completed just after the war, it took advantage of a central collection of documents, which today are either scattered in various archives or lost to history, and the fresh recollection of events in the minds of many of the subjects interviewed and consulted. Its meticulous accounting of air combat in the theater requires no duplication. Its principal weaknesses are lack of access to or discussion of what were still-classified subjects (such as the importance of Allied code-breaking to the campaign) and the excessive focus on strategic bombing as further justification for the new United States Air Force. This creates the somewhat awkward position of challenging a resource's biases while simultaneously relying upon it for evidence.

In the foreword to a 1983 reprint of the series, Richard Kohn, chief of the Office of Air Force History, acknowledged these biases when he wrote:

> Like all history, *The Army Air Forces in World War II* reflects the era when it was conceived, researched and written. The strategic bombing campaigns received the primary emphasis, not only because of a widely shared belief in bombardment's contribution to victory, but also because of its importance in establishing the United States Air Force as a military service independent of the Army. The huge investment of men and machines and the effectiveness of the combined Anglo-American bomber offensive against Germany had not been subjected to the critical scrutiny they have

since received. Nor, given the personalities involved and the immediacy of the events, did the authors question some of the command arrangements.[16]

Even though a number of historians have already reassessed the role of strategic bombing in relation to the conduct of the war, the topic has continued to dominate scholarship of the air war at the expense of tactical and operational assessments of the USAAF's role.

The most valuable manuscript collections have been those at the Library of Congress, which hold the papers of Henry H. "Hap" Arnold, the Army Air Force's Chief of Staff during the war, and Carl Spaatz, the senior American airman in the European theater, as well as those of his two principal subordinates, Ira Eaker and James H. "Jimmy" Doolittle. The Arnold Papers microfilms were consulted at the Clark Special Collections Branch of the McDermott Library at the U.S. Air Force Academy in Colorado Springs, which in addition holds other significant collections pertaining to the campaign. The Spaatz Papers, which have yet to be microfilmed, are an equally rich trove of documents and reports and are a tremendous resource for airpower historians.

Most of the important letters in the collection of Dwight David Eisenhower's Pre-Presidential papers were published in the mid-1960s under the guidance of editor David Chandler. On several occasions, I took advantage of the University of Kansas's relative proximity to the Eisenhower Presidential Library in Abilene to consult original documents, but I often found it was easier to cite the documents in published form so as to facilitate the work of other scholars. The published volumes are an incredible resource for any student of the campaign and a worthwhile addition to any personal or academic library. The Eisenhower Library's Lauris Norstad collection is another valuable resource for students of the air campaign in the Mediterranean.[17]

On the German side, Karl Gundelach's *Die Deutsche Luftwaffe im Mittelmeer, 1940–1945* (The German Air Force in the Mediterranean, 1940–1945) remains the best single-volume work, thought we still lack an English translation that would make it more widely accessible to scholars. Captured German records, especially those located in the National Archives and Records Administration's Record Group 242, offer insight into German production, allocation, and operational difficulties. The USAF's *The German Air Force Versus the Allies in the Mediterranean*, compiled in the 1950s by General der Flieger Hollmuth Felmy, is also useful, and James Corum's and Williamson Murray's published works on the rise and fall of the Luftwaffe have been especially helpful.[18]

For a theoretical construct, this book leans heavily on the ideas of Carl von Clausewitz. Although the master of military theory never saw an airplane, his ideas have demonstrated permanence despite advances in technology. Such technological leaps prompted the first airpower theorists—among them Giulio Douhet, William "Billy" Mitchell, and Alexander de Seversky—to depart from his earlier work and propose new theories based on perceived technological advantages. After more than a century of manned flight, it seems appropriate to reassess those ideas, as well as the campaigns conducted under their guidance, and to sift through the historical record for any missed evidence that might have provided a viable alternative to prevailing theories. Such an activity might demonstrate that, despite significant technological advancements, the fundamental nature of war has remained largely unchanged.

Theory and Doctrine During the Interwar Period

Since the end of World War II, many scholars have examined the theoretical, doctrinal, and technological developments that enabled the Allies to prevail in the skies. For the U.S. Army Air Forces, the force that entered the war displayed an almost schizophrenic split between body and mind. Even while the USAAF's leadership was firmly committed to the ideas of Giulio Douhet, Billy Mitchell, and Alexander de Seversky, embodied in the Air Corps Tactical School's (ACTS) so-called industrial web theory, the service was still equipped largely with fighter and attack aircraft designed for close support of ground forces. The service had also worked out a viable doctrine for effectively employing these aircraft, embodied in *Field Manual 31-35* (Aviation in Support of Ground Forces), a document that remained in use with only minor modification throughout the war and continues to influence existing doctrine today. Unable to completely demonstrate the value of the strategic mission, and unable to jettison the tactical one, the service evolved after the war into the U.S. Air Force; yet the dichotomy remained, in somewhat reversed fashion. The USAF inventory throughout the Cold War contained primarily aircraft designed to accomplish the strategic mission, but the refinement of a fully developed close support doctrine became the service's greatest, if least appreciated, intellectual asset. As a result of this split, the USAAF entered World War II with the goal of performing a strategic mission but was initially assigned to, and best equipped to execute, an operational campaign.

This dichotomy has led to much confusion among historians ever since. Some who served in or were affiliated with the ground forces have advanced the argument that the USAAF neglected its tactical mission, preferring instead to concentrate on the strategic one. Airpower advocates have countered that this was not a zero-sum game and that the USAAF performed both roles effectively. There is truth to both arguments. Some aspects of the surface campaign, particularly the anti–U-boat offensive, and, later, the invasion of Italy, suffered from shortages and misallocation of assets, especially heavy bombers. But throughout the North African campaign the U.S. Army benefited immeasurably from the USAAF's efforts, even if they were not always visible to the commanders on the front lines. The air superiority and interdiction campaigns enabled ground and naval commanders to operate largely uninhibited by aerial attack and against an enemy whose mobility and effectiveness were increasingly hampered by supply shortages and a lack of tactical mobility. Although the ground advance might have suffered from a lack of air support elsewhere in the latter stages of the war, particularly in the 1943–1945 campaign in Italy (which falls outside the scope of this study), the USAAF provided effective *operational* support throughout the entire campaign in North Africa.

During the war, air and ground commanders understood the word *support* generally to mean close support of the ground forces, either through tactical reconnaissance, air defense over the front lines, or what we know today as close air support (attacking enemy forces immediately opposite the front line). Here I use a broader definition of *support* to include anything that helps the ground and naval forces accomplish their assigned missions. This would include air superiority, as it protects the surface forces from attack, and interdiction well behind the front lines (in World War II parlance: "isolating the battlefield"), as well as reconnaissance and airlift.

Airpower Theory: Douhet, Mitchell, and de Seversky

In the original book *Makers of Modern Strategy*, published in 1943, Edward Warner identified Giulio Douhet, William "Billy" Mitchell, and Alexander de Seversky as the three most influential theorists affecting American air doctrine.[1] (Sir Hugh Trenchard's omission is warranted given the significant differences in British and American strategic theory.)[2] In citing these three disparate personalities, Warner argued that their collective influence had been codified in Army Air Forces doctrine and that they were either directly or indirectly influencing the conflict then under way. Although de Seversky's seminal work, *Victory Through Air Power*, was published the same year as Warner's essay, Warner still managed to capture the essential elements of the thinking of all three men and to place their ideas in proper relation to one another.[3] Through institutions such as the ACTS, these ideas permeated an establishment intent on contributing as much as possible to winning World War II through the skies and on making as strong a case as possible for an independent air force.

DOUHET

In his 1921 publication *Command of the Air*, Douhet outlined a future war uninhibited by any limitations, moral or otherwise. Once airplanes could unleash chemical weapons directly on enemy population centers, ground and naval forces would be useless in a conflict, except to guard airdromes against an enemy breakthrough. As a prelude to this attack, the first and most important goal of an air force was "to conquer the command of the air, that is to prevent the enemy from flying while assuring this freedom for oneself." Once this was achieved, air assets could be hurled at the enemy while completely protecting one's own bases.[4]

Douhet's vision of future war outlined in 1921 was found lacking in World War II. That conflict, however destructive, was not total, in that both sides decided not to use chemical weapons on the battlefield.[5] Although the United States did employ nuclear weapons in the closing stages of the conflict, those bombs were not ready until July 1945, meaning most of the war would be prosecuted with conventional munitions. As a result, Douhet's vision proved flawed, as it posited no roles for aircraft other than to gain command of the skies in order to facilitate chemical attack. Douhet's theory assumed that the static front lines of World War I would be an enduring feature of future wars, but this illusion was shattered by the restoration of mobility in World War II's opening stages.

Another flaw in Douhet's theory: It failed to emphasize the targeting process, which is critical to a successful strategic bombing campaign. Focusing on chemical attacks against enemy cities, Douhet likely saw no need for precise target identification or postmission damage assessment. Air planners during the interwar period who advocated a daylight precision campaign realized that they would have to identify more specific targets. But those same planners had not yet solved the problems of identifying critical nodes in national economic systems and the difficulties in successfully striking individual targets with the equipment currently available in all weather conditions.

By contrast and to his credit, de Seversky had at least realized that visibility would be a critical issue affecting the Combined Bomber Offensive. He likewise understood, after the opening campaigns of World War II, that "the 'panic' that was expected to spread through a city or even a nation as bombs began to fall had turned out to be a myth."[6] As a result, targeting of critical nodes would assume even greater importance.

Another flaw in Douhet's vision assumed a war against an industrialized opponent. Years later de Seversky realized that "total war from the air against an undeveloped country or region is well nigh futile" (as in the case of World War II–era China, for example).[7] Perhaps this was what led Allied leaders to employ heavy bombers in a tactical support role against shipping and airfields, rather than a more strategic role, in the North African campaign. As one historian observed, "In the desert there was no industrial base . . . and bombing sand piles would not break [the enemies'] morale or will to resist."[8] Although this insight did not otherwise play a direct role in World War II, in the years to follow it would play a major role in the way its lessons were applied.

In a concise but accurate summary of Douhet's vision, Williamson Murray found that Douhet posited a central role for bombardment aircraft: "All other missions would detract from this role and thus were considered counterproductive and a misuse of air resources." As a result, "Douhet excluded the possibility of air defense, denied fighter aircraft a place in future air forces, and argued that close air support and interdiction were an irrelevant waste of aircraft." Sadly, some US-AAF leaders shared this vision, establishing an intellectual conflict over resource allocation that would persist throughout the war. Even worse, according to Murray, Douhet "also argued that airpower eliminated the requirement for armies and navies; consequently, there was no need for interservice cooperation." This has been the most damaging legacy of Douhet's flawed vision—and the one most difficult to eradicate in the postwar period.[9]

ACTS AND RAF DOCTRINES

Subscribing to Douhet's twin beliefs that the bomber would be able to penetrate enemy defenses, and that the technological edge bombers enjoyed over fighter aircraft in the mid-1930s would remain, the Air Corps Tactical School began to deemphasize the role of pursuit aviation. In his analysis of the ACTS prewar curriculum, Robert Finney found that "pursuit instruction reached its all-time low during the period from 1934 to 1936." Pursuit was not without its defenders, though. Captain Claire Chennault, the American airman who would become legendary for leading the Flying Tigers in China, argued for the retention and continued importance of pursuit instruction. As an instructor of pursuit tactics from 1931 to 1936, Chennault "fought stubbornly to maintain pursuit as a vitally important element in the Air Force," believing that technology would eventually correct the disparity that had made the Boeing B-17 *Flying Fortress* heavy bomber appear impregnable. But Chennault's views were marginalized, and he was no longer on active duty when the war began.[10]

Although Chennault appeared to be a voice in the wilderness at the ACTS, there is evidence that his views were shared by others among the pursuit advocates. In 1931 Major John Cannon, ACTS class of 1936 and future commander of Twelfth Air Support Command in North Africa and all of Twelfth Air Force from 1943 to 1945, outlined his views in a letter to a fellow officer. In his duties as an instructor at the Pursuit School, Major Cannon emphasized the following:

- that attack and bombardment as at present operated are vulnerable to attack by pursuit
- that attack and bombardment missions will require pursuit protection for their successful accomplishment
- that a good proportion of attack, bombardment and observation missions can and will be intercepted by hostile pursuit
- that the possibilities and limitations of pursuit should not be judged by the performance of our tactical pursuit units during the last few years.[11]

Thus Chennault's views were not held in isolation and were perhaps indicative of a number of officers who served in the pursuit arm of the Air Corps. It is important to distinguish between the nature of Chennault's vision and Cannon's criticisms versus the theoretical views dominating the service at this time. The pursuit branch was not necessarily advocating a fundamentally different theory of airpower, only that pursuit aviation would be critical to the success of any planned strategic bombardment campaign. In the end they were proven correct—yet this did not alter the predominant Air Corps theory on the eve of World War II.

Across the Atlantic the Royal Air Force (RAF), which would heavily influence the USAAF's participation in the North African campaign, was struggling with many of the same issues. While most of the RAF in the interwar period performed "empire policing" missions, the service, and the nation it protected, was deeply influenced by the rise of aerial weapons that made the English Channel an ineffective barrier to attack. RAF Bomber Command embraced Douhet's theories, perhaps even more fully than the USAAF, primarily as a deterrent to aggression on the home islands, yet the RAF also boasted a number of officers experienced in providing air support for ground forces throughout the empire. In perhaps the most clearly articulated vision of the concept, J. C. Slessor's *Air Power and Armies*, published in 1936, mined the experiences of World War I to argue for direct and sustained support for ground forces. Developed from a series of lectures at the RAF Staff College at Camberley, Slessor's work provides further evidence that officers in both the British and American air services were resisting Douhet's siren song and thinking clearly and deeply about how to sustain ground forces in future conflicts.[12]

MITCHELL

Like Slessor, Billy Mitchell's early ideas on aerial warfare also evolved from his experiences on the Western Front in 1918. In organizing aerial armies to cover the St.-Mihiel and Meuse-Argonne offensives, Mitchell had first-hand experience in providing air assistance to ground operations. In his first published work, *Our Air Force* (1921), he echoed others in his assertion that an air organization could make the difference between victory and defeat in surface operations: "No navies can operate on the seas, nor armies on the land, until the air forces have first attained a decision against the opposing air forces."[13] The remainder of that work was a measured call for an all-around air establishment (specifically a Department of Aeronautics) that would not only encompass an air force but also coordinate the development of civil aviation (much as the Federal Aviation Administration does today). Mitchell saw prominent roles for the pursuit, attack, and observation aviation branches, as well as bombardment, and he expended a great deal of effort explaining how aviation can and does support surface forces. Unfortunately, Mitchell's ideas quickly devolved into the overstated claims that typify the early theorists. In his later publication *Winged Defense* (1925), Mitchell had fallen under the sway of Douhet's vision and had become an unabashed advocate for strategic bombing.[14]

Mitchell biographer Alfred Hurley believes that the legendary airman was "not an original thinker" but rather a synthesizer, and an advocate for airpower theory within an international community of like-minded colleagues.[15] Mitchell's ideas were certainly disseminated throughout the Air Corps, especially through the Air Corps Tactical School. In his history of that organization for the period 1920 to 1940, Robert Finney argues that Mitchell had a "most decided influence on the school," but the author also minimizes Douhet's impact, stating "it is doubtful that he had any profound influence on the thought at the school." This is difficult to believe. Douhet's theory of warfare posited a central role for the airplane, and his belief that airplanes alone could determine the outcome of war can be found at the core of ACTS doctrine of daylight precision bombing—the American half of the Combined Bomber Offensive over Europe in World War II. Although at the ACTS Air Corps officers had rejected Douhet's calls for chemical gas attacks on cities in favor of precision attacks on industrial and other key targets, there is no doubt that his ideas forced a reconsideration. Finney seems to agree but contradicts earlier statements: "The faculty and students did not confine themselves to a consideration of the application of the air weapon to traditional concepts of surface engagements; rather they explored the whole theory of warfare to discover whether or not this new, relatively untried weapon had altered the nature of war." As a result, even though Finney believes "Douhet was never really in vogue at the school," his ideas, through Mitchell, formed the foundation of American airpower theory during the interwar period.[16]

DE SEVERSKY

Alexander de Seversky attracted the least attention in Warner's article, but he had the greatest ability to influence operations. As the only living member of the legendary trio during World War II, de Seversky had the opportunity to incorporate lessons from the early missions into his thoughts on airpower. His insights into the campaigns in Norway, France, and Crete were prescient, as he recognized that airpower could play the determining role in the ground battle. In fact, he named the third dimension as the "key" to modern strategy.[17] Unfortunately, his seminal 1943 work, *Victory Through Air Power*, followed a familiar path for early airpower advocates and quickly devolved into an impassioned plea for an independent air force. Like Mitchell, to whom the book was dedicated (Mitchell had died in 1936), de Seversky believed that only airmen commanding an independent air force could properly employ aerial weapons and that the existing defense bureaucracy had repeatedly and deliberately undermined efforts to establish an independent air service in the United States.

De Seversky suffered somewhat from a conflict of interest in his writings. As the recently ousted president of Seversky Aviation (later Republic Aviation), he had seen his designs suffer from detrimental specifications at home and fail to secure sufficient buyers abroad. As a result of poor sales, he lost his place at the helm of his company. Even though some of his original designs, especially the Republic P-47 *Thunderbolt* fighter, turned out to be successful during the war, he lamented that the Army Air Forces had to enter the conflict with inferior equipment. The USAAF's insistence on substandard, liquid-cooled engines resulted in the underpowered Bell P-39 *Airacobra* and Curtiss P-40 *Warhawk* fighter airframes. (Presumably, the designer's fortunes would have been helped by a procurement program directed by an independent air service whose contractors might appreciate the potential of his work.)

Victory Through Air Power devolves from an insightful analysis of the first three years of the war into a polemic against not only the U.S. Navy but also bureaucrats throughout the defense establishment. As a World War I naval aviator (in the service of his native Russia), and as a consultant to Mitchell during the *Ostfriesland* trial of 1921, when Air Corps bombers successfully demonstrated their ability to sink the captured German warship, he correctly believed that the battleship was obsolete, yet he extended prejudice to the aircraft carrier as well. Once land-based aviation had developed the range to cross oceans, he espoused, carriers and their airplanes would be too vulnerable to air attack, and their embarked air wings would be unable to protect them. Although he spoke highly of "radio detection" (i.e., radar) and "rocket torpedoes" (rockets and missiles), he failed to see the combination of the two as an equalizer for ships against aerial threats. As a result, de Seversky's ideas lose some of their usefulness for predicting future warfare, but his principle that "no land or sea operations are possible without first assuming control of the air above" has stood the test of time in conventional operations.[18]

If Douhet, Mitchell, and de Seversky dominated thought on the employment of airpower at the outset of the war, it is easy to see why the USAAF struggled internally during the early years of the war. Air theorists were increasingly focused on the strategic use of airpower, but the army still controlled USAAF allocations, even in the face of its increasing administrative independence, and was firmly committed to the ground support mission. As a result, American airmen entered World War II most prepared for that mission, yet they were chafing for an opportunity to show what airpower could accomplish independently. These tensions remained throughout the war but did not become manifest until the USAAF had finally procured enough bombers to provide its theories a fair trial.

As a demonstration of the maturity of its ideas, the Army Air Forces issued a war plan in 1941 based solely on the concept of strategic bombardment. Air War Planning Document One (AWPD-1), written by advocates of the strategic concept for victory, contended that the US-AAF alone could bring about Germany's capitulation through strategic bombardment. (And in a further demonstration of the "scientific" precision of this theory, they even calculated the precise number of aircraft [68,416] necessary to execute the plan.)[19] In the rush to produce a comprehensive plan for defeating Germany (and lacking the time for a drawn-out internal battle) the U.S. Army accepted and incorporated AWPD-1 into its plans for the European Theater of Operations. Armed with this statement of their capabilities and intentions, USAAF leaders spent much of the war trying to prove them correct. Fortunately, their preference for an independent air campaign that could bring victory without an accompanying ground campaign was tempered by the U.S. War Department's senior leadership, especially Chief of Staff George C. Marshall, who remained skeptical of the airmen's claims but appreciated the potential benefits that even a strategic campaign could have in providing air cover for the ground forces.

The three principal American commanders assigned to the North African campaign reflected the broad range of thought during the interwar period. Carl Spaatz, the senior American air commander, remained a strategic bombing adherent throughout the campaign, although he proved skilled at directing what was largely a tactical effort. He served as General Eisenhower's principal American subordinate for air (Air Marshal Sir Arthur Tedder was Eisenhower's deputy for all Allied air forces) and was instrumental in deconflicting operations with the Eighth Air Force in the United Kingdom, which he commanded prior to moving to North Africa.[20] James H. "Jimmy" Doolittle, Spaatz's principal subordinate in the western Mediterranean, spent most of the interwar period as a civilian test pilot and, while preferring to focus on the technical aspects of flying, kept abreast of developments in air operations. However, as a civilian during most of the 1920s and 1930s, Doolittle was spared the service indoctrination he might have received at the ACTS and remained a flexible and independent thinker throughout the war. Doolittle was one of the first to earn an aeronautical engineering degree from the Massachusetts Institute of Technology and brought his years of expertise and technical knowl-

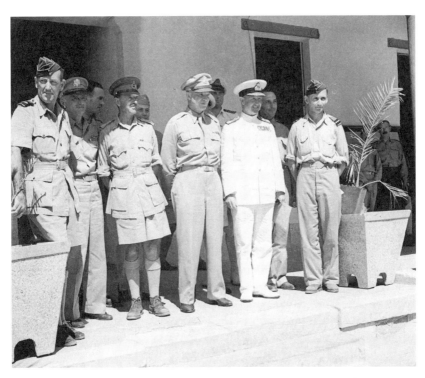

Allied Chiefs at Bizerte. Left to right: The Air Officer Commanding Tactical Air Force Mediterranean, Air Vice Marshal Sir Arthur Coningham; the Commander of the Northwest African Air Force, General Carl Spaatz; General Alexander; General Eisenhower; the Navy Commander-in-Chief, Mediterranean, Admiral of the Fleet Sir Andrew Cunningham; the Commander-in-Chief, Mediterranean Air Command, Air Chief Marshal Sir Arthur Tedder. (Courtesy of the Imperial War Museum)

edge to bear on the task at hand, but eventually he adopted enough strategic theory to earn command of the Eighth Air Force in Britain. The hero of the carrier-launched raid on Tokyo in April 1942, Doolittle was an excellent combat commander at lower levels, and he came into his own as a senior leader in North Africa.[21]

The third member of the team, Lewis Hyde Brereton, graduated from the U.S. Naval Academy in 1911 but transferred to the U.S. Army and served on Mitchell's staff during World War I. As the senior commander in the Philippines when World War II began, he shouldered some of the blame for the loss of his air force while it was still on the ground, but he escaped the islands and fought rear-guard actions in

Java and India before arriving in the Middle East. Though he, too, was well versed in strategic thought, having taught at the Air Service Tactical School when it was still at Langley Field, he also proved adept at directing a largely tactical campaign, drawing on his experience commanding an attack aviation unit in the early 1920s.[22]

Airpower Doctrine, the North African Campaign, and Historians

Two broad historiographical issues have thus far dominated discussion of the air campaign in North Africa. The first, less contentious issue involves the support that the RAF provided to the USAAF both generally and in getting up to speed in the early stages of the campaign. Despite some work suggesting that the influence was minor, historians now generally agree that the RAF played a major role in both material support as well as doctrinal development.[23] By mid-1942, the RAF had more than two years of experience in opposing the German war machine and in learning how to support ground forces. Although this period had seen more failures than successes, by mid-1942 the British had finally developed a robust system of close support for ground forces, backed by experiences in the Western Desert. American forces arrived just in time to take advantage of this expertise and benefited greatly from the British example.

The second, related issue involves the relative emphasis placed on close support doctrine during the interwar period. The standard charge is that the USAAF was too focused on strategic bombing to pay much attention to developing doctrine to support ground forces. Significant failures in the North African campaign have been used to support these charges, ignoring other factors, such as inexperience, weather, and logistic difficulties that hampered close support in the early phases of the war. This second issue is closely related to the first, as any credit accorded to the British for their leadership in doctrinal development correspondingly points to the deficiencies in the USAAF. But the two issues are not necessarily connected. The USAAF did pay attention to close support (under the auspices of the attack aviation branch) during the interwar period, but the Americans still had much to learn from the British, especially in the areas of intelligence and logistics. Likewise, emphasis on strategic bombing did not necessarily mean neglect for close support, as the USAAF was able to perform both missions satisfactorily fairly early in war. Most significant for the campaign in North Africa, the development of a heavy bomber benefited the ground forces by allowing airmen to conduct counterair and effective interdiction campaigns that immeasurably aided ground and naval forces in the theater. The air force might have been wedded to strategic bombing theory, but it willingly used those assets in a largely tactical role to support ground and naval forces in the Mediterranean.

Although historians generally agree on the basic ideas espoused by airpower theorists during the interwar period—and the impact these ideas had on the conduct of the war—there is wide disagreement about how these ideas were distilled into *doctrine* (essentially applied theory but more commonly defined as a set of principles that guide military operations) and how effective that doctrine was during the course of the war. Even though the USAAF remained focused on strategic theory, it had simultaneously worked out an effective ground support doctrine, which offers further evidence of the efforts made during the interwar period toward employing aircraft in the ground battle. The U.S. Army published *Army Field Manual 31-35: Aviation in Support of Ground Forces* (FM 31-35) on 9 April 1942, before any ground forces had been significantly engaged in any campaign save the disastrous losses in the Philippines. As the manual was in effect during the North African campaign, it can be taken as the relevant statement of official doctrine at the opening of the war.

FM 31-35 was a comprehensive document, outlining command relationships, support techniques, and communications procedures and emphasizing the importance of aerial reconnaissance (or "observation"). The manual was not deeply flawed, outlining a system of employment that endured with little substantial modification until the end of the war. Control concepts were especially well defined, and the importance of air assets being controlled by airmen but supporting ground forces was ensured:

> Designation of an aviation unit for support of a subordinate ground unit does not imply subordination of that aviation unit to the supported ground unit, nor does it remove the combat aviation unit from the control of the air support commander. It does permit, however, direct cooperation and association between the supporting aviation unit and the supported ground unit and enables the combat aviation to act with greater promptness in meeting requirements of a rapidly changing situation.[24]

The manual emphasized that "the basis of effective air support of ground forces is teamwork," and it cautioned that air support would not be immediately available in all situations, including enemy local air superiority, "distance from the airdrome to the point of action," and weather. Overall, the document displayed a well-defined concept of close support for ground forces. Army commanders in early campaigns might not have received the support they expected or felt they deserved, but *FM 31-35* demonstrates that undeveloped doctrine was not the chief cause.

In spite of *FM 31-35*, criticism of the Army Air Force's supposed doctrinal unpreparedness began even before the guns fell silent. Ground commanders in the war's early campaigns were quick to criticize the perceived lack of aerial support, and the first studies published during and after the war reflected this misperception. In 1944, Kent Roberts Greenfield began work on Study No. 35 in the "History of the Army Ground Forces Series." Published in 1948, *Army Ground Forces and the Air-Ground Battle Team* reinforced some of the rumors, which by then had earned wide acceptance at even the highest levels. Greenfield related that the commander of the Army Ground Forces, General Leslie McNair, incredulously observed that "it is absolutely true that the air helped the ground in Tunisia far less than in the [First] World War," and "he had just been informed by General Omar N. Bradley . . . that in Sicily there had been no improvement."[25]

McNair clearly did not understand that air assets had been instrumental to both the Tunisian and Sicilian campaigns by denying the enemy use of the skies above Allied troops, by disrupting enemy resupply and reinforcement, and by airlifting men and materiel to the battlefield. McNair may have been employing a narrow definition of "help," but he was wrong to suggest that biplanes had done better over the trenches of France.

McNair's frustration may have dated from the air arm's inability to participate in the stateside joint training exercises that he was largely responsible for. In 1941, both the Louisiana and Carolina maneuvers suffered from the absence of air assets, which was attributed to pressing requirements in building the force and conducting the required individual training to produce competent pilots.[26] The post-Depression buildup of the American air arm had come too late to permit assets to be stretched across the globe while simultaneously allowing fully prepared squadrons to take part in training maneuvers at home. But the roots of the poor working relationship likely ran much deeper. In his study, Greenfield attributed the lack of cooperation to the legacy of one individual, General Mitchell, whose 1925 court-martial for insubordination, which resulted in his resignation and "left an aftermath of bitterness which made it more difficult to arrive at agreements and decisions regarding the role of air power in the team of combined arms."[27] Although doctrinal issues may not have directly influenced the relationship, shortages of well-trained units, especially during the opening stages of the North African campaign, left the impression that the USAAF was neglecting ground forces.

As a result of the lessons learned in North Africa, the U.S. War Department on 21 July 1943 published a revised *Field Manual 100-20: Command and Employment of Air Power* (FM 100-20). Greenfield believed this document, which began "LAND POWER AND AIR POWER ARE CO-EQUAL AND INTERDEPENDENT FORCES; NEITHER IS AN AUXILIARY OF THE OTHER," amounted to a "declaration of independence" by the air force and was designed to replace *FM 31-35*, even though it referenced the older doctrine. In reality, the manual represented a codification of concepts already in existence and tested under fire in North Africa. But for those, especially in the U.S. Army, who had expected that air units would be apportioned to ground commanders, this represented a significant departure from prewar doctrine.[28] For all the criticism leveled at *FM 100-20*, it should be noted that the very successful system of air-ground cooperation worked out between, for example, General George Patton's Third U.S. Army and the USAAF's XIX Tactical Air Command during the drive across France in 1944, was guided by the precepts established in this manual. Greenfield also emphasized that the document "faithfully mirrored General Montgomery's statement of principles," a reference to the belief that the "new" principles had emerged from the Royal Air Force's experiences in the Western Desert.[29]

Greenfield's future service as the general editor of the U.S. Army's official history of the war, *The United States Army in World War II* (the famous "green books"), may have colored depictions in those volumes.[30] Authorized in 1946 and now including more than eighty volumes, the series often codifies these perceptions. For example, George Howe's 1957 volume on the North African campaign noted, "The Air Forces differed from the Ground forces in their conception of proper battlefield support and were disposed to concentrate heavily on strategic bombing." As a result, "the troops received insufficient training in air-ground co-operation."[31] Howe also reinforced Greenfield's belief that the remedy for the air arm's previously inadequate doctrine had emerged in British circles. He wrote that, in the advance from Egypt to Tunisia, General Sir Bernard Law Montgomery's ground forces and

Air Marshall Sir Arthur Coningham's air forces "had together tested a successful doctrine of air support."[32]

This account of American adoption of the British-derived system was almost unchallenged in the historiography of the war until the 1998 publication of David Mets's article "A Glider in the Propwash of the Royal Air Force," in Daniel Mortenson's edited volume *Airpower and Ground Armies*. Playing on John Quincy Adams's description of the early American navy as "a cock-boat in the wake of the British man-of-war," Mets asserted that, rather than adopting new British developments, "the main ideas already existed in the minds of many American airmen long before the beginning of the African campaign." Mets demonstrated that Carl Spaatz, the senior American air commander in the Mediterranean, had been an early advocate of attack aviation, and that the Air Corps had continued to develop attack types such as the Curtiss A-8 *Shrike* and Northrop A-17 *Nomad* light bombers throughout the interwar period. When the war began, a twin-engine attack aircraft, the Douglas A-20 *Havoc* light bomber (known in RAF circles as the Boston), was already in production and employed widely by both the RAF and USAAF in North Africa. The Air Corps even maintained an entire organization, the 3rd Attack Group, at a time when neither Italy, Great Britain, nor the Soviet Union boasted an attack formation in their air forces.[33] Mets even cites Robert Finney's 1955 study on the Air Corps Tactical School, which noted that "a subsection of the Air Force course was entitled Aviation in Support of Ground Forces, in which . . . the concept was taught that gaining air superiority was the most valuable contribution the Air Force could make to the ground campaign."[34] Although Finney suggested that there was a decline in the attention paid to air support of surface operations, the reduced level of attention was still sufficient to develop adequate doctrine and a specialized attack aircraft—even out of the miniscule budgets and reduced force structures of the interwar years.

Mets's initial assertion—questioning the impact of the RAF's assistance in getting the USAAF up to speed—remains one of the more contentious aspects of the campaign. American airmen repeatedly downplayed the RAF assistance they received for a number of reasons, including service and national pride, and in the attempt to deflect charges that they had neglected critical aspects of air-ground cooperation during the interwar period. The two arguments are not necessarily linked. One can (and should) be able to acknowledge the tremendous amount of assistance the RAF supplied to the USAAF during the campaign while still recognizing that the USAAF was prepared (at least as well as it is possible to prepare for war during peacetime) to conduct operations in support of ground and naval forces. The fact that initial efforts fell short should not be taken as an indictment of the level of effort during the interwar period. As an example, the U.S. Army spent a great deal of effort attempting to develop an effective antitank force during the interwar period, but it still had to modify doctrine and equipment after its initial employment in North Africa.[35]

Still, the army's position made many appearances in the postwar historical record. In 1950, perhaps sparked by events on the Korean Peninsula, *Military Affairs* published several articles on tactical aviation. Purdue University professor James Huston, an infantry major during World War II, provided a fairly balanced assessment that nonetheless reinforced the ground view:

> Ground commanders became concerned as they saw more and more emphasis being placed upon training and equipment for strategic bombing and thus relatively less effort being made to develop tactical support aviation. Strategically, Army Air Forces seemed bent upon pursuing its ambitious bomber offensive against Germany to prove its ability to force a decision against Germany from the air. Tactically, it seemed determined to concentrate air units outside the control of ground commanders, and as much as possible to avoid close support of ground units.[36]

Huston viewed doctrinal development as a zero-sum game. Any effort devoted to development of strategic bombardment was automatically a loss for tactical efforts. After this standard introduction, Huston went on to chronicle the admirable contributions airpower made throughout the rest of the war when it was instrumental to the success of ground combat, tempered with a few anecdotes of when it was slow to respond or inaccurate. One particularly relevant criticism was that "probably the greatest limitation on the scale of tactical air power was the competition for resources of the strategic bombing offensives."[37]

The newly formed United States Air Force (1947) was quick to address the emerging perceptions. In the same volume as Huston's article, Thomas Maycock, who worked on the USAAF's historical project during the war, offered the air view.[38] With regard to *FM 31-35*, he noted, "much of it, especially as regarded employment, differed little from principles invoked today."[39] Maycock offered a stout defense of

XII Air Support Command, the USAAF unit tasked with supporting American ground forces during the battle at Kasserine:

> XII Air Support Command was ill-equipped to demonstrate the effectiveness of any tactical doctrine. Its pilots by and large were inexperienced and no breaking-in period could be afforded. Proper employment of its light bombers and fighters was being worked out day by day. Worst of all, no air superiority had been won for it by any interceptor command and it lacked a radar net which could be used offensively.[40]

Moreover, "XII Air Support Command [was] obliged to devote a good share of its efforts to protective umbrellas." Maycock believed that the remedy came from British circles and noted that "the system adopted in Tunisia went through many refinements in subsequent operations against German-held Europe, but its doctrine did not change."[41]

In 1955, the same year Robert Finney's history of the Air Corps Tactical School was published, the U.S. Air Force also issued Thomas Greer's Historical Study No. 89, *The Development of Air Doctrine in the Army Air Arm, 1917–1941*. Greer's comprehensive work emphasized the importance that air officers placed on attack aviation after World War I and noted that General Mitchell was an early advocate. Greer further demonstrated that the effort persisted through the interwar years, noting that during the late 1920s and early 1930s "aviation in support of ground forces continued to occupy major attention in the Air Corps and at the Tactical School."[42]

However, by then the army's version was beginning to gain acceptance, even within U.S. Air Force circles. This could reflect the air force's preference for the strategic nuclear mission that now occupied its attention, or an attempt to distance itself from tactical aviation in the wake of the Korean War. At one point, Greer even repeated the mantra: "The development of the heavy bomber and its doctrine of employment, although the most important American airpower accomplishment of the 1930's, had a retarding effect upon attack, pursuit, and all other aviation activities."[43] Despite noting that "from 1939 on there was an increasing emphasis on the development of close support doctrine," in his final paragraph he asserted, "There was failure also to reach clear-cut agreement on the optimum type of equipment and tactics for ground support. The United States, as a consequence, entered World War II with inadequate preparation in this important branch of military aviation."[44]

Robert Frank Futrell, in his comprehensive review of airpower doctrine published in 1960, was more hesitant to accept the theory of neglect. In *Ideas, Concepts, Doctrine* he noted that in 1935 the Air Corps had four bombardment, three pursuit, and two attack groups and "initiated serious studies of ground support aviation." He also illuminated another potential cause of the dispute. A 1936 Air Corps Board recommendation affirmed the ground support mission, but it remained hesitant about the "proposed assignment of attack aviation as an organic part of an army," preferring that assets be centralized under the control of a single air commander. Later complaints by ground commanders about inadequate air support may have merely been frustration over losing direct control over an important asset. Futrell notes the July 1943 publication of *The Air Force in Theaters of Operations*: The "most ambitious and comprehensive doctrinal publication ever issued . . . conformed to the approved air-ground doctrine issued in FM 31-35," indicating that *FM 31-35* was considered adequate even after testing in North Africa.[45]

As the nation moved farther away from the events of the war, discussions of tactical doctrine development slipped into the background. The army had established a tactical support branch of its own, equipped largely with helicopters and the resuscitated observation-type fixed-wing aircraft, and the air force continued to invest in its strategic attack mission. The Vietnam War saw high-speed interceptors used as fighter-bombers and nuclear-capable Boeing B-52 *Stratofortress* strategic bombers employed in a tactical support role. The literature of this period is sparse, and it took a refocusing on air support for ground troops enshrined in the army's new AirLand Battle doctrine, published in 1982, to redirect attention to World War II. The next generation of scholarship would see the most prolific outpouring of research, as historians rediscovered World War II around the fiftieth anniversary of the conflict.

The first study to emerge after the publication of the AirLand doctrine was Daniel Mortensen's 1987 *A Pattern for Joint Operations*.[46] As the title suggests, Mortensen attempted to bridge the gap between the two opposing viewpoints. The study was commissioned jointly by the Office of Air Force History and the U.S. Army Center of Military History as part of a concerted effort to build interservice cooperation. In 1984, the respective branches' Chiefs of Staff issued a Memorandum of Understanding that attempted to patch up relations and "reaffirmed the Air Force's mission to provide close air support for the Army."[47] Mortensen's study demonstrated a significant effort during

B-24 Briefing, 1943: Bomber crews of the U.S. Ninth Air Force are given
a chalk talk before they take off on a mission to disrupt Axis shipping in
the Mediterranean. Giving the blackboard talk is Major Frank W. Delong,
squadron commander. (Library of Congress: Signal Corps Photo)

the prewar period to develop doctrine, refine tactics and techniques,
and procure aircraft for the ground support mission. In highlighting
problems in both services and emphasizing the further modification as
a result of the Tunisian campaign, Mortensen revealed that a spirit of
close cooperation had enabled both services to develop effective measures, yet his work focused almost exclusively on *tactical* employment
in North Africa and largely neglected the *operational* campaign.

Further investigation revealed other instances of effective cooperation. In 1990 the Office of Air Force History issued a more substantial volume, *Case Studies in the Development of Close Air Support*, edited
by Benjamin Franklin Cooling. Seven of the eleven essays focused on
World War II, and three highlighted the American experiences in Tunisia, Sicily, and the Southwest Pacific.[48] Perhaps most valuable was
Lee Kennett's overview of developments to 1939, which emphasized
the Air Corps' interest in interdiction, or "isolation of the battlefield,"
as an important source of support for ground forces. Kennett pointed
out that "at the end of 1939 the Air Corps Tactical School dropped the
designation 'attack' and substituted 'light bombardment.' The devel-

opment of this concept was a considerable gamble, but one which paid off once the war started."[49] The North American B-25 *Mitchell* medium bomber and Douglas A/B-26 *Invader* light bomber, which were used extensively in a tactical role throughout the war, were the logical successors to the A-20 *Havoc*, as all three aircraft were twin-engine types of similar design.

But the advent of light bombardment, as opposed to heavy bombardment, was viewed differently by advocates of the various positions. Attack enthusiasts likely benefited within the Air Corps establishment from the bombardment designation, whereas bomber advocates seemed willing to extend their circle to include light, medium, and heavy types. But ground commanders probably regarded this development merely as a loss of aircraft and support for the ground attack mission, despite the fact that such support would continue under the "bombardment" name. Semantics likely played a role in the debate.

Kennett's essay also ascribed to the British a significant role in American tactical development—but long before the American association with the RAF's Desert Air Force, the organization tasked with supporting the British Eighth Army in Egypt. In 1940 the British embarked on a crash program of air-ground cooperation as a result of their brief and unsuccessful experiences in the German invasion of France and Belgium. Hap Arnold, who had sent observers (including Spaatz) to Great Britain during the Blitz (the bombing of London and other targets by the Germans early in the war as a result of the Battle of Britain), was aware of the resulting program of ground controllers and, in 1941, created the Directorate of Air Support. Throughout 1941 the directorate "ordered tests, prepared training circulars, and issued field manuals" (including *FM 31-35*).[50] Despite noting these accomplishments, Kennett concluded that "the Air Corps generally neglected close air support and tactical aviation" due to "its pre-occupation with strategic bombing."[51]

The three essays appearing in Cooling's *Case Studies in the Development of Close Air Support* on the American experience in the war hew closely to this party line. David Syrett's "The Tunisian Campaign, 1942–1943" leaned heavily on Greenfield, who provided documentation for the assertion that "the AAF conducted operations according to its own concept of air power, without regards for the needs of ground forces."[52] Syrett further illuminated the origins of the air-ground dispute by extensively quoting Brigadier General Paul Robinett, commander of Combat Command B, U.S. First Armored Division. Robinett complained bitterly about the lack of close air support in Tunisia and believed "what was needed were not reports or photographs of ships being sunk, ports being smashed, or cities being bombed to ashes, but seeing Allied aircraft over front-line positions and attacking targets in the path of Allied operations."[53] However, Eisenhower's air deputy, Carl Spaatz, noted:

> The correct use of air power was not really close air support, but rather air superiority and interdiction operations, hitting enemy airfields, tank parks, motor pools and troop convoys—in effect, interdicting enemy supplies, equipment, and troops *before* they reached the battlefield. If he maintained a constant umbrella over one small portion of the front, then his available force would be dissipated without any lasting effect.[54]

Events would prove Spaatz's assessment to be more accurate than Robinett's. German tanks in front of Robinett's First Armored Division could have been engaged with tank destroyers or organic artillery (if the ground forces had developed and integrated effective antitank weapons during the interwar period), and Spaatz's air interdiction campaign would ensure that replacements and the fuel they needed to operate did not arrive in Tunisia. The Axis position in North Africa eventually collapsed under the combined weight of ground assault and Allied naval and aerial interdiction of already stretched lines of communication, and aircraft were best employed against the tenuous supply lines stretched across the Mediterranean rather than against isolated positions in the mountains of Tunisia. Despite his helpful observations on the correct use of airpower, Syrett also recognized that it originated with the British, who "imposed the doctrine of the Western Desert Air Force on all American tactical air units in Tunisia."[55]

Joe Gray Taylor's contribution, "American Experience in the Southwest Pacific," shows that the debate over close support and interdiction was not confined to the European theater. Close support was hampered by terrain, weather, distance, and interservice coordination with naval forces. After arguing "the most important factor affecting Air Corps disregard of and distaste for close support was the development of the doctrine of strategic bombardment,"[56] Taylor reported on the USAAF's successful interdiction of Japanese air, ground, and naval forces in the campaigns that wrested the Solomons and New Guinea from Axis control. The implication is that the Americans, unable to strike any strategic targets in the theater, were forced to conduct an operational campaign. The fact that they were already equipped with the aircraft and doctrine to do so seems to go unnoticed. Taylor believes that the early doctrine, particularly *FM 31-35* and *FM 100-20*, "played no role in the Southwest Pacific" and that "ground and air commanders in the Southwest Pacific looked pragmatically at the problems that arose and worked out solutions."[57] Taylor later notes that General Douglas MacArthur's senior air commander, General George Kenney, was one of the leading airmen involved in working out these "solutions," but he ignores Kenney's efforts in developing attack doctrine at the ACTS as somehow irrelevant to his later service. He does concede that "the Allied Air Forces of General Kenney developed techniques based on principles later set forth in FM 100-20, 'Command and Employment of Air Power,' well before that manual was released in July of 1943."[58] This statement calls into question both the reliance on Western Desert ideas in the formulation of tactical doctrine and the absence of well-developed tactical thought in the Army Air Forces prior to 1943.

Cooling's *Case Studies* volume, although reinforcing existing perceptions, was the first trickle in a flood of scholarship on the topic in the 1990s. Perhaps the successes enjoyed by aircraft equipped with precision-guided munitions during the 1990–1991 Operation DESERT STORM in Southwest Asia inaugurated the renaissance. In 1996, two volumes appeared that continued the discussion. In Williamson Murray and Allan Millet's *Military Innovation in the Interwar Period*, Richard Muller compared the German, British, and American experiences in close air support from 1918 to 1941. Muller offered a partial explanation for the strength of the army's version by revealing that the air force's official history of the war, Wesley Craven and James Cate's seven-volume *The Army Air Forces in World War II* (1949), "gives unjustifiably short shrift to tactical aviation."[59] Although Muller seems sympathetic to the argument that the USAAF was distracted by an overemphasis on strategic bombing, by highlighting the importance of the American tactical contribution he demonstrates the significant role interdiction played:

> While it would be an oversimplification to state that attack aviation fell into disrepute simply because "strategic bombardment" did more for the independent existence of the air corps, the suggestion of the subordination of air force units to the ground forces, coupled with the significant technical difficulty of the mission, forced

American attack doctrine away from a pure close support role into a mission more closely approximating the German concept of "indirect army support."[60]

Muller does agree that, in some respects, "the United States led the rest of the world during the interwar period in the field of close air support."[61] And though "leading the world" in aircraft technology in 1934 might be irrelevant on a 1942 battlefield, the effect on doctrinal development was more enduring. Presumably, some of this expertise, promulgated through the ACTS, permeated the minds of the generation of airmen who would direct American air campaigns in World War II.

That seems to be the point made by Thomas Hughes in his work, published in 1995, entitled, somewhat misleadingly, *Overlord*, but more correctly subtitled *General Pete Quesada and the Triumph of Tactical Air Power in World War II*. Hughes traces the career of General Elwood "Pete" Quesada, who graduated from the Air Corps Tactical School in 1936 and went on to lead Ninth Air Force's IX Fighter Command during the invasion of France and the drive across the continent during 1944–1945.[62] While clearly demonstrating that the pre-war Air Corps was capable of developing leaders who could effectively control and employ tactical assets, Hughes also chafes under the weight of the "bomber mafia." In characterizing the debate between strategic bombardment advocates, such as Harold George, and defenders of pursuit aviation, most notably Claire Chennault, Hughes believes that other topics atrophied. "Between the school's stress on bombardment and Chennault's vigorous defense of pursuit, there was little room for development of any other ideas. In lectures, class time and graded material, no topic suffered more than instruction in air-ground operations." Although such a course of events would certainly make Quesada's subsequent contributions seem more important, it may not have been strictly the case. Hughes believes "the subject in which Quesada received the least formal training was the one he later worked to revolutionize in World War II."[63] Although Hughes's emphasis on Quesada's contributions, important though they were, would be strengthened if his was an isolated case, there were other innovators who similarly devised creative solutions and directed tactical assets with great skill, including Kenney, Cannon, Otto Weyland, and Hoyt Vandenberg—all ACTS graduates. Clearly, there was something in the water at Maxwell AFB (Air Force Base) in Alabama that enabled the development of tactical airpower practitioners beyond the supposed short shrift the topic received in the curriculum.

Both Muller and Hughes served as faculty members at the Air Force School of Advanced Air and Space Studies (SAASS) at Maxwell AFB. Through this service school, their views began to filter down and are evident in some of the work completed by SAASS students. Gary Cox's 1995 thesis, "Beyond the Battle Line: US Air Attack Theory and Doctrine, 1919–1941," demonstrated both the depth of interwar thinking on attack and the important difference in interpretation between ground and air commanders. Whereas ground commanders preferred visible close air support, air commanders were already inclined toward interdiction (isolation of the battlefield). The differing definitions for the same term are another potential source of misunderstanding between wartime leaders. Cox also opened the first chinks in the armor of the theory that ground support had been neglected due to the emphasis on strategic bombardment. He demonstrated that the neglect was more apparent than real, as a result of the Air Force's interpretation, and concluded that "US attack theory and doctrine was adequately developed to be useful at the start of WWII."[64]

Perhaps army allegations that the air force was more concerned with strategic targets in Baghdad than supporting troops on the Kuwaiti border reopened the debate after a brief truce during the Ronald Reagan administration. A new generation of army officers led the investigation into the evolution of service doctrine during the interwar period. First to appear was David Johnson's 2003 *Fast Tanks and Heavy Bombers*, exploring the relationship between doctrine and equipment procurement and demonstrating that both ground and air commanders made flawed decisions during the 1930s. An emphasis on lightweight, faster tanks resulted in the armor branch suffering through the war with equipment that was consistently outmatched by the German tanks. Likewise, strategic bombing advocates made a series of miscalculations about the effectiveness of German defenses and the need for escort fighters that led to high casualties among bomber crewmen. Although Johnson appears to be equally critical of both, he also believes the services failed to develop air-ground doctrine during the interwar period. He notes, "In the months that followed the issuance of FM 100-20, little emphasis or direction was given to close air support by the Army Air Forces," a statement that belittles the significant effort expended in both the Sicilian and Italian campaigns and in the South Pacific. Johnson makes a strong case that the service's problems stemmed from institutional, rather than fiscal, neglect, but he does not acknowledge the significant doctrinal effort that did occur prior to the war.[65]

One potential source of the army's position came to light with the 2001 publication of Jonathan House's *Combined Arms Warfare in the Twentieth Century*.[66] The introduction reveals that the work originated as a locally published text used at the Army's Command and General Staff College since the early 1980s. House's work reveals an underlying assumption that airpower is most effective when it is closely integrated with the combined arms team, but it does not seem to consider that air may have important missions that remove it from the immediate battlefield. He believed that "proponents of strategic airpower such as William Mitchell in the United States and . . . Douhet in Italy made exaggerated claims that retarded the development of the tactical combined arms team."[67] On the surface, this is entirely true, as both Mitchell and Douhet did not view ground support as either the most important or effective use of airpower. But, like Warner in *Makers of Modern Strategy*, this characterization ignores much of the work that did occur during the interwar period in the development of ground support doctrine. House also believes the air force's developing interests in interdiction with light bombers "were oriented toward weakening the enemy air forces instead of meeting the needs of the ground forces," which is probably true as well. Emphasizing their ability to attrite the enemy air force would have given light- and medium-bomber advocates much more sway within the USAAF establishment.[68] But the destruction of the enemy air force would also provide tremendous assistance to the ground forces.

The debates have continued well into the twenty-first century. Two Canadian scholars entered the fray, addressing primarily the RAF's role in early American doctrinal development. Brad Gladman's 2002 essay "The Development of Tactical Air Doctrine in North Africa, 1940–43" focused primarily on Sir Arthur Coningham's contributions but observed that "in the early campaigns of the Second World War neither the RAF nor the United States Army Air Forces was able to provide effective air support. Their understanding of how to conduct such operations had largely vanished" since the successful days of World War I. Gladman believed that "some American and British airmen understood some of the elements of how to conduct air support, but the operational experience had disappeared and neither force had a fully developed doctrine." Against this blank slate, the miraculous developments in the Western Desert certainly appear stark, but Gladman minimizes the contrast by noting that "the preoccupation of many historians with the strategic bombing doctrine of both the RAF and the USAAC [Army Air Corps, the predecessor to the US-AAF] ignores the existence of some serious discussion by some influential members of both air forces about the importance of developing a doctrine for the application of tactical air power." Finally, historians seemed ready to move past the argument that tactical aviation suffered from the overemphasis on the strategic. Gladman recounts British development during the interwar period as a result of experiences policing the empire, but he does not return to American doctrinal development until 1942.[69]

In 2004, B. Michael Bechthold echoed his countryman Gladman in championing the importance of the British model. His article, in the *Journal of Military History*, relied exclusively on secondary sources and declared that "the ineffectiveness of Allied units in North Africa, both air and ground, American and British, led to a reorganization in 1943. For the tactical air forces, the key to the reorganization was the adoption of the British Eighth Army-Western Desert Air Force model of ground-air cooperation."[70] Disregarding Thomas Maycock's much earlier admonitions about operational constraints that prevent using the XII Air Support Command's work in North Africa as an effective doctrinal test, Bechthold believes that "FM 31-35 contained many good ideas, but it did not prove to be the guiding principle behind the employment of tactical air power in North Africa," and "as a result, the existing American tactical air doctrine was virtually discarded."[71]

Unlike Gladman, Bechthold spends considerable efforts tracing the development of American tactical doctrine during the interwar period, but he draws on Thomas Greer's work to conclude that attack and pursuit aviation suffered at the hands of the bombardment advocates. Interestingly, while most accounts (including Finney's) portray the Air Corps Tactical School as being controlled by the "bomber mafia," Bechthold believes it was "one of the few bastions of tactical aviation" but that "its 'progressive' ideas did not receive wide circulation." This is certainly a welcome development in the debate, but it does not square with Greer's work, which Bechthold cites in his preceding paragraph. Despite the supposed British origins of *FM 100-20*, Bechthold also notes that the ideas contained therein were already in circulation among American airmen in 1939. He reveals that "Montgomery and Coningham did not differ qualitatively from extant American doctrine. In fact, [their] speeches succinctly and accurately summed up the position held by the U.S. Army Air Forces." Despite the declaration in his abstract, it appears that the American difficulties were organizational rather than doctrinal. Bechthold eventually dissects the British contribution by observing "American airmen had developed a sound doctrine of their own, but they were unable to convince the army hierarchy of the applicability of their ideas. . . . This was where the British came in. . . . The American airmen became disciples of the British doctrine not because of its originality, but because they could use its success to convince the army leaders of its utility." The debate over British influence finally sheds some light on the U.S. Army–U.S. Air Force dispute.[72]

Since the end of World War II, air and ground historians of American tactical doctrine built a flimsy structure of tactical neglect due to strategic emphasis on the shaky foundation of the first generation of ground-focused historians. Phillip Meilinger, a retired air force officer, threatened to knock over the whole house of cards in his 2003 book *Airpower: Myths and Facts*.[73] In Myth No. 2 (second only to the myth that the Air Corps was adequately funded during the interwar period), Meilinger confronted the issue head-on. Myth No. 2 was titled "Entering World War II, the Air Corps's unbalanced doctrine and force structure leaned too heavily towards strategic bombing. Thus, air support of ground forces was inadequate and largely ignored by airmen." In toppling this long-perpetuated myth, Meilinger first assaulted the supposed bomber-heavy ACTS curriculum by revealing that in the 1935 curriculum only "44 out of 494 class periods (8.9 percent) were devoted to 'bombardment,'" compared to 158 for "equitation."[74] Next, Meilinger examined the Army Air Corps force structure, which one might suspect to be dominated by heavy bombers. Instead, when the war began in 1939, only twenty-six operational bombers were on the ramps. Of the 20,914 aircraft purchased in the remarkable buildup over the next two years, only 373 were strategic bombers.[75] Finally, Meilinger lists tactical air commanders who "rose to high rank during and after the war," including Kenney, Vandenberg, and Quesada.

Sadly, this historiographical debate is far from purely academic; it has real implications on the modern battlefield—and may have already affected the course of history. Disagreements between air and ground partisans hampered efforts to forge joint doctrine in the immediate postwar period. In his 2007 work *The American Culture of War*, Adrian Lewis lamented that "the Army and Air Force have never reconciled these beliefs that form the very core of their cultures" and that "the inability of the Army and Air Force to produce joint doctrine damaged the ability of the nation to effectively use military power to achieve political objectives, and arguably, caused the nation's first defeat in war."[76] The situation might have been averted had ground and air planners alike heeded James Huston's advice at the height of the Korean War: "Thorough analyses, free of personal bias and service prestige, need to be made of the whole story. The making of valid interpretations and of correct evaluations of the Army's experience with tactical air power in World War II already have become matters of life and death." The first step in reaching the level of joint air-ground cooperation achieved in the latter stages of World War II is to dispel partisan myths that have obscured the historical record. Only then can new relationships based on mutual trust and affinity be forged, which will undoubtedly multiply the combat effectiveness of both services.

Conclusion

In developing an air force capable of supporting ground forces during the interwar period, the USAAF had not neglected doctrinal developments. Charges that the USAAF had seriously slighted these areas in favor of strategic bombing are largely untrue, yet the emphasis on strategic bombing theory did result in the development of a heavy bomber, the B-17 that played a critical role in the campaign in North Africa. The USAAF also had a workable close support doctrine that proved successful with only minor modification. The combat aircraft first employed in summer 1942 were the exact same models that most of the RAF was then flying in North Africa, types that, as will be shown in Chapter 2, were proven to be highly effective in the Western Desert campaign.

But the USAAF had several shortcomings that would also be revealed in this first campaign against the German and Italian forces. In the Western Desert, the USAAF was almost entirely reliant on the RAF for both logistics and intelligence, two critical aspects of any air campaign. Although the USAAF was largely prepared in terms of front-line assets such as trained pilots and combat aircraft, it had neglected the establishment of an effective air intelligence service and suffered from serious logistical shortcomings.[77] Fortunately, in this, the first real test of the war, the flaws were masked by support from a well-equipped and combat-experienced RAF, as well as the existing infrastructure in Egypt and Palestine in the form of hard-surfaced and well-developed airfields and an established transportation network that could move supplies and personnel quickly from ships unloading along the Suez Canal to adjacent airfields. The proximity to the Middle Eastern oilfields and a developed distribution network also worked greatly in the Allies' favor and ensured that the USAAF would be successful in its first combat test against the Axis in Europe.

The Western Desert:
Learning with the British,
June to November 1942

Historians have frequently (and not without justification) minimized the role the United States Army Air Forces played in the see-saw battle for Egypt in the desert west of the Nile. The American contribution was belated and, when it did arrive, small compared to that of the Commonwealth, and it likely did not alter the eventual outcome of the Battle of El Alamein and the subsequent pursuit across Libya. The American contingent comprised less than 10 percent of Allied air assets in the theater and flew a similar percentage of the total sorties. British and Commonwealth forces, which included South Africans, Australians, New Zealanders, and Canadians, did most of the fighting in the air and suffered most of the casualties. But participation in the campaign was significant for the USAAF. For the first time, American airmen were directly exposed to the successful British method of employing tactical airpower and the demands of an operational campaign that trumped their desires to employ their weapons in the strategic mission. This is not to suggest that the British methods differed radically from American ideas, as David Mets has shown, but there is still a significant jump from theory to successful practice.[1]

In their initial employment against the European Axis powers, American airmen were forced to adjust their preference for strategic raids to attacks on tactical- and operational-level targets, including fielded forces, airfields, ports, and land and sea lines of communication. In doing so, the U.S. Army Middle East Air Forces, the US-AAF element assigned to the region, and especially the two heavy bombardment groups assigned to it, made a substantial contribution

to the defeat of Rommel's forces and likely hastened the eventual outcome and lowered the overall cost to the Allies. More important, these
first Americans to directly engage the Axis forces established a model
for the use of aerial assets in support of ground and naval forces that
would be successfully employed throughout the remainder of the war
against Germany and Italy.

The campaign demonstrated that the USAAF, during the interwar
period, had successfully developed a force that was capable of decisively influencing a ground campaign. By developing doctrine, acquir-
ing suitable aircraft and training pilots that were able to contribute to
the desert fight with minimal in-theater indoctrination and modification, the Army Air Forces had not neglected its responsibility to support ground forces. But at the same time, USAAF leadership remained
focused on a panacea of strategic bombardment that threatened to
undermine a successful air-ground team. By losing assets in a single,
risky, long-range raid; withholding reinforcements in order to build
the bomber force in England and seriously entertaining a Soviet request to base heavy bombers in the Caucasus, where they could reach
strategic targets in eastern Europe but would be unavailable to support
the ground and naval forces in North Africa, air leaders demonstrated
a clear bias towards strategic bombardment that could hamper air-
ground relations in the years ahead.

Army Air Forces in the Western Desert Before Pearl Harbor

American airmen were indirectly involved in the Western Desert campaign even before a formal declaration of war against the Axis powers.
The USAAF assigned advisers, representatives, and observers to the
American legation in Cairo to observe combat, to provide technical
assistance, and, even when not specifically requested, to offer their
suggestions on how to conduct the campaign.[2] Major General George
H. Brett conducted an initial inspection and provided the chief of the
Army Air Forces, General Hap Arnold, with a detailed update on the
battles on the Libyan-Egyptian border. In a lengthy report to Arnold
sent on 17 September 1941, Brett noted, "In all my investigations and
questions I keep constantly in mind, without mentioning it, the fact
that if the United States enters this war, this may be a theater in which
they will operate."[3] What exactly Brett meant was clarified in Air War
Planning Document-1 (AWPD-1), published that same month, which
"envisioned Egypt-based [Boeing B-29 *Superfortress* heavy bombers]

adding their weight to an ambitious bomber offensive against industrial Germany."[4] Although officially there to provide assistance to the RAF in their struggle against the Axis in the Western Desert, American airmen committed to a strategic campaign remained focused on the lucrative targets in Southern and Eastern Europe that would be within range of bombers based in North Africa. This attraction endured throughout the campaign on the northern shores of the African continent.

When hostilities opened in the desert in mid-1940, the Royal Air Force was at the height of the Battle of Britain and diverted few assets to the Mediterranean until that crisis had passed. Once Hitler reduced his aerial assault of Britain to preserve assets for the campaign against the Soviet Union, the RAF was able to transfer more aircraft, including some modern *Spitfire* and *Hurricane* types, to support the ground forces opposing the September 1940 invasion of Egypt by Italian forces from Libya. It soon became clear that British production would be insufficient to support the theater, and Air Marshal Sir Arthur Tedder requested Lend-Lease assets to help build the Western Desert Air Force (WDAF).

To rapidly move American aircraft from stateside factories to the British in Egypt, Pan-American Airways received a contract to establish an air route and to ferry aircraft and supplies across the South Atlantic to Africa. Ferry pilots could fly new aircraft from factories on the East Coast down to Florida, across the Caribbean to the coast of Brazil, and then across the narrows of the South Atlantic to the western coast of Africa. From there, a treacherous and unimproved air route crossed below the Sahara to Sudan, where a branch up the Nile offered access to British airfields in Egypt. By continuing east, the new ferry route also provided access across the Saudi deserts to Persia and on to India and the Pacific. When the Japanese temporarily severed the transpacific ferry route in early 1942, the African route provided the only access to Australia and Southeast Asia. The same route was later used extensively to provide aircraft to the Soviets from bases in Persia and Iraq and to reinforce Americans operating in the China-Burma-India theater.

Moving airframes across the Atlantic was only one step in providing the RAF with an adequate supply. Upon arrival, the aircraft had to be maintained, modified, and prepared for acceptance. In addition, American technical expertise was essential to train operators and maintenance personnel, and damaged or worn-out aircraft required facilities to enable them to reenter the battle. To accommodate all these functions, President Franklin Roosevelt on 13 September 1941 ordered the War Department to arrange for the "establishment and operation of depots in the Middle East for the maintenance and supply of American aircraft."[5] To oversee this growing commitment, the War Department created the United States Military North African Mission, under Brigadier General Russell L. Maxwell, on 27 September 1941. Brigadier General Elmer Adler was named chief of the mission's air section.[6] The mission's purpose was to "assure the timely establishment and operation of supply, maintenance and training facilities."[7] Adler's first task was to comply with Roosevelt's order to establish a repair depot. After considering several sites, Adler recommended Gura, Eritrea, liberated from the Italians in early 1941. With a facility just inland from the Red Sea, American technical experts could repair and modify aircraft flown across the ferry route and even assemble crated airframes shipped across the Atlantic, around the Cape, and up the Indian Ocean. This facility provided a valuable service to the British but, more important for the USAAF, gave the fledgling Middle East Air Forces a secure logistical base at a time when few additional assets could be spared from the United States. A later air depot at Rayak in Syria provided direct support to American forces in the theater, independent of British supply channels, but much of the logistical support during the active phases of the battle—including everything from rations to aircraft fuel to aircrew survival kits—was provided by the British. The secure, established system of maintenance and supply underwrote all of the Middle East Air Force's success in the Western Desert.

Initial Deployment and HALPRO

When hostilities opened at Pearl Harbor, the Middle East was pushed even farther back in importance, as reinforcements for the Pacific took center stage. The USAAF suffered a serious setback with the destruction of almost the entire Far East Air Force in the Philippines, under the command of General Lewis H. Brereton. Brereton had requested permission from General Douglas MacArthur to launch a preemptive raid on Japanese forces on Formosa, but MacArthur's chief of staff, Brigadier General Richard K. Sutherland, withheld authorization until attacking Japanese planes were already inbound. Before Brereton's bombers could arm and launch, twelve B-17s were destroyed on the ground, including three that were taxiing for takeoff.[8] After several weeks of unbalanced combat, the battered remnants of Brereton's force withdrew to the south. They later took part in the battle for Indonesia before finally seeking refuge in India. The few surviving B-17s would eventually be sent to the Middle East, augmenting the USAAF's heavy bomber force in Palestine.

Allied fortunes continued to ebb and flow in North Africa during late 1941 and early 1942. In early December the British Eighth Army relieved the garrison of Tobruk, forcing Rommel's Afrika Korps to retreat across the hump of Cyrenaica. By January British forces had reached Benghazi but were forced to evacuate the town later that month, as concerns about the security of Asian possessions took hold. Japanese attacks against Malaya and Singapore created pressure for the release of Australian and New Zealand ground and air units in the Western Desert, and by mid-February the lines had stabilized around Gazala. The situation was similar to the previous year, when the German deployment into Bulgaria and the invasion of Yugoslavia and Greece in early April 1941 had forced the British to withdraw additional forces from the desert in an ill-fated effort to help stabilize their Greek allies.

An American observer, Colonel Demas T. Craw, witnessed the invasion of Greece firsthand and even participated in several combat missions against the Germans, including bombing raids on Sofia and one on Skopje in which four of six aircraft were lost, before being forced to evacuate Athens. Upon his return, Craw shared his observations in a detailed report to the USAAF's intelligence section on 3 July 1942. In Craw's words, once the British and Greeks lost control of the skies, "a Ladies' Aid Society could have taken Greece without any difficulty." Craw was also emphatic that American heavy bombers could influence the campaign then unfolding in the Western Desert and observed that "the Royal Air Force in the Middle East had never been equipped with long range, four engine heavy bombardment airplanes." This was critical because, in the absence of a Royal Navy depleted by the evacuation from Greece and with the intensive Axis air attacks on Malta,

> the only thing available to the British to prevent the assembly of supplies and personnel in Libya by the Germans for an attack was modern, heavy bombers. The German attacks on Malta kept the available bombers (twin-engine *Wellingtons*) from operating, and permitted an uninterrupted flow of supplies from Italy to Bengasi and Tripoli. Had the British been in possession of a few B-17s [*Fly-*

ing Fortresses] or [Consolidated B-24 *Liberator* heavy bombers] it would have been impossible for Rommel to assemble in daylight the tremendous force which confronted the British in Libya before this campaign.[9]

By the time Craw returned stateside and made this report, the first American aircraft had already arrived in the Middle East.

In late May 1942, General Arnold and Rear Admiral John Towers, chief of the U.S. Navy Bureau of Aeronautics, traveled to the United Kingdom to discuss Allied aircraft allocation with Chief of the Air Staff Sir Charles Portal. The conference was officially requested by President Roosevelt, who on 12 May informed Prime Minister Winston Churchill that he was "anxious that every appropriate American-made aircraft be manned and fought by our own crews. Existing schedules of aircraft allocations do not permit us to do this."[10] Before the war, American officials had allocated large numbers of U.S.-built aircraft for Lend-Lease to the British at the expense of building up the US-AAF. Now that the United States had entered the war, Roosevelt was under heavy pressure from Arnold to revise the earlier agreements in favor of the USAAF. Portal had originally requested "three squadrons of Heavy Bombers [54 aircraft] and six squadrons of Medium Bombers [108 aircraft] equipped by American aircraft by April 1943" for the Middle East, but Arnold countered with an offer of only thirty-five heavies and 114 mediums, which Portal accepted.[11] The resulting Arnold-Portal-Towers Agreement, approved by the Joint Chiefs of Staff on 25 June, allocated a total of nine combat groups to the Middle East: one group of heavy bombers to be operational by October, the first of two groups of medium bombers to be ready by September, and six total groups of pursuit (480 aircraft), the first two to arrive in September and October, respectively. During the same time, the agreement allocated 700 heavy bombers and 800 mediums to Operation BOLERO, the buildup for operations in Northwest Europe.[12]

Subsequent diversions to Operation TORCH, the invasion of western North Africa, would limit the final allocation to the Middle East Air Forces to just four groups, including a second group of heavy bombers rushed over after the collapse of defenses on the Libyan border. The second pursuit group was not operational until after the Battle of El Alamein, so the entire American commitment during the vital stages of the Western Desert campaign consisted of the 57th Pursuit Group (three squadrons of P-40s—the 64th, 65th and 66th), the 12th Medium Bombardment Group (four squadrons of B-25s—the 81st,

82nd, 83rd, and 434th), and the 98th Bomb Group (four squadrons of B-24Es—the 343rd, 344th, 345th and 415th), as well as the heavy group originally specified in the Arnold-Portal-Towers Agreement. This unit, eventually redesignated as 376th Bomb Group, was an ad hoc formation created out of the Halverson Provisional Detachment (known as HALPRO, which included 24 B-24Es) and later reinforcements from India. The Halverson detachment, under the command of aviation pioneer Colonel Harry A. Halverson, had originally been created to attack Japan from bases in China. It lacked sufficient size to conduct a sustained operation, and its intended morale effect had been largely achieved by the Doolittle Raid on 18 April 1942. When the Japanese offensive through Burma in early 1942 made sustaining a supply route into China impracticable, the unit was instead diverted to the Middle East at the urgent request of Air Marshal Sir Arthur Tedder.

As Colonel Craw had observed, the British desperately needed long-range aircraft to support their battle against the Axis supply lines stretching across the Mediterranean, and Tedder "had long pressed for the diversion of a heavy bomber force to the Middle East, so far without success." In denying Tedder's request, Air Marshal Portal agreed "that long-range heavy bombers would be desirable in Egypt," but he "did not feel them to be essential." Portal was "absolutely opposed to diverting more heavies from the attack on Germany," which he believed, even then, was "really beginning to have great results."[13]

When the American and British Chiefs of Staff meet in Washington, D.C., for the ARCADIA Conference in January 1942, Portal had asked for a heavy bomber group for the Middle East, but Arnold denied the request at the time.[14] It should be noted that in May 1942 the British had 378 operational heavy bombers in Bomber Command and projected a total of 1,008 by the end of the year. There were none in the Middle East, and at that time the RAF did not propose to deploy any there until September, when they would send a single squadron of eighteen aircraft. By the end of the year, that number was projected to double to thirty-six. After the fall of Tobruk, the RAF did rush two squadrons to the theater and had sent a total of twenty-six *Halifaxes* and eighteen *Liberators* by the end of September.[15]

Without the British aircraft, the mission fell to Halverson's twenty-three remaining B-24s (one was lost in transit), which had spent the first few months of 1942 training at Fort Myers, Florida, and occasionally flying operational antisubmarine missions over the Gulf of Mexico. The unit was originally to have only ten crews but was expanded to twenty-four, largely at the expense of the 98th Bomb Group, also based at Fort Myers. The constant siphoning would lead to some hard feelings between the men in both units when the 98th Bomb Group later became the second American heavy bomber group stationed in the Middle East.[16] But the experience gained in overwater navigation and antishipping tactics would serve the unit well in its first months of war.

Halverson's crews were broken up into three flights of eight aircraft each for the transit across the southern ferry route. After leaving behind one damaged aircraft, the remaining twenty-three, with a total of 212 men aboard, began their journey to the Middle East. Each plane was stripped of unnecessary equipment to maximize range and to make room for two or three passengers, usually spare aircrew and a bare minimum of maintenance personnel. The absence of a dedicated maintenance unit was later offset by the incorporation of Australian ground crews from No. 458 Squadron, Royal Australian Air Force. Unable to obtain sufficient *Wellingtons* to equip the unit, the RAF had distributed the pilots of No. 458 Squadron to other operational units, leaving the maintenance personnel without a mission. When Halverson's crews arrived without their support personnel, Tedder readily assigned them to support Halverson's unit.[17]

Although the unit had been diverted to the Middle East to support the British campaign in the Western Desert, Halverson and the US-AAF still wanted to fulfill the original mission of striking a strategic blow against the Axis. Halverson and his men were not alone in this view, as Allied planners had long eyed the German petroleum facilities in Romania. From Fayid, HALPRO's new base in Palestine, the refineries at Ploesti were at the edge of the B-24s maximum range, but the complex was the single largest producer of Axis petroleum and represented a significant percentage of total production. Unable to pass up an opportunity, Arnold ordered Halverson to lead all available aircraft across the Mediterranean to strike this vital target.

On the morning of 12 June 1942, the thirteen operational B-24s lifted off from their base near present-day Tel Aviv to make the US-AAF's first raid on Axis targets in Europe. Lacking the fuel to return home, they planned to violate Turkish neutrality by overflying that country en route to Habbaniyah, Iraq. All thirteen aircraft reached the target but inflicted only minimal damage, largely due to cloud cover obscuring the target. During the return trip fuel shortages and battle damage forced down four aircraft in Turkey, three near Ankara, and one at Izmir, where they were interned by the unhappy Turks.

Two aircraft reached Aleppo, Syria, and three reached Iraq but landed short of Habbaniyah at Mosul, Ramadi, and Deir Ez Zor, with one aircraft damaged beyond repair on crash-landing. Only four of the original thirteen B-24s reached Habbaniyah and eventually returned to Fayid. The five aircraft permanently lost represented 38 percent of the aircraft launched on the raid and more than 20 percent of Halverson's total force. In the ensuing six months, the detachment flew sorties almost daily but never again launched as many aircraft on a single mission. The aircraft lost in the ineffective raid on Ploesti would be sorely missed in the coming campaign.[18]

Just three days later, Halverson was asked to enter the fray in the Mediterranean. In the early months of 1942, the British air and naval base at Malta had endured unrelenting attacks from German and Italian aircraft based in nearby Sicily. Stocks, especially of aviation fuel, were running low for the beleaguered defenders, and the British launched two convoys from either side of the Mediterranean in a desperate effort to resupply the garrison. The convoys were to depart from Gibraltar and Alexandria at roughly the same time so as to stretch the Axis air and naval resources and improve the chances that at least some of the ships would get through. Axis forces responded with continuous attacks against both convoys, which cost each a number of ships and depleted the defenders' antiaircraft ammunition. Emboldened by the Axis control of the skies, the Italian Regia Marina made a rare sortie in an attempt to intercept the westbound convoy and engage it in a surface action.

Halverson's detachment attempted to intercept the Italian fleet and launched seven B-24s, which found the ships in the Ionian Sea, just east of Malta. The rendezvous was difficult after a long flight to the target area, but Halverson's crews likely benefited from the long antisubmarine missions earlier in the year over the Gulf of Mexico. The group claimed five hits on the superstructure of a *Littorio*-class battleship and another hit on a *Cavour*-class battleship, as well as an additional near-miss. On the return trip, the bombers were intercepted and claimed to have downed a single German Messerschmitt Me-110, a twin-engine fighter.[19] Aircraft from RAF No. 39 Squadron, a *Beaufort* squadron based at Sidi Barrani, also participated in the attack and confirmed that the B-24s hit a battleship and had an apparent hit on a destroyer. Postwar reports indicate that the *Littorio* did sustain one hit on an armored turret but that the thick protection easily withstood the blast of the 500-pound bomb. Undaunted, the Italian fleet continued its pursuit of the resupply convoy, which was forced to turn back toward Egypt until reconnaissance aircraft could confirm that the Italian vessels had given up the chase. Unfortunately the delay cost the convoy precious time and further depleted ammunition stores defending against air attacks from Libya, and the convoy was forced to return to Alexandria.[20] The western convoy also suffered heavy casualties and managed to slip only two battered supply vessels into Malta's Valletta harbor. The loss of the fuel tanker *Kentucky*, an American ship with a British crew, was especially hard felt, as there was barely enough aviation gas on the island to keep the RAF squadrons there in the fight.

The battered state of the Malta garrison would make Allied sorties from Egypt even more important in the coming months for interdicting the flow of supplies across the Mediterranean. The initial American antishipping mission was surprisingly effective, especially when the results obtained by Halverson's group are compared with the disappointing USAAF efforts in the Battle of Midway the preceding week, when repeated sorties by B-17s from that island failed to hit any Japanese ships. Had the B-24s in Palestine been equipped with heavier bombs than the 500-pounders they were carrying, they might have been able to inflict significant damage on the Italian warships and forced them to turn back earlier, allowing the Malta-bound convoy to reach its objective. Despite slightly bettering the USAAF's record at Midway, the results paled in comparison to what a combined RAF–Royal Navy team was able to accomplish against the same battle group. Earlier in the day, Malta-based *Beauforts* of No. 217 Squadron had torpedoed and stopped the Italian cruiser *Trento*, which was later finished off by the British submarine *P. 35*.[21]

"Diversion" to Interdiction

After the Ploesti raid and the mission against the Italian fleet, HAL-PRO settled into the routine that would dominate activities for the coming months: almost nightly raids against port facilities at Benghazi and Tobruk. The Benghazi missions were especially important, as that harbor was now beyond the range of the British *Wellington* medium bomber, and could be struck only by the longer-range B-24s and the few *Liberators* of RAF No. 159 Squadron. These raids were conducted in close coordination with sorties by the WDAF, the British organization directly supporting the ground forces, which usually provided night-time illumination by dropping flares over target area. With artificial lighting on the typically clear North African nights, American aircrews were able to employ techniques originally designed for day-light bombing. On 21 June nine B-24s hit Benghazi, starting fires on the harbor's Cathedral Mole. On 24 June twelve B-24s launched, but two were forced to return with engine trouble, an early indicator of a chronic problem for bombers in the months ahead. The ten that continued on to Benghazi noted two explosions on the railway sidings, the critical link between the port and Rommel's forces pressing into Egypt. The next night four B-24s made the unit's first raid on Tobruk, as a diversion for a raid of Royal Navy Fairey *Albacores* of the Fleet Air Arm. HALPRO returned to Tobruk on 26 June with eight B-24s, as well as the British *Liberators* of No. 159 Squadron, and noted several explosions and a fire on the port's jetty. On 28 June nine aircraft claimed hits on shipping in Tobruk's harbor.

On its eighth mission on 29 June, HALPRO suffered its first casualties since the Ploesti raid when flak claimed a single B-24 and its six crewmembers on a mission to Tobruk. These casualties marked the USAAF's first losses to enemy action against the European Axis.[22] American attacks on the ports freed up more of the WDAF for attacks on airfields, which correspondingly decreased Eighth Army's losses during the retreat into Egypt. The RAF's official history also noted "the greater bomb load carried by the *Liberators* greatly increased the tonnage of bombs dropped per sortie, particularly at Tobruk." Between 21 and 30 June, *Liberators* flew thirty-four of the forty-three sorties to that port.[23]

As the calendar turned to July, Rommel's tenuous supply line across the Mediterranean assumed critical importance in the battle in the Western Desert. With supplies captured at Tobruk, Rommel was able to launch a serious drive into Egypt as the Eighth Army retreated before him. The WDAF played a vital role in preventing this retreat from turning to a rout, and General Claude Auchinleck, then commanding ground forces in the Western Desert, reported:

> Our air forces could not have done more than they did to help sustain the Eighth Army in its struggle. Their effort was continuous by day and night, and the effect on the enemy was tremendous. I am certain that, had it not been for their devoted and exceptional efforts, we should not have been able to stop the enemy on the El Alamein position, and I wish to record my gratitude and that of the whole Eighth Army to Air Chief Marshal Tedder, Air Marshal Coningham, and the air forces under their command.[24]

As the British fell back from positions at Mersa Matruh and raced to prepare what would become the line at El Alamein, a robust effort by WDAF fighters and light bombers stalled the Axis pursuit. Air cover allowed British ground forces to fall back without being harried by Junkers Ju-87 *Stuka* dive-bombers and Messerschmitt Me-109 fighters. This advantage cannot be overstated: Had British forces not been able to erect a solid defense at El Alamein, Rommel might have been able to break through to Alexandria and Cairo, terminating the North African campaign in an Axis victory. As it was, the exhausted British formations had time to incorporate reinforcements coming up from the Red Sea and to stall Rommel at the last defensible position before the Nile Delta. In the coming months, the British airmen responsible for this feat would train and employ units of the USAAF in its first ground support missions against the European Axis.

Early in July, the HALPRO detachment was reinforced by another hard-luck unit. In response to British appeals, on 23 June General Arnold ordered Major General Lewis Brereton, then commanding Tenth Air Force in India, to bring all available heavy bombers to Egypt to add their weight. Brereton's force had been chased by the advancing Japanese across the Southwest Pacific, from the Philippines to Java and finally to India. When he received the orders Brereton had only nine operational B-17s, but he loaded these aircraft with all available support and maintenance personnel and hurried to the Middle East.[25] Upon arrival, his aircraft, originally from 9th Bomb Squadron, 7th Bomb Group (Heavy), were merged with HALPRO to form the 1st Provisional Bomb Group under Halverson's command; Brereton was named commander of all U.S. air assets in the Middle East. Halverson's group now consisted of two squadrons; the B-24s, redesignated the Hal Squadron on 17 July, and the B-17s retaining their designation as the 9th Bomb Squadron.[26] The title "Provisional" underscored the ad hoc nature of this unit, thrown together from assets scattered around the globe to address the deteriorating situation in the Western Desert.

On 2 July four B-17s from 9th Bomb Squadron flew their first mission, accompanying a raid on Tobruk. For the remainder of July both squadrons, along with the few British *Liberators* of No. 242 Wing, threw their weight against Benghazi, Tobruk, and, when they could be located, convoys at sea. On 4 July six B-24s continued their remarkable success against shipping when they hit two ships of a convoy, including a tanker left afire. They followed up that success in the predawn hours of 6 July when eleven aircraft, the largest raid since

Ploesti, claimed the explosion of a vessel believed to be an ammunition ship in Benghazi's harbor. For the remainder of the month, almost daily raids by B-17s and B-24s hit Tobruk and Benghazi, frequently starting large fires on the docks and further reducing the capacity of Rommel's already strained supply lines. During July the 1st Provisional Bomb Group flew 120 B-24 and forty-five B-17 sorties against Rommel's ports and convoys. On 28 July nine B-24s and seven British *Liberators* ventured across the Mediterranean to Souda Bay on Crete (which had become an important staging area for convoys crossing the eastern Mediterranean), hitting two ships and damaging warehouses.

USAAF losses were not high, as the Luftwaffe was then heavily engaged in the Soviet Union and most of the B-24 missions were flown at night. The group lost three B-24s in fifteen July missions—two less than the single raid on Ploesti. During this period, Axis ground forces made their first attempt to break through the new position at El Alamein, but they were repelled by the British. Rommel's attack was limited due to fuel and ammunition shortages, and he pulled back briefly in an attempt to accumulate the reserves that would permit a sustained thrust.

The 1st Provisional Bomb Group was reinforced on 23 July with the arrival of the 98th Bomb Group (Heavy), which had trained alongside HALPRO at Fort Myers. Also equipped with B-24s, 98th Bomb Group contained a full complement of four squadrons. Even better, its entire ground component, along with additional support and maintenance personnel, were en route aboard the *Pasteur*, which arrived at Port Tewfik on 15 August. This bomber group tripled the weight of the American bombers in the Middle East and entered action quickly, flying its first mission on 1 August. Its arrival enabled the 1st Provisional Bomb Group to stand down briefly, from 6 August to 24 August, for much-needed rest and maintenance. During this time, Lieutenant Colonel George McGuire relieved Colonel Halverson in command of the 1st Provisional Bomb Group and Halverson returned to the United States. The older unit finished its first two months of combat with a flourish, as raids on 6 August left extensive damage on the docks at Tobruk. Seven B-24s, each carrying five 1,000-pound bombs, claimed to have left one ship at Pier 16T on fire. The Allied attacks reduced the port's capacity from 2,000 to 600 tons per day, and it never rose above 1,000 tons per day after the raid.[27] The 1st Provisional Group still flew sixty-two sorties during the month, all by the Halverson squadron's B-24s, while the 98th added 125 sorties. The additional weight made the almost daily raids against Axis supply lines even more effective.

USAAF Tactical Squadrons in the Western Desert

While the two groups of heavy bombers were heavily engaged in the interdiction campaign, the first two tactical groups promised under the Arnold-Portal-Towers Agreement arrived in the theater to augment the WDAF. The air components of both the 57th Pursuit Group (P-40s) and 12th Medium Bomb Group (B-25s) arrived in July but had to wait for the *Pasteur* to reintegrate their ground components. The 57th's journey to Egypt represented a significant commitment by the U.S. Navy. At a time when there was a severe shortage of fleet carriers in the Pacific, one of the Atlantic carriers, the USS *Ranger*, ferried the fighters of 57th Group from the United States to the western coast of Africa. P-40s lacked the range to make the transatlantic crossing and, without the carrier transportation, would have to be disassembled, shipped, and reassembled, significantly delaying their entry into combat. Without navy transportation, they likely would have missed the Alam Halfa battle in early September, and possibly El Alamein as well.

The 57th's odyssey began on 1 July, when seventy-two Curtiss P-40E *Tomahawks* left Mitchel Field in New York and were loaded on the *Ranger* at Quonset Point, Rhode Island. On 19 July, when still about 100 miles from Takoradi, Ghana, the aircraft took off from the carrier and began the journey across Africa. Ground crews, which had been moved by the southern ferry route in transport aircraft, followed the P-40s and their pilots across the continent, working nights to ready the aircraft for the next day's segment. By the end of the month all three squadrons were at Muqbelia in Palestine.[28] Two squadrons, the 64th and 66th, remained in the area to train while 65th Fighter Squadron was sent to Nicosia, Cyprus, to relieve overcrowding in the delta region. Brereton had previously made an inspection trip to Cyprus to investigate the island's use as both a training base and "an advanced base for heavies."[29] As the bombers could already cover the entire eastern Mediterranean, including the Greek coast, from their bases in Palestine, only raids into the European continent would have required the use of Cyprus as a forward base.

At the same time, the promised group of medium bombers also arrived via the southern ferry route. The 12th Bomb Group moved all fifty-seven B-25s to the Middle East without loss. Two squadrons, the 81st and 82nd, set up housekeeping at Deversoir, while the 83rd and 434th moved to Ismailia.[30] Both groups were fully trained and capable of delivering bombs against any target but required a thorough course on the RAF techniques employed in ground support in the Western

Desert. While the concepts were similar to those delineated in *FM 31-35*, the crews still required integration into the British system. The 57th began by rotating the squadron's most experienced pilots through British squadrons, then gradually attaching American squadrons to RAF formations until they were capable of flying missions on their own, a capability achieved prior to the breakout from El Alamein.[31]

The British support system in the Western Desert had evolved continually since the first attacks against Italian-occupied Libya in September 1940.[32] By mid-1942 the RAF operated a series of "tentacles", with the forward ground units that funneled information back to the mobile Army Air Support Control (AASC), usually located at the combined ground and air headquarters.[33] The AASC processed requests for support and also disseminated near real-time intelligence passed from either ground-intercept (known as Y) units or from airborne observation assets via the new VHF radios. Using this information, as well as status reports from the air units on the number of available assets, the AASC would then allocate units to the most lucrative targets. Additional command-and-control measures, such as the establishment of a so-called bomb line (based on geographic landmarks and beyond which targets were assumed to be enemy) and an illuminated, changing letter of the alphabet at night provided reference points for pilots and enabled them to strike Axis ground targets more effectively.

On 22 August, Brereton sent Arnold three copies of a report titled "Direct Air Support in the Libyan Desert," covering the period from 26 May to 22 August 1942.[34] Brereton wrote: "While I realize the operations being conducted in this theater must be adapted in the greatest degree to circumstances of terrain and weather, nevertheless many of the conclusions and recommendations contained herein will apply to direct support operations in any theater."[35] The report provided USAAF leaders the first description of the British system then in use in the Western Desert. The report arrived two full months before the next USAAF units would enter combat in North Africa, providing the service ample time to indoctrinate the green units in these methods. Unfortunately, this opportunity seems to have been missed.

The report began with a broad assessment of the situation in the Western Desert during the period covered, including a summary of forces available and their organization and equipment. (Almost 600 RAF aircraft, including 300 fighters, and another 200 light and medium bombers were opposed by an estimated 500 German and Italian planes, including more than 200 fighters.) The report included information on serviceability and tactical formations but, most important, outlined the function and request-approval process employed by Air Support Control, including the establishment of a bomb line. It also commented on the difficulty of identifying friendly forces, and the measures introduced to remedy this defect, including colored smoke signals (which were as yet unavailable), ground panels, and colored lights, all of which were deemed unsatisfactory.

In its conclusions, the report found that "fighter-bomber operations are markedly successful, particularly continuous attack against dispersed motor units and tanks." It continued: "In spite of deficiencies in equipment and training, technique used for direct support by air has been successful, but failure to provide proper means of identification—or failure to use those provided—has resulted in attack on friendly troops. . . . Communications are difficult and have proved the most serious obstacle to developing the full power of air support." It concluded that "success achieved in direct air support operation is primarily due to fine cooperation and mutual understanding between air and ground command echelons."[36]

One of the keys to this cooperation was the assignment of two RAF Army Liaison Officers (ALOs) to each fighter group. In an interview conducted on 17 June 1943, at the end of the campaign, Major P. R. Chandler, the intelligence officer assigned to 66th Fighter Squadron, described the importance of ALOs and believed that without them "we couldn't have done anything." The men were

> British officers who had considerable experience out in that area. Our Army liaison officers had both been in Africa for going on three years. They were very carefully chosen. Our men had the difficult job of selling themselves and their personality, as English officers, to the American pilots. They did a swell job of it. They stayed with the group and would come around and visit the squadrons quite frequently. They had with them a wireless link which kept them in frequent communication with Air Support control.

With this radio link, ALOs could keep the group abreast of changes in the ground battle and would provide the pilots with the most current bomb line, "sometimes once a day and sometimes five or six times a day. The ALO got it and would phone it to the squadron or come around himself and help post it on the squadron situation map." In turn, ALOs monitored the intelligence debriefs of returning crews and obtained "from the air units matters of immediate interest to the Army." Chandler reported that "a friend of mine, who worked at Air

Support control said frequently the same information would come through to one trailer via the ALO link 20 minutes before the trailer next door got it from the regular intelligence channel." ALOs, and their dedicated communications links, greatly facilitated the flow of real-time intelligence from air to ground units, and later in the war the USAAF reciprocated by providing trained pilots as air liaison officers to ground units to provide many of the same functions, including direct control of supporting aircraft.[37]

The British ALOs also provided critical feedback to the air units, maintaining their morale and willingness to engage in the often dangerous close support mission. Chandler related one incident during the battle when:

> The boys went on bomber escort—one of the numbers that we had. I believe they were themselves carrying 500-pounders on the mission. They frequently did and dropped them along with the bombers. Anyway, they went out with the bombers to an assigned point, dropped their bombs and came home. They came into the tent after a little while. You can generally tell when there's been a good mission or a bad one. This was a bad one. "Why 211 Group ever sent us to that patch of sand, I don't know—wasted time and effort." They had nothing to report. "Let's get on back up to the Mess." I dressed that report up suitably to pass inspection: "Results not observed, target not observed." Then I talked to the Army liaison officer on the telephone and he said: "Please convey to your pilots the sincere appreciation of the Army for what they did. Immediately following the bombing 200 Germans came out of their trenches and surrendered." I called the mess and told the boys. They said, "Maybe it was a good job after all. We are glad to know it."[38]

Both the newly arrived fighter and medium bomber groups completed their familiarization in time to join the two heavy bomber groups in the coming battle of Alam Halfa. On 9 August, Brereton reported the strength of all four groups in the delta region. Together, the 98th and 1st Provisional Heavy Bomb Groups numbered thirty-five aircraft and 1,663 personnel (barely the strength of a single heavy group later in the war). The 12th Medium Bomb Group had fifty-seven aircraft and 1,540 men, and the 57th Fighter Group numbered eighty aircraft and 930 men. In addition, the 323rd Service Group, with 900 men, was working to set up an air depot at Rayak, Syria.[39]

The 12th Bomb Group (Medium) was the first of the tactical units to see action in the Western Desert. Initially, B-25s were used as medium bombers on night missions alongside WDAF *Wellingtons*. On 15 August nine B-25s of 81st Bomb Squadron, each armed with four 500-pound bombs, left Deversoir for the hourlong run to Mersa Matruh. Fleet Air Arm *Albacores* provided illumination for the targets, which included barracks and supplies at the port. The 82nd Bomb Squadron had to wait until 22 August for its first mission, also to Mersa Matruh, alongside two *Wellingtons* of No. 40 Squadron. This time the bomb load was increased to six 500-pound bombs. On the return to the delta region, one aircraft was shot down by an RAF *Beaufighter*. The crew evidently failed to follow the correct procedures for returning to the area at a time when Axis bombers still made occasional raids. Two crewmen were lost in this unfortunate accident. The next night, the 81st Bomb Squadron flew its second mission, this time accompanying twelve *Halifaxes* of No. 10 and No. 76 Squadrons to Tobruk. The targets included a tanker and a merchantman that had just arrived in the port. One American aircraft was lost when it reportedly blew up over the target. During 24–26 August, the two squadrons flew nightly missions to the Axis airfield complexes at El Daba. The group's commander, Colonel Charles Goodrich, recognized that B-25s were unsuited for the night mission because the aircraft lacked flame dampeners on the engine exhausts, which made it very easy for the Axis gunners on the ground to track them in the darkened sky. As a result, the B-25s were reassigned to the WDAF's No. 232 Wing, where they flew alongside the RAF and South African *Baltimores* and *Bostons* (the export version of the A-20 *Havoc*) in daytime close support missions. Later, when crews had perfected the techniques of close support, they flew missions independently.[40]

Rommel knew that he could not win a long-term supply race, as Allied reinforcements sent after the disaster in Libya were already en route to Egypt, yet he hoped that one final push would carry him through the defenders before these reinforcements arrived. He timed his assault for the first week of September, when the moon phase would be favorable for night operations but before the bulk of the British supplies would complete their sixty-day transit around the Cape. The resulting Battle of Alam Halfa would be his last chance to break through the defensive cordon and reach the Suez Canal. The American tactical squadrons saw their first action in this battle, making a small but noticeable contribution, but, more important, demonstrating that they had absorbed the lessons of their mentors and were able to provide effective support of ground troops. Meanwhile, the heavy groups continued attacks on the supply lines, denying Axis forces the supplies, especially petroleum, needed to win the battle.

The switch from night interdiction to daytime close support missions came just in time for the 12th Bomb Group to participate in the Alam Halfa battle. Rommel opened his offensive on 31 August, and the WDAF took advantage of concentrated and exposed ground forces to initiate what became known as shuttle bombing. B-25s joined the South African Air Force (SAAF) No. 24 Squadron on all three missions that day, attacking troops, transports, and motor transport concentrations. In the following days, the formations, which typically consisted of fifteen SAAF *Bostons* and three B-25s, became known among the Germans as *Die Sture Achtzehn* ("The Eighteen Imperturbables"). In two raids on 1 September, three on 2 September, five on 3 September, and four on 4 September, 12th Bomb Group made its contribution to the failure of Rommel's attacks. While there were five *Bostons* for each B-25 on a raid, the B-25s carried 2,500 pounds of bombs, while the smaller *Bostons* carried only 1,000 pounds. As a result, the three B-25s increased by half again the ordinance dropped on each raid, magnifying the striking power considerably. The escorted attacks took place at medium altitude, between 7,000 and 9,000 feet, above the light flak but below the heavier weapons, and involved all four squadrons of 12th Bomb Group. At night, RAF medium bombers pounded the Axis positions, generating the first true around-the-clock bombing of the war.[41]

Some of the escort missions were flown by P-40s of 57th Fighter Group. While 65th squadron remained in Cyprus, the 64th and 66th were pressed into service escorting the shuttle runs over the battle area. The 66th was the first to see action, when four P-40s joined aircraft from No. 260 Squadron, as well as No. 2 and No. 4 SAAF Squadrons, in escorting eighteen *Bostons* and two B-25s over a concentration of motor transports. During the next week, the 64th Fighter Squadron flew eighty-three sorties while the 66th Fighter Squadron added eighty-seven, including up to four missions a day at the height of the battle. Due to the light opposition and the nature of the escort mission, the two squadrons did not lose any aircraft during the battle, but they did not claim any victories over enemy aircraft.

The escorts typically consisted of eight fighters in close formation, while another eight provided top cover. Later, one of the groups would also be equipped with 500-pound bombs to increase the weight of the attacks, then revert to their fighter role if any opposition was encountered. The British had only recently pioneered fighter-bomber tactics in the Western Desert, first with obsolete *Hurricanes* and later, in May 1942, with modified P-40s, but the fighter-bomber mission was new to the USAAF at that time.[42] Prewar doctrine had focused on escort of heavy bombers and interception of enemy bomber forces as the primary missions for pursuit aircraft. Close support was supposed to be accomplished by either attack aircraft, or else light or medium bombers like the A-20. According to Brereton, "Fighter-bomber technique was not taught in the States. Indeed, there existed a school of thought prior to our entry into the war which considered such employment uneconomical and ineffective."[43] During the prewar period, the Army Air Corps had even prohibited the installation of bomb racks on fighter aircraft.[44] Fighter-bomber tactics evolved to the point where, by war's end, the less maneuverable and more vulnerable dive-bomber, which had dominated the war's opening stages, was obsolete. Future fighter designs emphasized aircraft that could perform both roles, and existing fighter aircraft, most notably the American P-47 and the British Typhoon, were adapted to this role. Today, there are few fighter aircraft that do not possess an air-to-ground capability.

It is difficult to underestimate air's role in halting the offensive at Alam Halfa. First, it must be recognized that the bulk of the Luftwaffe was, at that time, supporting the drive into the Caucasus and the developing battle around Stalingrad.[45] Rommel felt their absence keenly. He noted "air attacks . . . have caused considerable losses in personnel and material." The Afrika Korps *kriegstagebuch* (war diary) reported losses of sixty-four tanks, 571 men, 145 vehicles, and nine guns completely destroyed and claimed "the high rate of losses in men and equipment was due mainly to enemy air attacks." The RAF's history noted that "the victory at Alem Halfa—even more than at El Alamein—proved a turning point of enemy fortunes during one of the most critical periods of the whole war. Basically, it was a battle of all arms in which Navy, Army and Air Force played their parts." Further, "victory would depend more than anything else on the correct employment of air power."[46]

At the same time, Rommel failed to use the aircraft he did have in an effective manner. There was never a sustained program to either build the Luftwaffe to sufficient strength to provide effective support or to challenge the growing RAF for control of the skies. Axis logistics were far worse than the Allies, and in-service rates were much lower due to both supply shortages and the extreme distance of the forward airfields from the ports and supply bases. The few aircraft available were often engaged in uncoordinated raids on the British front-line position, raids that were frequently broken up by effective resistance. While the RAF (and its few USAAF elements) deserve much of the credit for organizing an effective air campaign, it must be remembered that they were opposed by a weak and uncoordinated enemy in the air.

General Sir Bernard Law Montgomery, commanding British Eighth Army, recalled that "the Desert Air Force continued to cause great damage and confusion to the enemy." On the significance of Alam Halfa, Montgomery stated, "I think that this battle has never received the interest or attention it deserves. It was a vital action, because, had we lost it, we might well have lost Egypt. In winning it we paved the way for success at El Alamein and the subsequent advance to Tunisia."[47] Rommel blamed his failure on two factors: the "non-stop and very heavy air attacks by the RAF whose command of the air has been virtually complete," and lack of fuel. He reflected: "We had learnt one important lesson during this operation, a lesson which was to affect all subsequent planning, and, in fact, our entire future conduct of the war. This was that the possibilities of ground action, operational and tactical, become very limited if one's adversary commands the air with a powerful air force and can fly mass raids by heavy bomber formations unconcerned for their own safety." It is worth noting that, while these remarks reflected a frustration at the Luftwaffe's lack of support, they were also made during the early stages of the war. Rommel's experience in France, where Germany had enjoyed air superiority, and in Africa, where it had not, is instructive. In many theaters of the war, command of the air was a vital prerequisite for the success of ground and naval forces. Rommel was referring to Alam Halfa when he wrote that "anyone who has to fight, even with the most modern weapons, against an enemy in complete command of the air, fights like a savage against modern European troops, under the same handicaps and with the same chance of success."[48]

The USAAF at El Alamein

After Alam Halfa the tide turned against the Axis. Allied reinforcements continued to arrive in the Nile Delta, while Rommel's supply lines suffered crippling attacks. Two more months of attrition set the stage for the final battle in the Western Desert. Rommel's logistics also suffered from factors other than Allied interdiction. The battles in the Caucasus siphoned off men and equipment, especially aircraft that could have been used to protect either Rommel's forces or his vulnerable supply line. At the same time, the few supplies allocated to Rommel did not always make it from Italy to Egypt. After two years of war in the Mediterranean, the Italian merchant marine was showing signs of exhaustion. Allied aircraft and ships had taken a heavy toll, and the shortage of escorts delayed the ships that were available. British aircraft from Malta, and especially submarines of the Royal Navy, did much of the work to interdict the strained supply lines, but American heavy bombers added their weight and scored a few noticeable successes in the months leading up to El Alamein. As Rommel monitored the progress of each vessel, especially the critical fuel tankers that attempted to run the gantlet, even the loss of a single ship could have significant implications for the front lines. In his examination of the struggle, Alan Levine notes that Rommel "lost only 20 percent of his supplies on the route to Africa in September, but no less than 44 percent in October."[49] In *Supplying War*, Martin van Creveld argues that Rommel still received sufficient fuel in Africa but had difficulty transporting it from ports to the front lines.[50] If so, then the damage to the forward ports is magnified, as any reduction in port capacity would have to be made up at facilities farther to the rear, such as Tripoli, which increased the strain on an already extended logistics network.

The 98th and 1st Provisional Bomb Groups continued raids throughout September and October. In these two months, the heavy groups flew a combined fifty missions, totaling 417 individual sorties. Tobruk and Benghazi were still rich targets, but as the damage there accumulated the bombers ranged farther in search of other lucrative targets. The groups frequently visited the Greek coast, including the Cretan ports of Candia and Souda Bay, the airfield at Maleme, and Navarino Bay on the Peloponnesus. The ports were important staging areas for convoys prepared to make the run to North Africa, and Maleme held both convoy escorts and transport aircraft that were pressed into service to relieve the now critical shortages. A 16 September raid by seventeen B-24s and seven British *Liberators* on Benghazi heavily damaged the 3,500-ton transport *Ravello*. On 22 September, nine B-24s of the Hal Squadron, along with nine more aircraft from the 98th Group, hit Benghazi at dusk from 24,000 feet. The crew observed a fire and large explosions on a large merchant vessel, followed by "a large volume of black smoke." The crews had found the 7,949-ton *Apuania*, a large merchant vessel with ten tanks, 350 tons of rations, and 500 tons of ammunition. British codebreakers at Bletchley Park had evidently reported the ship's arrival. The resulting explosion severely damaged the main pier, known as Harry, and sank an adjacent wreck being used as an unloading platform.[51] By mid-October, the Army Air Forces comprised 80 percent of the heavy bombers in the Middle East. While they never destroyed as much shipping as the RAF or the Royal Navy, they complemented British efforts by preventing an unopposed end run around Malta through the eastern Mediterranean and further strained Rommel's supplies while freeing WDAF assets for other missions.

After a brief stand-down to recover from the Alam Halfa battle, tactical groups were soon back in action, intercepting German forays over the Eighth Army's lines and paying return visits to Axis airfields. While the USAAF and RAF had the advantage of improved airfields in the delta area, Germans and Italians operated from primitive strips near El Daba and Fuka. These sand and dirt fields had performed well during the dry summer months, but the change in seasons revealed their flaws. The flat, open areas that were so attractive for landing grounds also suffered from poor drainage and quickly turned to mud after even a light desert rainstorm. In early October, one such storm immobilized the Axis pilots, while Allied airmen were still able to operate from their all-weather fields in the delta region. Knowing his adversary would be stuck on the ground, Air Marshal Sir Arthur Coningham, commander of the Western Desert Air Force, planned a surprise visit for the early hours of 9 October. Although the results proved disappointing—with only ten aircraft destroyed and another thirteen damaged—the American squadrons were fully integrated into the attacks. For the first time, the 57th Fighter Group mounted a group mission, with all three squadrons contributing a total of forty-five sorties. The P-40s escorted the bombers to their targets and then strafed the airfields at Landing Grounds 21 and 104. The group claimed seven trucks, as well as one gun emplacement destroyed, and scored its first aerial victory, with a claim of one Me-109 downed.[52]

The 12th Medium Bomb Group contributed sixteen B-25s to the operation. Armed with eight 250-pound bombs each, the *Mitchells* made an afternoon raid from 10,000 feet. They were intercepted by a dozen Me-109s but reported no losses. The mission was the group's first since a costly raid on enemy airfields on 14 September. In what became the group's last nighttime mission, four B-25s were lost over Sidi Haneish. Alerted defenders and the visibility of the flame dampeners contributed to the losses. The groups attacked three separate airfields at twenty-minute intervals, with sufficient time for the defenders to respond and offer strong resistance. One of the casualties was the group commander, Lieutenant Colonel Goodrich, who became a prisoner of war. The 12th flew few combat sorties between Alam Halfa and the Alamein battle but continued to rest and train to ensure it would be ready when it was needed most.[53]

As Montgomery prepared for his attempt to break through Rommel's defenses, the Allies gradually gained the upper hand in the air. On 10 October, Fliegerfuhrer Afrika, the German air headquarters on the continent, had at their disposal only thirty-nine bombers (twenty-eight operational), 131 fighters (seventy-two operational), and 170 transports (100 operational). At the same time, the WDAF had 420 fighters alone, but only fifty were *Spitfires*; less-capable *Hurricanes* made up almost half the force. The light-bomber force had suffered serious losses in the months of continuous combat. *Wellington* numbers dropped from 130 in July down to seventy. At the same time, Bomber Command contained 970 aircraft, including more than 600 medium and heavy bombers. Tedder felt this discrepancy keenly and cabled Portal that he was "becoming increasingly concerned at my Wellington situation and feel I must ask for reconsideration of present Air Ministry policy."[54] At this time, the USAAF comprised only 10 percent of the WDAF but accounted for 33 percent of its light bombers and 70 percent of its heavies.

The air pattern for the Alamein battle followed very closely that of Alam Halfa two months earlier. The light bombers, escorted by fighters, attacked troop and motor vehicle concentrations by day while British mediums continued the assault by night. The heavy bombers continued to range far behind the battle lines, striking ports and shipping and adding to Rommel's woes. The heavies had been organized into three striking forces, with two squadrons of the 98th Group at St. Jean d'Acre (sixteen B-24s), the other two squadrons of the 98th at Ramat David (sixteen B-24s), and the 1st Provisional Group at Lydda (sixteen B-24s and ten B-17s). Ideally, each strike group would operate every third day, ensuring a sizeable force was available daily to respond to taskings, weather permitting.[55] On 1 November, the 1st Provisional Bomb Group was brought up to strength by the addition of three full squadrons sent out from the United States and was redesignated as 376th Bomb Group. The former Hal and 9th squadrons became 513th Bomb Squadron, still equipped with B-17s and B-24s, while the 512th, 514th, and 515th Bomb Squadrons rounded out the new group. On the next night, five B-17s scored 376th Group's first official tally by sinking the *Brioni* at Tobruk with 255 tons of ammunition onboard. This ship was the sole survivor of an emergency convoy rushed through to Rommel when the Alamein battle began. Five B-17s repeated this success on 6 November when they sank the 2,153-ton freighter *Etiopia* at Tobruk, while the B-24s set afire the 6,424-ton tanker *Portofino* at Benghazi. On 4 November, Generalleutnant Otto von Waldau, commanding the German air forces in Africa, commented in his diary, "The fate of the Mediterranean hung more or less on these three ships."[56] With his men already on half-rations and the gas tanks and ammunition racks in his panzers running empty, Rommel was unable to contain the determined British breakthrough and was forced to retreat. Unfortunately, the weather turned against the Allies, as autumn rains turned desert tracks to mud and hampered pursuit. When they could get airborne, crews reported that the entire length of the road from Gazala was "crowded with enemy transport," and they did their best to stall the retreat. According to Montgomery, "The Desert Air Force operated at maximum intensity and took every advantage of the exceptional targets which the fleeing enemy presented."[57]

In the fortnight-long battle, the WDAF had provided valuable close support. Coningham's light bombers and fighters resumed shuttle services, concentrating over any critical point on the battlefield, breaking up Axis counterattacks, and covering Montgomery's offensive. During the battle, the 12th Medium Bomb Group was attached to No. 232 Wing, along with the British *Baltimores*. From 19 October through 5 November, the group flew fifty-eight missions totaling 428 sorties, again at a rate of three to four missions per day. Seven aircraft were put out of commission by battle damage, but all crash-landed at friendly airfields. Another B-25 and crew was lost in a midair collision with another aircraft. At times the ground crews had the turnaround times down to twenty minutes, including refueling for the two-hour roundtrip to the front and loading on eight more 250-pound bombs. The WDAF preferred to operate with an even number of subordinate units, so 66th Fighter Squadron was folded into No. 239 Wing, with a British and two Australian squadrons. The other two American fighter squadrons fought under 57th Group's headquarters, assigned to No. 211 Group. While the Americans comprised less than 10 percent of the assets, and flew only slightly more than 10 percent of the sorties, they provided important assistance throughout the battle. They likely did not change the outcome, but in facilitating the success of Eighth Army they helped save British lives. Axis forces suffered 75,000 casualties during the battle in killed and captured, while the British lost 13,500. In the air, the losses were more even, as the WDAF lost ninety-four aircraft to all causes, including seventy-one fighters, against a German and Italian loss of 105.[58] By this time, Allied production rates could easily replace their losses while the Axis units, especially the Italian squadrons, were significantly understrength.

As Axis forces moved west out of Egypt, Allied air and ground forces followed. On 13 November, the same day that 57th Fighter Group entered Libya and reoccupied the landing grounds at Gambut, 98th Bomb Group displaced forward from Palestine to bases in Egypt. The day before, Brereton's headquarters in Egypt had been designated as Ninth Air Force, comprising all four groups that had participated in the battle, as well as the newly arrived 79th Fighter Group (P-40s) and the 316th Troop Carrier Group equipped with the Douglass C-47 *Sky-train/Dakota* and five full service groups. In the months ahead, Ninth Air Force would continue to support Eighth Army in the pursuit across Libya. The heavy bombers would eventually settle into airfields in Cyrenaica, where they could reach Axis ports in Italy, Sicily, and Tunisia. The following summer, they would even return to Ploesti from airfields liberated in the campaign in the Western Desert.

Results—and the Mission to Moscow

Allied airmen were impressed with and appreciative of the American contribution. Tedder reported "co-operation between fighters and bombers and between British and Americans in the desert is first class." Arnold cabled Brereton, "Brilliant operations (by the) 9th Air Force in Egypt represents outstanding achievements. The unexcelled support given the Ground Forces, the destruction of enemy ships and naval vessels, the destruction of 45 enemy airplanes with loss of only 6 American planes, and the relentless destruction of enemy communications has unquestionably contributed largely to present victory. . . . The courage and loyalty of all officers and men is evident. . . . Your cooperation with the British is very gratifying."[59] But the lessons learned and skills acquired in the skies over Egypt were more important than the comparatively small contribution to the eventual outcome of the Western Desert campaign. American airmen had demonstrated that they had the equipment to effectively support ground campaigns and, with important assistance from British circles, could quickly adapt to the tactics they were then employing. As one noted airpower historian has observed, "In all likelihood, the *truly* progressive characteristics of airpower are those that allow *ground* power to succeed more quickly and cheaply than it otherwise would."[60] Such was the case in the Western Desert. Unfortunately, many of these same lessons would have to be relearned in the next major American undertaking, the invasion of French North Africa, launched on 8 November, just as the pursuit began from El Alamein. There was simply too little time between the Alamein battle and Operation TORCH to fully incorporate the wealth of experience gained in the Western Desert into the green units supporting the new operation. Eventually, the two air forces would merge in Tunisia and finally have an opportunity to share what they had learned.[61]

But perfected techniques of ground and naval support were insufficient to deter the Allies from pursuing a campaign that promised a quicker and easier path to victory. As the Soviet situation deteriorated in the summer and early fall of 1942, Soviet premier Josef Stalin asked the Allies if they would be able to accelerate the shipment of Lend-Lease aircraft. As it was unlikely that the Soviets would be able to train sufficient aircrews to pilot the new planes, Stalin was even willing to consider basing Allied squadrons on Soviet territory. This concession reflects the importance of the Caucasus region, especially the oilfields along the Caspian Sea. On 10 October, Marshall cabled Brereton to begin planning for the diversion of one heavy bomber group and one transport group to the Caucasus, to arrive around the first of the year. Brigadier General Elmer Adler was selected as the American representative to a mission headed by the Australian-born Air Vice Marshal Peter Drummond, Tedder's deputy, and traveled with the delegation to Moscow in late November to work out the details with the Soviets. By that time, the Soviets had sprung their trap around Stalingrad, and a counteroffensive in the Caucasus had greatly reduced the threat to the Soviet oilfields. As a result, Stalin began to backtrack on his initial offer and stalled Drummond's mission. After several weeks of impasse, the delegation finally left, but Ninth Air Force had been deprived of the services of its most experienced logistician for more than a month. Fortunately, the proposed diversion of strategic bombers never came to pass, and they were allowed to continue their excellent service in support of the ground campaign in North Africa.[62]

Conclusion

This examination of the USAAF role in the Western Desert challenges some prevailing interpretations while reinforcing others. First, it refutes the suggestion that the USAAF so focused on the strategic bombardment mission that it neglected tactical developments during the interwar period.[63] In the Western Desert, American fighters and medium bombers were capable of providing excellent support to British ground forces with existing equipment and minimal training. However, there is an element of truth to the assertion of a British and American obsession with the strategic mission for heavy bombers. While B-24s and B-17s did excellent work interdicting Axis supply lines, this was not the role air leaders envisioned. At the same time that the WDAF and Ninth Air Force struggled to obtain replacement aircraft, engines, and pilots, the buildup of Bomber Command and Eighth Air Force proceeded almost uninterrupted. Only critical needs for Operation TORCH, the invasion of Morocco and Algeria, and General Eisenhower's insistence that they be adequately supported with all types of aircraft succeeded in prying loose B-17s and their escorts (twin-engine Lockheed P-38 *Lightnings*) from missions over Western Europe. At the time, many airpower advocates regarded the North African campaign as an unnecessary diversion and a serious delay in the Combined Bomber Offensive, but, like Ninth Air Force, the assets sent to North Africa would make a substantial contribution to the successful conclusion of that campaign.

3

TORCH and Twelfth Air Force:
June to November 1942

Just three days after Rommel's forces broke in front of the El Alamein line, American and British forces landed on the western end of the North African shore. Operation TORCH placed land and air forces in Morocco and Algeria, with the hope of quickly seizing Tunisia, securing valuable air bases for the protection of Malta-bound convoys, cutting the shipping distance to the Far East by reopening the Mediterranean via the Suez Canal, and sealing off the escape route for the Axis forces now retreating toward Libya. The U.S. Army Air Forces played a minor role in the landings themselves, as most direct air support came from British and American carrier-based aircraft, but it played a major role in the subsequent campaign. By establishing and providing trained units and personnel for Twelfth Air Force, the USAAF facilitated the overall success of the joint operation.

Many in the American defense establishment opposed the decision to land in North Africa, which would involve the transfer of units from Eighth Air Force, which was building up to strength in the United Kingdom, to the Twelfth, for support of operations in the new theater. Even today, many supporters of the Combined Bomber Offensive suggest that this diversion delayed the effects of the heavy bomber campaign by preventing Eighth Air Force from reaching a critical mass, whereby it could overwhelm German air defenses and destroy vital targets with minimal losses. But the decision to send escort fighters, airlift assets, and especially heavy bombers to North Africa was correct, as it enabled the Allies to further attrite German air and ground strength and resulted in both the conquest of the North African shore and the eventual capture of more than 200,000 Axis troops. By fully and effectively supporting the campaign, the USAAF made the strongest possible contribution to winning the war.

The USAAF and Antisubmarine Warfare

Neither Operation TORCH nor the buildup of an air force in the United Kingdom could have been accomplished in the face of heavy opposition from German U-boats. The Battle of the Atlantic was, therefore, a vital prelude to both campaigns. While heavy bombers themselves could be flown directly to the United Kingdom, the fuel and bombs they carried, as well as the immense logistical support the campaign required would have to cross the North Atlantic in ships. The loss of just a single ship, the SS *Oklahoman*, in July 1942 off the coast of South Africa had cost Ninth Air Force valuable equipment and delayed full operation of the depot at Gura, Eritrea, by six months.[1] Likewise, all of the troops participating in Operation TORCH would have to cross U-boat–infested waters in order to reach their objectives. The US-AAF's role in the antisubmarine campaign therefore deserves some exploration in order to comprehend both the effectiveness of aircraft in antisubmarine warfare and the USAAF's institutional resistance to using heavy bombers in this role.

The airplane's value as an antisubmarine weapon had been realized as early as World War I.[2] By the beginning of World War II, most navies possessed antisubmarine aircraft, and many air forces were developing capabilities, including airborne radar, to support the battle under the waves. Most U.S. Navy antisubmarine aircraft were short-range assets, either due to a requirement that they be able to operate from carriers, or because of an agreement that allocated the majority of longer-range and shore-based missions to the U.S. Army. As a result, there were a number of gaps in aerial antisubmarine coverage which most naval aircraft could not reach. There were two ways to effectively close these air gaps, which served as U-boat sanctuaries in the mid-Atlantic: carrier-borne aircraft, and very-long-range (VLR) land-based aircraft, which, in the American arsenal, included the B-17 and B-24 types.

But the USAAF desperately needed these same aircraft types to build up the bomber forces in Britain. In an unsatisfactory compromise, it agreed to use the heavy bombers to attack both the U-boat building yards in Germany and the operating bases on the French Atlantic coast. The USAAF was reluctant to assign bombers to these targets because such targets were not deemed critical enough to cause severe dislocation in the German economy and, therefore, did not represent a vital node in the German industrial web. But, by compromising, the USAAF retained control of the heavy bombers and could use them on missions that would approximate the later strategic raids, providing the crews and leaders valuable operational experience. Unfortunately, the raids largely failed to achieve their primary objective: a diminution of the German U-boat force. VLR aircraft operating over distant areas of the Atlantic destroyed many more U-boats than the raids on yards and bases, even when the disastrous RAF raid on Hamburg (Operation GOMORRAH) in July 1943 is taken into consideration. Despite burning out most of the city, raids destroyed only three boats, although "dislocation of shipyard workers at the Blohm & Voss plant caused a loss in production of twenty-five to thirty" additional boats.[3] In that same month, Allied forces at sea destroyed thirty-seven U-boats, many by aircraft, and most of which were lost with their entire crews.[4] Even the USAAF's official history agreed, noting, "attack from the air against the U-boat at sea had been the most effective single factor in reducing the German submarine fleet," and that "bombing of bases had contributed relatively little in that direction."[5] Many of the four-engine bombers used in the USAAF's thirty-seven different raids on U-boat yards and bases during the first year of operations would have been better assigned to antisubmarine squadrons and trained and equipped for that mission.[6]

As aircraft carriers remained in short supply due to demands and losses in the Pacific, the U.S. Navy embarked on a building program for smaller convoy-escort carriers, which would eventually prove very effective in the campaign, but these would not be available until mid-1943. To remedy this deficiency, early in the war naval planners requested an allocation of VLR aircraft from U.S. production. On 20 February 1942, Admiral Ernest J. King, commander-in-chief of the United States Fleet, wrote General Hap Arnold to request 200 B-24 type aircraft from USAAF production allocations, to be delivered by 1 July 1943, and an additional 200 B-24s to be delivered by 1 July 1944. King also requested a total of 900 medium-range B-25 bombers and explained, "We are now in a position to utilize these airplanes to advantage, particularly in the Atlantic Fleet in northern bases."[7] In a supplemental letter, Rear Admiral John Towers, chief of the U.S. Navy Bureau of Aeronautics, explained that "naval aircraft missions such as convoy escort, observation, scouting and patrolling over the sea, and the protection of shipping in the coastal zones, could not be accomplished by seaplanes based on ice-bound northern bases in the Atlantic." Towers added, "A study of the purely naval operations of the Coastal Command of the Royal Air Force led to the conviction that for operation from prepared fixed bases, multi-engined landplanes have certain characteristic advantages in performance, operation and maintenance, inherent in any type, which rendered it advisable that the Navy procure a considerable number of this type for its similar functions."[8]

Arnold drafted a reply and forwarded it to the Army Chief of Staff, General George C. Marshall, for a coordinated response. Arnold took umbrage not only at the potential loss of badly needed assets, which he noted was "critically short by 1190 planes of the barest needs to meet the United States Army Air Forces requirements," but also the potential for "duplication of aircraft types and hence a duplication of functions, in the air components of both the Army and the Navy." In his response to King, Arnold suggested that transferring such a large number of planes of this type would require the navy to develop, maintain, and defend large shore-based facilities, which would eventually "deny the essential differences between armies and navies." Arnold offered to continue to support fleet actions with USAAF heavy bombers, relieving the navy of the need to maintain duplicate establishments—but apparently missing the nature of the antisubmarine mission, which required specially modified aircraft and specifically trained crews. Most likely, Arnold was using the specter of duplicate missions to protect assets he badly needed to build up the bomber force and mission outlined in AWPD-1.[9]

By March 1942, losses to U-boats had become so heavy that RAF Bomber Command had to divert significant assets to the Bay of Biscay, where U-boats were most easily and successfully attacked as they transited to and from their French bases. On 31 March, British prime minister Winston Churchill requested an additional 100 heavy bombers to make up for those flying antisubmarine missions.[10] On 19 May, Sir John Dill was still emphasizing the need for additional assets. At the twentieth meeting of the Combined Chiefs of Staff, he noted, "At present we have not enough long-range aircraft in the United Kingdom for this extension (over the Bay of Biscay) and additional aircraft would greatly enhance our prospect of success." The committee also reviewed a proposal to focus heavy bomber attacks on submarine bases and building yards to help win the Battle of the Atlantic and noted that "upon arrival, of U.S. bomber forces in the UK, it would be necessary to consider the most useful targets for both them and the RAF to attack."[11]

In April 1942, Arnold informed the outgoing chief of naval operations, Harold Stark, of the USAAF's planned strength and dispositions by 31 December of that year. Of a total force of 1,469 heavy bombers, 525 were to be concentrated in the United Kingdom, with eight assigned to the Atlantic bases of Newfoundland, Iceland, Greenland, and Bermuda.[12] But the navy persisted, and in August a report of the Joint U.S. Strategic Committee recommended 500 aircraft of all types be allocated for antisubmarine work. The USAAF objected "on the grounds that this deployment represents a diversion of much-needed air striking forces from combat areas where their use would be much more decisive and employs them on relatively ineffective operations." The navy responded that it did not feel that "sufficient aircraft have been deployed for anti-submarine patrol duties in the U.S.-South America-Caribbean theater," and it estimated that twenty-four U-boats were then operating in the Western Atlantic and Caribbean.[13]

In October 1942, the USAAF acquiesced in the formation of the U.S. Army Air Forces Anti-Submarine Command, primarily to keep the heavy bombers allocated to antisubmarine work under its direct control. Although Arnold envisioned the Anti-Submarine Command as "a Coastal Command, within the Army Air Corps, which will have for its purpose operations similar to Coastal Command, Royal Air Force," the setup was far from ideal.[14] The units assigned to the Antisubmarine Command were taken from First Air Force's Bomber Command. As part of a stateside numbered air force, I Bomber Command had the dual responsibility of patrolling the coastline and training units for the bomber offensive in Europe. While on occasion the missions overlapped, there were important differences. First, strategic bombing was planned to be conducted during daylight and at high altitude. Antisubmarine work was most effective at night, when the U-boats surfaced to recharge their batteries, and at low altitudes, where aircraft could detect and attack the submarines. Assigning both missions to the same force would inevitably lead to a conflict of interest, and the air force's commitment to heavy bombing meant that "this situation prevented it from concentrating as fully on the anti-U-boat war as the nature of the conflict required."[15] The airmen assigned to this new command tried to obtain the assets they needed to accomplish their mission, but they were often unsuccessful. On 18 October, just three days after the command had been established, its headquarters estimated that it would require 228 B-24 aircraft with ASV 10 (the new 10-centimeter airborne radar developed by the British, which the Germans were unable to detect) and envisioned a force of nineteen squadrons of twelve aircraft each. Of the 148 aircraft then assigned to I Bomber Command, there were only twelve B-17s and three B-24s, with the balance made up by smaller aircraft types with much shorter ranges. Even by that time "it had come to be recognized that the long-range B-24 was especially well suited to the demands of antisubmarine warfare, and . . . would thereafter become the principal reliance in the USAAF's antisubmarine effort."[16]

In the United Kingdom, General Dwight D. Eisenhower, the overall commander TORCH, remained concerned about the submarine threat throughout the planning stages. On 18 October, General Marshall advised him that he was investigating the "practicability of forming antisubmarine patrols off straits (of Gibraltar) to a distance of 600 miles by ASV equipped B-17's and 24's," undoubtedly from the new Anti-Submarine Command, and requested information from Eisenhower on whether these aircraft could be based at Gibraltar from a week prior to a week after the scheduled invasion date and if suitable crews and equipment, especially depth charges, were available in the United Kingdom for twelve B-17s and four B-24s.[17] In December 1942, when U-boats continued to threaten resupply convoys for North Africa, Churchill requested an additional thirty ASV-equipped *Liberators* from the United States to provide additional coverage of the transit from the United Kingdom to North Africa. The U.S. sent all twenty-one aircraft then available and further diverted two Eighth Air Force B-24 squadrons already in the United Kingdom to antisubmarine work.[18] Had the USAAF been more willing initially to dedicate aircraft and crews to the antisubmarine mission, it is unlikely it would have found its combat units barraged for piecemeal requests later on.

At the Casablanca Conference in January 1943, the question of long-range antisubmarine aircraft continued to occupy the interests of the Combined Chiefs of Staff. At the fifty-fifth meeting on 14 January, General George C. Marshall stated that "the U-boat menace is the paramount issue" and that "everything must be done to combat it from the place of manufacture of submarines to the places where they are used." Sir Charles Portal, RAF Chief of Staff, agreed and observed that the "defeat of the submarine menace must be given first priority in the use of air power." Portal also expressed his appreciation for the twenty-one U.S. *Liberators* sent to augment the forces patrolling the Bay of Biscay.[19] At the next meeting, Portal emphasized that "air had proved the most effective weapon against the U-boat." General Arnold wanted to know if it was possible to use flying boats for antisubmarine work, in order to "avoid the use of valuable long-range bombers." Portal explained that VLR aircraft were essential, as flying boats lacked speed and sufficient payload and were not equipped with radar that could detect submarines at night and in poor visibility. Portal estimated that the United Kingdom still required 120–135 long-range bombers to cover the required area. Still, Arnold insisted that Eighth Air Force wanted to attack Germany but had been directed to concentrate on the U-boats by Eisenhower in order to support TORCH.[20]

As the U-boat campaign intensified in early 1943, the attacks again garnered the attention of the Combined Chiefs, who convened a special conference to address the festering issue. On 19 March the group observed that fifty-seven ships had been sunk in the preceding eighteen days, and it pressed for more VLR aircraft to close the air gap in the mid-Atlantic. General George Stratemeyer, filling in for General Arnold, promised to deliver twelve aircraft immediately and make another thirty-six available, but Admiral William D. Leahy, then functioning as the equivalent of the Chairman of the Joint Chiefs of Staff, believed that 128 aircraft were needed. The following week, when air requirements for Operation HUSKY, the invasion of Sicily, were being briefed, Arnold argued against sending another two heavy bomber groups to the Mediterranean to support the six already there on the grounds that it would detract from the antisubmarine campaign; he preferred to use them to augment forces in the United Kingdom. He had support from Sir John Dill, who concurred that the two additional groups could not be spared due to the U-boat threat and added that the British were using all of the B-24s from their allocation for antisubmarine work. Persuaded, General Marshall agreed to defer allocation of the two additional groups, which were not sent to North Africa until July, and then primarily to participate in the second raid on Ploesti.[21] Arnold did allocate a total of twelve aircraft per month from new production for each of the next three months, but Admiral Leahy expressed his view that 255 were required by 1 July 1943, with seventy-five allocated to the USAAF, fifteen to the Royal Canadian Air Force (RCAF), sixty to the U.S. Navy, and 105 to the RAF.[22] The loss of an additional 700,000 tons of shipping in March forced the deployment of two VLR squadrons to the Western Atlantic, and by the end of April there were twenty-eight aircraft in Newfoundland, three in Iceland, but still none in Greenland. Arnold promised that an additional forty-plus would be available in May, prompting the Combined Chiefs of Staff to direct weekly reports on the status of the VLR aircraft in the Atlantic.[23]

At the same time, the U.S. Navy and Royal Navy turned up the pressure to acquire additional VLR aircraft. On 14 March, Admiral King endorsed a staff memo that stated, "The only means for quickly increasing the effectiveness of our ASW [antisubmarine warfare] measures is to divert heavy bombers from other assignments. In view of the situation in the several theaters of active warfare, it seems the only possibility is to divert these planes from the bombing of Germany." The U.S. Navy had already diverted fifteen of its B-24 replacements from the South Pacific, and the RAF was shifting replacements for the Middle East and India to its Coastal Command. But the USAAF strongly resisted the diversion of existing bombers to the antisubmarine units and offered to make up the difference out of new production. On 26 March, General Frank Andrews, commanding all U.S. forces in the United Kingdom, cabled General Marshall: "Although I fully concur that defeat of submarines is a high priority defensive objective of our efforts, I urge that every endeavor be made to procure necessary VLR aircraft from sources other than planes now bombing Germany, which themselves are frequently engaged against targets affecting the enemy submarine situation." In a separate cable on 30 March, Andrews lobbied to build the VLR antisubmarine force:

> Over 160 additional long range bombers would thus have to be diverted from (their) present primary mission of bombardment of Germany unless obtained elsewhere. I consider such diversion unsound because diversion of over 160 long range bombers would nullify present United States power for bombardment of German targets, now severely strained due to lack of density of missions necessary to disperse fighter protection . . . I would be opposed to any consideration of Bay of Biscay proposal which would affect existing bombing policy or build up of Air Strength in this theater.[24]

On 14 April, Arnold recommended "no reductions from heavy bomber commitments to 8th Air Force."[25] The USAAF did modify B-24 allocations to the antisubmarine mission for the next four months, allocating fifty-six of 142 B-24s produced in March, seventy of 195 in April, eighty of 297 in May, and seventy-one of 333 in June.[26]

The following week the group noticed a decrease in the number of merchant ship sinkings, which Admiral Sir Percy Noble, then head of the British naval delegation in Washington, attributed to both the availability of extra escorts freed from convoys bound for the Soviet Union and the increased number of VLR aircraft. By June the Allied counteroffensive against the U-boats at sea had broken the back of the German submarine force. Admiral King reported that the German submarines had recently been hit hard and that "large numbers of submarines had been withdrawn" from the battle due to the high loss rate. The allocation of increasing numbers of long-range ASV-equipped aircraft played an important role in the final victory in the Battle of the Atlantic. Sir John Dill believed that the "success now being achieved against enemy submarines were due largely to the increase in VLR aircraft."[27] Indeed, the statistics provide support for this argument. Of the 118 U-boats sunk or damaged during the decisive period from May until August 1943, fifty-five were attributed to land-based aircraft and another six to a combination of ships and shore-based aircraft.[28]

These numbers correspond with an increased deployment of VLR aircraft in the Atlantic Basin. Between 14 April and 31 June, the number of VLR aircraft in the Atlantic increased sevenfold, from thirty-three to 233, with the largest increases coming in the United Kingdom and Iceland (from seventeen to eighty-four), the Northwest Atlantic (from twelve to forty-two), and the U.S. Atlantic Coast (from zero to thirty-five). VLR aircraft were also deployed for the first time to the Caribbean, South America, Bermuda, and Ascension Island, closing many of the air gaps available as sanctuaries to U-boats. Of the 233 aircraft available on 30 June, the Army Air Forces operated eighty-eight, the RAF seventy-one, the U.S. Navy fifty-nine, and the RCAF fifteen. These increases were achieved at the modest cost of ninety-six B-24s from April production and another ninety-four in May.[29] Had the USAAF been willing to make these concessions in production earlier, it might have accelerated the eventual victory in the Battle of the Atlantic, thereby speeding the delivery of troops and supplies to the United Kingdom and saving countless lives on the perilous North Atlantic run.

The USAAF's parochialism in this respect was shortsighted. In late 1942, one heavy bomb group of B-24s sat virtually immobilized in the United Kingdom because of bad weather and because Eighth Air Force did not like to mix formations of B-17s and B-24's due to speed differences in the aircraft. The 93rd Bomb Group's aircraft would undoubtedly have been better used in an antisubmarine role, and two of its squadrons were later detailed for just this purpose. Unfortunately, the aircraft were not equipped with ASV radar, and their crews were not specifically trained for the mission. In early 1943, the USAAF built additional B-24 groups in the United Kingdom instead of allocating this production to the Anti-Submarine Command or to the U.S. Navy, RAF, or RCAF, where they could have been applied against the U-boat. When ASV-equipped VLR aircraft were finally deployed in numbers—alongside increased numbers of escorts and the appearance of escort carriers—they made a substantial contribution to breaking the back of the U-boat force. As one authority on the air war in Europe observed, "The failure in the Atlantic was to a large extent due to the failure to get air forces committed early enough and in large enough numbers to have a decisive influence."[30] Another survey of the war found astonishing

> the obdurate unwillingness of the Allied air forces to devote the re- sources necessary to close the gap in air cover over the Central At- lantic. Except for Coastal Command, the RAF leadership opposed the commitment of long-range aircraft to protecting convoys with a fervor that bordered on fanaticism. And the airmen maintained this position throughout 1942 and into 1943, when finally their po- litical masters forced their hand. The result was the unnecessary loss of hundreds of ships and many, many lives.[31]

One authoritative study of the U-boat campaign found that "had the War Cabinet assigned more of Bomber Command's four-engine, long-range, radar-equipped, land-based aircraft to Coastal Command from the summer of 1942 on, the 'U-boat peril' could have been re- duced dramatically."[32] The same myopia blinded USAAF leaders on their side of the Atlantic.

Eighth Air Force and "Junior"

Most of the units that would eventually form Twelfth Air Force in North Africa came from Eighth Air Force, then building in the United Kingdom. Advocates for the Combined Bomber Offensive— then and now—suggest that the diversion of the Eighth's most highly trained and experienced units to North Africa set back the bomber of- fensive by at least a year. The same advocates ignore that, at the time, the strategic forces in the United Kingdom lacked the technology to play a decisive role in the war effort. The Eighth's heavy bombers did not yet possess an effective all-weather bombing capability and, most important, a long-range escort fighter that would allow them to reach the most sensitive targets deep in Germany without excessive losses. The game-changing North American P-51 *Mustang* did not en- ter combat until late in 1943, limiting strikes before then to either shallow penetrations that could be escorted by existing fighters, or un- escorted raids that resulted in heavy losses, such as the Schweinfurt-

Regensburg raids of 17 August 1943 and the "Black Thursday" mission of 14 October 1943.

Many of the targets the Eighth did attack on the shallower raids were related to the Battle of the Atlantic, including U-boat operating bases and construction yards. Lieutenant General Ira Eaker, who commanded Eighth Air Force throughout 1943, labeled even this a diversion of effort and constantly appealed for more bombers in order to build his force to a critical mass that he believed would be capable of defending itself. But the Army Air Forces wisely allocated significant portions of the available force to support operations in the North African theater. The gains made along the shores of North Africa were more significant and did more to further the Allied cause than anything a concentrated bomber force in the United Kingdom could have accomplished during the same time.

Ironically, Eighth Air Force itself was initially formed to support a planned landing in North Africa. Under the code-name GYMNAST, the Allies explored a landing in early 1942 in order to deny Africa's Atlantic Coast to the Axis and to involve U.S. forces in the European war at the earliest opportunity. When GYMNAST was postponed indefinitely, the Eighth became the parent headquarters for all U.S. air forces in the United Kingdom, with the mission of attriting German air strength over the continent and supporting either of the two operations then being planned for landings on the French coast. Operation SLEDGEHAMMER was an emergency operation designed to provide immediate relief for the Soviet Union if collapse appeared imminent. It envisioned seizing a port along the Channel coast (Cherbourg on the Cotentin Peninsula was frequently mentioned as an objective) in order to establish a ground force on the continent within range of air bases in the United Kingdom. Operation ROUNDUP was a full-scale invasion, originally planned for 1943, and eventually executed in modified form as Operation OVERLORD on 6 June 1944.

The units assigned to Eighth Air Force reflected this dual mission. The Eighth was initially organized as a composite air force, containing bomber, fighter, air-support, and service commands. The first units assigned were the B-17 heavy bombers of the 97th and 301st Bomb Groups; four groups of fighters: the 31st and 52nd Fighter Groups, initially flying Bell P-39 *Airacobras* but later reequipped with British *Spitfires* in exchange for more P-40s for the RAF in the Middle East, and the 1st and 14th Fighter Groups, equipped with P-38s; and the 60th Troop Carrier Group, flying C-47s. The 60th was to have a dual mission of training the airborne units assigned to the United Kingdom, as well as supporting the air forces by providing logistic support around the country. The Eighth's commander, General Carl Spaatz, began to assemble his units in the northeastern United States to prepare them to cross the Atlantic via the newly opened northern ferry route. From New Hampshire and Maine, the planes would fly first to Canadian bases in Newfoundland, then jump to one of two new bases on the southern coast of Greenland. From there, the planes could reach Iceland and then continue on to bases in Scotland and Northern Ireland. The northern ferry route was treacherous, even in summer, and provided little margin for error in weather forecasting or navigation for the new crews. Because the fighters were single-pilot, each flight of four would be led by a B-17 in order to take advantage of its dedicated navigator.

Just as the groups were preparing to make this journey, naval intelligence revealed that the Japanese were embarking on a major operation that would result in the naval battle at Midway. The USAAF had established only a small garrison of medium and heavy bombers on that Pacific island, and naval authorities clamored for reinforcements. The only forces available were those already en route to the United Kingdom, and the 97th Bomb Group and 1st Fighter Group were ordered to redeploy to the west coast. Transports from the 60th Troop Carrier Group were unloaded in order to help with the move. Spaatz was not pleased by the delay. He reported to Eaker, already in England, "Four groups, the 1st and 31st Pursuit, the 97th Heavy Bombardment and the 60th Transport were all concentrated at full strength about ready to move when several Japanese fishing and other boats moving in the general direction of our west coast from Japan scared everyone to death."[33]

While the Japanese fleet contained more than a few fishing boats, Spaatz was correct in the view that his units were unlikely to affect the outcome. The fifty-five B-17 sorties and four B-26 sorties by USAAF aircraft stationed on Midway did not hit a single combat ship, despite wildly inflated claims by their crews of twenty hits, including some on carriers "set afire" or "hit and slowed."[34] The inaccurate reports, and their subsequent release to the press, led to much ill feeling between the U.S. Navy, whose aircraft had actually sunk four carriers, and the USAAF after the battle.[35] In a widely publicized rebuttal to these false claims, Lieutenant Commander John S. Thach, who commanded a navy fighter squadron at Midway, was quoted in the *Washington Times*: "There's a theory that the war can be won in an easy way without in-fighting by a fleet of long-range bombers that can fly high and far and drop their loads and then come back and wait for a radio report of surrender of the enemy. That won't work. To capture a spot there must be a landing of men, preceded by fighter planes to clear the way and followed by other planes to keep it clear."[36]

During the delay, Spaatz returned to Washington and met with, among others, Sir Charles Portal, who reported that a P-51 trial with a Rolls-Royce Merlin engine had yielded airspeeds of 428 miles per hour at 25,000 feet. It was a development that would have significant consequences for the Combined Bomber Offensive.[37] On 9 June, Spaatz and the forty-eight B-17s of the 97th Bomb Group were finally released to continue on to the United Kingdom, but it took several weeks to reassemble the force and move it across the Atlantic. In the interim, it had been decided that the 31st and 52nd Pursuit Groups would leave their P-39s in the United States and be reequipped with British *Spitfires* upon arrival. The move was a significant upgrade for the groups in terms of equipment but would delay their entry into combat while they became acclimated to their new aircraft.

On 26 June, just a week after arriving in the British Isles, Spaatz had his first meeting with General Eisenhower. This was to be among the most significant command relationships of the war, perhaps rivaled only by that between Eisenhower and Sir Arthur Tedder. Of Spaatz, Eisenhower would later say, "He was never long absent from my side until the last victorious shot had been fired in Europe. On every succeeding day of almost three years of active war I had new reasons for thanking the gods of war and the War Department for giving me 'Tooey' Spaatz."[38] The two had been separated by a year at West Point and had worked together in the War Department, but this was their first combat pairing. Two days later they met again, in what would become almost daily meetings, and they began to outline the relationship between the air and ground forces.

Spaatz was wedded to a separation of tactical and strategic airpower, a division that he would help to firmly establish later in the war; it would persevere for another half-century within the U.S. defense establishment. He told Ike, "All Air Forces except heavy bombardment forces and 10 pursuit groups [will be] in close support under (the) Air Support Commander—remainder operates under Eighth Air Force general support." The view reflected Spaatz's desire to segregate the strategic assets, and their escorts, from the control of the ground commander. Rather than establishing a composite air force that was capable of performing any mission the theater commander desired, Spaatz and his contemporaries preferred to isolate the close support mission by assigning assets, usually the less capable fighters and the light and medium twin-engine bombers, to each numbered air force's Air Support Command.

On 6 July, Spaatz outlined for Eisenhower and General Mark Clark, commanding ground forces in the theater, the force he needed in order to attain the degree of air supremacy required for Operation ROUNDUP (the OVERLORD precursor). It included seventeen groups of heavy bombers, six groups of mediums, another six groups of light bombers, twelve pursuit groups, eight transport groups, and six observation groups. These were ambitious plans for a force that included only eight B-17s, seven P-38s, and five C-47s on that date. Spaatz wrote Arnold that he envisioned "observation, transports and light bombardment" in the Air Support Command, with P-39s assigned primarily for strafing.[39] This would prevent ground commanders from gaining control over the heavy bombers, which were kept free to attack distant targets. The struggle over these assets would continue for the rest of the war. For its part, the Army Air Forces eventually established numbered air forces by type: the Eighth and the Fifteenth, established in Italy in November 1943, would have the heavy bombers and most capable fighters; the lighter bombers and less-capable fighters would be grouped in the Ninth and Twelfth Air Forces. Theoretically, the heavy bombers would be available to support ground forces in an emergency, as in the landings at Salerno and the breakout from Normandy, but isolating them in their own organization, later under Spaatz's direct control as commander of the U.S. Strategic Air Forces (USSTAF), made it more difficult to divert them to supporting surface forces.

With only a small force building in the United Kingdom, both Spaatz and Eisenhower were about to be pulled by events outside of that theater. Their British hosts were transfixed by the collapse of their position in the Western Desert and the subsequent retreat to the El Alamein line. Arnold wrote Spaatz and correctly speculated that "the surprising turn of events in the Middle East must have absorbed a great deal of your time."[40] On 26 June, Spaatz reported that "the Prime Minister was urging the President to throw everything in the Middle East and General [Asa] Duncan [Spaatz's predecessor in charge of Eighth Air Force and now his Chief of Staff] feared that the Eighth Air Force would suffer by this untimely diversion."[41] While no Eighth Air Force units were sent directly to the Middle East, the crisis would lead to a resuscitation of the old GYMNAST plan. Unable to get the British to approve SLEDGEHAMMER and wanting to get the

country into the fight against Germany before the nation became fix-
ated on the Pacific, President Roosevelt was receptive to Churchill's
overtures for a landing in French North Africa, in which forces built
from Eighth Air Force would play a prominent role.

Before committing to the North African operation, Roosevelt sent
a team of advisers to try to convince the British to commit to SLEDGE-
HAMMER in 1942. The group included Harry Hopkins, Admiral Ernest King, General George Marshall, and Colonel Hoyt Vandenberg.
When it became clear that their efforts would be unsuccessful, the air
commanders in the United Kingdom began to see some advantages
in the North African campaign. On 22 July, Spaatz, Vandenberg, and
General Howard Craig drafted a letter to General Marshall expressing
their views. At the time, Marshall was inclined to write off operations
in the European theater and begin shifting assets to the fight against
the Japanese in the Pacific. In an effort to continue the buildup of
Eighth Air Force they noted, "Because the Middle East is the next
most decisive theater against the major enemy, all or part of the re-
distribution of air forces should be allotted to that theater." The move
was likely a strategic ploy by these men, who realized that it would be
much easier to get assets returned to the United Kingdom from North
Africa than from Australia (if in fact they were sent to fight Japan).
They added, "The Middle East should be considered as a valuable
complement of the Western European Theater since it permits striking the same enemy from the air. In this connection ground crews and
supplies of the Air Force should be placed there in order that heavy
bomber air planes from the U.K. can operate against the major enemy
from either side, taking advantage of favorable weather."[42] The words
were to prove prophetic, as bombers operating from North Africa,
and eventually from Italy, were to enjoy much better flying weather
and, consequently, much higher effective sortie rates than those in the
United Kingdom.

Meanwhile, Spaatz was under intense pressure from Arnold to begin
combat operations with Eighth Air Force. Arnold was also concerned
that the Pacific theater, where combat operations were already under
way in New Guinea and set to open the following month in the Solo-
mon Islands, would begin to pull assets away from Eighth Air Force.
Earlier, he had promised the Chief of the British Air Staff, Sir Charles
Portal, that Americans would be operating combat sorties from the
United Kingdom by 4 July 1942. To help Arnold keep his promise, on
that date four American crews from the 47th Light Bomb Squadron,
flying British *Bostons* (A-20s), participated in a raid on an airdrome

on the Dutch coast. Two crews were lost on the sortie, and another plane, piloted by Captain Charles Kegelman, lost an engine and nearly crashed, actually bouncing off the ground before Kegelman regained control and nursed his wounded ship back home. During the recovery, he was able to line up his gunsights on a machine-gun tower and reportedly destroy it with a long burst. For these actions, Eisenhower personally awarded Kegelman the Distinguished Flying Cross.[43]

This raid, the first by American aircraft over Western Europe, did not receive the same amount of attention as the next mission, the 17 August attack by twelve B-17s of the 97th Bomb Group on the rail yards at Sotteville near Rouen, France. The USAAF's official history allotted an entire section to the raid, whereas the 4 July mission received less than a page. The disparity seems to fit with an overemphasis on strategic operations. The 17 August raid featured the B-17, the aircraft most closely identified with the strategic offensive against Germany, against a transportation target, whereas the July mission used a ground support aircraft, the A-20, in a tactical role. Further, the raid on Rouen was completed successfully, as crews hit their target and suffered no losses, thanks to a heavy escort and good weather over the target, whereas the A-20 mission in Holland lost two planes and their crews. The Rouen raid also featured two of the best-known airmen of the war: Lieutenant Colonel Paul Tibbets, who would later pilot the *Enola Gay* on the atomic mission to Hiroshima, led one section of six aircraft, and General Eaker personally led the other.[44] While neither mission inflicted serious or even permanent damage on Axis targets, it seems clear which one the USAAF wanted to remember and why.[45]

It should be noted that the USAAF's desire to build and operate a strategic bombing force in the United Kingdom did not stem purely from a selfish desire to win independence. The service, and the men directing it, honestly believed that the bomber offensive was the best way to win the war. Many air leaders in World War II had also participated in World War I. They were aware of the horrors of trench warfare and sought a way to save ground forces from such slaughter. By destroying German industrial capacity, they hoped to spare the army from another ground campaign across France. Their theory, while unproven, told them that it was possible, and they were desperate to prove it correct.

The 97th Bomb Group's second mission would more accurately foreshadow how the group would spend the next year of the war in the Mediterranean. On 19 August, twenty-four B-17s attacked the airdromes at Abbeville-Drucat in support of the amphibious raid on Dieppe and inflicted serious damage on the dispersed Luftwaffe aircraft on the field.[46] *Spitfires* of the 31st Fighter Group escorted the raid but suffered serious losses in their first combat action, as one pilot was reported killed, another seriously wounded, with four missing.[47] For the remainder of the month, the 97th gained valuable experience in an additional six raids against airfields, shipyards, and factories along the French and Dutch coasts. By later standards, the raids were small affairs and did little permanent damage to either the installations attacked or the Luftwaffe fighters defending them, but they did provide valuable experience for the crews.[48]

In September, operations took a step backward, as only three missions reached their targets, totaling eighty-three effective sorties, four less than in August. Poor weather was most often to blame, although timing difficulties in rendezvousing with escort fighters also stopped one mission. Targets were again airfields, ports, and rail yards. In October, the Eighth was ordered to attack the German U-boat bases on the western coast of France, a target set that would dominate the next six months. By the end of the month there were five operational heavy bomber groups in Eighth Air Force, but they again mustered only three effective missions, totaling only 138 sorties. The first raid on the submarine base at Lorient came on 21 October. But seven of the eight missions in November were against the U-boat bases at Brest (one raid), St. Nazaire (five missions), and Lorient (one mission) each with a force of at least fifty bombers.

The new targets were a direct result of Eisenhower's concern for the security of the initial assault convoys for TORCH, as well as the follow-up convoys that would build the force and bring sufficient supplies for the drive on Tunisia. The airmen were initially less than enthusiastic about the assignment, preferring to hit the construction yards in Germany, but they realized that they lacked the escort fighters to make even shallow penetrations into German airspace. Eisenhower had first broached the subject at a meeting with Spaatz on 25 September but wrote again on 13 October to clarify:

Confirming prior verbal communication, I want you to know that I consider the defeat of the submarine to be one of the basic requirements to the winning of the war. In fixing priority of air targets from this theater, I realize that the German Air Force must be constantly pounded in order to give our own Air Forces freedom of action in carrying out fruitful missions. Of these missions, none should rank above the effort to defeat the German submarine. As a specific and immediate target, I am extremely anxious, for reasons of which you are well aware, to obtain effective action against the submarine ports in the Bay of Biscay.[49]

Eaker, for one, seemed enthusiastic to give the mission a try. On 14 October, he wrote Spaatz:

Whether the pens themselves, with their 11-foot thick reinforced concrete roofs and heavily reinforced sides can be cracked by 1,600-lb. AP (armor-piercing) and 2,000-lb. GP (general purpose) bombs remains to be seen. This is one of the interesting bits of data we shall glean from our experiment. It is unnecessary, however, to demolish these sheds in order to render these bases unusable. The power, the turntables, the operating personnel, the machine shops—are all vital supporting accessories and all are destructible by aerial bombardment.[50]

Spaatz reported his concerns with the new target set to Arnold, noting that he expected higher loss rates due to the intense antiaircraft artillery surrounding the targets and the lack of escort fighters. He also pointed out, "The concrete submarine pens are hard and maybe impossible nuts to crack. . . . However, the bombing of the surrounding installations should seriously handicap the effective use of these bases."[51]

Eaker and Spaatz soon realized that the roofs on the concrete submarine pens were indeed impermeable to existing ordinance, making it impossible to damage or destroy the U-boats within their shelters. But in order to keep the bombers engaged against a strategic target that would provide valuable training and experience for aircrews, they argued that the raids could still have important effects. While the biggest prizes, the boats themselves, were well protected, they argued that many of the essential aspects of the U-boat campaign were housed in the surrounding workshops and warehouses, where skilled craftsmen performed essential repair work and critical supplies were stored. The men were encouraged by a report from inside France just after the first raid, on Lorient on 21 October. According to a source who had visited the yards, two large submarines outside the pens had been damaged, the floating docks were rendered useless, and the surrounding workshops had been completely destroyed, with more than 240 casualties, which unfortunately included some French workers.[52]

By mid-November Eaker was reporting to Spaatz that "the Admiralty was most enthusiastic about the results which have been accomplished by our bombing of the submarine bases."[53]

Unfortunately, the raids, while individually effective, were too infrequent to seriously handicap the U-boat campaign. Later analysts determined that while the raids "leveled the cities of St. Nazaire and Lorient," they "at most only slightly inconvenienced the U-boat force" and did not significantly extend the turnaround times for U-boats in port.[54] Eighth Air Force's willingness to participate in the campaign, while somewhat self-serving, was at least encouraging, but the aircraft would have been far better employed by the dedicated antisubmarine commands.

Twelfth Air Force and Operation TORCH

The new organization formed out of the Eighth Air Force would play only a minor role in the initial landings on the North African coast, but the units allocated to the new organization would play a major role in the eventual victory in Tunisia. The bomber, fighter, and transport groups represented the best the Army Air Forces had to offer and ensured that the ground forces and their commander received the best possible support. This is not to suggest that there were no failings during the campaign. Direct air support was lacking, often due to factors beyond the USAAF's control, such as weather and logistics bottlenecks, but also because units were properly focused on the air superiority and interdiction campaigns that would play a larger role in determining the outcome compared to the close support mission. While ground commanders would complain at times about lack of direct support, the theater commander, also a ground officer, wisely never directed his air force to abandon the interdiction and air superiority campaigns in order to provide more close support. While flying General Eisenhower from England to Gibraltar just before the landings took place, Lieutenant Colonel Paul Tibbets engaged the general in a two-hour discussion of the operation. Tibbets observed that Eisenhower "recognized that air power would have a major role" in the operation and "disclosed a keen understanding of air power and its uses."[55] Tibbets was not the only airman who noticed Eisenhower's aptitude. After an inspection visit the previous August, General Ira Eaker wrote that he was "tremendously impressed with Gen. Eisenhower's keenness for air operations."[56]

Because of airdrome crowding at Gibraltar and the extreme range from there to the three landing sites in Morocco and Algeria, USAAF aircraft could not make round-trip sorties to the battle area. However, once airfields had been seized, USAAF fighter and attack aircraft would be flown in immediately to take over the air defense and close support missions from the U.S. Navy and Royal Navy carrier aircraft in order to permit those ships freedom of action to leave the U-boat–infested waters. As the airfields around Casablanca, Oran, and Algiers were the primary objectives of the landing forces, the USAAF allocated an entire transport group to the airborne mission designed to acquire the two fields at Oran. Because the transports could not be staged at Gibraltar due to congestion there, they would make a one-way flight from the United Kingdom and land on the fields once the paratroopers had gained control. This was to be the USAAF's most important contribution to the landings themselves, the one that demonstrated the most potential for future operations. While the operation did not go exactly as planned, the first American combat use of airborne troops was successful enough to merit their inclusion in every subsequent major amphibious operation in the European theater, including the landings on Sicily, in Italy, and in France.

The 60th Transport Group was one of the first three combat groups to arrive in the United Kingdom. Equipped with C-47s, the unit had the dual mission of providing intratheater airlift of personnel and spare parts, as well as training with and providing airlift for the airborne forces assigned to Operations SLEDGEHAMMER and ROUNDUP. The USAAF considered the unit essential to the bomber campaign, as the bomber's operating bases would be located as far forward as possible in the United Kingdom in order to provide maximum range into Germany, while the units' repair and parts depots would be well behind the lines in order to protect them from the Luftwaffe. The bomber bases, eventually concentrated in East Anglia, were several hundred miles from the Eighth Air Force's main supply depot at Burtonwood, near the shipping center of Liverpool, and the two could be connected much more quickly by the assigned C-47s than by trucks or trains when operating units required parts or equipment on short notice. Early in the planning process for TORCH, air planners recognized that supply difficulties would be even more strained on the North African shore and prudently included a total of three transport groups in the allocations to Twelfth Air Force. The planes would be used to connect rear-area depots in Morocco with front-line units in Tunisia, a distance of more than 1,000 miles. They would also provide airlift to the small airborne force allocated to TORCH, the 503rd Parachute Infantry Regiment, initially commanded by Colonel Edson Raff.

The airborne operation itself failed to achieve its immediate objective: the capture of the military airfields at Tafaraoui and La Senia, just south of Oran. But the failure stemmed largely from confusion at higher echelons than from any conceptual problems with airborne operations in general. The 556 men of 2nd Battalion, 503rd Parachute Infantry Regiment, were to be ferried in thirty-nine C-47s from 60th Troop Carrier Group. Due to the uncertainty about French resistance, Colonel Charles Bentley, commanding the 60th, briefed two separate plans to his group. Under the "War" plan, the group would drop the paratroopers at Tafaraoui and then circle until daylight, when they would land on the secured field. Under the "Peace" plan, the aircraft would land unopposed directly at nearby La Senia after daylight. The proximity of a large, dry lakebed, the Sebkra d'Oran, provided a nearby emergency landing strip if there were complications with either plan. Based on assurances from contacts in North Africa, the group launched under the "Peace" plan, and the paratroopers expected to disembark rather than jump into North Africa. Unfortunately, complications arose during the trip and the "War" plan was implemented, but the airborne force was never notified and would have to adapt and improvise on the spot.[57]

The thirty-nine aircraft left two fields in the southwestern corner of the United Kingdom, St. Eval and Predannock, in four flights. Flight A, composed of ten aircraft led by Bentley, and Flight B, of nine planes, departed from St. Eval at 2120 local time on 7 November; flights C and D, of ten planes each, left Predannock at 2105. The four flights assembled over Portreath at 2200. All four were to join into a single formation for the transit across the Bay of Biscay and the Iberian Peninsula, but poor weather, faulty communications, and burned-out formation lights left the aircraft widely scattered. Bentley placed a navigator trained in celestial navigation aboard each plane, but they varied widely in quality. Evidently some did a commendable job, while others were described as "dead weight."[58] The group transited the Bay of Biscay safely but began to scatter upon reaching the Mediterranean. Three aircraft eventually landed in Spanish Morocco, where they and their passengers were interned by Spanish authorities until February 1943. One of these aircraft, piloted by Captain William Raymond, was running low on fuel and dropped its paratroopers over

Einzoren, in Spanish Morocco, and then landed to find that "there were only two Spanish soldiers in the fort and the paratroopers had things well in hand." Raymond's crew was able to contact six other C-47s by radio and successfully warn them not to land. When a much larger force of 400-plus Spanish soldiers arrived, Raymond and his men wisely went into captivity without resistance and were eventually reunited with the pilots and paratroopers of two other C-47s, as well as three *Spitfire* pilots from 52nd Fighter Group who had likewise landed on neutral territory. A fourth stick of paratroopers had also been dropped in Spanish Morocco by an aircraft that continued on to Oran. By mid-February, Spanish authorities had released the sixty men, who returned to their units in Algiers by way of Gibraltar.[59]

Two other aircraft eventually landed in French Morocco and a third at Gibraltar, with the result that only thirty-three loaded C-47s successfully reached Algeria. A beacon light intended to direct the planes to their objective was extinguished when the "Peace" plan was briefed, and a shipboard electronic homing signal was broadcasting on a frequency of 460 kilocycles, rather than the 440 that was briefed, as several crews discovered when they checked adjacent frequencies after hearing nothing on the one assigned.[60] After receiving a hostile reception from Vichy forces over their assigned airfield, twenty-eight of the transports either dropped their paratroopers or landed with them on the western end of the dry lakebed. Losses would have been much worse had the carrier-based aircraft of the Fleet Air Arm not already worked over the fields heavily, destroying an estimated seventy Vichy aircraft at La Senia.[61] After forming up, the infantry joined an armored force moving inland from the beachhead and arrived at the airfield the following day. Upon learning that Tafaraoui was secure, the remaining C-47s flew from the dry lakebed to the airfield and arrived at the same time as the first two squadrons of American *Spitfires* from Gibraltar. The crews of three transports that had landed closer to the airfields, including Colonel Bentley, went briefly into captivity but were released by French authorities after the capitulation on 11 November.

Permanent losses to 60th Troop Carrier Group totaled seven aircraft, the three interned by the Spanish and four destroyed by French fighters on the Sebkra, but these were made up by the arrival of ten replacements from the United Kingdom on 20 and 21 November, giving the group forty-two aircraft and keeping it up to strength.[62] While the airborne mission failed to seize the airfields before the amphibious forces arrived, they did provide the theater commander

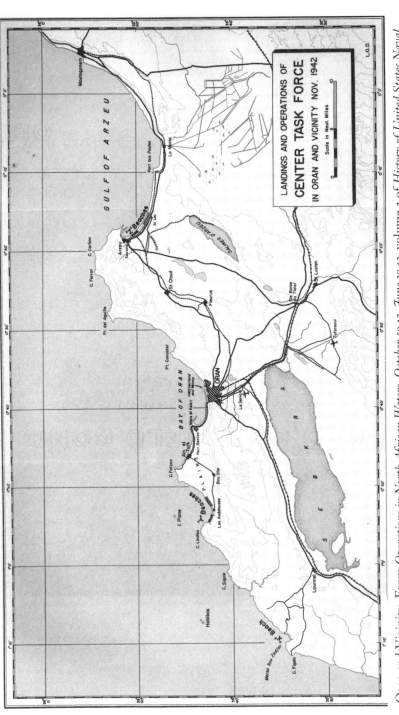

Oran and Vicinity. From *Operations in North African Waters, October 1942–June 1943*, volume 2 of *History of United States Naval Operations in World War II*, by Samuel Eliot Morison, Copyright © 1947, 1950 by Samuel Eliot Morison. By permission of Little, Brown and Company. All rights reserved.

with a relatively intact force that could be used in the advance east toward Tunisia. On 11 November, just three days after the initial assault, thirteen planes carried 134 paratroopers east to Maison Blanche airfield at Algiers, where they joined 64th Troop Carrier Group with thirty-eight aircraft and 456 British paratroopers. Both units would go on to play an important part in the drive for Tunis by seizing airfields close behind the battle lines. The next day 64th Troop Carrier Group, protected by twelve *Spitfires* of 52nd Fighter Group, dropped 312 British paratroopers on the airfield at Bône. On 14 November, twenty C-47s of 60th Troop Carrier Group dropped 350 American paratroopers at Tebessa, near the Tunisian border, seizing an airfield that would be used extensively in the Tunisian campaign. Two days later, the 64th leapfrogged 384 paratroopers to the airfield at Souk el Arba.[63] The distances covered by the Allied airborne forces during the first week of the drive on Tunis would not be equaled for the rest of the campaign.

General James H. "Jimmy" Doolittle, commander of Twelfth Air Force, had high praise for the pilots of the three transport groups allocated to TORCH. In a letter to Arnold, he stated, "I cannot speak too highly of the work that the boys flying the transports are doing. Most of our transports are now working directly for the (British) First Army and are flying directly into the Hun's backyard to drop parachutists, carry troops and bring supplies. They are escorted when fighters are available. Theirs' is the job of greatest hazard and least glory. A fine bunch."[64]

While the troop carrier groups made the most identifiable contribution to the landings, several of the USAAF's tactical units also played a small but important role. The 31st Fighter Group's *Spitfires* entered combat on D-Day and quickly established shore-based fighter cover for the invasion forces there. The group left Gibraltar as soon as it received word that the airfield at Tafaraoui was in Allied hands and arrived overhead late in the afternoon. Four French Dewoitine De-520s, which the American pilots had mistaken for friendly British *Hurricanes* from the carrier force, attacked just as the last four *Spitfires* were landing, shooting down and killing one pilot. The remaining *Spitfires* gave chase and claimed three of their enemy.[65] Again, Vichy fighter opposition would have been much heavier without the support from the carrier-based aircraft. Doolittle acknowledged their role in his first report to General Arnold, noting, "The American carrier borne Navy Aviation at Casablanca and the British Fleet Air Arm at Oran did the major part of the air fighting. By the time airports were secured, they had destroyed either in the air or on the ground the majority of French aviation."[66]

On 9 November, the ground echelon of the 31st, which had landed with the invasion forces, reached the airfield with maintenance and support personnel. With an established base, the air echelon was able to provide material aid to the forces converging on Oran. A reconnaissance flight discovered a column of the French Foreign Legion approaching the airfield from their base at Sidi Bel Abbès. Three flights of four *Spitfires* each immediately attacked the ten-mile-long column, forcing it to turn back, sparing the airfields and protecting the rear of the forces investing Oran.[67] The French column lacked air protection of its own, as most of the remaining French planes were by then en route to Morocco, and lost five lightly armored tanks and a number of unarmored trucks in the attacks.[68]

The 31st was joined by the other American *Spitfire* group, the 52nd, the same day, and both groups continued to provide cover for the advance, silencing several artillery batteries but also mistakenly attacking Allied ground forces, which shot down two of the attackers and thereby demonstrated that ground forces were capable of defending themselves from some air attacks. Doolittle attributed this unfortunate incident to communications errors and the lack of training for both the ground and air forces, which had not had extensive opportunities to train together in the buildup for the invasion.[69] He took prompt action to correct the matter, even having American mechanized units visit the airfields so his pilots could inspect their equipment from both the ground and the air. The two fighter groups lost a total of six aircraft in the assault, one to French fighters, two to friendly ground fire, and another three to enemy ground fire.[70] While arriving units were rapidly shipped east to help in the push for Tunis, the shorter-range *Spitfires* were unable to reach the front lines from the rear airdromes and consequently were assigned air defense and coastal patrol duties during the following month. The 52nd Fighter Group's 4th Fighter Squadron, based at La Senia, and 5th Fighter Squadron at Maison Blanche, near Algiers, spent most of November and December engaged in antisubmarine patrols and convoy escort missions to facilitate the critical movement of supplies to the forward areas. A month after the landings the group's 2nd Fighter Squadron had only eleven planes in commission out of an original twenty, while the 5th Fighter Squadron was down to eight.[71] The high rates of attrition and lack of immediate replacements would hamper USAAF operations throughout the Tunisian campaign.

The USAAF and the Western Task Force

The landings in Morocco did not derive any direct benefit from US-AAF participation but were critical to establishing a secure and robust base area for the future advance on Tunisia. The immediate objectives included the airfield at Port Lyautey, the only all-weather strip along the Atlantic Coast, and the airfield at Casablanca itself, which would host Twelfth Air Force's rear echelon supply and repair depots for the duration of the campaign. The invasion plan again called for fighters to be flown in as soon as airfields were available—but from U.S. Navy escort carriers off the coast. In another remarkable display of interservice cooperation, the USS *Chenango* ferried seventy-seven P-40s of Colonel William Momyer's 33rd Fighter Group, while the USS *Archer* later brought an additional thirty-five, specified as "advance attrition" for the 33rd Fighter Group. These actions ensured that the 33rd would be in a position to provide essential support during the drive into southern Tunisia, although Marshall hoped that they would play a role in the amphibious assault itself. On 18 September he wrote Eisenhower, "The use of P-40's . . . to my mind play a decisive part in affecting a landing on the West Coast. These planes, backing up the tanks to go into Safi by sea train offer the possibility of an immediately available striking force which can play a vital part in the seizure of airfields and breaking down the rear defenses of Casablanca."[72] The 33rd Fighter Group had initially been assigned to the American air forces in the Western Desert, but it was reassigned to North Africa in exchange for replacement P-40s sent to the Western Desert to bring Coningham's squadrons up to strength for the El Alamein battle.[73]

Early invasion plans recognized the deficiency of land-based air support for the initial invasion and sought to make up the difference with robust carrier-based air coverage. The assignment of the USS *Ranger*, one of the U.S. Navy's three surviving fleet carriers at that time, provided the critical margin for the landing forces. *Ranger*'s planes were airborne before dawn on D-Day, conducting antisubmarine patrols and attacking French aircraft in the air and on the ground. Planners estimated the Vichy forces would have 135 bombers and 170 fighters available in the Casablanca area but, recognizing the difficulties of obtaining reinforcements from other areas, believed that the force would fall off rapidly after several days.[74] *Ranger* and three escort carriers, *Sangamon*, *Santee*, and *Suwanee*, totaled only 171 aircraft including fighters, dive-bombers, and torpedo-bombers, although all were of improved types generally superior to the French

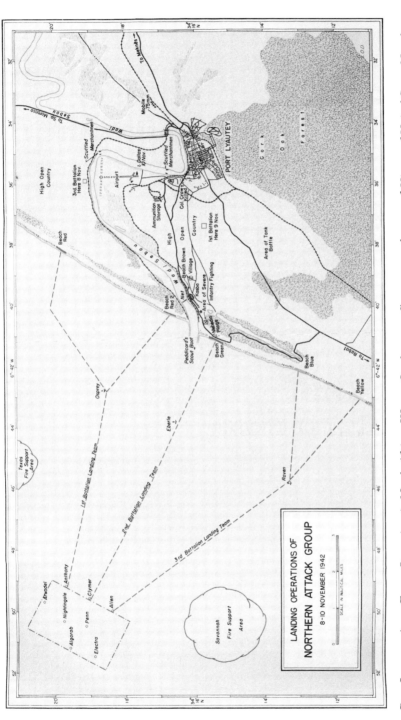

Port Lyautey Area. From *Operations in North African Waters, October 1942–June 1943*, volume 2 of *History of United States Naval Operations in World War II*, by Samuel Eliot Morison, Copyright © 1947, 1950 by Samuel Eliot Morison. By permission of Little, Brown and Company. All rights reserved.

aircraft. Their weakness was their carriers, which could remain in the hostile waters only for a short period, making it essential to establish airpower ashore as quickly as possible so that the carriers could depart before Axis submarines concentrated in the area. *Ranger* was attacked by hostile submarines on several occasions during the assault but luckily escaped damage.

The 33rd Fighter Group's ground support personnel would be required to participate in the initial landings as ground troops in order for them to be at the airfield when the fighters arrived, and to quickly service, refuel, and rearm them so that they could participate in operations around Casablanca.[75] Ultimately, Twelfth Air Force personnel would comprise almost 2,000 of the 9,000 troops assigned to the objective.[76] Unfortunately, the Air Force support personnel evidently received little training to prepare them for their temporary combat role. Once ashore, an airman holding a submachine gun even asked General Lucien Truscott, commanding the Northern Attack Group, "General, we have never shot these things. Couldn't we try them out and see how they work before we have to fight?"[77]

As the western invasion progressed, rough surf, troops landed on the wrong beaches, poor coordination with naval gunfire support, and stout French resistance conspired to delay progress toward the airfield. As Lieutenant General George Patton and his air commander, Brigadier General John Cannon, monitored progress from reports received aboard the cruiser USS *Augusta*, Cannon elected to proceed to the landing site to hasten progress. By float plane and landing craft, Cannon arrived at the Port Lyautey airdrome in late afternoon on 10 November, just as American tanks had repelled a French counterattack and secured the airfield. As the first P-40s arrived, Cannon was speaking with a lieutenant who commanded the armored force when both observed another tank coming over a hill onto the field. Neither could identify the vehicle and, as French Renault light tanks were known to be in the area, the lieutenant asked Cannon what to do. Cannon later explained that he "told him to turn his guns on it and blow it up. He immediately got into action and let it have it. The tank turned tail and disappeared over the hill in a cloud of dust. I later found out that General Truscott was in this tank. It is rather fortunate that the lieutenant's gunnery was not better."[78]

The operation was not without risk, as evidenced by the tragic fate of Colonel Demas T. Craw, the air officer assigned to General Truscott's force charged with the landings in the Mehdia–Port Lyautey area. Craw and Major Pierpont M. Hamilton landed at dawn with the first wave and proceed by jeep under a flag of truce to the commander of the French garrison in hopes of negotiating an early end to hostilities. As they neared the town, Craw was killed by a burst of fire from a concealed machine gun. Ultimately, USAAF personnel would suffer sixty-seven casualties in the landings, including forty-one killed. Cannon lamented these losses, especially of his senior staff members, noting, "Nick Craw was killed in action the day of the landings. It is too bad because I needed him to help here." Craw was awarded a Medal of Honor for his efforts on 8 November 1942, but his absence left Cannon's staff shorthanded.[79]

With the airfield secure and the P-40s available to support operations, Cannon devoted his energies to the ground establishment necessary to sustain flight operations. On 19 November, General Doolittle, commanding Twelfth Air Force, reported that "Joe Cannon . . . has done an outstanding job" and had more than 100 P-40s available, as well as the first B-25s, and that "Joe and George Patton have the western situation well in hand and are getting along together beautifully."[80] When General Spaatz visited Casablanca on 20 November, he too commented favorably on Cannon's efforts to establish an air depot, noting one hanger filled with machine tools and even "skilled, friendly Frenchmen to operate the machines."[81]

On 13 November two squadrons of U.S. Navy Consolidated PBY *Catalinas* arrived at the Port Lyautey airfield from England and were assigned to patrol the Moroccan coast for hostile submarines. Unfortunately, the aircraft arrived too late to prevent several attacks. The day before, three German U-boats in the area, *U-173*, *U-130*, and *U-515*, sank a total of four transports, demonstrating that Eisenhower's concern for the safety of his forces at sea was justified.[82] Losses might have been higher had most of the U-boats in that area of the Atlantic not pursued a convoy sailing between Sierra Leone and the United Kingdom. Fortunately, all of the troops and a large percentage of their supplies had been offloaded before the transports were destroyed. The U.S. Navy would continue to handle antisubmarine duties in Morocco until augmented by the USAAF's 480th Anti-Submarine Group in March 1943. On 22 March 1943, just three days after their first operational sortie, one of the group's B-24s sank *U-524* just west of the Canary Islands. While the U.S. Navy's PBYs could range only 400 miles from shore, the B-24s could reach up to 1,000 miles over the sea and were an unwelcome surprise for U-boat crews plying the mid-Atlantic.[83] The antisubmarine aircraft based on Africa's northern shore provided essential escort for Mediterranean-bound convoys and further restricted the safe operating areas for Axis submarines, fulfilling one of TORCH's objectives.

Conclusion

Between June and November 1942, the USAAF built up a force in Western Europe capable of influencing the outcome of the campaign in Tunisia. Against some opposition, the majority of that force was allocated to support the invasion of North Africa, either directly by supporting the invasion forces or indirectly by attacking the German submarines that threatened its safety. While the USAAF was focused on building a sufficient heavy bomber force in the United Kingdom in order to attack German industry and other strategic targets, it wisely devoted a significant portion of its available assets to ensure the success of the Allies' first major joint operation of the war. Eaker and Spaatz lamented the loss of so many trained personnel and almost half of Eighth Air Force's planes, but they were receiving reinforcements, especially heavy bomber groups, and were also opening a theater that would allow some of these planes to escape the poor weather of the British Isles and operate against the Axis from the better conditions along the African shore. In the months-long campaign that followed, the USAAF, alongside aircraft of the RAF and ships of the Royal Navy, conducted a decisive interdiction campaign that would lead to a major Allied victory in Tunisia and cost the Axis ground forces more than 200,000 casualties and their air forces hundreds of valuable planes.

The Tunisian Campaign:
November 1942 to May 1943

The USAAF units allocated to Operation TORCH would go on to play an important part in the campaign that concluded in Tunisia in early May 1943, with the loss of more than 200,000 Axis troops. They supported the advance of the Allied ground forces by largely clearing the skies of Axis aircraft, helping naval forces interdict the flow of reinforcements and supplies into the Tunisian bridgehead, and performing a variety of other missions, such as land and sea reconnaissance, airlift, and close support of ground troops. While Eighth Air Force in the United Kingdom received the preponderance of heavy bomber assets and supported the campaign by forcing the Luftwaffe to begin to divert fighter and flak assets to the defense of the Reich, the four heavy bomber groups assigned to Twelfth Air Force, along with the two earlier sent to Ninth Air Force in the Western Desert, were employed in an operational campaign that inflicted serious casualties on Luftwaffe forces in the Mediterranean and, along with elements of the RAF and Royal Navy, seriously hindered the Axis supply effort, eventually forcing its collapse. While this air campaign did not mesh with prewar visions of how the B-17 and B-24 should be employed, the results for the combined air, ground, and naval forces clearly demonstrate that the USAAF provided essential and valuable support to the battle in Tunisia.

The pace of the Allied ground advance largely mirrored the buildup of Allied air forces in the theater. (See Figure 4.1.) The forces initially assigned to TORCH were only sufficient to establish a lodgment along the North African shore, but not to win air superiority over the Axis reinforcements rushed into the theater after the landings. The departure of the naval aircraft assigned to cover the

A-20s over Tunisia. (National Archives and Records Administration, Signal Corps Photo)

landings further reduced Allied air strength, making it inadequate to provide the support necessary to capture Tunisia in the initial thrust. Critics of the campaign have suggested that an Allied landing farther east in Algeria or even in Tunisia itself would have guaranteed a quick and early conclusion to the campaign. But this criticism ignores several important developments. First, Axis air strength in the central Mediterranean made a landing any farther east of Algiers a very risky proposition. Earlier in 1942, reinforcement convoys for Malta had suffered devastating losses in the very sea lanes that would have to be traversed to put the troops ashore, and where the supply convoys would have to spend days unloading, all within easy range of Axis air formations on Sardinia and Sicily that were experienced in antishipping attacks and would have been largely immune to a fledgling Allied air effort. Within days of the landings, and while Allied transports were still in the highly vulnerable offloading stage, the Luftwaffe shifted assets from as far away as Norway to the Mediterranean islands in order to employ them against Allied shipping and ports.[1] Some of these aircraft were already en route before the

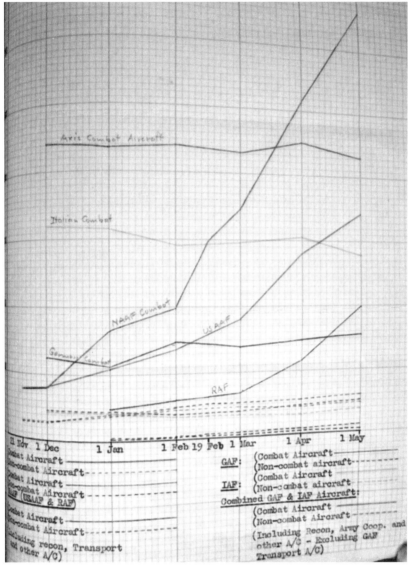

Figure 4.1: Relative strength of Axis and Allied Aircraft in Northwest Africa (Y-axis in 500-plane increments) (Reproduced courtesy of the National Archives and Records Administration, College Park, MD). *Source:* Carl Spaatz to Henry H. Arnold, 24 May, 1943, Folder 312.1-D, Operations Letters, Box 194, Central Decimal Files, 1942-1944, Entry 294A, Serial 312, Record Group 18, Records of the Army Air Forces, NARA 2, College Park, MD.

landings occurred, interpreting the impossible-to-conceal buildup at Gibraltar as another attempt to force a convoy through to Malta. Second, Allied air forces lacked the logistics infrastructure to counter this threat. The Luftwaffe operated from fixed bases in Sicily and Sardinia and, once Tunis had been taken without any Vichy resistance or damage to existing facilities, from developed fields there. Their supply lines across the Sicilian Strait were much shorter and initially more secure than Allied ones that stretched back at least to the United Kingdom and as far as the Eastern Seaboard of the United States. Allied air forces would have to win a preliminary air campaign against Axis air forces in the theater before Allied ground forces could reach their objective.

Some have even suggested that a quick conclusion to the Tunisian campaign would not have materially advanced the Allied schedule in the Mediterranean. Instead, by allowing the Axis to build up the Tunisian bridgehead, the Allies inflicted a much higher eventual cost on the Axis forces squeezed into the bottleneck. Douglas Porch believed "the loss of the Race for Tunis worked to Allied advantage. The Axis decision to reinforce Tunisia had proved disastrous."[2] Even an early capture of Tunis would have left intact large Axis ground and air forces in Sicily, Sardinia, and southern Italy—which would have delayed the eventual landings in Sicily.

In the six months leading up to the fall of Tunisia, the Luftwaffe sustained serious air losses in the Mediterranean, losses it was unable to replace due to insufficient production and strong pressure on other fronts. In *Strategy for Defeat*, Williamson Murray estimates that the Germans alone lost more than 2,400 aircraft, including almost 900 fighters, in the Mediterranean from November 1942 to May 1943 (a full 40 percent of their front-line strength at the time of TORCH), and that overall losses in this theater exceeded those in the skies over Western Europe in each month from January to May 1943.[3] While the Combined Bomber Offensive was unable to inflict serious damage to the *Luftwaffe* in an air-only campaign, tactical air forces operating as part of a combined-arms team destroyed large numbers of German aircraft and killed or captured many highly trained pilots and maintainers and their essential equipment. By May 1943, the few squadrons still operating in Africa were forced to abandon most of their equipment and many repairable aircraft and, in some cases, could evacuate vital ground crews only by stuffing them into cramped storage spaces behind the cockpits of the surviving fighters.[4]

Allied Buildup and the Failed Drive on Tunis

When the Vichy French forces in Morocco and Tunisia finally ended their resistance on 11 November, most USAAF units assigned to the Twelfth Air Force were still in the United Kingdom. Some had not even left the United States, or were strung out along the northern ferry route across the North Atlantic, which would soon close due to winter weather, or the southern ferry route across the Caribbean and the South Atlantic. The capture of Morocco was timely, for it allowed the southern ferry route across the waist of Africa to open a branch up the continent's western coast toward Morocco and, eventually, on to the United Kingdom. The route, while longer, enjoyed better weather and was much more secure, leading it to eventually replace the shorter but much more hazardous northern route for forces destined for the Mediterranean. Negotiations with French officials in French West Africa opened ferry stops at Dakar and made the airdrome at Marrakech, Morocco, an important terminus of a route that would be used heavily throughout the North African campaign. The opening of a secure, all-season air route from the United States to North Africa and on to the United Kingdom was one of the major accomplishments of Operation TORCH. Unfortunately, French officials in Morocco and Dakar did not finalize an agreement to use the airfields there until 2 December, so it was impossible to open the route until after the initial drive on Tunis had been halted.[5]

Having a secure ferry route did little to accelerate the initial flow of complete units and replacements for Twelfth Air Force. Units that had already started across the northern route had to be recalled and sent south. Those units already in the United Kingdom had a difficult transit across the Bay of Biscay to North Africa, made even more difficult for single-engine aircraft by the lack of a suitable emergency airfield between England and Gibraltar. Several P-39s that were to equip the fighter and observation groups assigned to Morocco encountered strong headwinds and were forced to land in Portugal, where they were interned. Those units that arrived safely remained scattered across the North African coast, with some held in French Morocco as insurance against any incursion from Spanish Morocco, while others were pushed forward into the battle area in Tunisia. Losses in combat and from accidents took a heavy toll, increasing the requirement for replacements at a time when shipping schedules were already strained and the logistic network was nearly at its breaking point. Many units soon dropped below nominal operating strength and were forced to make do for an extended period with only the planes and pilots they had available when they arrived.

The Twelfth Air Force was officially assigned to support the American ground forces, which, with the exception of 2nd Battalion, 503rd Parachute Infantry Regiment, were still in rear areas. But the shortage of Allied aircraft over the front lines quickly drew the USAAF into the fight. RAF Eastern Air Command, supporting the British First Army's drive into Tunisia, was short of both aircraft and forward bases. As a result, American units moved up into the battle area. In the two weeks after the landings, the 97th Bomb Group had two of its four B-17 squadrons at the Maison Blanche airfield near Algiers and flew its first mission from there on 19 November, striking the El Aouina airdrome near Tunis.[6] But Axis counterstrokes soon forced the bombers back to Tafaraoui, near Oran, and eventually to Biskra, far south of Algiers on the edge of the Sahara. (See map on page 89.) An Axis raid on Maison Blanche on 20 November, which destroyed ten aircraft, cost the unit one B-17 on the ground, and a second Axis raid on 21 November claimed another aircraft. On General Spaatz's recommendation, the bombers were pulled back the following day.

From Tafaraoui, heavy bombers continued to hit targets in Tunisia and even attempted to reach Axis airfields on Sardinia, but they were turned back by weather. In late November, the 301st Bomb Group joined the 97th, giving the Allies a potent striking arm of two groups of heavy bombers. When escorted by P-38s from the 1st and 14th Fighter Groups, the B-17s could hit the airfields and docks in Tunisia with few losses, but only when the poor weather of the North African rainy season permitted. The move to Biskra in December eased some of the overcrowding in Oran and Algiers and gave bombers a drier and more secure base from which to operate, but it did not change the weather over the target.

USAAF fighters moved forward onto the recently captured airfields at Bône and Youks les Bains, but these were just as far, or farther from, the front as were the British airfields. Neither field was improved, and the heavy rains turned them to mud while thick clouds and poor visibility prevented effective sorties. The forward airfields were also at the end of a tenuous supply line and were often maintained only by air. C-47s of the 62nd and 64th Transport Groups kept the Allied fighters in the air by flying in fuel, ammunition, and spare parts, and they even executed another airborne mission. On 28 November, forty-four planes dropped 530 British paratroopers at Depienne in an unsuc-

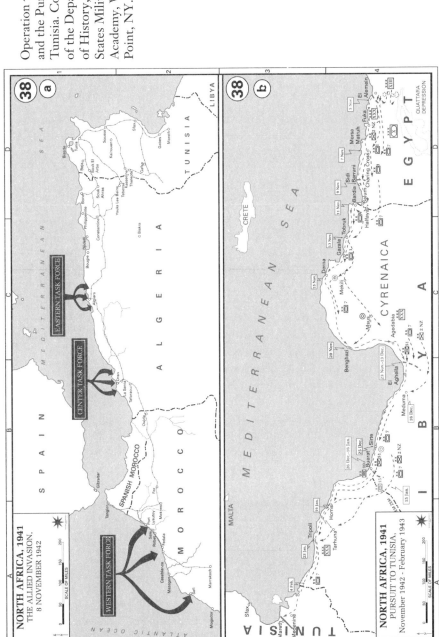

Operation TORCH and the Pursuit to Tunisia. Courtesy of the Department of History, United States Military Academy, West Point, NY.

cessful attempt to take and hold the airfield at Oudna, ten miles from Tunis, until ground forces could link up with them. Unfortunately, Allied ground forces were encountering heavy resistance, both on the ground and in the air, and the surviving paratroopers were forced to retreat back to their own lines with heavy losses.[7]

Despite the Allied advances, the Axis fighters and bombers still controlled the skies over Tunisia. On 3 December Eisenhower reported to the Combined Chiefs of Staff:

> In the pell mell race for Tunisia, we have gone beyond the sustainable limit of air capabilities in support of ground forces. Result is that although air forces have been working at maximum pace, without even minimum repair and supply and maintenance facilities, the scale of possible air support is not sufficient to keep down the hostile strafing and dive bombing that is largely responsible for breaking up all attempted advances by ground forces. The air commanders report that from two days to one week more of present scale of operations, under existing conditions, will leave them near or at complete breakdown, and yet this scale of air support is not sufficient.

Eisenhower noted that the air logistic network had to be built up and had to deliver adequate supplies and personnel to the forward areas before the advance could continue. A final push, scheduled for 9 December, was later postponed and eventually cancelled. He concluded, "This force had only enough 'tail' in initial shipments to capture ports. We gambled that with what we had we could grab Tunisia." This was more than true for the air forces, which had been thrown into an offensive air campaign without providing for an adequate logistical base or time to wrest control of the skies from the enemy.[8] Eisenhower was fully aware of the risks he had accepted and that they contradicted sound military precepts. On 7 December he wrote General Thomas T. Handy of the War Department staff, "I think the best way to describe our operations to date is that they have violated every recognized principle of war, are in conflict with all operational and logistic methods laid down in text books, and will be condemned, in their entirety, by all Leavenworth and War College classes for the next twenty-five years."[9]

In an attempt to remedy the situation, Eisenhower asked for more heavy bombers to help interdict the Axis buildup in Tunisia. His first request was for the temporary assignment of the remaining B-17s and an entire group of B-24s from Ninth Air Force, then still operating from the Nile Delta.[10] While it is unclear who suggested these resources, their concentration in North Africa would have been the first step in retrieving these assets from the Middle East and moving them closer to England. Such a move would have fulfilled Arnold's and the USAAF's desire to concentrate as many heavy bombers in the United Kingdom as possible. Unfortunately for them, Ninth Air Force's heavy bombers were already gainfully employed. On 6 December, Air Marshall Tedder replied that "B-17s and B-24s are the only effective means of striking at Rommel's main port of entry by attacking Tripoli." He added, "Rommel's position has been considerably weakened through the efforts of this striking force. Our ability to continue striking at the supply line on which the entire Libyan campaign will largely depend will be gravely limited if this force is weakened through the prospect of withdrawals to North Africa." In explaining that the bombers were already moving forward toward a planned base near Benghazi, he reported that that location would "afford the best position from which to attack lines of communication and bases from which the Axis forces in North Africa are supplied, as well as attack Rommel's supply line. The attack on Naples today (4 Dec 1942) demonstrated that assistance is afforded to the North African campaign as well whenever the opportunity is presented."[11] In addition to eliminating merchant shipping, the 4 December attack sank the Italian light cruiser *Muzio Attendolo*, which had been damaged by a submarine the previous August during the attempt to push through the Pedestal convoy to Malta, and heavily damaged two other cruisers, *Raimondo Montecuccoli* and *Eugenio di Savoia*. Ninth Air Force's raid prompted the *Regia Marina* to move its remaining capital ships, including three battleships, from Naples farther north to Spezia, relieving somewhat the concerns of Allied naval commanders.[12]

Instead of drawing on Ninth Air Force, the USAAF wisely decided to add reinforcements from the bombers idled by bad weather in the United Kingdom. On 7 December, the Eighth Air Force sent the 93rd Bomb Group's B-24s, which it preferred not to use in mixed formations with B-17s, but which threatened to introduce a new type of aircraft into the Twelfth Air Force's supply channels.[13] In the first instance of cooperation between the two American numbered air forces in North Africa, Tedder apparently convinced Eisenhower to send 93rd Bomb Group on to General Lewis Brereton's Ninth Air Force in Egypt, which was already operating two groups of B-24s, in exchange for the remaining B-17s of Brereton's 376th Bomb Group (the original refugees from Tenth Air Force in India). Tedder's "ample stocks of fuel (from the Middle Eastern refineries) and bombs" in the Delta region and the ability to move them forward into Libya no doubt played a large part in the decision.[14] This exchange gave Brereton a homogenous force of three groups of B-24s and allowed his remaining B-17s to reinforce the 97th and 301st Groups, simplifying somewhat Twelfth Air Force's network of supplies, maintenance, and spare parts. The end result was that the USAAF now had five groups of heavy bombers supporting the campaign (two B-17 groups with Twelfth Air Force in Algeria and the three B-24 groups with Ninth Air Force in Libya), only one less operational group than Eighth Air Force had in the United Kingdom at the time.

This employment evidently meshed with the views of the Air Staff in Washington. On 2 December, the acting Chief of the Air Staff, General George Stratemeyer, gave Spaatz a summary of a meeting with Arnold on 1 December. In it, Arnold told his staff, "I don't want you all to be 'parrots' and just go along with what my views are on winning the war. It might be that you have different ideas and I would like to hear different ideas. It may be that I am wrong and you can show me where I am wrong." Arnold then went on to outline his views:

We must assemble in the European Theater all the bombers we can get our hands on—all the bombers we don't need to hold the Japs— and have them under one command so they can be moved around. I can't see this business of holding two thousand bombers in England. I think you must always have a limited number there to meet emergencies. The rest should go to North Africa, the Middle East and possibly to Turkey if she gets in the war, but all under one command. By doing that I believe that we can break German morale . . . by breaking German morale, it will make the final show comparatively simple for our ground troops.[15]

In order to make this vision a reality, Arnold also began a push to have Spaatz join Eisenhower in the Mediterranean as the overall American air commander in the European theater. By doing so, it would be much easier to shift assets between the Eighth and Twelfth Air Forces, either to take advantage of better weather in Africa or to concentrate forces in the United Kingdom.[16]

On 12 November, Eisenhower wrote Spaatz to thank him for Eighth Air Force's efforts in making TORCH a success but added that he did not think the time had yet arrived for Spaatz to visit and discuss future plans. But the next day, Eisenhower relented, and Spaatz arrived for an inspection tour on 17 November.[17] Two days earlier, Arnold had written Ike to express his views and urge him to name Spaatz as his overall air commander. The same day, he asked Spaatz, "How much of our heavy bombardment strength should we retain in England during the bad weather months where the weather prevents operations more than once or twice a month and how much should we send down to the Northern Mediterranean where the weather is normally good and we can operate at least two or three times every week with greater effectiveness?" He also wondered, "Might it not be necessary to have provisions made for assembling large numbers of heavy bombers, we will say, in Cairo or in the Caucasus, or moving them down again to Tunisia, or perhaps moving them all back again to England?"[18] By 3 December, Eisenhower had recognized the need for an overall commander for both Twelfth Air Force and RAF Eastern Air Command, both operating in Tunisia, and designated Spaatz as his "deputy for air operations in this theater." Spaatz's departure from Eighth Air Force in England gave that command to Lieutenant General Ira Eaker.[19] By 9 December, Spaatz was already engaged in straightening out supply difficulties and in the allocation of replacement aircraft between Eighth and Twelfth Air Forces. He planned to send the first twenty-eight replacement B-17s to the 97th and 301st Groups in North Africa but allocated the next forty-six to Eighth Air Force.[20] Despite his new assignment, Spaatz remained committed to the strategic campaign. On 9 December he wrote Arnold, "To just what extent the operations here over the long pull are going to interfere with our Heavy Bomber build up in the UK, I cannot foresee at present."[21]

But the number of aircraft was a minor problem, compared to the lack of prepared fields and the acute shortage of supplies and maintenance personnel to keep them in the air. In a 30 November letter to Marshall, Eisenhower explained in detail just how strained his lines of communication were. He observed, "Even by using transport airplanes for supply of critical items, the logistics situation is one to make a ritualist in warfare go a bit hysterical." He explained that the small rail line along the coast was capable of handling only nine trains per day, with two required to haul coal for the railroad and one to keep the population from starving. "This leaves 6 for military purposes, and since we have been trying to crowd troops forward, particularly armor, and to supply what we already have there, you can see that reserves of munitions and rations are almost to the vanishing point." Use of the coast highway was hampered by a shortage of vehicles, and coastal convoys continued to suffer from Axis air attacks. Eisenhower noted, "Our greatest concern is to keep the air going efficiently on inadequate, isolated fields."[22]

Even a two-week operational pause was inadequate to build the air and ground forces to sufficient strength to overcome the Axis forces now firmly established in Tunisia. Without command of the air, the Allies could not successfully interdict the flow of Axis troops and supplies or ensure the safety of their own. The successful conclusion to the campaign would require an extended period of buildup, and attrition of the Axis forces, before ground forces could resume their advance in Tunisia. On 25 December, an obviously frustrated Doolittle outlined his estimate of the situation for General Spaatz: "Let's stop our wishful thinking, abandon our present 100% bitched up organization, stop trying to win the Tunisian War in a day, and through forward planning, sound organization and an appreciation of what air power, when properly utilized, can do, put the God Damn thing on ice." To remedy the situation, Doolittle was "firmly convinced that a new and radically different course of action must be adopted in order to exploit fully and effectively the Allied forces in this theater." His plan recognized that "an intensive build-up will be necessary before a successful combined ground-air offensive can again be undertaken." He advocated "making available to the Air Force, airport sites and the transportation necessary to bring in required supplies and equipment to permit them to execute their maximum continuous effort in the forward area." The first requirement was to "Attain definite air superiority," which would enable the ground forces to build up to sufficient levels. To do this, he proposed to "limit the enemy's air operations by (A) Destruction of enemy aircraft in the air and on the ground (B) destruction of essential air installations and supplies." His plan required "working first on docks, marshaling yards, stores, boats, airports and airplanes, not only in Tunisia, but Sardinia, and Sicily as well, and then on all concentrations of troops and if necessary the cities of Tunis and Bizerte using high altitude precision day bombing, low altitude bombing, torpedoes and strafing. Only after this period of 'softening up' can the ground troops move in." In short, Doolittle was calling for an *operational* campaign that would use both tactical and strategic assets to enable the ground forces to achieve success.[23]

The failures in front of Tunis also generated the first significant episode of friction between the ground and air forces. Colonel Paul M. Robinett, who had commanded Combat Command B of the 1st Armored Division at Oran and was later pushed forward into Tunisia to reinforce Lieutenant General Kenneth Anderson's First British Army, wrote directly to General Marshall on 8 December to express his frustration with the lack of air support during the stalled drive. He blamed the failure on both the lack of support, which was largely due to reasons beyond the USAAF's control, and the lack of coordination between ground and air forces, which stemmed from an inadequate communications network but also reflected a lack of training in this critical area for both the ground and air forces. Robinett felt "there will be no coordination until all ground and air elements bearing on a common objective are effectively placed in the hands of a single commander."[24] For Robinett, that would likely be the ground commander, although, in the Western Desert, the British had demonstrated that it was possible to obtain effective coordination by close cooperation between independent ground and air commanders.

Robinett concluded with his equally faulty suggestion for the employment of air forces in the theater. "I have talked with all ranks possible and am sure than men cannot stand the mental and physical strain of constant aerial bombings without feeling that all possible is being done to beat back *the enemy air effort* [emphasis in original]. News of bombed cities or ships or ports is not the answer they expect." But the interdiction campaign against Axis shipping, which first required reduction of the Axis air effort, was precisely what would bring the Tunisian campaign to a successful conclusion. Robinett was correct that the USAAF's green units had much to learn about offering effective close air support, but he was wrong to suggest that air be used as a defensive shield to protect ground troops instead of offensively to attack Axis airfields, ports, and shipping that the enemy air and ground efforts both depended on.

Fortunately, Robinett's views did not prevail. Marshall forwarded the letter to Arnold, who seized the opportunity to reinvigorate the effort to achieve coordination between the ground and air arms. In a letter to his director of air support, he railed, "This is something I have been pounding on now for over a year—apparently with little success. I have emphasized time and time again the urgent necessity for having perfect team play between the Air Support units and the Ground troops." While acknowledging that "our troops in the North African venture went over there only partially trained," Arnold ordered his deputy to "impress upon all concerned not only the necessity for absolute teamwork between the Air Support and Ground elements, but also the very thorough step by step training necessary in all of the Air Support elements in order to develop the technique and procedure so essential to bring such teamwork about." Arnold's sincerity is attested to by the near-perfect coordination achieved during the drive across France in 1944.[25] At the same time, Arnold sent a copy of Robinett's letter to the War Department's A-3 (assistant Chief of Staff for operations) with the request that it be "brought to General Eisenhower's attention, with the request that he comment upon it, to the end that the Army Air Forces may most efficiently prepare new units for their roles in theatres of operations." It included the qualifier that "General Robinett, as a regimental commander, may not have been aware of all the problems confronting the Theatre Commander in the employment of Army Air Forces units."[26] Months later, Eisenhower wrote Marshall that Robinett "has made the best fighting record of any Combat Commander on the front. However, I will never recommend him for a promotion until he learns to control his tongue. He seems intelligent but entirely without judgment."[27]

But Robinett's frustrations stemmed from real failures in air-ground support during the early phases of the campaign. Eisenhower's headquarters had attempted to clearly outline what was expected, issuing a six-page operations memorandum on 13 October, less than one month before the landings. The memo, titled "Combat Aviation in Direct Support of Ground Units," reflected USAAF influence by stating, "As a general rule, only those targets which cannot be reached quickly and effectively by artillery should be assigned to combat aviation." But it equivocated: "This should not be interpreted as prohibiting the concentration of all available means, including combat aviation, against the decisive objective." It anticipated the requirement for both prearranged and on-call support, as reported by either aerial reconnaissance or the ground forces themselves, and relied on both the U.S. *Field Manual 31-35* and the British "Army Training Instruction No. 6" for guidance, believing "the US and British systems of communication for obtaining direct air support are quite similar." It noted that U.S. air support parties were intended to perform essentially the same functions as the British "tentacles" and that the American "Air Support Control" was virtually identical to the British "Army Air Support Control." But the document failed to incorporate valuable lessons from the Western Desert. It relied on ground identification panels that had already proven unworkable, and protection of friendly troops was supposedly assured by the designation of a bomb line, but the recommendation of using "easily recognized land marks, such as a river, highway or railroad" reflected that planners had not fully considered the difficulties the British had encountered in the nearly featureless Western Desert. In short, the document, while supported by a strong theoretical foundation, reflects the haste with which the entire operation had been planned and the lack of incorporation of lessons learned at great cost in Libya and Egypt.[28]

Ninth Air Force and Allied Pursuit Across Libya

While the western forces stalled before their objectives in Tunisia, the British forces to the east were demonstrating what could be accomplished after a period of buildup, a decisive battle, and complete mastery of the air. As Axis forces streamed west across Libya, the British Eighth Army pursued, using the fighters and bombers of the Western Desert Air Force to break up roadblocks, including the strong defensive position at El Agheila, harass road-bound columns, and interdict resupply efforts.[29] The American air units assigned to the WDAF continued to operate alongside RAF units. In November the P-40s of 79th Fighter Group joined those of the 57th, which had participated in the Alam Halfa and El Alamein battles. The 79th rotated its pilots into the 57th in order to provide experience for the new crews while also granting a respite from the intense activity of the battle and pursuit for the older ones.[30] By the end of the year, a third P-40 unit, the 324th Fighter Group, joined the other two groups, giving Ninth Air Force a potent force of fighter-bombers and interceptors. The 12th Medium Bomb Group was likewise reinforced with the addition of a second B-25 unit, the 340th Bomb Group, and both units continued to work with the light and medium bombers of Sir Arthur Coningham's WDAF, providing significant support in the breach of the Mareth Line the following March.[31]

But the most important contributions to the air effort in Libya came from the heavy bomb groups and a new unit, the 316th Troop Carrier Group. Initially assigned to transport and supply air units that were to support the Soviets in the Caucasus, the four squadrons of the 316th became available to the WDAF when that mission was cancelled. Although the air echelon was available on 7 December, the ground component did not arrive until the following February.[32] The 316th could not have arrived at a better time. As units leapfrogged across the southern shores of the Mediterranean, British supply lines expanded from the compact area in the delta and eventually stretched over one thousand miles to Tripoli and beyond. With only a single road stretching across much of this expanse, and coastal shipping hampered by

B-25 *Mitchell* in the WDAF, 1943. B-25 bombers of the United States Army
Air Forces and *Baltimore* bombers of the South African Air Force flying
in formation on their way to attack Rommel's position in North Africa.
(National Archive and Records Administration, Still Pictures Division,
Photo 208-MO-48-N-9009-AC)

extensive demolition and bomb damage in the Libyan ports, the C-47s
became a valuable addition to both Ninth Air Force and the WDAF.
The unit's fifty-two C-47s were used to move supplies, personnel, and
emergency parts and fuel so that the WDAF could continue to apply
pressure to the retreating elements of the Afrika Korps. The C-47
was the only aircraft in the Western Desert capable of carrying drums
of fuel and frequently helped keep WDAF aircraft in the air, hauling
130,000 gallons forward for the attack on the Agheila position.[33]

Moving by the southern ferry route, the unit reached Egypt between 23 and 25 November and immediately began moving supplies to
the west. Although one squadron was temporarily detained in West
Africa to help the Air Transport Command alleviate a backlog of supplies that had accumulated there, the entire unit was available to the
WDAF by mid-December and materially aided the advance. The RAF
did not field a large transport aircraft like the C-47, instead relying on
the smaller Lockheed *Hudson* and an extremely efficient network of
ground transportation to move units forward. The American groups

An Air Transport Command plane flies over the pyramids in Egypt, 1943. Loaded with urgent war supplies and materials, this plane is one of a fleet flying shipments from the United States across the Atlantic and the continent of Africa to strategic battle zones. (National Archives and Records Administration, Still Pictures Division, Photo 111-SC-179564)

lacked sufficient numbers of motorized transport and became dependent on the 316th to relieve their overstretched supply lines.

The Ninth's two assigned heavy bomber groups displaced forward from Palestine to the Delta area as soon as WDAF units occupying those fields moved off to the west. The 98th and 376th Groups, augmented by *Liberators* of the RAF's No. 160 Squadron, began staging through Gambut, near Tobruk, on 21 November in order to extend their range sufficiently to reach Axis shipping at Tripoli while still enjoying the established maintenance and repair facilities in the canal area. By using fuel on-loaded at Gambut, the B-24s eventually extended their reach to Tunisia, Sicily, and even the Italian mainland.[34] During the coming months, these raids would inflict serious damage on the Axis supply lines stretching into Tunisia, materially assisting the campaign there. By January, estimates revealed that the Tunisian ports of Sfax, Sousse, Bizerte, and Tunis were operating at anywhere from 20 percent to 50 percent of capacity. By the end of January, the Libyan fields were sufficiently well established to move the B-24s there permanently, saving the shuttle run to the Delta area on each mission.[35]

With a secure base area, an established—if temporarily strained—logistics network and, counting the temporary reinforcements from the Eighth Air Force's 93rd Bomb Group, which returned to the U.K. in February, three highly experienced long-range bomb groups, Ninth Air Force was ideally suited to carry the brunt of the interdiction campaign during the winter months. From Gambut and, after the end of January, Benghazi, the B-24s paid frequent visits to the Tunisian ports and became a regular caller at Naples. The effort began with a raid on Tripoli on 21 November in an attempt to keep Rommel's forces, especially his air arm, too short of fuel and ammunition to effectively oppose the pursuing British ground forces. Although only fourteen aircraft of the twenty-three sent reached their target due to poor weather and mechanical difficulties, they caused serious damage to the port's warehouses and the principal mole. A return visit on 26 November was limited by poor weather, but a follow-up on 29 November again inflicted heavy damage to the port. RAF Liberators of No. 160 Squadron continued the effort at night, significantly reducing the port's capacity and thereby reinforcing the Axis decision to shift most of its supply effort to the comparatively safe ports in Tunisia. Solly Zuckerman and a team of RAF operations analysts conducted extensive bomb-damage surveys once Tripoli was liberated and found that "despite the many night sorties which the R.A.F. had directed at the harbour, only two ships had been put out of action completely, whereas four big enemy vessels had definitely been sunk by a relatively small number of American daylight sorties in the last weeks of November and the first week of December 1942." This further demonstrated the value and efficacy of the USAAF's contribution to British air forces in the Middle East.[36]

In December, B-24s made two raids on Naples, losing one aircraft to heavy flak on 12 December but disrupting the supply network at its source. A heavy raid on the railroad roundhouse at Sfax on 16 December completely destroyed the target, interrupting rail transportation down the Tunisian coast. Sousse, Tunis, and Naples were hit in the following weeks, causing further disruptions and significantly reducing port capacity. In January, Palermo and Bizerte were added to the target list, and repeat visits to Naples and Tripoli kept the Axis from building up sufficient supplies for a strong striking force within the Tunisian bridgehead. Even though the raids were unescorted, losses were kept low by timing the strikes for dusk and departing the target area over the sea, where fighters were loath to follow. In December 1942 and January 1943, the 93rd, 98th, and 376th Groups flew more than five hundred separate sorties and lost only six aircraft. As Ninth Air Force began to strike targets in and around Tunisia, Twelfth Air Force reciprocated by hitting targets in Libya. On 18 January, B-17s escorted by P-38s participated in a series of raids on the Castel Benito airfield near Tripoli. Now that the two forces were within supporting distance of each other and striking the same targets, a new command structure would be required to improve coordination.[37]

The Casablanca Conference and the Battle of Kasserine Pass

The meeting of the Western Allies at the Anfa camp near Casablanca in mid-January provided a number of significant developments for the air forces. The most commonly cited is the decision to implement a Combined Bomber Offensive from the United Kingdom, with Eighth Air Force's bombers attacking using visual means during daylight hours while RAF Bomber Command struck at nighttime. The decision resolved a great deal of tension between the two air forces, as the RAF had been pressuring the USAAF to shift to night operations, based on the high RAF losses incurred during daylight raids earlier in the war. But American advocates were convinced that with a more heavily armed bomber and a precision bombsight they could achieve results in daylight with acceptable losses and without endangering civilian populations in surrounding areas. The resulting agreement largely set the stage for the remainder of the air war in Northwest Europe.

But the conclusion was not foregone. Entering the conference, several officials were open to suggestions for where and how to employ the USAAF's heavy bombers. On 14 January, Charles Portal, Chief of the RAF, suggested that "one of the most important questions before the present conferences is to decide on where the United States bombers are to be used." In response to suggestions that North Africa promised a better operating environment, he responded, "Before deciding to build up a strong bomber force in North Africa, it is desirable to be certain that this action is more advantageous than concentrating them in the United Kingdom." Portal appears to have been convinced of the wisdom of around-the-clock bombing from the United Kingdom, in which the American daytime sorties would increase the effectiveness of the British nighttime sorties, and vice-versa, by not permitting German defenders any respite in which to prepare for the next attack;

and he was reluctant to diminish this effort by concentrating too many bombers in North Africa, where they could not reach industrial targets deep inside Europe.[38]

The plan to continue operations in the Mediterranean was equally as important as the decision to implement the Combined Bomber Offensive. By agreeing to the invasion of Sicily, code-named Operation HUSKY, the Allies acknowledged that "aid to Russia is regarded as being of paramount importance in order to assist the Russian Army to absorb the strength of the German ground and air forces." (See map on page 159.) The Allies clearly realized that, without the Soviet forces tying up the bulk of German ground and, for the time being, air strength, they would have little prospect of a successful return to the continent. Sir Alan Brooke, chief of the Imperial General Staff, pointed out that by continuing to press in the Mediterranean "airplanes which normally leave Russia during the winter months and participate in operations in the Med would be unable to return in the spring."[39] This had already happened after TORCH, as the landings has forced the redeployment of more than one hundred bombers and forty fighters from the German air forces around Stalingrad.[40] By mid-January, the Soviets and Germans were then locked in the final stages of that battle, which would consume large numbers of German transport aircraft, and it appeared wise to attempt to stretch the Luftwaffe to, and past, the breaking point, in order to facilitate the ground advance on both fronts.[41] The large Allied air commitment to the Mediterranean accomplished this objective in a way that a bomber-only offensive from the United Kingdom could not. As the German air force was committed to using its assets in support of ground forces, the bulk of it could only be successfully engaged in a campaign where ground forces were active. The substantial Luftwaffe losses incurred in trying to support Axis forces in Tunisia, and in protecting and supplying the Tunisian bridgehead, more than justified the Allied decision to engage the Axis powers there.

On 15 January, Eisenhower traveled to Casablanca to brief the Combined Chiefs of Staff on operations in Tunisia and his plans for the future. At the time, Eisenhower hoped to attack toward Sfax, on the coast south of Tunis, in order to drive a wedge between the Axis forces around Tunis, commanded since November by Generaloberst Hans-Jürgen von Arnim, and Rommel's Afrika Korps, approaching from the south. After reviewing the weak state of the American forces holding that sector, and the slow speed of Montgomery's pursuit, the plan was abandoned. In light of future events, it is probably a good thing that it was. A salient projecting between the two forces would have been sticking a neck into a noose and provided Axis forces with an ideal scenario for a *kesselschlacht* (cauldron battle) that might have inflicted serious damage. Sir Alan Brooke, chief of the Imperial General Staff, accurately observed that such an offensive invited defeat in detail. During his presentation, Eisenhower noted that "every effort had been made to build up for an attack in the North by increasing our air-power" but that the "appalling conditions of the airfields and the bad weather had largely closed down air operations."[42]

During this operational pause, the initiative swung to the Axis powers, giving them freedom to prepare and execute a counterstroke against U.S. forces in southern Tunisia, culminating in the battle that became known as Kasserine Pass. The air forces would take their share of criticism for failing to detect the assault and their inability to halt it due to poor weather. But the steady attacks on Axis supply lines ensured that Rommel lacked the supplies he needed for a more damaging penetration than the one he actually achieved.

The air support provided by the Army Air Forces was often inadequate, for several important reasons. First, the units assigned to XII Air Support Command, the organization responsible for supporting the American ground forces in southern Tunisia, were understrength and equipped with less-capable types of aircraft. Twelfth Air Force initially deployed P-38 fighters to the newly won airfields on the Algeria-Tunisia border, but these were withdrawn in order to provide escorts for the heavy bombers involved in the interdiction campaign. The 33rd Fighter Group, equipped with P-40s, had landed in Morocco during Operation TORCH but had been worn down by two months of heavy action in southern Tunisia. It was withdrawn on 6 February and replaced by the American *Spitfires* of the 31st and 52nd Fighter Groups. These *Spitfires* lacked the range to effectively perform the heavy bomber escort mission but were more than capable of protecting the light bombers and P-39s. The P-39s of the 81st Fighter and 68th Observation Groups were so inferior to the Luftwaffe's Me-109s and Focke-Wulf 190s that they themselves had to be escorted by the *Spitfires* on their strafing and fighter-bomber missions.

Twelfth Air Force correctly reserved its most capable assets, the B-17 bomber force and P-38 escorts, and applied them to the interdiction campaign. The medium bombers, which now included squadrons from the experienced 12th Bomb Group transferred from Ninth Air Force, also remained focused on the air-superiority and interdiction campaigns. Both decisions had important results for the Kasserine battle. The Germans never achieved air superiority over the battlefield and, thanks to the interdiction campaign, lacked the logistical "tail" necessary to make the thrust a serious threat to Allied rear areas. While the decision was not popular with the ground troops who suffered heavy losses in the Kasserine battle, the decision to remain focused on airfields, ports, and shipping was justified. As General Robinett's comments indicated, this did little for the morale of the ground forces, who could not see the "bombed cities or ships or ports," but the reduced Axis effort was undoubtedly in their long-term best interest.[43]

The second reason that American air support was lacking during the battle was that the ground forces had been unable to protect the forward landing grounds where the few assets dedicated to close support were based. A total of five fields stocked with precious supplies had to be abandoned, limiting the effectiveness of close-support missions. On 11 February, just three days before the battle opened, Eisenhower wrote General Kenneth Anderson, commanding all ground forces in Tunisia, that "your mission will now be as follows: (a) To protect the airfields at Souk el Khemis, Tebessa and Thelepte (No. 2) so that our air forces may operate continuously from them."[44] Anderson did protect the first two airfields, as Souk el Khemis was never threatened, and Tebessa held, just barely, although operations were hampered by partial evacuations. But Axis ground forces captured Thelepte on 17 February with the loss of eighteen inoperable aircraft (five damaged beyond repair) and 60,000 gallons of aviation fuel.[45] These were substantial losses, as they represented supplies brought forward at great costs over the strained logistics network. It also points to the USAAF's overreliance on air transport, as aircraft bringing up essential supplies from the rear could not be diverted quickly enough to evacuate supplies at the threatened airfields. A larger allocation of ground transportation, as in the RAF establishment, might have saved more of the supplies, but even those vehicles allocated to USAAF units had been requisitioned to support the overall logistics effort.

The rainy Tunisian winter further impacted the USAAF's ability to directly attack leading elements of the German offensive. When the clouds cleared, XII Air Support Command, units of RAF No. 242 Group, assigned to support units to the north, and the Western Desert Air Force, still tasked to support Montgomery's Eighth Army, just now investing the Mareth Line to the south, took advantage of a reorganized command system to combine their efforts against Axis ground forces. Units struck truck and tank columns, destroying vehicles and forcing advancing columns to deploy for defense, slowing their progress, and giving Allied ground forces valuable time to prepare defenses.

But during 18–22 February, the most critical phase of the advance, the USAAF's lack of an all-weather capability grounded its aircraft, limiting it to four missions on 18 February, none on 19 and 20 February, and only limited efforts on 21 and 22 February.[46] For their part, the Germans appeared to have learned this lesson well, timing their own offensive in the Ardennes in December 1944 (the Battle of the Bulge) to coincide with a period of poor weather that again limited the USAAF's response.

The 52nd Fighter Group's experiences during 14–20 February illustrate all three factors. After receiving reports of the German breakthrough at Faid Pass, early on 15 February the group cancelled all scheduled missions and pushed forward twelve *Spitfires* each from the 2nd, 4th, and 5th Fighter Squadrons. The 2nd and 4th went to Thelepte, Tunisia, while the 5th settled in at Youks les Bains, just across the border in Algeria. By that afternoon, all three squadrons were flying sorties, escorting P-39s on reconnaissance and strafing attacks. On 16 February the group flew a total of eighty-two sorties that included airdrome defense, reconnaissance missions, and escort for light bomber attacks on German tanks and artillery positions. But that night the 2nd and 4th Squadrons received evacuation orders, and by 1000 local time the next morning everything was gone except for three unflyable *Spitfires* that had to be burned. En route to their new home at Youks les Bains, eight aircraft strafed gun positions while twelve more escorted another attack. After joining the 5th Fighter Squadron at Youks, where foxholes provided the only accommodations, the 2nd and 4th continued to fly escort and reconnaissance missions and found a traffic jam of German vehicles held up by a demolished bridge near Feriana. Within two hours, twelve *Spitfires*, six A-20s, and four P-39s had arrived on scene and inflicted considerable damage. On 18 February poor weather closed in, limiting the group to only fourteen reconnaissance sorties and costing it one pilot in a collision with a mountain peak in the rugged terrain. Poor weather completely precluded flying on 19 February but did bring a second evacuation order, as Youks was then being threatened by the ground advance. On 20 February, as Germans poured through Kasserine Pass, the group again evacuated to Telergma and Chateau d'un du Rhumel, this time by C-47. The group was again in action on 22 February, the critical day, escorting A-20s in sustained attacks on the enemy's lead elements, thereby helping the ground forces finally halt the offensive.[47]

Another factor inhibiting the USAAF's response was a reorganization that finally combined the British and American air elements in

Northwest Africa under a single commander. This development, while much needed and long delayed, was poorly timed and took effect on 18 February, at the height of the battle. While it did not appear to prevent any sorties by aircraft already grounded by rain and fog, it did serve as a distraction for higher echelons. The new command, the Northwest African Air Force (NAAF), headed by General Spaatz, was to be but one component of Sir Arthur Tedder's Mediterranean Air Command, the overall Allied air headquarters in the theater, along with the RAF forces in Malta and the Middle East. (See Appendix 2 for a complete description of the new organization.) This placed all of Twelfth and Ninth Air Forces (but not Eighth Air Force) under a single commander, facilitating cooperation between the two but removing the heavy bombers still in the United Kingdom from Spaatz's operational control.

While uniting the British and American air forces in Algeria, Morocco, and Tunisia, the Northwest African Air Force also segregated them by type and function and placed these under separate commanders. Doolittle's Northwest African Strategic Air Force (NASAF) retained the heavy and medium bombers and their escort fighters and remained focused on the air-superiority and interdiction campaigns, while Sir Arthur Coningham's Northwest African Tactical Air Force (NATAF) would finally bring the lessons and expertise of the Western Desert Air Force (and its capable commander) to the American and British units that landed with TORCH. Coningham applied his experience with the WDAF to both No. 242 Group and XII Air Support Command, which retained their identity alongside the WDAF under NATAF. By splitting the air defense mission, which primarily involved ports and convoys, off to the Northwest African Coastal Air Force (NACAF), Coningham ensured that the maximum number of fighters would be available for ground support in the forward area. Other refinements included a focus on soft-skinned vehicles rather than harder to destroy tanks, as well as better coordination between light bombers and escorting fighters.[48]

Unfortunately, the separation of NATAF and NASAF also codified the distinction between the two missions. While in North Africa this proved to be a positive development, allowing NASAF to complete the interdiction campaign, it also set the precedent for segregating heavy bombers in a separate command and formalized the idea that they were not intended, except in emergencies, to support surface forces tactically. Heavy bombers dedicated to an *operational* objective could influence the outcome of the North African campaign. But had these same bombers been allocated to the *strategic* campaign, they likely would have been sitting idle in England, or attacking industrial targets producing weapons and munitions destined largely for the eastern front, which would not have had an immediate impact on the campaign in North Africa. In reflecting on the campaign, Field Marshall Albert Kesselring, who held overall command of the Axis forces in Tunisia, felt that the interdiction campaign was "the decisive factor, namely, that under the weight of concentrated air and sea attacks on ports and airfields, our supply lines and accordingly whole resistance would break down."[49]

Allegations of a lack of support by the USAAF are particularly disconcerting when one considers what the units of Twelfth Air Force *were* doing during the difficult winter months in Tunisia. In addition to the interdiction and air-superiority campaigns, which limited the strength of Axis land and air forces in the theater, the airlift units, lacking a troop-transport mission, were used almost exclusively in bringing supplies forward. The difficult conditions and rudimentary and unreliable road and rail networks also gave rise to a new, important, and enduring mission—that of medical evacuation of wounded casualties. Empty transport aircraft, on their return trips to supply areas to the rear, began carrying wounded troops to more secure and better-equipped and better-staffed hospitals in Oran and Algiers, increasing their chances for survival and freeing front-line medical units to focus on new casualties. From 16 January to 18 February, the 51st Troop Carrier Wing (which included the 60th, 62nd, and 64th Groups) evacuated 887 patients from the forward area.[50] Troops could be moved by air between hospitals at the front and those in Algiers in five hours, and Oran in less than seven, while travel by train took three and six days, respectively.[51] Eventually, surgeons and nurses flew out and back on the aircraft to provide care en route. This efficient and effective service had a positive effect on both the survival rate and morale of the ground forces involved in the Kasserine battle. Consolidation of all cargo aircraft into the Northwest African Troop Carrier Command (NATCC) further improved the overall efficiency of the air transportation system.

USAAF units, especially within XII Air Support Command as part of NATAF, continued to provide support to ground forces, but not all of it was of the close support variety. In the period after Kasserine but before Eighth Army's breakthrough at the Mareth Line, XII Air Support Command refocused its combat objectives:

These objectives now were: (1) "to defeat the enemy by fighter sweeps and escort for intensive bombardment of airdromes"; (2) "to provide visual and photo reconnaissance along the II Corps front"; (3) "to give direct support to ground forces by attacks on enemy supply columns, vehicle concentrations and enemy armor units." It soon became apparent that objective (1) was first priority. The command's effort was henceforth predominantly devoted to counter-air force operations.[52]

Thus, the organization primarily devoted to ground support was involved mainly in the air superiority mission.

But the new focus did not seem to impact the quality of support provided. On 24 March, the II Corps commander, Lieutenant General George Patton, wrote the commanding general of XII Air Support Command to express his "great appreciation for the superior manner in which the XII Air Support Command has assisted the operations of this Corps. We feel that each day mutual understanding between air and ground improves, with great benefit to ourselves, and greater and greater unhappiness and destruction to the enemy."[53] But just a week later Patton had changed his tune, after a particularly unfortunate episode that created one of the more serious incidents between both air and ground forces, as well as between the British and Americans, of the entire campaign.

On 1 April, one of Patton's most trusted personal aides was killed in a German air attack on an American observation post. Feeling the loss keenly, Patton issued a situation report that complained that the "forward troops have been continuously bombed all morning" as a result of the "total lack of air cover for our units." Sir Arthur Coningham, commander of NATAF, took offense at the allegation, especially considering the heavy support his forces were then providing, including 260 sorties over Patton's sector of the front lines. But he chose to respond to the allegation publicly, claiming in his own report that Patton was using the lack of air support as an excuse for the failure to advance on the ground, and added further insult to injury when he suggested that II Corps, which Patton had commanded only since the Kasserine battle, was "not battleworthy in terms of present operation."[54]

On 2 April a mortified Spaatz wrote Eisenhower, "I have seen signal Special 40 of April 2 from AOC, NATAF [Coningham]. I am gravely concerned at certain comments which that message contains. . . . I take the gravest exception to the broadcasting in his message of comments which are entirely outside his competence and are calculated seriously to affect the growth of the mutual good will and confidence between land and air forces which is essential for success."[55] Eisenhower seemed to take the incident particularly hard, laboring, as he had, to bring about harmonious relations between ground and air forces but more importantly between the Allies. On 5 April he wrote Marshall, "This past week as been a very trying one and was notable for one incident that disturbed me very much. This involved a very unwise and unjust criticism of the II Corps by a senior member of the British Air Force. Unfortunately, this criticism received very wide circulation. . . . There were, of course, as usual, two sides to the story but there was really no excuse for the thing happening."[56]

Eisenhower also addressed his concerns to Patton directly and, while feeling that Patton was right to take offense to Coningham's charges, deplored the manner in which the dispute had aired publicly. He insisted that "when we have anything we feel compelled to report that smacks of criticism of another Service or of any collaborating agency, we must see that the matter is handled in a purely official manner and given in the nature of a confidential report to the next military superior *only*." He hoped that Patton would drop the matter, writing, "*the great purpose of complete Allied teamwork must be achieved in this theater* and it is my conviction that this purpose will not be furthered by demanding the last pound of flesh for every error."[57]

The incident did not appear to have lasting consequences for inter-Allied relations, or further cooperation between the ground and air forces, although Coningham later demonstrated a lack of respect for Spaatz's authority as commander of NAAF when, according to Solly Zuckerman, while visiting Spaatz at his headquarters in Tunis:

> [He] suddenly got up and moved into the garden where we could see him picking blossoms from a hibiscus bush. He then returned and bent down on one knee in front of Tooey [Spaatz] saying, as he proffered the flowers, 'Master, I bring you these.' Tooey was not amused. He knew well enough that the gesture was Mary's [Coningham's] way of indicating that he had nothing to learn from an American general who had been in the war less than a year.[58]

Interdiction and Final Victory in Tunisia

While the tactical assets of the RAF and Twelfth Air Force attempted to slow down the Kasserine offensive, the strategic bombers remained focused on the interdiction campaign, although they were assigned one mission designed to hit elements of the Afrika Korps as they retreated through Kasserine Pass. Accustomed to bombing ports with their easily identifiable land-water contrast and patterns of settlement, locating a single mountain pass in the Eastern Dorsals in poor weather proved beyond many navigators' capabilities. In an effort that foreshadowed later attempts to use strategic bombers on close support missions, the flight spent an hour of searching for the target before finally bombing friendly forces at Souk-el-Arba, inflicting a number of civilian casualties.[59] While the USAAF leadership complained of the diversion from the strategic mission in the United Kingdom, and U.S. Army leadership demanded more direct support for ground forces, the B-17s and P-38 escorts remained properly focused on the operational targets that would eventually make the greatest contribution to the end of the Tunisian campaign.

Since the second week of November 1942, elements of the 97th and 301st Bomb Groups had been raiding Bizerte and Tunis, as well as targets on Sicily, Sardinia, and even the Italian mainland whenever weather permitted. Initially, these forays were hampered by the same obstacles that limited the air effort elsewhere in North Africa. Inadequate airfields turned to mud in the winter rains, forcing bombers to be parked on the limited space on inactive runways between sorties. A new, all-weather complex was under construction at Biskra in the drier desert, but it was not ready until late January 1943. Bombs and fuel were constantly in short supply, with missions often launching with the last of the reserves on the base, depending on C-47s to fly in replacements in time for the next mission.[60] While apparently an efficient form of supply-chaining, this was not an ideal arrangement with the tenuous logistics infrastructure in North Africa.

By February 1943, the base and logistics network had expanded sufficiently to accommodate additional bomber groups in Twelfth Air Force, and Eisenhower requested the deployment to North Africa of 91st and 306th Groups, then in England but originally allocated to Twelfth Air Force. Faced with the prospect of losing another two experienced B-17 groups, the Eighth Air Force's commander, Lieutenant General Ira Eaker, rushed off a letter of protest to the War Department and requested that he be allowed to retain those two groups. He wrote, "We were just getting up off the floor from the loss of our P-38 fighters, when we received cables indicating the diversion of our next two groups to Twelfth Air Force. I have an idea that your answer to those diversions is that they can make better use of these planes and need them worse than we do." But in an unfortunate display of paro-chialism, Eaker still implored Arnold to "do what you can to prevent the other Air Forces from stealing all our planes and pilots."[61]

On 8 March, Arnold's chief of staff, General George Stratemeyer, wrote to calm Eaker, telling him that the inexperienced 2nd and 99th Bomb Groups, then completing training in the United States, would be sent to North Africa instead and that "you are keeping the 91st and 306th which would have gone to North Africa if the other two had not been diverted from this end."[62] The two new groups, while lower-ing the experience level in Twelfth Air Force's heavy bomber arm, at least doubled its size, and by March all four groups were pounding the trans-Mediterranean supply lines and beginning to inflict serious damage to Luftwaffe forces as far away as Sicily. Control of the sky freed Allied convoys from air attack and allowed air and surface vessels to further constrict the Allied supply line without fear of interference by Axis aircraft.

The 301st flew eighty-eight total missions between November 1942 and 13 May 1943 and then, after only a week's respite, resumed its work against airfields, docks, and rail yards in Sicily and on the mainland. In March alone, the group flew fifteen missions with a total of 384 sor-ties, striking Axis landing grounds in Tunisia and Sardinia six times, ports in Tunisia and Sicily six times, and convoys at sea three times.[63] By comparison, the entire Eighth Air Force in England completed only five missions that same month.[64] The 301st's 4 March mission against a convoy at sea claimed four of the six ships sunk. The next mission, on 7 March, also claimed a vessel in Sousse's harbor. Photos of the 22 March raid by twenty-four B-17s, escorted by twenty-seven P-38s, on Palermo captured the explosion of a tanker or ammunition ship, and the resulting blast sank three other ships and destroyed "thirty acres of waterfront," restricting the harbor's capacity for weeks.[65] The next mission on 24 March claimed a 470-foot-long am-munition ship at Ferryville's harbor, near Bizerte. While the crews' claims were always subject to correction, photographic evidence pro-vided conclusive proof of ships destroyed. On 6 April, twenty-three 301st Group B-17s caught a small convoy just off Bizerte. The skies were clear, and prestrike photos clearly showed two transports, later determined to be *Rovereto* and *San Diego*, both laden with ammuni-tion.[66] At least one of the 262 500-pound bombs dropped scored a direct hit on *Rovereto*, and the resulting massive explosion was caught on film. The striking image was later reproduced in the USAAF's of-ficial history.[67] Two of the attacking aircraft, which were only 10,000 feet above the surface of the sea, were damaged by the blast. The *San Diego*, carrying more ammunition and petroleum, was also hit and set afire and exploded a few hours later.[68] A final raid on 10 April targeted two surviving Italian heavy cruisers, now anchored at La Maddalena. Sixty B-17s sank *Trieste* and heavily damaged *Gorizia*, forcing it to seek shelter at Spezia.[69]

Despite early difficulties in moving aircraft into the theater, by the end of March the Twelfth Air Force had assembled a potent force of five groups of medium bombers. Two groups, the 310th and 321st, were equipped with B-25s, while the other three, the 17th, 319th, and 320th, operated B-26s. In the Western Desert, and later in the war in France and Germany, medium bombers were assigned to the tactical air force for use in interdiction and close-support missions, but in the Tunisian campaign they were grouped with the heavies in Doolittle's Northwest African Strategic Air Force. Early operations enjoyed some success, such as a 22 January attack on El Aouina airfield near Tunis, when forty B-17s, accompanied by thirty B-25s and B-26s, destroyed thirty-one German aircraft, but events soon proved that the mediums were unsuited for the strategic mission.[70] The aircraft could reach the most important targets in Tunisia and Sicily but lacked the high-altitude capability to evade the heaviest flak concentrations. Low-level attacks on the well-defended ports of Tunis and Bizerte resulted in unacceptably high losses, resulting in the mediums being redirected against the smaller and less well defended ports and airfields.

The mediums eventually proved most effective attacking ships at sea.[71] The switch from medium- to minimum-altitude attacks, perfected in the Southwest Pacific, enabled medium bombers to use skip-bombing, where the bombs would literally skip like rocks along the surface of the water into the sides of their targets, and strafing with forward-mounted machine guns to disable merchant ships on the Tunisian run.[72] The first significant success came on 20 January when six B-25s, escorted by twelve P-38s, sank the 5,000-ton tanker *Saturno* en route to Tunis. The mediums followed that up by sending the 3,100-ton *Vercelli* to the bottom near Bizerte.[73] On 7 March, six B-25s of 310th Bomb Group intercepted a convoy containing the *Ines Corrado*, loaded with tanks, trucks, and gasoline. Attacking at low altitude, the bombers scored several hits and left the ship "a flaming wreck." It later sank, and the two other large vessels in the convoy were also lost, one to a mine and the other to a B-17 attack the following day.[74] On 22 March, the B-26s joined the act when thirteen hit a convoy off of Cap Bon, sinking the *Monti*, of 4,300 tons, and setting the *Ombrina* afire, although it managed to struggle into Bizerte before blowing up. During the last three months of the campaign, USAAF aircraft sank ten ships at sea and another forty-three in port, for a total of more than 150,000 tons, far surpassing the totals amassed by surface ships (four), submarines (thirty), and mines and other causes (eight). By this time, most of the shipping was confined to the narrow channel between Sicily and Tunisia, which was protected on both sides by substantial minefields, making it difficult for the naval craft to intervene. The losses of merchant shipping, combined with the low probability of making a successful run, was also a significant factor in the capture of virtually the entire Axis garrison in Tunisia.[75]

As their naval supply lines became seriously reduced by damage to ports and losses of shipping, Axis forces placed even greater reliance on their fleet of transport aircraft to make up the difference. Tedder had witnessed this tactic in the Western Desert, during the battle for and pursuit from El Alamein, and began to plan for a concentrated action against this lifeline.[76] Intelligence intercepts provided him with detailed information about transit times and routes, and his staff planned to strike the transports both in the air and on the ground as they unloaded their critical cargoes, which by mid-April consisted largely of fuel. In an operation code-named FLAX, fighters of the WDAF and Twelfth Air Force patrolled the likely corridors between Sicily and Tunisia, hoping to intercept the inbound flights and their escorts, while heavy bombers prepared to strike the arrival airfields to catch as many of the survivors as possible on the ground before they could unload their cargoes.

The operation opened on 5 April when a group of longer-range P-38s sweeping the Sicilian Strait encountered between fifty and seventy transports and two dozen escorts and claimed eighteen transports and thirteen among the escort with a loss of six P-38s. Later that morning B-17s hit the Sidi Ahmed airfield, near Bizerte, and El Aouina, near Tunis, which were packed with transports. A separate formation of twenty-two B-17s from 301st Bomb Group ventured to the Bocca di Falco airdrome on Sicily and found more than 150 aircraft on the field. The group watched their 2,448 twenty-pound fragmentation bombs fall among the parked aircraft and claimed more than fifty destroyed and another twenty-six damaged.[77] The Sicilian airfields at Trapani and Bo Rizzo received similar treatment from additional groups of heavy and medium bombers. Photo interpreters estimated that the bombers destroyed more than 200 aircraft on the ground, a large number of them transports.[78]

Later in the week fighter sweeps again encountered large formations of transport aircraft over the Sicilian Strait and claimed twenty-
five (actually just four) on 10 April and twenty-six (actually eighteen)
on 11 April. But the real damage came on 18 April in what became
known as the "Palm Sunday Massacre." On that day, P-40s of the
Ninth Air Force's 57th and 79th Fighter Groups, with top cover from
RAF *Spitfires*, encountered more than one hundred enemy transports
trying to sneak into Tunisia before sunset. In a running battle that left
German Junkers Ju-52 and Messerschmitt Me-323 transports strewn
across the Gulf of Tunis and its beaches, the Allied pilots claimed an
astonishing seventy-three transports destroyed (actually only thirty-
two) and another nineteen damaged and downed sixteen of the accompanying fighter escorts.[79] Despite these losses and desperate for
supplies, the Luftwaffe was able to put up another large formation the
next day, which cost it twelve more transports. The operation closed
on 22 April when RAF *Spitfires* and *Kittyhawks* (the British name for
the P-40) intercepted twenty-one giant Messerschmitt Me-323 transports loaded with gas, and downed sixteen. In all, the Axis air forces
lost 200–300 transport aircraft, in addition to a large number of escorts during the operation. In the six-month campaign, Allied intelligence experts correctly estimated that the Axis lost more than 2,000
aircraft between 8 November 1942 and 11 May 1943, at a cost of 770
Allied machines. Given the disparity between Allied and Axis production, this was a rate of exchange that the Axis could ill afford and did
much to facilitate the ground and naval campaigns and to win control
eventually of the skies over Europe.[80]

In little more than two weeks, Allied air forces had broken the back
of the Luftwaffe's North African transport service and, when these
losses were combined with similar results in the Stalingrad pocket earlier in the year, rendered the German air transport network largely
impotent for the rest of the war.[81] German ground commanders could
no longer count on aerial resupply or large-scale airborne operations,
and the losses denied Luftwaffe units rapid logistics support. With
both the sea and air lines of supply severed, resistance inside the Tunis
pocket collapsed in less than a month. But this is not to imply that the
air forces won the campaign by themselves. As several authors have
pointed out, interdiction campaigns required sustained pressure in order to bring supply shortages to a crisis point.[82] By actively pressing
against Axis forces inside the bridgehead, Allied ground forces forced
the German and Italians to consume their remaining stocks, leaving
them unable to resist the final ground offensive. The interdiction

campaign was a success because of the *combined* effects of the Allied
land, air, and naval forces. It is not surprising that future historians
labeled the campaign "A Pattern for Joint Operations."[83]

In the course of the interdiction campaign from 1 July 1942 to 11
April 1943, Allied planners estimated Axis shipping losses at more
than a half-million tons. Of these, submarines claimed eighty-two
ships totaling 224,000 tons, surface ships another thirty totaling
55,000 tons, and aircraft seventy-one totaling 247,000 tons.[84] Thus,
Allied aircraft accounted for destroying almost half of the tonnage of
all enemy surface ships attempting to run across the middle sea. In
addition, by attriting the Axis air forces, they enabled the naval units
to operate without excessive losses. RAF forces operating from Malta
claimed a large number of these ships, but the USAAF, which operated almost all of the heavy bombers in the theater, made a substantial
contribution.

The naval and aerial interdiction campaigns benefited from a well-
established intelligence system that was largely imported from the
Western Desert. As Brad Gladman has demonstrated in his work *Intelligence and Anglo-American Air Support in World War Two*, the Allies
lacked an effective intelligence network early in the Tunisian campaign.[85] British codebreakers in the United Kingdom had penetrated
German secure communications encrypted on ENIGMA machines. The
resulting intelligence, code-named ULTRA, provided invaluable assistance to Allied operations throughout the war. To prevent compromise of this important resource, ULTRA information was not widely
released and had to be confirmed through another source (such as
aerial reconnaissance) before it could be acted upon.[86] With the infu-
sion of British units and leadership from the Western Desert came
experienced intelligence officers who mirrored the radio-intercept
and communications units in the WDAF and set up a highly effective similar structure in the NAAF. NATAF especially benefited from
information on tactical troop movements, while NASAF used sailing
schedules and Luftwaffe timetables to increase the effectiveness of interdiction sorties.

British methods developed in the antishipping strikes conducted
by the WDAF in Libya were adopted by NASAF for the Tunisian
and Italian ports. A study of Twelfth Air Force's intelligence activities
found:

On shipping targets where accurate pinpoints are essential an idea
has been borrowed from R.A.F., Middle East. Black and white

First Army Pursuit Plane, a P-40, to take off from the USS *Chenango*
(ACV-28) near Casablanca, Morocco, during the U.S. campaign in North
Africa. (National Archives and Records Administration, Still Pictures
Division, Photo 80-G-30512)

charts were obtained of every harbor of importance in enemy hands
in the theater. These are gridded and each given a code designation. When shipping is the next day's target exact ship sizes and
locations from the day's photo reconnaissance are passed by tele-
phone or TWX in the clear to the groups, based on chart grids,
and this information in turn transposed to the target chart of each
bombardier.

Such a system enabled "rapid dissemination of vital combat intelligence" to the operating units.[87]

Within the USAAF, observation units assigned to the Air Support
Command quickly proved inadequate to meet the ground troops' demands. Spaatz wrote their requiem in a letter to Arnold on 25 February 1943: "It is now evident that observation groups, as we know them,
will never serve a useful purpose when the enemy is equipped and operates as the German air and ground forces [have] in this theater."

He recommended that "no further effort be wasted in training and equipping observation groups as such for this or similar theaters. Our whole concept of support aviation has been altered radically by the past month's fighting in Tunisia. . . . It is suggested that the air staff study the operations of the 8th Army [British] and of the operations of the Western Desert Air Force [RAF]."[88] He further recommended that light bomber squadrons in the observation group be combined with the other light bomber units, that the P-39s be employed in strafing and tactical reconnaissance missions, and that all photo reconnaissance equipment be reallocated to the photo reconnaissance wing.

Light aircraft indigenous to each battery met the requirements for aerial spotting for artillery, but other requirements—especially aerial photography—proved more difficult. The Twelfth Air Force's 3rd Photographic Reconnaissance Group, commanded by the president's son, Lieutenant Colonel Elliott Roosevelt, was equipped with three squadrons: the 3rd Photographic Squadron (Light) and 12th Photographic Squadron (Light) with forty F-4 and F-5A (modified P-38) aircraft, and the 15th Photographic Squadron (Heavy) with four B-17s and, later, British *Mosquitoes*. After the reorganization of 18 February, the 3rd Photographic Reconnaissance Group was combined with RAF No. 682 Photographic Reconnaissance Squadron into the Northwest African Photographic Reconnaissance Wing (NAPRW), still under Roosevelt's leadership.[89] Once equipped with an improved communications network and fully integrated with RAF photographic reconnaissance units, the NAPRW was eventually able to respond to immediate requests for photographic surveillance of front-line positions and have processed photographs in ground commanders' hands before any attack began. While it took most of the campaign to reach this level of proficiency, the development was critical and would provide greater assistance in the campaigns ahead.

Roosevelt particularly distinguished himself in command of the unit. One pilot of the 12th Photographic Squadron reported that "Col. R. has more hours time over the lines than anyone else. . . . He is courageous, a splendid leader and has a brilliant mind . . . lives with the gang, slept in the mud with us, eats with us and is a thoroughly democratic fellow, regardless of politics . . . deserved everything he has earned. . . . [He] has contributed materially to the organization and advancement of wartime photo reconnaissance."[90] Roosevelt's superiors agreed with the assessment. In a 1944 letter to Spaatz, Arnold explained that he could not grant Roosevelt a pilot's rating (Roosevelt was a navigator-observer) because "it would be letting the bars down too much to grant a waiver for his physical defects," but that "Roosevelt has done an excellent job over there and I am most grateful to him for the assistance he has rendered to the Army Air Forces."[91]

Like much of the air-ground cooperation developed in Tunisia, it is unlikely that the ground and air forces would have recognized and corrected this deficiency had the assets been held in the United Kingdom and used to support an air campaign alone. Even so, some fighter groups in North Africa complained that the intelligence officers assigned to support them were trained more to identify strategic targets and to interpret bomb damage from photographs rather than to help fighter pilots combat enemy aircraft and tactics. Lieutenant Richard Kremer of 325th Fighter Group complained that "Harrisburg [i.e., the USAAF's Intelligence Officer School in Pennsylvania] turns out a pretty good Bomber Intelligence Officer; but nobody seems to know a damn thing about fighters."[92] This bias extended to the highest levels of command. In early March, General Spaatz directed his assistant chief of staff for intelligence to conduct a survey of the intelligence apparatus of all American units under his command. The resulting survey provided detailed information on NASAF, where all the bombers were located, but "lack of time prevented a complete coverage of units of Tactical and Coastal Air Forces," where most of the fighter units were located.[93]

Conclusion

American air forces were properly employed by playing such a large part in the interdiction campaign that ultimately led to the Axis defeat. Many within the USAAF establishment would have preferred that heavy bombers remain in the United Kingdom and conduct true strategic raids on Germany. It is worthwhile to consider, therefore, the relative contributions of Eighth and Twelfth Air Forces during this period. Between January and October 1943, Twelfth Air Force's heavy bombers launched 13,974 sorties, for a rate of 5.8 sorties per aircraft assigned. During the same period, Eighth Air Force launched 17,187 sorties, for a rate of only 2.8 per aircraft assigned.[94] But when one considers *effective* sorties, the Twelfth Air Force completed 11,675 (83 percent effective) while Eighth Air Force had only 11,599 (67 percent).[95] Thus, with only a fraction of the force allocated to the United Kingdom, the bombers in North Africa actually completed more effective missions.[96]

The force deployed to North Africa also gave the USAAF a greater return on the substantial investment it made in training aircrews. Crews assigned to Eighth Air Force rotated out of the theater after completing their twenty-fifth mission. Due to high losses, few crews reached this milestone. In North Africa, due to the higher sortie rate and relatively lower level of opposition, the bar was set at fifty missions before returning home. Even then, some airmen exceeded this number, as replacements were not immediately available. Thus for every aircrew member sent to North Africa, the USAAF received more than twice the return on their training investment.

The transfer of air units to North Africa was critically important for the eventual success of Allied arms in the theater. When Axis forces controlled the skies over Tunisia, Allied aircraft were unable to interdict the flow of supplies or to influence the land battle, and Axis forces were capable of limited offensive action. But as Allied air strength grew and exceeded that of the Axis, the Axis supply line was no longer safe, and Allied ground forces could safely build up to a point where they were able to win the campaign. More significant, Allied dominance of the skies, and therefore of the seas, prevented any Dunkirk-style mass evacuation, with the result that most of the Axis troops rushed into North Africa between November 1942 and May 1943 became casualties, either killed, wounded, or captured.[97] The USAAF tracked this trend and compiled the relative strength of all four air forces engaged in a single graph. (See Figure 4.1.) It is striking to note that the rising line of Allied (i.e., NAAF) strength in combat aircraft crosses that of the declining line representing Axis combat aircraft in mid-March 1943. From that point on, Axis forces were barely able to maintain their strength, both due to combat losses and to demands in other theaters, while the Allied air forces continued to grow. Once the Allies were able to establish a superior air force in the theater, success on the surface followed rapidly.

The decision to send a large percentage of the USAAF's available strength to support the North African campaign, even at the expense of the Combined Bomber Offensive, was undoubtedly correct. The territory gained enabled the Allies to reopen the Mediterranean to shipping, saving countless days and ships from the passage around the Cape and achieving the campaign's primary objective. It removed any Axis threat to the Middle East's oilfields and precluded the potential use of Vichy bases in Morocco and Dakar to support the U-boat offensive in the Atlantic. It also removed large numbers of Axis ships, planes, and soldiers from the war. Italian losses in North Africa were so heavy that they were largely unable to defend their own shores, as the July 1943 invasion of Sicily would demonstrate, and Italy was rapidly losing the stomach to continue the fight. Germany had expended a small percentage of its total ground strength yet a significant portion of its available air forces. Each winter, when weather largely closed down operations on the Eastern Front, the Luftwaffe had shifted large formations to the Mediterranean. During the winter of 1941–1942, this buildup had enabled a sustained campaign against Malta that crippled the island forces and permitted the Axis buildup in Libya that eventually brought Rommel to El Alamein. But in the winter of 1942–1943 the Axis enjoyed no such success. Unable to disengage from the Eastern Front due to the siege of Stalingrad, and forced to begin reassigning fighters to protect the homeland, the Luftwaffe was unable to transfer large formations again to the Mediterranean. Those they did send were forced to fight at a numerical disadvantage and eventually wore down past the point of effectiveness. In his study of the organization's demise, Williamson Murray found that "the commitment to Tunisia placed the *Luftwaffe* in a position where it had to fight at great disadvantage with a resulting high rate of attrition."[98] By mid-July 1943, the Axis air forces in the Mediterranean were too weak to prevent the second major Allied amphibious invasion in the European theater: Operation HUSKY, the invasion of Sicily.

5

The Sicilian Campaign:
May to August 1943

While Allied ground forces enjoyed a two-month respite from combat following the conclusion of operations in Tunisia, the air forces immediately began the next phase of operations in the Mediterranean. After an intensive monthlong bombing campaign against Pantelleria, a tiny island off the North African coast garrisoned by Italian troops, resulted in a near-bloodless surrender to invading forces, air commanders touted the success as evidence that airpower could win campaigns alone and allowed it to bolster their desire to prove this assertion on a larger scale against Italy and Germany. While the USAAF continued to provide effective support to ground and naval forces throughout the campaign, it was also further distracted by a desire to strike strategic targets at the expense of support for the surface forces.

The USAAF rendered effective support to the amphibious invasion of Sicily by protecting the fleet from air attack and by reinforcing the landing troops with airborne forces, but a breakdown in interservice cooperation plagued the operation and resulted in the unnecessary deaths of many Allied paratroopers. And while aircraft such as the newly developed North American A-36 *Apache* dive-bomber provided extremely accurate close air support during the ground campaign across the island, the USAAF's reluctance to use the heavy bombers of Twelfth Air Force, and especially those of Ninth Air Force, to interdict the Strait of Messina resulted in an incomplete Allied victory. Many of the Axis forces that fought in Sicily avoided a Tunisia-style capitulation and escaped to the Italian mainland, where the Germans rebuilt and successfully employed them in the fall campaign that stalled long before the Allies approached Rome. Some credit for a skillful extrication must go to the German commanders and Italian authorities responsible for the evacuation, but the lack of an intensive

Pantelleria-style effort by heavy bombers against ferry terminals and beaches at Messina and Reggio di Calabria deserves much of the blame for the Allied failure. During the critical month prior to the Axis evacuation of Sicily, the USAAF withdrew all of Ninth Air Force's B-24s from combat, including three additional groups sent from the United Kingdom, to either prepare for or recover from the disastrous 1 August raid on the oil refineries at Ploesti, Romania, while Twelfth Air Force often employed its four groups of B-17s against targets that did not directly impact the evacuation.

Operation CORKSCREW: The Capture of Pantelleria

Planning for Operation HUSKY—the invasion of Sicily—had been under way since the Combined Chiefs of Staff approved the operation at the Casablanca Conference in January 1943. One of the main factors in favor of the Sicilian operation, as opposed to one against Corsica, Sardinia, or even the Dodecanese, was the availability of air bases in close proximity to the objective. From the newly won fields in northern Tunisia, as well as from Malta, aircraft could easily reach the landing beaches and provide critical air cover to both the invasion fleet and the landing forces. The only logistical factor limiting this support was the number of bases that engineers could rehabilitate and make available in the two months after their capture and these airfields' capacity to support large numbers of aircraft.

After the loss of Tunisia, the small island of Pantelleria, just fifty miles northeast of Cap Bon and astride the invasion route to Sicily, stood as the southernmost Axis holding left in the Mediterranean. In addition to its small airfield, Pantelleria and a neighboring island, Lampedusa, also supported radar stations that could detect the launch of an air or naval armada and alert Sicily's defenders to an invasion. Several factors combined to make an amphibious assault a daunting task. The island itself was surrounded by rocky cliffs and offered few suitable landing sites other than a direct attack against the well-defended harbor. There, the 10,000 Italian defenders would have had a concentrated target and could have been expected to inflict serious casualties on the British amphibious troops tasked with taking the island.

Unwilling to risk high casualties in an immediate seaborne assault, General Eisenhower instead approved a plan to soften up Pantelleria's defenses as a test of what airpower could do to prepare the way for landings against hostile shores. In explaining his rationale to General George C. Marshall, Ike wrote, "I want to make the capture of Pantelleria a sort of laboratory to determine the effect of concentrated heavy bombing on a defended coastline. When the time comes, we are going to concentrate everything we have to see whether damage to materiel, personnel and morale cannot be made so serious as to make landing a simple affair."[1] Eisenhower was also concerned about the large quantities of munitions to be expended in the effort and the potential loss of aircraft "at the very time when I was concerned with the build-up of bombing potential at our Tunisian bases to support the invasion of Sicily." In a later assessment, he observed that the campaign was "expensive in total bomb load," though not in aircraft. "For 5,255 effective sorties the loss of Allied Aircraft of the NAAF was only 16 damaged and 14 missing, but a total of 6,313 tons of explosives had been dropped." Despite these reservations, Eisenhower approved Operation CORKSCREW on 11 May, and attacks against the island began the following week.[2]

Eisenhower clearly had the future OVERLORD landings in mind, but his air planners saw it differently. They hoped to use CORKSCREW to demonstrate that a sustained air campaign, scientifically applied with precise calculations of the tonnages required to damage each gun emplacement, would make the amphibious invasion unnecessary by forcing the island to capitulate. The original plan for CORKSCREW called for a gradual escalation of air attacks that would steadily increase pressure on the garrison, with periodic halts to give the defenders a chance to surrender.

The island had sustained light attacks as part of the Tunisian campaign, but CORKSCREW officially did not get under way until 18 May, when a combination of medium bombers and fighter-bombers made the first heavy attack on the island.[3] Fighter-bombers continued assaults for the next week, until a heavy raid by twenty-two RAF *Wellingtons* on 24 May opened the next phase of the operation. This pattern continued until 1 June, when the heavy bombers of the Northwest African Strategic Air Force added their weight to the attacks. On that day, more bombs fell on Pantelleria than had been dropped in the entire theater during the month of April.[4] From that point on, the attacks escalated gradually in intensity (see Table 5.1) with two significant pauses to allow the Italian defenders time to respond to demands for surrender dropped by leaflet. The first pause, a six-hour armistice on 8 June, yielded no results, so attacks continued until a second ultimatum, followed by a three-hour pause, was delivered on 10 June—

Table 5.1: Tonnage (in pounds) Dropped on Pantelleria by Date*

18 May	194,500	1 June	283,500
20 May	5,000	2 June	265,500
21 May	6,680	3 June	229,500
22 May	5,720	4 June	405,000
23 May	153,420	5 June	232,000
24 May	93,180	6 June	463,000
25 May	13,240	7 June	1,193,050
26 May	8,100	8 June	1,398,500
			(first bombing pause)
27 May	13,000	9 June	1,644,350
28 May	12,000	10 June	3,141,600
			(second pause)
29 May	168,000	11 June	2,032,060
			(halted by surrender)
30 May	240,500		
31 May	181,000		

*"The Air Effort Against Pantelleria," Field Operations Bulletin, 3 June 1943, Box 12, Norstad Papers, Eisenhower Library, Abilene, KS.

the day before the scheduled amphibious landings by the British 1st Infantry Division. That evening the island's governor, Admiral Gino Pavesi, cabled Rome to request permission to surrender. As justification for his decision, he claimed the lack of water on the island made further defense impossible. Later investigations supported Pavesi's claim, finding,

> Pantelleria has only three wells and their mechanism was destroyed. Otherwise the island relies on rain traps with which almost every house is equipped [the bombing destroyed most of the island's houses, and presumably their "rain traps" as well]. The problem, however, was not so much to find water as to transport it from the source to the place where it was needed. With all roads destroyed and transport reduced to mule back this was increasingly difficult, although not insuperable.[5]

A postattack assessment found that "the two main wells were rendered inoperative early in our attacks. There were, however, sufficient scattered supplies of water on the island to see to the requirements of the military and civilian population, if means of transport could have been found."[6] Considering that there were still almost 20,000 people on the island, finding a means of transport to supply a daily ration of water was a Herculean task, especially while under constant bombardment.

Unaware of these developments, the landing forces boarded their boats as scheduled and, after air and naval vessels gave one last preparatory bombardment, began their run toward the island. Shortly thereafter, the radio station on Malta intercepted a request for surrender, and aircraft observed a white flag atop one of the island's hills and a white cross painted on the airfield. The troops moved ashore against virtually no resistance; the forward defenders, who had not yet received word of the surrender due to a breakdown in communications, fired only a few shots before they were overwhelmed.

The near bloodless conquest of Pantelleria vindicated the faith Eisenhower placed in his airmen and demonstrated that air forces, especially heavy bombers, could and did make vital contributions to the advance of ground and naval forces. B-17s flew 679 sorties against the island, only 13 percent of the total, but dropped almost one-third of the total bomb tonnage. Unfortunately, the victory almost immediately descended into an interservice squabble that in some respects continues to this day. The day after the surrender, General Doolittle, commanding the NASAF, released the following statement to the press: "The predominant force in warfare is the Air Force. No successful operations of a major nature are possible unless control of the air has first been obtained. If the air power can be applied directly against the heart of the nation concerned, no other force is necessary."[7] Eisenhower responded immediately, drafting a statement for Spaatz, which read, "My attention has been invited to a quoted statement made to the press by General Doolittle upon completion of the Pantelleria operation. Unfortunately this statement escaped proper action by the censors." Eisenhower explained that the statement not only violated his policy that "senior American officers avoid issuing quoted statements, at least until they had been carefully checked with Allied Headquarters" but also that he thought it "highly unwise, therefore, to issue statements that generalize and develop a doctrine of war from incidents that may happen in our theater."[8]

Statements like Doolittle's ignore a number of factors. First, the USAAF conducted the test of Pantelleria under optimum conditions. Concentrated into a small area, defenders could not escape the raids except by going into underground shelters, which they did successfully. During the entire campaign, the island suffered less than 200 casualties. If the defenders had been committed to defending the is-land, they could have emerged from their underground shelters and inflicted heavy losses on the landing troops. Second, Allied planners did not have to worry about dispersing their effort to disguise the in-tended point of landing, as they would during the Normandy landing. An intensive, two-week bombing of Omaha Beach certainly would have been welcome, but it also would have telegraphed the Allies' plans to land in that area, allowing the defenders to position reinforce-ments close by. Third, air and naval forces imposed a blockade that isolated the island garrison from resupply, preventing reinforcements from arriving in the battle area and cutting off all hope of escape for the beleaguered defenders. Finally, the Allies had largely won control of the skies over and around Sicily, so the attacks proceeded without the need for robust escort and without appreciable interference by units of the German and Italian air forces on Sicily and Italy.

An article in *Time* magazine the week after the attack recognized these limitations and incorporated a subdued comment from Doolittle:

> Air enthusiasts, greeting the surrender as a historic achievement of all-out air warfare, were quick to recall Winston Churchill's re-mark before Congress in May, that the idea of bombing Germany into submission was "worth trying." Soberer heads recognized this as a victory of air power, but a victory won under laboratory condi-tions. The island fell because it was possible to isolate it completely from supporting bases on the mainland. This was the decisive fac-tor, not the sheer weight of bombs. Malta in three years of war had taken many times the weight of bombs dropped on the Italian out-posts; it still stood because its supply lines were never severed. Said Major General James H. Doolittle: "In simple terms, if you destroy what a man has and remove the possibility of his bringing more in, then in due course of time it becomes impossible for him to defend himself."9

But in his memoirs Doolittle was undeterred and returned to his original argument: "What was significant about Corkscrew was that it was to be the first attempt to conquer enemy territory with air power," a claim often repeated by airmen both during the war and in the years that followed. Doolittle remained defiant long after, writing in 1991 that, after being chastised, "to appease my critics, I revised my statement to conclude that it was a 'combined naval and air victory.' In view of the statistics, I wish now I hadn't given in and said all that."10

These comments ignore the important role naval forces played not only in isolating the island and in ferrying the ground troops to their objective but also in transporting across the treacherous Atlantic the bombs, fuel, and personnel necessary to build and maintain a strong air force in North Africa.

The timing of the surrender made it difficult to determine whether the prospect of an imminent invasion figured into Admiral Pavesi's decision to surrender. Allied forces did not see the white flag until the landing force had already embarked in their landing craft, but an interviewer shortly after the battle claimed that Pavesi's view of the invasion force had been blocked by haze and dust from the raids and that he thought the gathering naval force was simply repeating an earlier naval bombardment mission. The interviewer, Lieutenant Commander G. A. Martelli of the Royal Navy, asserted that "when he hoisted the white flag, the Admiral had no idea that a land attack was impending." This version of events enabled Martelli to conclude, "It is clear that the reduction of the island was achieved as planned, exclusively by aerial bombardment, assisted by naval blockade and psychological warfare, and that the arrival of the land forces had no influence on the decision of the enemy to capitulate."[11]

Anxious to prove the efficacy of their bombing, the Northwest African Air Force sent a team of observers and inspectors to tally the damage. Solly Zuckerman, a British biologist of South African birth, led this effort and compiled a detailed report the following month. The findings demonstrated that, while the weight of the attacks had certainly been impressive, the damage inflicted, especially on pinpoint targets such as the coastal gun positions, left much to be desired. Only two of eighteen batteries had been hit directly, and only forty-three of eighty guns were placed out of commission. Nevertheless, Zuckerman believed, "by common consent, the capture of the island was essentially due to the bombing. Naval fire had very little effect, and the soldiers had only to walk in."[12]

Despite the disappointing material results, Spaatz and others believed the *morale* effect had been devastating and had induced the Italian garrison to surrender. A week after the capitulation, Spaatz wrote a friend, "The application of air power available to us can reduce to the point of surrender any first class nation now in existence within six months from the time that pressure is applied."[13] The theory was classic Douhet, but it was already being disproved both by the attacks on the United Kingdom during and after the Battle of Britain and by the heavy raids on Germany. The following month, the Allies launched heavy raids with most of their available force on the German city of Hamburg, which burned much of the city and killed tens of thousands of civilians, yet these and other more devastating attacks failed to produce a collapse of the German state. But the USAAF continued to draw erroneous conclusions from what should have been a vindication of the use of air assets in a joint campaign. In 1945, the USAAF's official report on the campaign continued to cite the attacks on Pantelleria as "history's first example of territorial conquest by air action."[14]

Pantelleria, which is often barely a footnote in most histories of the war, was clearly a story the USAAF wanted to be remembered and retold.[15] In 1947, the service devoted an entire study (115 pages) to the operation and likewise an entire chapter (thirty pages) in the official history of the war, almost as much as the entire Sicilian campaign (forty pages, including seven devoted to the Ploesti raid).[16] The version did not go unchallenged. The U.S. Navy, in particular, was quick to emphasize its role. In Samuel Eliot Morison's history of the naval war in the Mediterranean, he characterized the discussion as a "whodunit" and corrected the airmen's emphasis on bombing to the exclusion of other members of the joint team.[17]

It is possible that the success enjoyed against Pantelleria influenced future air campaigns in later wars, especially if the air force clung to the notion that it had been effective. The idea of escalating air pressure, punctuated with bombing pauses to give the enemy time to comply with demands, was echoed in the ROLLING THUNDER air campaign conducted against North Vietnam from 1965 to 1968, although on a much larger scale and under less favorable conditions.[18] The air leadership in that war included General William Momyer, who commanded Seventh Air Force in South Vietnam and whose 33rd Fighter Group had participated in the attacks on Pantelleria and was later based on the island during the Sicilian campaign.

Current studies of air warfare, particularly of the USAAF in World War II, continue to emphasize the campaign, but authors continue to misstate the results.[19] In 2002, Herman Wolk wrote in *Air Force* magazine that at Pantelleria "the aerial offensive marked the first time in history that an enemy land force was compelled to surrender in the absence of an accompanying ground invasion,"[20] which completely ignores the invasion force that was approaching the beaches as the white flags went up. And airmen (and their political leadership) continue to attempt to achieve cheap victories through the use of airpower alone. In 1999, a largely British and American air force operating under the auspices of the North Atlantic Treaty Organization attempted to induce Serbian leader Slobodan Milosevic to halt a campaign of ethnic cleansing in Kosovo through air strikes on key Serbian infrastructure. After three months of attacks, Milosevic finally agreed, leading one British historian to exclaim "the capitulation of President Milosevic proved that a war can be won by airpower alone."[21] The statement ignored a number of other factors, such as the failure to actually halt ethnic cleansing during the air campaign, the role of international diplomacy in forcing Milosevic to back down, and the increasing threat of ground-force intervention.[22]

But one significant bright spot in the Pantelleria campaign was the introduction into combat of 99th Fighter Squadron, the first of the Tuskegee Airmen. The squadron had arrived in North Africa in April as a separate unit and was attached to Momyer's 33rd Fighter Group. Spaatz visited the unit on 19 May and reported that 99th's commander, Lieutenant Colonel Benjamin Davis, "impressed me most favorably." Spaatz further noted, "This squadron will be attached to the 33rd Group, to be used for ground support in [the] tactical [air force], and will be given all the consideration, as they have been, of a white squadron."[23] While Spaatz may have been incorrect regarding the "consideration" given to the squadron, considering that Eighth Air Force had already rejected it largely out of racial concerns, Spaatz did not discriminate against it in terms of assignments or missions during the campaign for Sicily.

Invasion of Sicily

Immediately after the fall of Pantelleria, the USAAF resumed its mission of preparing the way for landings in Sicily. The most serious threat, once the troop- and supply-laden convoys had safely crossed the Atlantic, came from Axis aircraft based on Sicily, Sardinia, and the boot of Italy. Mediterranean Air Command's first task was to clear the skies of Axis bombers and fighter escorts in order to provide protection for the invasion convoys and the landing troops. To accomplish this mission, the Allied air forces now held an overwhelming superiority in the theater, thanks in large part to the increasing weight of the bomber offensive from the United Kingdom, which was diverting a significant percentage of the Luftwaffe's fighter strength to defense of the Reich.[24] In the twenty-nine days between the end of resistance on Pantelleria and the invasion of Sicily, Allied air units largely accomplished this task. While a few Axis aircraft did attack the invasion convoys and sank several ships, they never seriously threatened the outcome of the invasion, and in little more than a month the Allies had evicted the Axis forces from the island. After gaining control of the air, Allied aircraft participated decisively in the land battle, first by providing the ground commanders with detailed photographs of the entire island, then by augmenting the assault landings with airborne forces and by restricting the flow of supplies and reinforcements onto the island, and finally by providing effective close air support for the advance.

Between 11 June and 10 July, the NAAF flew thousands of sorties against targets in Sicily, Sardinia, and Italy. By far the most effective weapon was the six groups of heavy bombers assigned to the Mediterranean. Twelfth Air Force's four groups of B-17s (2nd, 97th, 99th, and 301st) concentrated on the western part of the island, while Ninth Air Force's two groups of B-24s (98th and 376th) worked over the eastern half as well as airfields in Italy as far north as Foggia. Eisenhower correctly anticipated that these aircraft would be extremely effective and, as early as April, wrote the Combined Chiefs of Staff to request that an additional two groups of heavy bombers be assigned to the Mediterranean for a period from three weeks prior to three weeks after the invasion date. He noted, "The excellent work done by the B-17 groups now operating give good prospects of obtaining crippling results against aerodromes, communications, and shipping targets providing sufficient weight of attack can be applied at the right time and place. I cannot overemphasize the vital importance of my having available the maximum possible scale of air effort to offset to some extent the increased defense organization which is clearly being built up in [Sicily]."[25] Two days later, General Arnold wrote General Frank Andrews, then commanding the European Theater of Operations in the United Kingdom, to reassure him that the requested transfer would not take place. He referenced the "attempt being made now by Eisenhower to *borrow* two of your groups for a period of 42 days," then justified his recommendation for refusal by asserting: "Such procedure would deprive you of the service of those groups for a minimum of four months and the absence from your operations would come during a period when the weather in Continental Europe is such that you could make the best employment of them. I hope that I have been able to squash any such diversion." He added: "Personally, I can not see how they could use two [additional] heavy groups with all the airplanes they already have there."[26] On 1 June 1943, Twelfth Air Force had 178 B-17s, with 129 (72 percent) serviceable, while Eighth Air Force had been promised 912 heavy bombers by the end of June.[27] Nevertheless, Arnold was successful, and Eisenhower's air forces did not receive any further reinforcement until July, when two new B-24 groups destined for England and one already there joined Ninth Air Force, but only for raids on the Messerschmitt factory at Wiener-Neustadt, Austria, and the oil refineries near Ploesti, Romania.[28] Both Spaatz and Arnold were anxious to attack German aircraft production facilities (the target of the massive Regensburg raid in August 1943), and Spaatz hoped that "we will soon be in a position to do our share of that from this end."[29]

As it was, the NAAF made excellent use of the assets assigned. The medium bombers augmented the heavies in the airfield attacks, and fighter-bombers patrolled the island to search for hidden dispersal fields where the Luftwaffe tried to escape the daily pounding of their main airfields. The effort was disguised for most of the month, as the Allies then had several cover plans in place to deceive the Axis into thinking that the large invasion fleet then gathering in North Africa was destined for the Balkans or Greece.[30] As Spaatz later explained to Arnold:

> after the fall of Pantelleria, our bomber effort was distributed over a wide area without too much attention to Sicily, in accordance with a prearranged plan. Commencing on D-7 [seven days before the landings] we started operating against Sicilian airdromes, the greater part of the effort with fragmentation clusters. This was continued as the primary and almost sole object until the night of D-day. As D-day approached, we shifted to demolition type bombs and attempted to put the airdromes out of commission. These counter-air force operations were apparently more successful than we had hoped, and as a result, the air effort against us has been on a rather low scale.[31]

Again, heavy bombers played an important role. A USAAF summary of operations against Sicily found that USAAF heavies had flown more than 100 sorties per day between 3 July and 9 July, while the mediums added 1,289 for the week.[32] To keep defenders from getting any meaningful rest, RAF *Wellingtons* added another 378 nighttime sorties.[33]

A massive raid on 5 July on the airfield complex around Gerbini inflicted serious damage despite a massed defense by more than 100 German fighters. The heavy bombers and their escorts claimed thirty-five victories against only two losses. Oberstleutnant Johannes Steinhoff, commanding Jagdgeschwader (Fighter Wing) 77, one of three German fighter groups still on the island, was shot down that day and lost one of his most experienced Gruppe commanders. He witnessed the attack on Gerbini and remembered seeing "brown fountains of earth and all at once the whole of the vast plain seemed to erupt into eerie motion. On the fighter-bomber group's airfield, where continuous sticks of bombs were plowing up the ground, all hell was evidently being let loose." The Me-109 that Steinhoff lost that day was his third in a little over a week, the other two being destroyed on the ground at Trapani on 25 June and at Comiso on 27 June.[34]

Even the few Axis raids that did reach North Africa were hampered by the counterair campaign. On 6 July, as the Allied invasion fleet was assembling in Tunisian harbors, the Luftwaffe launched seventy-five aircraft in an attempt to destroy the transports at their berths. No ships were hit, with only light damage in the ports and few casualties, as Allied antiaircraft gunners and RAF night-fighters knocked down several of the attackers.[35] The interrogation of one Junkers Ju-88 crew captured near Bizerte is particularly revealing. The crew was from Kampfgruppe (Bomber Wing) 30 and had been transferred from Norway at the beginning of May. It was currently based at Viterbo on the Italian mainland, sixty miles north of Rome, as the Sicilian airfields had become untenable. The prisoners stated that all of the German bomber units in the central Mediterranean were then based in northern Italy or southern France, greatly increasing the operational range of each mission and complicating the difficult rendezvous over the target in which bombers from scattered bases would attempt to arrive simultaneously to overwhelm the defenders. The group had lost a number of their aircraft on the ground when they were based in Sicily, and a raid on Allied shipping at Bône on 29 June had cost them their squadron commander and the most experienced crew remaining in their group. Of the forty-three crews with the group when they arrived in Italy only nine remained, and replacement crews were being returned to Germany because they were untrained in nighttime flying.[36]

As the attacks intensified, resistance continued to decline. The only response against the invasion fleets now assembling from Algiers to Alexandria was the attack on Bizerte on 6 July by seventy-five aircraft. Once the invasion was under way, the ships were subjected to moderate air attacks at their anchorages off the southern coast of Sicily, but these declined each day as the NAAF continued to work over Axis ports and airfields. Fighter opposition became sporadic and weak. Enemy sorties declined from an estimated 200 on 11 July to 150 on 12 July, seventy-five on the 14 July, and only thirty on 15 July.[37] During this period, Axis bombers sank only five ships, but the casualties incurred, most notably the destroyer *Maddox*, which sank on D-Day with more than 200 of its crew, and on one of the LSTs carrying the antitank guns for the 18th Infantry Regiment of the 1st Infantry Division, coupled with numerous attacks that resulted in near-misses, left a bad taste in the navy's mouth, even though the high number of attacks and near-misses coupled with the low number of ships sunk strongly suggest a lack of experience on the part of the attacking aircrews. In his after-action report, Admiral Kent Hewitt, commanding the Western Naval Task Force, opined that "if the 12th Air Support Command had taken a more active part in the initial planning of the campaign and had been less desirous of showing its independence vis-à-vis the Army, difficulties might have been obviated."[38] This is undoubtedly the source of the allegation in the introduction to Samuel Eliot Morison's volume in the U.S. Navy's official history of the campaign (and for which Morison consulted Hewitt) that "air operations, too, contributed greatly to victory in the Mediterranean, although the aviators' desire to fight the war in their own way made their contribution less than it might have been under a more resolute control, such as both Admiral Nimitz and General MacArthur exercised in the Pacific."[39] Such statements cast doubt on the value of an otherwise excellent series of works, but they reflect the interservice rancor of the early 1950s, when the navy felt that the newly independent U.S. Air Force had gained too large a share of defense budgets under President Eisenhower. At the very least, Eisenhower's knowledge and handling of the air assets assigned to his theater compares favorably with General Douglas MacArthur, who allowed his heavy bomber force to be destroyed on the ground during the initial attacks on the Philippines. For his part, Admiral Chester Nimitz controlled very few USAAF assets in the drive across the Central Pacific, but he did gain the Marianas as an air base for the USAAF's heavy bombers—an achievement not unlike what Eisenhower eventually accomplished in the Mediterranean.

In the end, both Hewitt and Morison were forced to acknowledge that the USAAF's counterair campaign had been effective. Later in his report, Hewitt admitted that "the destruction or neutralization of enemy air forces within range of the operations . . . was, by and large, successful," but he still recommended that "where practicable, naval aviation should be used for close support in amphibious operations.

Where this is not practicable, Army dive bombers should be assigned under the operational control of the Naval Commander."[40] This was not practicable in the amphibious assaults on Sicily, Salerno, Anzio, or Normandy because the navy's fleet carriers were all assigned to the Pacific theater. While there were undoubtedly coordination failures between the elements of the joint force, placing air assets under the command of a surface officer was not likely to resolve them. Morison summarized the air campaign as follows: "The Air Forces certainly performed valuable and vital services before Operation HUSKY even started. They won air supremacy over the Axis, which otherwise might have decimated the amphibious forces."[41] The U.S. Army's official history of the campaign agreed, noting "the air raids interfered but little with the landings."[42] Eisenhower commented later, "The real preliminary to the assault was a vast bombing operation by air. Entirely aside from the success in defeating the enemy air forces, it so badly battered the enemy communications in Sicily and southern Italy that the mobility of his forces was severely lowered and the supply of his troops a most difficult process."[43]

One final case of the exemplary support provided to the ground and naval forces in the invasion is the efforts of the Northwest African Photographic Reconnaissance Wing, still commanded by the president's son, Lieutenant Colonel Elliott Roosevelt. In the weeks leading up to the invasion, the group's three squadrons and attached RAF photographic aircraft flew more than 500 missions and "mapped the entire 10,000 square miles of Sicily."[44] NAPRW's customers were truly joint, as it provided photographs of the invasion beaches to ground commanders, reconnoitered Italian naval ports for the Allied naval forces, and maintained coverage of the island's principal airdromes to provide the strategic air forces with precise information on which fields were in use and what effect their strikes had on each one. Even Morison was forced to acknowledge that "the Northwest African Photo Reconnaissance Wing covered important Axis-held ports from Spain to Corfu, photographing Spezia and Taranto twice daily to discover if the Italian navy had sortied." But he still found room to complain that "no adequate photos of Sicily could be had from the Northwest African Photo Reconnaissance Wing, since the aviators could not be persuaded to give proper attention to beach gradients and approaches."[45]

Shortly after the invasion, Roosevelt returned to the United States at Arnold's request to brief air planners on how to set up additional photographic units. Spaatz reported that:

He has been doing a perfectly splendid job and has, in my opinion, a better grasp of aerial photography in all of its phases than anyone here, including RAF, our own Air Forces, and both Armies. . . . I hope his opinions will be given justifiable weight. Do not get too mad if he finds too much wrong with what has been done. This is an expression of the intensity of his purpose, and probably the typical Roosevelt method of getting results.

Spaatz hoped that Roosevelt's stay would be brief, as "he is badly needed here in connection with our further operations."[46]

Airborne Assaults

The USAAF committed significant assets to the airborne assaults designed to help the amphibious forces break out from the beachheads and hasten the advance inland. The large numbers of pilots trained to fly these aircraft (each C-47 transport aircraft was dual-piloted) and the industrial production allocated to cargo aircraft could have been used to produce more heavy bomber groups, but the USAAF correctly allocated these still scarce assets to develop a significant airlift capability, one unavailable elsewhere in the Allied arsenal. In a preview of the airborne operations in Normandy a year later, almost every available transport aircraft carried British and American paratroopers to drop zones behind each nation's sector of the landing beaches. While the operations were technically successful, they were also marred by inaccurate drops and high casualties, mostly as a result of friendly antiaircraft fire, especially from ships as the aircraft passed over the invasion convoy. Air planners for Operation OVERLORD took advantage of this learning experience by routing the ingress route for that operation far to the west of the Cotentin Peninsula, well away from the invasion fleet then gathering off the coast.

By July 1943, the Northwest African Troop Carrier Command had been doubled in size with the addition of the 52nd Troop Carrier Wing, comprising three new groups. The 61st, 313th, and 314th Troop Carrier Groups did not arrive in theater until June and had their training cut short after only one practice drop with troops from the 82nd Airborne Division. NATCC's more experienced wing, the 51st, still comprising the 60th, 62nd, and 64th groups, which had been active in the theater since the TORCH landings, was assigned the more difficult mission of towing most of the 147 gliders filled with troops from the

British First Airlanding Brigade to their objectives near Syracuse. Unfortunately, the higher experience level of the 51st Wing's pilots was offset by the inexperience of many of the glider pilots, some of whom made errors that resulted in their aircraft landing in the sea.[47] During the first week after the invasion, both troop carrier groups flew a total of 666 sorties but lost a total of forty-five planes, roughly the equivalent of one of the six groups involved.[48]

The first two missions, flown on the night before the invasion, largely escaped the high losses that plagued the two follow-on missions. In the British sector, all 134 American tow aircraft launched returned safely to their bases in North Africa, but only twelve of the 134 gliders reached their assigned landing zones, and an estimated forty-seven crashed in the sea, after casting off from their tugs while still too far from the coastline. Only seventy-three troops reached their objective, the Ponte Grande bridge over a canal south of Syracuse, but even this small force was sufficient to hold the bridge until 1530 the following day. At that time, the nineteen remaining unwounded men were forced off their objective by an Axis counterattack, but troops of the British 5th Infantry Division, advancing from the beaches, retook the bridge before the enemy could destroy it. Two weeks after the landings, more than 600 of the airborne troops were still missing.[49]

Appalled at the high losses, Eisenhower appointed a commission of Allied officers to investigate the operations.[50] Their report found that a thirty-knot headwind had played havoc with the operation and that "the high wind was not allowed for sufficiently either during navigation or for the height and distance from the coast gliders were cast off." In addition, "judgment of distance out to sea from a coast line had not been practiced sufficiently. A coast line appears to be almost underneath the aircraft when flying at 1,500 ft and 3,000 yds out to sea." Further, navigation by the inexperienced glider pilots was "generally bad," and a number of the tow pilots had not reached their assigned cast-off points.[51]

The initial operation in the American sector, in which 3,405 men of the 505th Parachute Infantry Regiment and the 3rd Battalion of the 504th Parachute Infantry Regiment jumped behind the American beaches at Gela, was also widely scattered due to inexperienced pilots. The 220 C-47s making the drop also escaped heavy losses, losing only eight of their number, largely because the invasion fleet had been warned of the operation and because the fleet itself had not yet been detected at sea or attacked by Axis aircraft. But navigation errors, induced by both the high winds and from smoke from an earlier bombardment that obscured key landmarks, left paratroopers scattered across the southern half of the island. Of the 3,400-plus men actually dropped (some aircraft had been lost or returned to Tunisia), less than 200 arrived on the primary objective: the high ground east of Gela near the village of Piano Lupo. The terrain feature held several critical road intersections that would enable paratroopers to protect the landing beaches from an expected counterattack until the seaborne forces had built up sufficient strength to fend for themselves. Paratroopers detected the expected counterattack the following day and began to apply "friction" in the form of numerous, localized, but still annoying roadblocks. Elsewhere on the battlefield, isolated units of paratroopers attached themselves to whatever friendly troops were in the area and attacked the defenders wherever they were found, increasing the entropy in the Axis command. The commission's final report found that "the operation had a decisive effect on the successful landing and the advance inland of the seaborne forces. There is little doubt that the action of the American airborne troops speeded up the landing and advance inland by at least 48 hrs."[52]

If these two operations had been the full extent of Allied airborne operations in Sicily, they might well have been judged a success. Both groups had reached their nominal objectives in at least some strength, all the paratroopers that reached the island played an important role in the quick escape from the beachheads, and the airlift forces were still relatively intact. But Allied planners, encouraged by this limited success, overplayed their hand and hastily scheduled two additional large follow-on missions—again, one each in the British and American sectors—that resulted in heavy losses and largely failed to achieve their objective of providing the ground commanders an immediately available reserve to meet the growing Axis counterattacks.

On the night of 11 July, 144 aircraft of 52nd Troop Carrier Wing carried the remainder of the 504th Parachute Infantry Regiment, plus attached artillery and engineer units—more than 2,000 men in all—to reinforce the beachhead near Gela.[53] As there were not enough aircraft in theater to transport the entire division in the initial lift, planners envisioned a follow-on mission but left the timing open in order to have the flexibility to drop the paratroopers where they were needed most. Unfortunately, this flexibility came at a cost. There was insufficient time to ensure that the other elements on the battlefield, particularly the ground and naval forces that would inflict most of the casualties, would know when and where the paratroopers would be crossing their formations. The airborne mission arrived overhead just after the naval forces had beaten off an attack by a flight of Axis bombers. The still-nervous gunners immediately opened up on the friendly aircraft, scattering the formation; some aircraft brought their loads back to North Africa, and others dropped their cargoes further inland and then ran the gauntlet of fire back to their bases. One pilot reported that "evidently the safest place for us . . . while over Sicily would have been over enemy territory." Twenty three aircraft failed to return, and many of those that did were badly damaged.[54] Despite suffering more than 20 percent casualties in the two drops, both regiments of the 82nd Airborne Division were consolidated with another infantry regiment and played an important part in protecting Seventh Army's flank in the subsequent drive across the island. Perhaps more important, both the airborne forces and NATCC had gained valuable experience that would pay dividends in more critical situations at both Salerno and in Normandy. Ignoring the potential for improved training exercises and better pre-attack coordination, the 82nd Airborne Division's commander, Major General Matthew Ridgway, believed, "diplorable [sic] as is the loss of life which occurred, I believe that the lessons now learned could have been driven home in no other way."[55]

A second mission in the British sector on the night of 13 July met similar results. Here 124 transports, plus seventeen gliders, carried additional elements of the British First Airborne Division toward their objective, a bridge over the Simeto River that would permit Montgomery's Eighth Army to debouch onto the relatively open plain near Catania. Again heavy antiaircraft fire from fleet and shore elements resulted in only fifty-six aircraft reaching the vicinity of the drop zone. Twenty-four were scattered across the area, while another twenty-seven returned to base without dropping their cargoes. Eleven of the transports (9 percent) were lost. Only about 200 troops reached the bridge, but they were able to capture it and remove the demolition charges. As in the earlier mission near Syracuse, they were eventually forced off their objective, but the advancing ground forces were able to retake the bridge before it could be destroyed. Montgomery later estimated that the assistance from the British airborne division had accelerated his advance by one week.[56]

The issue of friendly fire had dogged the Allies throughout the Tunisian campaign. On 2 June, General Arnold wrote the commander of the Army Ground Forces, General Leslie McNair, to express his concern with the number of aircraft that had been fired on by friendly ground and naval forces and suggested that, given the preponderance of Allied aircraft in the theater, ground troops should assume that all unidentified aircraft were friendly unless they displayed hostile intent. McNair replied on 15 June and confirmed that "I have received many reports from observers in North Africa citing occasions on which troops have fired on friendly aircraft, and airplanes have attacked friendly ground troops." He believed that "the mental 'conditioning' caused by the fact that in the early stages of the campaign most of the aircraft seen by ground personnel were hostile was a contributing factor" to the ground forces "itchy fingers," but even increased recognition training of pilots and ground personnel had merely "alleviated, but never entirely eliminated, these unfortunate incidents." While acknowledging Arnold's suggestion that unidentified aircraft be assumed to be friendly, he countered that "such a mental attitude would be extremely hazardous in situations where control of the air was in dispute and enemy aviation was engaged actively."[57] A final suggestion involved enlarged or specific identification markings on aircraft, both of which were adopted. In summer 1943, the USAAF added a white horizontal bar to its insignia (a white star inside a blue circle) to better distinguish it from both the German swastika and Japanese rising sun, all of which tended to blur into an unidentifiable circular shape from a distance.[58] Just before the D-Day landings in Normandy in 1944, Allied aircraft were also painted with alternating white and black bands on the undersides of the wings and fuselage to further assist in identification, but neither of these measures would be effective for aircraft flying at night, when most of the transport losses occurred.[59]

During the preinvasion planning sessions, Brigadier General Paul Williams, a veteran of the TORCH airborne mission and commander of NATCC, and Major General Matthew Ridgway, commanding 82nd Airborne Division, had raised their concerns about flying large formations over friendly naval forces, but they "were informed that the Navy would give no assurance that fire would not be delivered upon aircraft approaching within range of its vessels at night." Ridgway pressed his case, even threatening to "recommend against the dispatch of airborne troop movements," and eventually received assurances that the naval forces would issue "instructions in the sense desired." Ridgway likewise took steps to ensure that the ground troops, especially antiaircraft gunners, could recognize the C-47 transports and the Waco CG-4A Hadrian assault glider and felt that "the danger of having friendly fire directed on our airborne forces was recognized, and strenuous efforts were made to eliminate it long before the operation was to take place." Unfortunately, according to Ridgway, the views of NATCC and the 82nd Airborne Division "were not shared by higher echelons, particularly those in the naval command." But Ridgway did feel that "the responsibility for loss of life and material resulting from this operation is so divided" that efforts at disciplinary action would lead only to "acrimonious debates."[60]

Despite the high casualties among both the paratroop forces and the troop carrier elements, the airborne forces played an important part in protecting the landings, breaking up counterattacks, and facilitating the movement of amphibious forces out of the beachhead. The USAAF's significant investment in both transport aircraft and in developing airborne tactics had paid its first real dividends on the battlefield. While the results left significant room for improvement, in both the training of the transport aircraft and in interservice cooperation, they did prove, for the Allies, what had until then been only a theoretical capability and added yet another weapon to the theater commander's growing arsenal.

Air Support in Sicily

While the USAAF devoted considerable assets to the air-superiority, interdiction, and airlift efforts in the battle for Sicily, it did not neglect close support of the advancing ground troops. In both the British and American sectors, the "immediate objective of the assault forces must be the airfields both in the southeast and in the west to provide the extension of air cover essential for the capture of the ports."[61] This would save supporting aircraft the long flights from Tunisia or from the Mediterranean islands. Fighter units moved to these newly captured airfields and began rendering support in less than one week after the landings.[62] But some historians of the campaign latched on to later statements by the principal commanders, including General Omar Bradley, commanding the U.S. II Corps, who wrote, "The air support provided us on Sicily was scandalously casual, careless, and ineffective."[63] As with Admiral Hewitt's criticism, Bradley implied that an air force possessing, and using, a potent heavy bombardment arm was incapable of using other assets in effective close support. Like Hewitt, Bradley was mistaken. Most of the Twelfth Air Force's fighters and medium bombers provided ample and important support for Seventh Army's drive across the island. Even the U.S. Army's official history agreed, describing the advance on Palermo as "little more than a road march. Swarms of planes struck at targets of opportunity." The capture of Palermo itself on 22 July provided further evidence of the efficacy of the interdiction campaign. The wrecks of forty-four ships blocked the harbor.[64]

To augment the Northwest African Tactical Air Force, Spaatz diverted two groups of long–range P-38 *Lightning* fighters from the strategic force. These two groups joined two groups equipped with an airplane that was new to the theater, the A-36 *Apache* dive-bomber, operated by the 27th and 86th Light Bomber Groups. The A-36, a modified P-51 equipped with dive brakes and bomb racks, proved to be one of the most accurate close support weapons of the entire war. Tedder recognized the importance of both of these types, reporting to Portal that "the [P-38] *Lightnings* and the [P-51] *Mustangs* [actually A-36s] have been invaluable for freelance work on communications. They are, of course, ideal types for the job."[65] Only the P-51 model's even greater utility as a long-range escort prevented more A-36s from being employed. Its main flaw was a liquid cooling system that limited the airplane to only two or three minutes of flight if the engine was hit and the coolant lost.[66] Another new fighter, then being operated exclusively by Eighth Air Force in the United Kingdom, was the P-47 *Thunderbolt*, equipped with a large air-cooled radial engine that was not as susceptible to ground fire but lacked the range to escort the heavy bombers deep into Germany. During the last two years of the war, the two fighters eventually switched roles, with most of the P-51s gravitating to Eighth Air Force and serving as escort fighters while the P-38s and P-47s remained in the tactical air forces, such as the Twelfth Air Force in the Mediterranean and the reconstituted Ninth Air Force in the United Kingdom, largely flying ground support missions. The P-51 had originally been slated to replace the P-40 groups in the Mediterranean, but when USAAF leaders recognized its value as an escort fighter, as well as the great need for it in the United Kingdom, the P-51s were sent to Eighth Air Force; P-40s were replaced with P-47s instead.[67]

The two A-36 groups provided effective service throughout the Sicilian campaign. Lieutenant Colonel Dorr Newton, who commanded 27th Bombardment Group (Light), provided a summary of his group's contributions from 1 July to 1 August 1943, which included 1,971 effective sorties that destroyed 353 motor vehicles and seven tanks, one entire train and twelve railroad locomotives, four ships and seventeen small boats, and numerous fuel dumps, gun positions, supply dumps, and troop concentrations. In a demonstration of how tactical reconnaissance had matured, Dorr related one attack that neutralized a gun position that was invisible from the air:

It has been found that photographs of the target or an accurate pin point location considerably enhance the chances of success. On 31st July 1943, 12 A-36s of this [27th] Group were sent against a gun battery in position of four guns that had been causing our ground troops much trouble. A pin point location was given, and the squadron was carefully briefed on the terrain to be expected. The guns could not be seen although the flight circled the location three times. The pin point location was bombed regardless, and a congratulatory message from the 1st Division stated that all 4 guns had been hit and knocked out.

Dorr credited the A-36s success during the campaign to the "extreme accuracy" of ordinance delivered in the A-36s near-vertical dive and the fact that "since the A-36 is fundamentally a fighter" it was capable of taking care of itself and did not require any fighter escort, which improved both the flexibility of scheduling missions and the survivability of the aircraft flying them.[68]

The A-36s remained active in the fight for the city of Troina, launching a number of effective sorties in the following days, but the Allied struggles continued with target identification and friendly fire. One A-36 pilot continued to press an attack on an Allied tank column despite their releasing yellow smoke—the identification signal for a friendly unit. The ground forces eventually returned fire, downing the aircraft. Upon questioning, the pilot revealed that he was unaware of the significance of the yellow smoke signal. In another incident, A-36s attacked a British corps headquarters.[69]

Twelfth Air Force's seven groups of B-25 and B-26 medium bombers (including the two groups transferred from Ninth Air Force in late July) continued their tactical support role, though, unlike in the early stages of the Tunisian campaign, the supported units and objectives were no longer segregated by nationality. The strongest German units gravitated toward the path of Montgomery's Eighth Army, which directly threatened the critical logistics lifeline across the Strait of Messina. Accordingly, American airmen flew a significant percentage of their close support sorties in the British sector, perhaps another source of the American ground commanders' complaints about the lack of close support. In one case, twelve B-25s of 340th Bomb Group destroyed a battery of three German 88mm guns that were holding up the advance of Canadian troops near Adrano. While the mediums were often used in the continuing interdiction campaign on the mainland, they also provided valuable direct support to the ground troops in Sicily.

Despite their excellent performance record in the campaign for Sicily, the medium bombers lacked strong support from the USAAF's leadership. On 14 July, Spaatz elaborated on his earlier proposal to convert four groups of medium bombers to heavy bombers in order to alleviate anticipated crew shortages in the training pipeline. He wrote, "Our results here indicate that the B-17 does the most accurate bombing and can, without excessive losses in this area, proceed unescorted on its missions if necessary. If crews are a bottleneck, it would be, I believe, most expedient to transform progressively four of our medium bomber groups to B-17 groups. . . . The disposition of our medium bombers thus made available can, as suggested before, take care of some of our commitments to foreign nations." At the time, the French were pressing for bombers to reequip their air force to augment the successful transfer of a number of P-40s to French squadrons in North Africa. Spaatz recognized this would be unpopular with ground commanders, as

> there are many objectives to be attacked with Ground Armies which must be bombed at altitudes below 10,000 or 11,000 feet, and further, weather conditions do not always permit high altitude bombing. In this connection, the B-17 is too slow to operate in the altitude bracket at which the B-25 and B-26 operates. I am sure that if we attempted B-17 operations in such altitudes our losses of B-17's would greatly exceed our present losses of B-25's and B-26's.[70]

Thus, Spaatz was advocating for an increase in the heavy bomber force at the expense of additional assets for the tactical air forces. The effect would be heightened after 1 November 1943, when all of the heavy bombers in the Mediterranean were segregated in the Fifteenth Air Force and assigned primarily to strategic targets, while the medium bombers remained with Twelfth Air Force and, along with the fighters deemed unsuitable for bomber escort, would comprise the bulk of its tactical assets. Fortunately, Arnold rejected the idea of converting the medium bomber groups to additional heavy groups and informed Spaatz of his decision on 20 August.[71]

In the immediate aftermath of the campaign, ground commanders generally expressed satisfaction with the air support they received in Sicily. On 30 July, Spaatz reported to Arnold that the P-38 and A-36 had proved very effective against vehicles. "Also impressive was the damage done to aircraft and airdromes as well as to the harbors. . . . As the extent to which the air has assisted the ground action becomes more widely known, increasing demands are made for its employ-ment."[72] On 3 August Spaatz observed, "General Patton [commander of Seventh Army, the parent command of all American ground forces involved in the campaign] was quick to state that the success of the landing and the rapid march over land was due to the fine air support given his Army." Two days later Spaatz visited with Patton person-ally and reported, "He stated that he is thoroughly satisfied with air cooperation."[73]

A Failed Interdiction Campaign

For all its successes in setting the conditions for the Allied advance onto and across Sicily, the final stages of the campaign were marred by the USAAF's failure to successfully interdict either the early re-inforcement of the island's garrison or the successful evacuation that left several German divisions intact. These troops would go on to play an important role in the defense of the Italian peninsula and contrib-ute to the Allies' failure to reach Rome until almost a year later. The Axis defenders had a number of factors in their favor, but a dedicated and sustained air campaign, coordinated with the naval forces, could have made Sicily a much more complete victory and possibly acceler-ated the Allied advance.

The failed interdiction campaign stemmed from three main causes: favorable geography, poor interservice coordination, and the absence of the heavy bombers that could have made a substantial contribution. The Axis defenders benefited from the favorable geography of Sicily itself. Instead of a sixty-mile expanse of open sea, Axis supplies had to cross the Strait of Messina, only two miles wide at its narrowest point. But this factor could have also been turned to the Allies' fa-vor. Instead of searching for Axis convoys anywhere between Naples and Bizerte, as they had during the Tunisian campaign, Allied airmen had been given a single chokepoint, especially in the latter stages of the Sicilian campaign when the Allies held all of the other important ports on the island. While the Axis could, and did, make use of the surrounding beaches to conduct the evacuation, the entire area was still confined geographically and subject to attack. But the Axis turned this to their advantage, as they were able to concentrate their anti-aircraft defense in a small area, making it difficult, if not impossible, for fighter-bombers and medium bombers to operate without sustain-ing heavy losses.[74] The U.S. Army's official history of the campaign

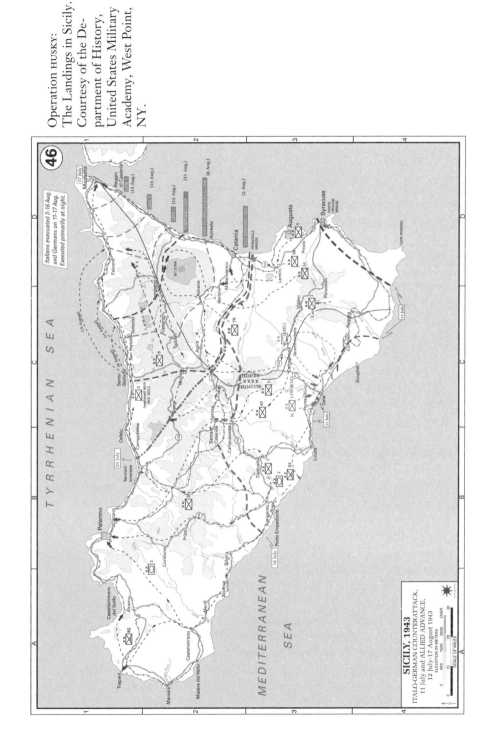

Operation HUSKY:
The Landings in Sicily.
Courtesy of the De-
partment of History,
United States Military
Academy, West Point,
NY.

found that "the single weakness in [the German] antiaircraft defense system was the limited range of his guns. A large number would not be able to reach high-flying Allied bombers, aircraft like the B-17, the B-24, and the British Wellington."[75] While it would have been difficult for the fighter-bombers and medium bombers to operate against targets protected by concentrated antiaircraft fire, the heavies could still make a substantial contribution. To avoid daylight bombing attacks, the Germans planned to carry out most of the evacuation at night, but even these operations could be interrupted by the RAF's fleet of *Wellington* bombers, which specialized in nighttime attacks. Finally, the Axis forces benefited from a geographical advantage, as the northeast corner of Sicily tapered to a point at Messina, which enabled the Germans and Italians to withdraw troops from the front lines in stages, while maintaining the overall density of their defensive formations in a reduced frontage.[76]

An inability to integrate naval, land, and air forces into an effective combined force also contributed to the interdiction failure. The initial plan for the landings had Montgomery's British Eighth Army driving up the eastern shore of Sicily and seizing Messina, blocking the Axis escape route. But Axis ground commanders, especially the German general Hans Hube, recognized this threat to their supply lines and Hube quickly moved his two strongest divisions, the Hermann Goering Division and the 15th Panzer Grenadier Division, into Montgomery's path, stalling the advance. This left western Sicily open for the exploitation of Patton's Seventh Army but resulted in both forces pushing the defenders back toward Messina rather than imposing their forces between them and their source of resupply.

While the ground forces were unable to reach Messina ahead of the Germans and Italians, Allied naval forces might still have interdicted the strait had they received effective support from air forces. The Italians had erected strong coastal defense batteries on both sides of the narrow passage and blocked access at either end with mines, preventing Allied warships from entering the area where the transports operated. But a sustained effort to render the coastal batteries ineffective, such as that delivered on Pantelleria in the final days before that island's surrender, might have suppressed the coastal fire long enough for Allied minesweepers to clear the channel and permit Allied warships to make a foray into the shipping channel, sinking a number of the boats used in the evacuation. In fact, such an effort was exactly what the Allied naval commander, Admiral Sir Andrew Cunningham, had in mind when on 3 August he requested Tedder's assistance in silencing the coastal batteries in order to bring his warships into the strait.[77] But Tedder never acted on Cunningham's request, and between 11 and 16 August the Germans brought out more than 38,000 troops and almost 15,000 tons of supplies, all of which would be put to good use in defending against the subsequent invasion of the Italian boot.[78]

The exact reasons for Tedder's failure to act are unclear, but an examination of the Mediterranean Air Command's operations in the month prior to the evacuation, especially those of the strategic bombers, makes it obvious that the priorities lay elsewhere. On 19 July, the heavy bombers launched a large and destructive raid on Rome's rail marshaling yards, ostensibly to interdict supplies headed for Sicily but in reality designed to deliver a shock to the Italian government and force it out of the war. Spaatz prepared an eighteen-page report on the raid for Arnold, detailing the damage done and demonstrating the great care that NAAF had taken to avoid damage to any significant religious sites within the eternal city in order to refute any Axis propaganda.[79] Benito Mussolini's forced resignation one week later appeared to vindicate this belief and provided more fuel to the theory that governments could be coerced by air action alone. Arnold wrote Spaatz on 11 August to congratulate him on the attack and pass along his belief that it "probably had a very great weight in the overthrow of the Fascist regime," ignoring the almost complete impotence of the Italian military after three years of sustained war and the impending loss of Sicily, the last bastion between the Allied forces and the Italian mainland.[80] Despite Mussolini's ouster, Italian troops on Sicily continued to resist, although the Germans began to question their ally's resolve and plan for both the evacuation of Sicily and the occupation and defense of the rest of the Italian mainland.

Following the strike on Rome, Ninth Air Force withdrew all of its B-24s from operations to complete training for Operation TIDALWAVE, the planned strike on the oil refineries around Ploesti, Romania. That raid, carried out on 1 August and discussed in detail in Chapter 6, cost the five groups involved fifty-four aircraft and inflicted heavy damage on the remainder, putting them out of action for almost two weeks. They did not return to action until 13 August, at the height of the evacuation from Sicily, with a raid on German fighter factories near Wiener-Neustadt in Austria. On 16 August the B-24s hit the airfield complex at Foggia, despite the fact that the Luftwaffe was already too weak to provide any significant support to the evacuation.[81] The five groups (the two original Ninth Air Force groups, plus three others diverted from Eighth Air Force in the United Kingdom), which at the time made up more than half of the heavy bomber assets in the Mediterranean, were thus removed from the battle just when their efforts were most needed.

To their credit, Eisenhower and the Combined Chiefs of Staff had foreseen this possibility and attempted to delay the attack on Ploesti until well after the invasion of Sicily. During the Casablanca Conference in January, Air Chief Marshal Sir Charles Portal stressed that the value of attacks on German oil facilities had to be balanced against the needs of HUSKY, but the group agreed that the attacks should be launched as soon as other commitments would allow.[82] The subject emerged again in March, when the group discussed a proposal to send two additional groups from the United Kingdom to reinforce the Mediterranean prior to invading Sicily, but the Combined Chiefs of Staff determined that no additional bombers could be spared from the anti–U-boat campaign. In noting that there were already six groups of heavy bombers then in the Mediterranean, the group "did not consider it necessary that this force should be augmented" prior to launching HUSKY.[83] At the eighty-seventh meeting of the Combined Chiefs of Staff on 18 May, during the TRIDENT Conference in Washington, D.C., Portal again reminded the conferees that, in planning for Ploesti, the "effects on HUSKY must be borne in mind," and he suggested that the group solicit the theater commander's views "in light of the necessity for concentrating our air resources in support of Operation HUSKY." Sir Alan Brooke, chief of the Imperial General Staff, agreed and "stressed the disadvantage of the dispersal of air forces prior to HUSKY."[84] As early as 5 June, Eisenhower had asked for the TIDALWAVE operation to be delayed until it would not detract from the weight of the invasion of Sicily. He agreed that the Ploesti operation was both "important and desirable" but did not want to release the force until the invasion of Sicily had been assured of success.[85]

But Eisenhower was far more concerned with gaining the initial lodgment and did not himself foresee a requirement to use the force as the campaign wound down. In the same letter, he projected that the Ploesti operation should take place by the "end of July with a total of five heavy bomber groups" but that "they should be available for operational use" while they underwent training in North Africa.[86] Even after the three additional groups arrived in North Africa in early July and began training at their desert base near Benghazi, Libya, Eighth Air Force tried to have the raid cancelled and the bombers returned to the United Kingdom, where there were already eighteen other operational groups. Such an action would have avoided the disastrous raid on Ploesti but would not have materially helped the bomber shortage in the Mediterranean. General Ira Eaker, commanding Eighth Air Force, pressured his theater commander, General Jacob Devers, to appeal to the Combined Chiefs of Staff to cancel the attack on Ploesti and to return the bombers to the United Kingdom at once.[87] Eisenhower and Spaatz, with Marshall's and Arnold's assistance, resisted this appeal, and the Ploesti mission went ahead as scheduled.

Eisenhower had also repeatedly asked for reinforcements for his heavy bomber arm but had been denied. While his original request had asked for only two groups, and then only for a period from three weeks before until three weeks after the initial landings (essentially mid-June until the end of July) and therefore might have been released even before the evacuation was under way, they would have at least been in theater and possibly held for an additional two weeks in order to help block the escape.[88] In late July, he again appealed for reinforcements for his heavy bomber arm, this time to help prepare for the invasion of Italy, only a little more than a month away. On 28 July, he reported to the Combined Chiefs of Staff that

> of all types of additional strength that could now be made available to us to assure a reasonable success in the whole venture, a temporary doubling of our heavy bomber types would be the most effective. Had we such strength, we believe that we could practically paralyze the German air effort in southern Italy and almost immobilize his ground units. If the Combined Chiefs of Staff should find it possible to direct several heavy groups of Eighth Air Force to shift their base of operations to this area from now until September 15, it appears to us that the chances for achieving a decisive success in this region would be tremendously enhanced.[89]

When the Combined Chiefs of Staff, at Eaker's urging, refused this request, Eisenhower asked to keep only the three additional B-24 groups that had participated in the Ploesti raid.[90] That request was also refused, and the surviving bombers of those three groups returned to the United Kingdom in late August.

Even without the five B-24 groups, Twelfth Air Force in Tunisia still had four groups of B-17s, which could have been used in a sustained campaign in the strait or to suppress coastal batteries and let the naval forces make an attempt. But after two raids on Messina during the first week of August, the B-17s were withdrawn, leaving fighters and medium bombers to shoulder both the support missions for the ground forces and the interdiction campaign against the increasingly well defended strait. The bombers had sustained a high operations tempo for the preceding two months, and many crews, even in the two new groups that arrived in March, were already approaching their fifty-mission limit.[91] On 30 July, Spaatz wrote Arnold, "Weather almost never interrupts flying and between 70% and 80% of our airplanes are kept in commission." As a result, "combat crew fatigue has become the main problem."[92] The requirement to support the landings on the mainland the following month with a sustained campaign against a growing German bomber force, including units released from the Eastern Front after the failed Battle of Kursk, added a sense of urgency to the crew shortage and a growing backlog of deferred maintenance. Doolittle speculated either that operations would have to be curtailed or that the flow of replacements increased.[93] But the bombers still found the time and crews to strike targets not directly related to the evacuation of Sicily. On 13 August, in the middle of the evacuation, 107 B-17s returned to Rome for a second raid on the rail yards there.[94] The decision to inflict further destruction on the Italian rail network would restrict the German efforts to reinforce the area around Naples but, at the same time, allowed the German troops in Sicily to escape with light losses. On 17 August, the day the evacuation ended, 180 B-17s attacked a Luftwaffe buildup at the Istres–Le Tube and Salon airdromes, northwest of Marseille, France. While the attack helped to reduce German bomber strength in the theater, destroying an estimated ninety-four aircraft on the ground, the strike also demonstrated that strategic bombers had their attention focused on areas other than the Strait of Messina.[95]

As these aircraft returned to their bases in North Africa, they were joined by almost 200 B-17s of Eighth Air Force. In an attack timed to commemorate the first heavy bomber raid on Rouen exactly one year earlier, and to highlight the results of the yearlong buildup in the United Kingdom, Eighth Air Force had launched simultaneous heavy raids on the Messerschmitt factory at Regensburg and the ball-bearing production facilities at Schweinfurt. Rather than return to England through an alerted German air defense network, the Regensburg force continued on to Twelfth Air Force bases in North Africa. While the raid demonstrated that the two theaters could be mutually supporting when required, they also temporarily overwhelmed Twelfth Air Force's supply and maintenance facilities. Ground crews assigned to support Twelfth Air Force bombers were put to work servicing and repairing those of the Eighth, many of which had suffered heavy damage. Months later, a number of these planes were still on North African fields awaiting repair. Colonel Curtis LeMay, who had flown to Africa to lead the survivors in a second raid on their way back to the United Kingdom, "found that servicing and then re-assembling widely-dispersed aircraft was an almost impossible task."[96]

With the heavies employed elsewhere, and the mediums and fighter-bombers forced by the dense flak to too high an altitude to be effective, the only significant resistance Allied aircraft offered to the evacuations came from the RAF's force of *Wellington* medium bombers. By flying at night, when the Axis gunners were unable to offer effective resistance, the *Wellingtons* flew an average of ninety daily sorties during 8–13 August and inflicted such heavy losses on the evacuation beaches that on 12 August the Germans shifted their operations back to the daylight hours.[97] But even this highly effective force was under pressure from the UK-based Combined Bomber Offensive. Tedder later recalled that he had "asked for the loan of these three [RCAF] Wellington squadrons for the six weeks ending 31 July and quite realized that it would not be easy for Portal to prolong their stay in the Mediterranean. He had, in fact, given a personal promise to [Sir Arthur] 'Bomber' Harris [commander of RAF Bomber Command] that the squadrons would return to him." The issue created some friction between Portal and Tedder, not least because Portal implied that Allied air superiority in the Mediterranean was largely the result of the Combined Bomber Offensive in the United Kingdom, a remark that Tedder challenged and that Portal later withdrew.[98] While the Combined Bomber Offensive had forced the Luftwaffe to begin redeploying assets to Germany, Tedder's British and American aircraft had expended significant effort in reducing the German air forces already present in the theater.

Although the primary failure to prevent the evacuation of Axis forces from Sicily lies with the inability of the theater commander to develop and implement a joint operational plan, the USAAF's reluctance to participate played an important role and demonstrated, for the first time, that the USAAF's preference for strategic attack, on both distant targets in Italy and as far afield as Ploesti and Regensburg, was beginning to impact operations on the ground and at sea. The U.S. Army's official history accurately noted that "almost one-half of the available Allied air power—the 869 aircraft that belonged to NA-SAF—was used in only a limited way to stop the evacuation."[99] The growing heavy bomber forces in the United Kingdom did play a part in the campaign by drawing German aircraft and antiaircraft guns away from the Mediterranean, but the desire to keep these aircraft isolated in a strategic-only force focused exclusively on that mission robbed airpower of one of its inherent strengths: the flexibility to be used whenever and wherever it can be most effectively employed.

Conclusion

The air phase of the campaign for Sicily was significant for several reasons. The Allied air forces, especially the USAAF's six groups of heavy bombers, had further demonstrated that they could be a decisive force in land and naval campaigns. When resistance ended on Sicily on 17 August, Eisenhower released the following statement to the press:

> During the Tunisian battle, Air Forces coordinated with Ground and Naval action, proved decisive. Since then this force has been applied against Pantelleria and later against Sicily with its culminating phase today. The movement of great numbers of surface craft through the Mediterranean, carrying thousands of troops against a hostile shore, was made possible by complete domination of the air. After the landing, the action of our air forces prevented the launching of significant counter-attacks, and insured the steady progress of our ground forces. The possession of air supremacy will enable us to continue a relentless air offensive, which will ensure the success of any future military operations we may undertake.[100]

Yet at the same time, the USAAF's heavy bombers in the Mediterranean began to be drawn into the orbit of the growing strategic bomber force in the United Kingdom. Three days after Eisenhower's statement demonstrating the air force's effectiveness as part of the joint team, Spaatz wrote the War Department's assistant secretary for air, Robert A. Lovett (future secretary of defense under President Harry Truman), "I am becoming increasingly convinced that Germany can be forced to her knees by aerial bombardment alone."[101]

Despite the fact that the USAAF would undoubtedly be the greatest beneficiary of an invasion of the Italian mainland and the capture of both the port of Naples and the airfield complex at Foggia, the USAAF began to display a reluctance to being committed heavily to the advance of ground forces. Many of the Axis units that were successfully evacuated from Sicily made the landings at Salerno, less than a month later, the closest the Allies came during the entire war to defeat in a major amphibious operation. Only the intervention of naval gunfire support, another airborne operation to reinforce the beachhead, and massive raids by heavy bombers diverted from strategic targets saved the invasion force from being overrun and pushed back into the sea. The USAAF had played a significant role in the Allied advance from Cairo and Casablanca to Messina, but it was becoming increasingly more interested in the strategic campaign and less interested in using strategic assets to attack tactical targets that sped the advance of ground forces.

6

Ploesti and Salerno:
August to September 1943

As the Allied attackers backed Sicily's defenders into the tiny north-east corner of the island, Allied airmen took advantage of their hard-won ascendancy in the skies over the middle sea to embark on one of their pet projects: a long-distance raid on the oil refineries surrounding Ploesti, Romania. The target, attacked unsuccessfully from Palestine more than a year earlier by Harry Halverson's tiny force, continued to produce large quantities of Axis petroleum, including high-octane aviation gas that fueled Hitler's Luftwaffe. Less than two weeks into the battle for Sicily, Allied commanders pulled the five B-24 groups in the theater (two from Ninth Air Force, along with three other groups that had been loaned from Eighth Air Force in the United Kingdom) out of combat and began to train them for a single mission to attack the refineries. From 20 July to 13 August 1943, these five groups, which then comprised more than half of the Allied heavy bomber as-sets in the Mediterranean, flew only a single mission: the low-level attack on Ploesti on 1 August 1943. Fifty-three of the 178 bombers that took part in the raid (30 percent) failed to return, and another sixty were so badly damaged that they never flew again.[1] After the raid, the three Eighth Air Force groups returned to the United Kingdom, but the remaining Ninth Air Force groups were still so weak that they were unable to provide substantial support to the invasion of the Ital-ian mainland. In mid-September, the three B-24 groups in the United Kingdom were rushed back to the Mediterranean to help support the landings at Salerno, but they were too late to avert the near-disaster there. In one stroke, the Army Air Forces had taken the cream of their heavy bomber force in the Mediterranean and thrown a large portion of it away on a single target.

The Ploesti Raid

The refineries at Ploesti had long captured the attention of Allied airmen and leaders on both sides of the Atlantic. The facility was featured prominently in the USAAF's Air War Planning Document 1942 (AWPD-42), which, like AWPD-1, advocated for a bomber force large enough to wage a strategic campaign against the Axis in Europe. The report contained detailed assessments of each of the nine major refineries surrounding Ploesti, with most of the figures being lifted verbatim from an earlier British report on the target set.[2] The desire to hit Ploesti had driven the diversion of the HALPRO project to the Middle East, after Japanese forces overran their projected bases in China, and resulted in the June 1942 attack by thirteen B-24s of that group that inflicted no damage but cost Halverson a large portion of his available bomber force (see Chapter 2). Determined to atone for the earlier failure, the USAAF continued to plan for a strike on Ploesti and waited for an opportunity to send another wave of bombers after the Romanian oil.

The Combined Chiefs of Staff took up the topic at the Casablanca Conference in January 1943. On 19 January, at the sixty-second meeting, Sir Charles Portal responded to the USAAF's proposal for the raid by noting that "it would be a mistake to make light and sporadic attacks on Ploesti, which would do little harm and only result in an increase of the German air defenses. It would be better to wait until we had the Turkish air bases."[3] General Arnold countered Portal's suggestion by noting that Ploesti was equidistant from Sicily, Benghazi, Cairo, and Aleppo (Syria) and that attacks could be made from any of those locations with less than 4,000 pounds of bombs. While Portal's hopes for Turkish cobelligerence would remain unfulfilled, he had accurately forecasted the results of the 1 August raid. While not designed to be either light or ineffective, the raid did result in a further strengthening of German defenses and made the sustained raids from April to August 1944 even more costly.

Portal was already fully committed to the Combined Bomber Offensive in the United Kingdom and therefore to the buildup of American bomber forces in the British Isles, and he was likely arguing against the operation in order to prevent what he perceived as a further dispersion of effort. But he was right to suggest waiting until the Allied ground advance had obtained air bases within a feasible operating range, although they would be in southern Italy instead of

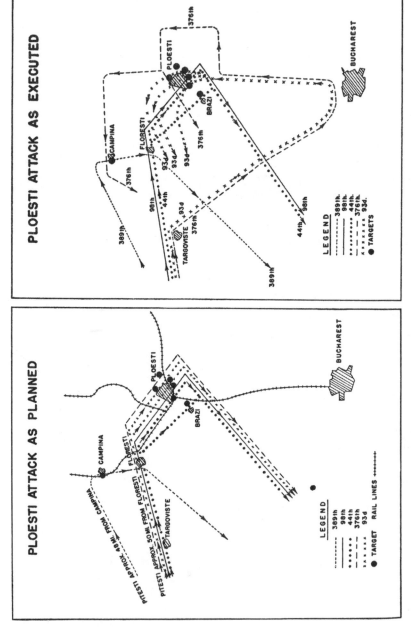

The Attack on Ploesti. From Wesley Craven and James Lea Cate, *The Army Air Forces in World War II*, 7 vols., Volume 2: *Europe: TORCH to POINTBLANK, August 1942 to December 1943*, p. 480.

Turkey. By launching a long-range raid from North Africa, the US-AAF would have to cut bomb payloads in order to carry additional fuel tanks in the bomb bays, and would have to forego fighter escort, which might have dealt successfully with the still small number of Axis fighters deployed in Romania, largely an inactive front for the Luftwaffe. Waiting until the Allies held the bases in Italy would permit escorted attacks with much heavier bomb loads, as demonstrated by the sustained raids in summer 1944 that inflicted such serious damage on the refinery complex that the target was essentially destroyed.

In a second argument to derail the proposal, Portal pointed out that the Allies lacked detailed weather information over the Balkans. This deficiency would have a significant impact on the 1 August 1943 raid in both the planning and execution stages. The first raid on Ploesti—the HALPRO raid in June 1942—had been foiled by clouds over the target, causing the bombers to dump their bombs blindly or on alternate targets, such as the Black Sea port of Constanta. As a result, planners argued for a low-level attack in 1943 in order to evade German radar detection that would alert the defenders and slip below any clouds that might obscure the target from high-altitude bombers, but weather still conspired to defeat the purpose. As the bombers approached the Adriatic coast, towering clouds obscured the Yugoslavian mountains that the bombers would have to cross in order to reach Romania, forcing the formation to climb above the clouds and reveal itself to Axis radar stations in the area. By the time the bombers reached Ploesti, defenders were fully alerted and waiting to meet them. Weather also contributed to the scattering of the attack formation by obscuring ground checkpoints, breaking it into two separate groups and preventing the single coordinated attack the planners envisioned that might have temporarily overwhelmed the defenders' capabilities.

Portal's final objection centered on the potential impact on the invasion of Sicily. He inveighed, "The value of attacks on German oil had to be balanced against the needs of HUSKY." In this line of argument he was slightly more successful, as he succeeded in delaying the raid from its initial date in early June until early August, saving two months in which the bombers could be used to support the softening-up period and the invasion itself. Unfortunately, the raid still occurred during the latter stages of the invasion and just before the Axis evacuation, preventing the participating bombers from being used to oppose it. General George Marshall "emphasized the importance of making great efforts against German oil if we could be sure that it formed a really critical target." As current intelligence data revealed that Ploesti was then supplying 33 percent of Germany's oil, the committee believed that Marshall's criteria had been met and concluded the meeting by recommending that "attacks should be undertaken as soon as other commitments allow."[4]

With a clear mandate to conduct the attack, Arnold then turned over planning to one of the members of his inner circle at USAAF Headquarters in Washington. Colonel Jacob Smart received the assignment and immediately set out to make the single attack as successful as possible. Smart had graduated from West Point in 1931 and spent the remainder of the interwar years in flight training, as a pursuit pilot in a squadron charged with defending the Panama Canal, and as a flight instructor. Shortly after the war began, he was ordered to Washington to help with the massive expansion of the USAAF's training program. A biographer found, "In these endeavors he competed with both the Army and the Navy, which required the same aluminum, steel, and production capacity to build their respective tactical units."[5] As a reward for Smart's successful work in this area, in July 1942 Arnold assigned him to his Air Corps Advisory Council, a sort of brain trust that would help Arnold manage the myriad details involved in building and employing the nation's air forces. In the performance of his duties, he allegedly found "it was also imperative to keep the service's best interest and potential growth in mind."[6] Smart was not the only member of the air staff to view weapons procurement as an interservice competition for resources. In September 1942, Laurence Kuter wrote Spaatz to complain of the ground and naval forces plans to "continue to build phenomenal numbers of light, medium and heavy tanks and big, beautiful battleships. . . . It is clear we cannot build the AWPD-42 program (nor the AWPD-1 program) and at the same time build unlimited quantities of Monitors and Merrimacs [sic] or infinite quantities of the shields, spears and chariots that are listed in the Leavenworth reference data."[7]

Shortly after being tasked with leading the planning effort for the Ploesti strikes, Smart seized on an idea that he believed would enable the bombers to achieve maximum effectiveness with a single strike, negating the requirement for follow-up missions. Realizing that any error in accuracy was magnified as the altitude above the target increased, Smart suggested that the bombers strike at a minimum altitude, both to ensure the element of surprise and to guarantee that the bombs fell precisely on the targets. Low-altitude attacks would have the additional advantages of minimizing the effects of weather that might obscure the target from higher altitudes and fighter interception, as the bombers' crews would have to fend off attacks from one-half of the normal sphere around the aircraft.[8] As no attacks could be expected from below, maintainers could modify the B-24s (at an additional cost of time) by removing the turret on the bottom of the aircraft, saving weight that could be used to extend range. Unfortunately, attacking at low levels also significantly increased the aircrafts' susceptibility to ground fire, which contributed to the majority of the casualties on the raid. Low-flying aircraft were in range of even the smallest-caliber antiaircraft weapons that were incapable of reaching heavy bombers at higher altitudes. In addition, the advantage of lower altitudes for bombing accuracy also worked in the gunners' favor. Any errors in aim at high-altitude targets would be negated by low-flying aircraft, which the gunners could attack at almost point-blank range. These factors were well known to airmen in both the United Kingdom and North Africa who had tried and abandoned low-level attacks as too costly.[9]

Unfortunately, Smart's plan carried the blessing of the USAAF's Chief of Staff and, after the May 1943 TRIDENT conference in Washington, that of the Combined Chiefs of Staff as well, making it extremely difficult for the group commanders who would fly the mission, and their local commanders, to oppose what they unanimously agreed was a flawed plan.[10] On 13 May at the Combined Chiefs of Staff's eighty-third meeting, Smart presented his plan for discussion. In supporting the plan, General Joseph McNarney, an air officer who served as Marshall's deputy, argued that the attack "would render any further operations against the refineries unnecessary for a period of some six months." Marshall responded that it appeared to be "well worth the gamble," as the "effective use of air power might enable us to economize in the use of ground forces in the Mediterranean."[11] Marshall's comment revealed a frustration with British proposals, then under discussion, to extend ground operations to Italy after the invasion of Sicily. Marshall believed that Allied ground forces should be withdrawn and shifted to the United Kingdom to begin preparing for the cross-Channel attack in 1944. He apparently seized on the USAAF's willingness to operate against strategic targets in Southern Europe as an opportunity to reverse the operations of the two European theaters. He wanted to make the United Kingdom, which was then an air-only theater, the focus for Allied ground operations, while turning the Mediterranean, where the Allies had made a significant investment in ground forces, into an air-only theater, with sufficient ground troops only to protect the bases. While both theaters remained active in both air and ground operations for the remainder of the war, Marshall largely got his wish, as the primary ground effort had shifted to Northwest Europe by mid-1944.

The Combined Chiefs of Staff again took up the topic at its eighty-seventh meeting on 18 May. McNarney briefed Smart's plan, which envisioned 155 aircraft carrying between 3,000 and 6,000 pounds of bombs each.[12] McNarney opined that the "losses might be heavy, but would be more than offset by results," and he advocated that the attack take place prior to Operation HUSKY for the "morale effect." The raid had little chance to influence the success of HUSKY at that late date, but it might contribute to Soviet successes on the Eastern Front—the destination for the majority of Ploesti's oil and gas. As it was, the Allied invasion of Sicily itself provided a sufficient shock for Hitler to halt his only planned offensive for summer 1943, the long-delayed Operation ZITADELLE, which resulted in the Battle of Kursk, and shift some of his most capable units to southern Europe to watch the situation there.[13] At the 18 May meeting, Portal again reminded the convened group that the "effects on HUSKY must be borne in mind," then solicited the commander's views "in light of the necessity for concentrating our air resources in support of HUSKY." Sir Alan Brooke, chief of the Imperial General Staff, supported Portal and "stressed the disadvantage of the dispersal of our air forces prior to HUSKY." For the second time, Portal succeeded in delaying the attack until after the success of the landing had been assured, but the committee did approve Smart's plan for the strike.[14]

Armed with these assurances, Smart left for England, where three of the five groups that would participate in the raid were already assembled. They began to practice low-level flights in the ungainly B-24, much to the chagrin of farmers in the English countryside. At the end of June the three groups traveled to North Africa to join the two Ninth Air Force groups then at Benghazi. As usual, the commander of Eighth Air Force, General Ira Eaker, strenuously objected to the move. On 8 June 1943, he wrote Arnold,

> I am greatly disturbed about the diversions which have come up to the Combined Bomber Offensive. The combined Chiefs of Staff have approved it, but there is evidence that the force will be dispersed and we will be prevented from accomplishing it by these continual diversions. The latest concerns the sterilization of our two B-24 groups for SOAPSUDS [an early code-name for the Ploesti raid], and the information we received yesterday that one of our

Heavy Groups due in July [the 389th, also slated for Ploesti] is to be retained in Africa. I imagine you fight these things as hard as you can, but I believe it is only fair for me to state now that if these diversions are to continue it will be impossible to accomplish the result anticipated, simply because the force required will not be furnished.[15]

Eaker still had more than a dozen B-17 groups at the time and remained reluctant to use the B-24 groups in the same formations as B-17s due to different flying characteristics. The loss of the B-24s did not seriously impact the maximum size of a raid he could launch against Germany, although the B-24 groups could have been (and often were) used as diversions to pull German fighters away from the primary formations.

Upon arrival in North Africa, Smart revealed the details of the operational plan and target to the assembled force. Brigadier General Uzal B. Ent, commander of Ninth Air Force Bomber Command and by then a veteran of a number of B-24 missions in North Africa, immediately protested and prepared a second plan for consideration by Ninth Air Force's commander, General Lewis Brereton. Brereton, therefore, had the final authority but chose the plan presented by Smart.[16] But after the raid, Ent wrote to Arnold, "Colonel Smart by his personality and steadfastness of purpose was responsible for the Ploesti attack being made at low level. Almost to a man from the 8th Air Force, North African Air Force to the Ninth Air Force, he was opposed but he stuck to his guns."[17] Brereton's decision would continue a string of questionable judgment calls throughout his career. In December 1941, he had been responsible for the air defense of the Philippines but had allowed most of his fighters and bombers to be destroyed on the ground, largely as a result of squabbling with General Douglas MacArthur's chief of staff. After arriving in the Middle East from Asia in June 1942, he assumed command of Ninth Air Force from his headquarters in Cairo, but during the campaign in the Western Desert he was personally admonished by General Marshall. On 14 September 1942, the Army Chief of Staff wrote Brereton that "information, official and otherwise, reached me indicating that your relations with your secretary have given rise to facetious and derogatory gossip in India and Egypt. . . . I wish you to release your secretary and if practicable see that she returns to her permanent residence. You will not permit members of your command to have their women secretaries accompany them on their official trips."[18]

Once ordered to execute the low-level attack, Ent and his five group commanders buried their opposition and put their full energies into making the mission a success. During an intensive, ten-day training period in late July, the B-24s honed their low-flying skills and demonstrated, on a mock target constructed in the Libyan desert, that they were capable of executing the attack with pinpoint precision. Unfortunately, while the mock target was perfectly visible in the clear desert skies and undefended, far different conditions prevailed when the bombers arrived at their target in Romania.

The bombers launched from their bases around Benghazi in the early morning hours of 1 August. With a minimum of fourteen hours of flying ahead of them, the crews would not return to North Africa until late in the evening. One aircraft lost an engine on takeoff, a not-uncommon occurrence on the desert fields where sand and dust cut the service lives of engines by well over half, and the heavily laden bomber crashed while attempting to return to base. Another aircraft inexplicably spun into the Mediterranean off the coast of Corfu, and several others experienced mechanical difficulties and peeled off of the formation as well. On making landfall, the bombers encountered thunderstorms and climbed over them, providing the Axis defenders at Ploesti confirmation of the formation's route and destination. (The launch had already been reported by radio operators in Greece who had broken Allied codes, eliminating the element of surprise.)[19] When the bombers reassembled on the other side of the storms, the formation had been split into two elements. The first two groups, the 376th and 93rd Bomb Groups, were now almost sixty miles ahead of the other three. But upon approaching their initial point on the bomb run, the two lead groups made a navigational error and turned short of their target. This put them on a course directly toward Bucharest, southeast of Ploesti. They did not realize the error until they approached the capital's outskirts and then made a belated turn north toward Ploesti. As they were now attacking in a direction directly opposite to that which had been briefed, the crews in the first two groups were largely unable to identify their assigned targets and delivered their bombs onto refineries assigned to the trailing three groups. (See map on page 170.)

These three, the 98th, 44th, and 389th Bomb Groups, were now led by the 98th's commander, Colonel John R. Kane, who had earned the nickname "Killer" for his fierce demeanor. Kane's formations attacked almost exactly as planned and inflicted the heaviest damage of the raid. Unfortunately, their efforts were complicated by the earlier attacks of the two wayward groups, which not only had fully alerted the defenders but also had dropped delayed-action bombs in the targets, which began to explode as the second wave arrived at their targets. Smoke was so heavy that Kane initially thought a thunderstorm was obscuring the area. Despite these obstacles, Kane and Colonel Leon Johnson, commanding 44th Bomb Group, brought their bombers directly into the target area. Both men were later awarded the Medal of Honor for their efforts.[20] The War Department awarded a total of five such medals for the raid, and every airman, save one, participating in the mission earned a Distinguished Flying Cross.[21]

Flak, fighters, and barrage balloons in the target area took a heavy toll, claiming an estimated twenty-one bombers. A number of the survivors were heavily damaged and had lost crewmembers who would have manned the defensive guns, making them more susceptible to fighter interception. Bombers leaving the target headed for the nearest friendly territory and wound up being scattered across the Mediterranean from Sicily to Cyprus. German fighters based in Greece intercepted those bombers that set a course directly for Benghazi and shot down four more. Kane's aircraft was damaged beyond repair in a crash-landing on Cyprus, although the crew escaped injury. When he returned to Benghazi a few days later, Kane found seventeen aircraft on his group's strength report, but only three were fit to fly a combat mission.[22] Kane later recalled, "One of the few times I ever cried in my adult life was after that mission. I cried because of all the fine men we lost that day and wondered if their sacrifice had been worth it."[23] In ten missions during the month of July, 98th Bomb Group averaged twenty-eight aircraft per mission. After the Ploesti mission on 1 August, in which the group lost twenty-six of the thirty-one planes that reached the target, the group did not fly again until 13 August, and then put up only six planes. For the rest of the month, the group averaged only seventeen planes per mission. One survey found that "the loss of many crews and aircraft was a staggering blow to the Group and had a decided effect on the morale of the men."[24]

Of the 532 highly skilled aircrew who failed to return from the mission, a postwar accounting found that 330 of them were killed, more than 100 were prisoners in Romania, and another seventy were temporarily interned in Turkey. Another study concluded that TIDALWAVE (the final code-name for the Ploesti operation) "was the end of the Ninth Air Force as a heavy bomber command."[25] In its entire operational period before the raid (the thirteen months between June 1942 and July 1943), Ninth Air Force had lost forty-four heavy bombers while flying 4,869 operational sorties. On 1 August 1943, on a single raid of 178 sorties, the Ninth's heavies, including those attached from Eighth Air Force, lost fifty-three bombers—more than in the entire previous period combined.[26]

After the raid, Colonel Smart was called back to Washington and testified on the raid's effectiveness before the Joint Chiefs of Staff at the QUADRANT conference in Quebec. On 16 August he described the damage reported by the crews flying the mission and testified that "early reports indicate that destruction there has resulted in a 70% reduction in output," and that a follow-up attack was not required.[27] In reality, the planned follow-on missions had been "postponed in favor of direct support to the coming operations in Italy" on Air Chief Marshall Tedder's orders.[28] But based on Smart's assessment, the Joint Chiefs recommended that the additional B-24s dispatched from Eighth Air Force be returned, as they believed their assigned mission was complete, despite Eisenhower's efforts to retain them in the Mediterranean to support the upcoming invasion of Italy.

Damage assessments completed immediately after the raid by RAF photo-reconnaissance *Mosquitoes* of the Northwest African Photographic Reconnaissance Wing provided the first poststrike assessments, but these were incomplete. Two refineries, the large Romano-Americana and the Unirea, had escaped damage altogether. Another facility, the Concordia Vega, sustained only minor damage and was actually exceeding its prestrike production in a month's time. Of the five refineries that sustained heavy damage, only one did not resume production for the remainder of the war, while another two were out five and eleven months, respectively. Two others suffered less severe damage, as the Astra-Romana had several storage tanks destroyed and lost a distillation plant, while Phoenix Orion also lost several storage tanks and had its boiler damaged. Further photo-reconnaissance on 19 August revealed that an older distillation plant at the Astra-Romana plant had already been brought back online, enabling production to resume at that facility.[29] (See Table 6.1.)

Back in the United Kingdom, General Ira Eaker, who to his credit had launched a last-ditch effort to stop the raid but was overruled by Eisenhower, was upset with both the heavy losses his forces sustained in the raid and the fact that they had not received any of the credit in the early press reports. On 3 August he wrote Spaatz:

> This is Tuesday and we still have no report from General Brereton on the work of our groups on Ploesti, or as to the losses our groups sustained in the operation . . . no mention was made of the fact, nor

Table 6.1: Results of the Ploesti Mission*

Target Designation	Refinery	Estimated Capacity (Tons)	A/C- Unit Assigned	Units Bombed	Damage	Losses
White I	Romana Americana	1,170,000	28-376th	None	Undamaged	3-376th
White II	Concordia Vega	1,450,000	21-93rd	376th-6 a/c	Out 1 month	13-93rd
White III	Standard Petrol/ Unirea Sperantza	485,000 440,000	18-93rd "	None "	Undamaged "	
White IV	Astra Romana/ Phoenix Orion	1,750,000 730,000	48-98th "	93rd/98th	Out 1 month "	20-98th
White V	Colombia Aquila	535,000	16-44th	93rd/44th	Out 11 mos.	9-44th
Blue	Creditul Minier-Brazi	535,000	21-44th	44th	Destroyed	2-44th
Red	Steaua Romana-Campina	1,500,000	26-389th	376th/389th	Out 5 mos.	6-398th
Totals		8,595,000	178 (163 reached target)			53 a/c (532 crewmembers)

*Data compiled from several sources, including "A Report on Battle Damage and A/C Losses for the Mission of 1 August 1943 Against the Roumanian Oil Refinery Installations," Report No. 10, 17 August 1943; IX Bomber Command, Operations Analysis Section, AF-HRA 533.04, Maxwell AFB, AL; Earl Cruickshank, *The Ploesti Mission of 1 August 1943*, Historical Study No. 103 (Maxwell AFB, AL: USAAF Historical Division, 1944); James Dugan and Carroll Stewart, *Ploesti: The Great Ground-Air Battle of 1 August 1943* (New York: Random House, 1962); Leroy Newby, *Into the Guns of Ploesti* (Osceola, WI: Motorbooks, 1991); and report, "Monthly Crude Through-put of Principal Ploesti Refineries," in Folder "Ploesti (1)," Box 19, Norstad Papers, Eisenhower Library, Abilene, KS, all of which disagree to some extent. Author has made the best estimate based on the reliability of the various sources.

has there been any since that our groups had a large share in the undertaking. The present reports indicate the losses were pretty high. I am concerned to know what the status of our groups is and whether they would be in good shape to go forward.[30]

When his forces finally returned, Eaker compiled a complete report on his air force's contribution to the Ploesti mission and other operations in the Mediterranean. In their two months in North Africa, his three groups had lost sixty-nine aircraft and 499 airmen. Of the 144 aircraft dispatched in late June, he received only fifty-eight back, while an additional seventeen remained in North Africa awaiting repair. Eaker complained of the Combined Chiefs of Staff, "They approved our Combined Bomber offensive and they are rapidly making it impossible for us to accomplish it by taking our forces away from us. We lost one-third of our present operational strength on [Ploesti]."[31]

Early on-the-ground intelligence reports seemed to confirm Smart's optimism about the raid's success. A 4 September report from the U.S. Office of Strategic Services in London announced a 50 percent production drop at Ploesti. A more detailed report issued later that week found that production for August decreased between 120,000 to 150,000 tons, "nearly 30% of up to now monthly quantity of refined oil." The report optimistically suggested that it would take eight months to repair all damage and achieve the original level of production. Damage estimates might have been deliberately inflated by Axis agents hoping to spare further attacks on the facility. As it was, much of the damage had been repaired, except at the two surplus facilities that were written off, and production had already reached prestrike levels. But the Allies, convinced of the raid's efficacy, left the facilities off target lists for another seven months.[32]

An even more detailed report on 29 September revealed that the rail damage had been relatively light, resulting in a minor interruption of service, but provided greater detail about each refinery targeted. It judged three refineries as "offline for a considerable time": the Creditul-Minier facility at Brazi (540,000 tons), the Steaua Romana at Campini (1,240,000 tons), and the Colombia Aquila (540,000 tons) in Ploesti proper, one of the smaller facilities of the eight there. The report elaborated, "This loss may appear serious but not dangerous since refining capacity was double the actual production. Against the refining capacity of 11,000,000 tons, crude production was 5,485,000 in 1941 and 5,649,560 in 1942, thus one half of the refining capacity remains unused." The report indicated that the Romanian government had temporarily prohibited the export of petroleum products except gasoline and crude and, as of 16 September, was "making every effort to recondition petroleum refineries which had been damaged and also those who had been previously abandoned."

By mid-January 1944, intelligence estimates were already advocating for a return to Ploesti combined with additional attacks on other refineries to prevent crude from being transferred there for processing. The assessment advocated

> further attack on the refineries at Ploesti calculated to destroy refining capacity of five million tons a year. The relation of refining capacity to available crude at Ploesti is such that this would not result in a reduction in the amount of *production* [emphasis in original]. It is estimated by the Enemy Oil Committee that, if this destruction of capacity at Ploesti could be effected and could be followed by later attacks on certain Italian and North German refineries to prevent the crude at Ploesti being transferred to Italy or North Germany for treatment, Germany would be deprived of approximately one and one half million tons of refined petroleum products during the ensuing six month period.

But the effects would not be instantaneous: "The experts of the enemy Oil Committee estimated, taking into account stock piles and other factors, that the effect of this curtailment of production would begin to make itself felt in actual consumption after a period of about five months from the completion of the destruction at Ploesti." This forecast proved to be quite accurate. The German petroleum situation deteriorated rapidly around the beginning of 1945, an effect often attributed to Spaatz's "Oil Plan," which targeted Germany's synthetic petroleum plants, but also coinciding almost exactly with the elapsed five months after the sustained attacks against Ploesti in summer 1944 that culminated with the Soviet occupation of Romania in late August. There is no doubt that the two events combined to stretch the German oil position past the breaking point, but there is some disagreement on which of the two made the larger contribution.[33]

In April 1944, the RAF's weekly intelligence summary admitted,

> The enemy's liquid fuel supplies did not suffer in the second half of 1943 from any major interruption by bombing. The attack on Ploesti by American heavy bombers at the beginning of August put out of action some of the most efficient units of the Romanian re-

fining industry, but did not reduce total throughput capacity below the current level of crude output. . . . Shipment of crude oil
to refineries outside Romania has helped to tide over an awkward
situation.[34]

Allied bombers based in Italy returned to Ploesti later that month to
finish the job. Between April and August 1944, the newly established
Fifteenth Air Force flew more than twenty separate missions, totaling
5,479 heavy bomber sorties, against Ploesti and inflicted heavy damage on the refineries, reducing the output to less that 20 percent of
capacity. These raids cost the Allies an additional 300 planes and almost 3,000 airmen.[35] More than 1,000 of them were eventually repa-
triated, along with more than a hundred survivors of the 1 August 1943
mission, when Romania left the Axis in August 1944. But "many vital
parts of all refineries were still standing at Ploesti when the Germans
were driven north." Intelligence experts believed "the only way to
keep the Hun from using what he needs is to keep bombing it," demonstrating the sustained nature of attacks required to render a target
impotent if it is impossible to physically occupy it by seizing it with
ground forces.[36]

Had the raid succeeded in accomplishing its objective, the cost
might have been worth it. In fact, the Ninth Air Force's commander,
General Louis Brereton, told the crews the night before the mission
that if they destroyed the target but lost the entire force the mission
would be considered a success.[37] But they did not, due to a series of
errors, including a poor plan authored by a staff officer with no combat experience, and faulty execution by one of the group commanders
flying the mission. Despite putting a large number of bombs on several of the targets, the airmen succeeded in damaging less than half of
the refineries' productive output. Worse, because there was a much
greater refining capacity than available crude, the losses had almost no
effect on the Axis war effort. German engineers and forced laborers
quickly repaired damaged facilities, returned idled plants to production, and shifted crude to undamaged facilities, allowing a return to
full production in little more than a month. In the interim, the Axis
shipped excess crude to other refineries elsewhere in Europe, minimizing even the temporary production losses. As a result of the ill-
conceived raid, the USAAF lost the services of a significant portion of
its combat strength in the theater during the vital stages of the battle
for Sicily for very little to no gain. The 1 August 1943 raid on Ploesti,

while a worthy target and technically within the USAAF's capabilities, was poorly timed and poorly executed. The bombers likely could have been used to greater effect in a sustained campaign to prevent the evacuation of Sicily and to prepare for the landings on the Italian mainland the following month, which would lead directly to the capture of airfields that could be (and were) used to put the target out of commission permanently.

Salerno

The effective loss of Ninth Air Force's heavy bomber force at Ploesti left Twelfth Air Force's four groups of B-17s with the full responsibility for supporting the Allied landings in Italy. Unlike the invasion of Sicily, when the Allied air forces had two full months after the fall of Tunisia to prepare for the landings, less than three weeks elapsed between the end of resistance on Sicily and the main landings at Salerno. This was insufficient time for a sustained air campaign, even if the full heavy bomber force had been available. But Twelfth Air Force's four B-17 groups were falling below strength, partly because of a push to replace Eighth Air Force's losses after the disastrous Schweinfurt-Regensburg raids of 17 August. In early September, Arnold visited Eighth Air Force and immediately cabled Marshall for replacements. He wrote, "The total number of B17's in the 8th Air Force is less than the total number in the month of July and not sufficient to maintain operations of past strength." He believed that the Eighth's heavy bomber groups required an additional 200 B-17s, above the 217 they were scheduled to receive in September, because "the battle losses, battle damage and operational losses to the heavy Bombers have cut down [the] number available to the organized units so that they can not even approximate a total of 35 planes per group ready for service."[38] The trip did, at least, finally convince Arnold of the need for long-range fighters. He wrote Marshall, "Operations over Germany conducted here during the past several weeks indicate definitely that we must provide long range fighters to accompany the daylight bombardment missions."[39] Leaders in Twelfth Air Force had been aware of this requirement for months, but it took the heavy losses of the 17 August raids to finally convince USAAF leadership. Only a month earlier, Arnold had written Eaker and suggested that his high losses to enemy fighters were because the bomber "formation is so dispersed that it affords very little opportunity for mutual protection in warding off enemy aerial attack."[40] Arnold was still convinced that tighter defensive formations and more and better defensive armament would enable bombers to fight their way through to targets, although he did propose building up an escort arm to deal with "long range firing, the overhead bombing and other forms of attack outside of [the] reach of the .50 caliber guns installed in bombers."[41]

With only a fraction of the force available in the United Kingdom, Spaatz's headquarters outlined the following objectives for the Northwest African Air Force's support of the landings on the Italian mainland: neutralize enemy air forces by air bombardment; provide air cover for convoys and invasion beaches; isolate the battlefield from enemy reinforcements; transport and drop the airborne forces; and support Operation BAYTOWN (the British landing across the Strait of Messina).[42] The NAAF estimated that it would have 346 heavy bombers available to fulfill these tasks, a number that included the two groups of Ninth Air Force. Even though the tactical air force's fighters had been rapidly moved up to the captured airfields on Sicily, the Salerno beaches were still at the extreme edge of their operating range. Only the strategic air force's P-38 escorts, as well as NATAF's A-36s and *Spitfires* equipped with drop tanks, could operate for any length of time over the beaches, making the longer-range medium and heavy bombers comparatively more valuable and important. (See map on page 185.)

Eisenhower recognized that the rush to take advantage of a possible Italian surrender was compressing his timeline to prepare for an invasion properly. Without additional time to conduct a preparatory air campaign, he instead sought to augment his bomber force to achieve maximum results in the short time available. On 12 August he cabled the American Joint Chiefs of Staff:

> In view of the critical situation in Italy, we consider that the B-24 force which carried out the attack on TIDALWAVE [Ploesti] and which is now awaiting suitable weather conditions for attack on JUGGLER [the aircraft factories at Wiener-Neustadt, Austria] coordinated with B-17 force from 8th Bomber Command should, immediately on completion of JUGGLER, be concentrated on targets in Italy. We consider that at this juncture every available force should be brought to bear against Italy and the German in Italy. Once we are established in Italy follow up attacks on TIDALWAVE will from every point of view be easier to carry out than they now are from African bases.[43]

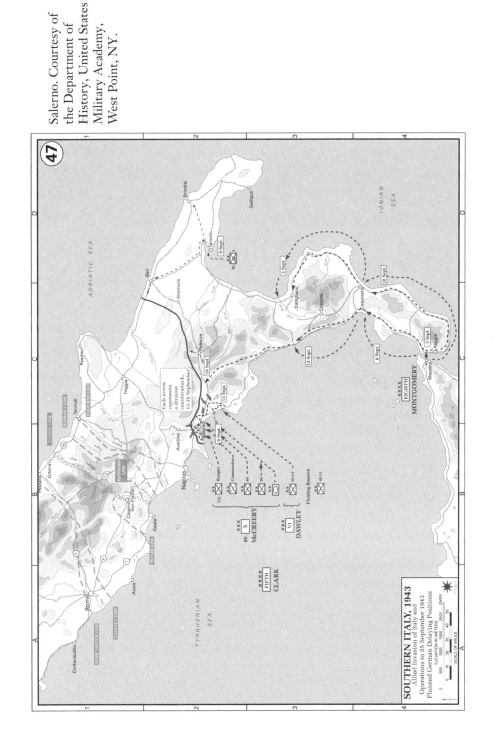

Salerno. Courtesy of the Department of History, United States Military Academy, West Point, NY.

Eisenhower's point about follow-on attacks was entirely accurate. From the heel of Italy, heavy bombers could reach Ploesti with a full bomb load and a fighter escort, greatly reducing the high casualties suffered in the long-range raid from Libya. The air force would be best served in the long run by fully supporting the ground and naval forces that would seize one of their most valuable base areas of the entire war. But the Combined Chiefs of Staff again denied Eisenhower's request, and afterward the U.S. Air Force's official history of the war opined, "This request of Eisenhower's raised a knotty question of priority in which the immediate requirements of a critical tactical situation almost prevailed over the less dramatic needs of strategic bombardment."[44]

As it was, the invasion almost failed and was the closest the Allies came to being hurled back into the sea in a major amphibious assault. The inadequate air preparation contributed substantially to this situation but also provided some relief. Resurgent Luftwaffe forces scored a number of hits on the invasion fleet, enjoying particular success with the new radio-guided glide bombs, but were unable to halt the invasion or disperse the fleet. On this point the navy again disagreed, arguing that the attacks were highly disruptive, but the buildup ashore proceeded on schedule.[45] Opposite the beachhead, German divisions that had escaped from Sicily, including the 15th and 29th Panzergrenadier and the Luftwaffe's Hermann Goering and 1st Fallschirmjaeger (Parachute) Divisions, concentrated quickly against the bridgehead and delivered a near-fatal counterattack. Air attacks had slowed the concentration, delaying its arrival and reducing its impact, but they were unable to prevent it.

As a result, Eisenhower ordered the NAAF to again divert its heavy bombers from interdiction targets farther up the boot to direct battlefield support. Heavy raids on 14 September, including 170 by B-17s and 300-plus by the medium bombers, broke up German assembly areas and took the steam out of the counterattacks. Eisenhower later recalled, "This great air attack was delivered with precision and effectiveness on the morning of the fourteenth. So badly did it disrupt the enemy's communications, supplies, and mobility that, with the aid of naval gunfire, the ground troops regained the initiative and thereafter German counterattacks were never in sufficient strength to threaten our general position."[46] But it would be wrong to give air most of the credit for the repulse. The ground troops that actually did the fighting and the extremely accurate naval gunfire were equally important.

Salerno again demonstrated what was possible when all elements worked together as part of the joint team.[47]

Eisenhower's deputy ground commander, Sir Harold Alexander, expressed his appreciation for the air effort in a letter to Spaatz on 17 September. He wrote, "Not only have your tremendous air attacks added greatly to the morale of the ground and naval forces but, in addition, have inflicted on the enemy heavy losses in men and equipment. They have seriously interfered with his movements, interrupted his communications and prevented his concentration of the necessary forces to launch large-scale attacks. You have contributed immeasurably to the success of our operations." During the invasion period, the NAAF flew 4,014 sorties, dropping 3,822 tons of bombs, but NAAF's most effective weapon—the heavy bomber—flew only 407 of these sorties and dropped only 852 tons, less than one-fourth of the total.[48] Still, the effect in the immediate battle area was tremendous. The carpet bombing had placed an estimated 760 tons per square mile on the German counterattack and played an important role in the battle.[49]

As the "number of troops available to man the long front was . . . dangerously small," Allied planners had also ordered an airborne mission to reinforce the beachhead.[50] Only the paratroopers of the 82nd Airborne Division could arrive in time to influence the battle, as seaborne troops would take days to reach the lines and all available shipping was already in use unloading and supporting the divisions that were already ashore. On the night of 13 September, less than twelve hours after receiving notification, the 52nd Troop Carrier Wing dropped more than 1,000 troops of the 504th Parachute Infantry Regiment, with no loss of aircraft. Most of the men were assembled on the front lines before dawn. The next night 125 C-47s inserted another 2,000 men of the 505th Parachute Infantry Regiment into the battle, again with no losses. Unlike the Sicilian operation two months earlier, both missions were highlighted by accurate drops and minimal casualties from friendly ground fire, thanks largely to the development of radar beacons employed by pathfinders, who directed the formations to the drop zones, and ingress patterns that avoided the concentration of naval vessels offshore. After the crisis had passed, the men of 82nd Airborne led the breakout from the beachhead with an assault on Altavilla on 16 September.[51]

With Ninth Air Force's two B-24 groups still understrength as a result of the Ploesti mission, and with his ground forces meeting heavy German opposition in Italy, Eisenhower finally received reinforcements from Eighth Air Force in the United Kingdom. From 16 September until 4 October 1943, the three Eighth Air Force B-24 groups that had participated in the Ploesti mission returned to North Africa to augment the heavy bomber force there. But the eighty-four bombers (twenty-eight each from the 44th, 93rd, and 389th Bomb Groups) were too late to participate in the battle at Salerno. Instead, they flew only three missions, a 21 September raid on the docks at Leghorn, a 24 September attack on the rail yards at Pisa, which was aborted due to weather, and a 1 October attack on the Messerschmitt factory at Wiener-Neustadt, Austria, which cost fourteen bombers lost and another fifty-two damaged. At the end of the three-week sojourn, only sixty-three of the original eighty-four aircraft returned to the United Kingdom from North Africa, further increasing Eaker's ire at the repeated diversions.[52] During November and December 1943, the two remaining Ninth Air Force B-24 groups in the Mediterranean (the 98th and 376th) suffered a loss rate three times higher than that of Twelfth Air Force's B-17s, possibly a result of the loss of experienced crews after Ploesti.[53]

In less than a month after the landings at Salerno, the U.S. Fifth Army had taken the important port of Naples, while the British Eighth Army liberated the airfield complex around Foggia. While work continued to rehabilitate the logistical base and develop the airfields, the Allies had gained important ground that would play a major role in the developing air campaign.[54] Between early October, when British forces liberated the Foggia area, and late December, when the heavy bomber squadrons finally moved onto the continent, the USAAF built forty-five airfields despite severe shortages in equipment and supplies and the ever-present Italian mud. At the same time, engineers built a pipeline capable of providing 160,000 gallons of 100-octane aviation fuel per week. They also rehabilitated roads and rail lines while transportation companies labored to ensure that bombs and bullets arrived in time to equip the next mission. All of this was a well-choreographed ballet that overcame the countless instances of fog and friction inhibiting the Allied effort.[55] By 1945, the USAAF was much more enthusiastic about the invasion of southern Italy and Fifteenth Air Force's contribution to the war effort from the bases established there. In the service's annual report, it gushed, "The capture of the air bases on the plains of Foggia in the early stages of the Italian campaign may go down in military annals as one of the keys to the liberation of Europe."[56]

Epilogue: Fifteenth Air Force

Allied leadership had long been interested in the possibility of air bases on the Italian boot, largely as a means to defeat the poor winter weather in the United Kingdom, which had held up the Combined Bomber Offensive during the winter of 1942–1943. Eisenhower had recognized this limitation after his first four months in the United Kingdom. On 29 October 1942, he wrote Marshall, "The one great weakness of daylight precision bombing is its dependency upon excellent weather, which must be continuous, vertically over the target, to great heights. Time after time we have been disappointed in this regard and it is obvious that more than one practicable base should be available to a bomber force."[57] In May 1943, Tedder gave Eisenhower a lengthier substantiation:

> The establishment of air bases in central Italy would bring within range of our heavy bombers the main Axis industrial centres in southern Germany, etc., also the Roumanian oil fields. This is true, but the main advantage of using Italy as a base is omitted. The main value of such an air base is that heavy bomber attacks on the majority of the most vital centres in Germany, and other Axis countries, pass through routes which completely evade the great belt of fighter and AA defenses which Germany has set up along the whole North and North Western approaches. These defenses are exacting an increasing toll on our bomber offensive. It would be quite impossible from every point of view for the enemy to create a similar organization covering the southern approach, and a bomber offensive directed from the South, especially when co-ordinated with that of U.K. would have enormously increased material and moral effects.[58]

The wisdom of maintaining the air offensive from the hard-won fields in southern Italy was also becoming apparent at the highest level of the USAAF. General Carl Spaatz had been an early advocate of the endeavor, reporting in his diary that at a 1 June 1943 meeting with British prime minister Winston Churchill, chief of the Imperial Staff Sir Alan Brooke, and General George Marshall at the heavy bomber base at Chateau d'un, Tunisia, he "emphasized the necessity for using North Italy as a base for air operations against Germany."[59] On 30 July, Spaatz had written Arnold, "If operations are to continue in this theater to include heavy bomber bases in Italy, I believe that consideration should be given to the possibility of increasing considerably the number of heavy groups operating here. . . . Though weather conditions will be the same over the target area, the frequency of operations will be greater from bases in Italy than from the U.K."[60]

On 14 August, Arnold replied, "Let me again refer to the matter of a planned and sustained strategic bombing attack on German key industrial targets from Mediterranean bases. The cumulative effect of this program both upon the enemy's ability to resist and his will to resist will be severe and would appear to justify this type of bomber effort as being rated a #1 priority." Arnold also reported that his efforts to pry the heavy bombers away from the ground campaign were beginning to bear fruit. On 1 August he wrote Spaatz, "I feel that you will be pleased to learn that the Plans Division has prepared a complete paper which may result in a CCS directive to you to place your longer range elements in the combined bomber offensive on the same basis that Ira's forces are employed."[61] But, after seeing the plan, Spaatz had reservations. On 30 August, he wrote Arnold that he had met with General Doolittle, who had a letter from General Hoyt Vandenberg outlining an overall command for both the Mediterranean and the United Kingdom but that he could not "agree wholeheartedly with [the] proposed plan because weather conditions make it impossible for the responsibility of coordinating attacks to rest with one man."[62] But Arnold won out, as the Fifteenth Air Force, which absorbed all of the heavy bomber groups from Ninth and Twelfth Air Forces, along with Eighth Air Force would eventually fall under Spaatz's direct command as the U.S. Strategic Air Forces Europe. Spaatz was supposed to cooperate closely with the theater commander, Eisenhower, in support of his objectives, but removing the strategic assets from the theater commander's direct control led to a number of acrimonious debates later in the war, particularly over the theater commander's desire to interdict the Axis road and rail network in advance of the Normandy landings (the "Transportation Plan"), while air leaders preferred to direct their efforts against Axis petroleum refineries and synthetic fuel plants (the "Oil Plan"), which they believed could cause the German economy to collapse. While this debate has received much attention in the annals of the war, the incredible size of the bomber force available by 1944 ensured that both target sets could be attacked successfully.

Sir Charles Portal was another strong supporter of establishing Fifteenth Air Force. At the 106th meeting of the Combined Chiefs of Staff on 14 August, he elaborated on his views: "The key to the situation from the air point of view, would be the placing of strong offensive air forces in Northern Italy. From there all [of southern] Germany would be within comfortable range and above all two of the largest German aircraft factories which between them produced nearly 60% of the German fighters. . . . Ploesti . . . could be attacked at much shorter range from the heel of Italy. . . . To protect their Southern Front against a similar scale of attack to that being made from the U.K. they would require half the fighter forces on the Western Front."[63]

Not surprisingly, Ira Eaker, commander of Eighth Air Force, was one of the chief opponents of the plan to build a heavy bomber force in the Mediterranean. Many of the bombers that would be used to build up Fifteenth Air Force were already allocated to Eaker's force. Having unsuccessfully fought a yearlong battle against diversions from his command, Eaker felt the plans would be a fatal blow to his goal of building up a force large enough to overwhelm German defenders. He outlined a number of his reasons to General Haywood Hansell, one of the architects of the Combined Bomber Offensive (as one of the authors of AWPD-1) and a member of Eaker's staff at the time. He began by noting that 100 percent of the critical targets in Germany, including those in the heavily industrialized Ruhr Valley, were closer to England. In addition, UK-based bombers damaged over Europe could "glide down to the North Sea," where they could be rescued. Damaged bombers based in Italy would be unable to cross the Alps in returning to their bases (Eaker did not explain why the Italy-based bombers could not also turn toward England and be rescued from the North Sea). Eaker also argued that the repair and logistics facilities in England were already well developed, whereas those in Italy, including ports and rail lines, would require extensive rehabilitation.[64]

At the same time, Eaker was advising Hansell to protect these Eight Air Force assets from the new tactical air force then being set up in the United Kingdom. Base overcrowding that threatened to overwhelm the islands as the Allies built up for the cross-Channel attack would have actually provided a justification for basing more bombers in Italy. Eaker summed up his opinion by stating, "There is no question in my mind that all targets in Germany can be more efficiently and economically attacked out of UK bases."[65] But Spaatz disagreed, telling Arnold that the USAAF should add more heavy groups to Italy because "the frequency of operations will be greater from bases in Italy than from the UK."[66] Spaatz estimated that Italy's weather, which he erroneously assumed would approximate that in North Africa, would allow fifteen group missions per month, requiring an increase of 25 percent in the replacement rate for aircrews. Spaatz's assumptions about the Italian weather were not entirely correct, but Fifteenth Air Force did enjoy a higher mission rate than the Eighth during the last years of the war. But Eaker's argument persisted in the postwar official history, which noted that any additional heavy bombers sent to the Mediterranean were "likely to be diverted to purely tactical purposes."[67]

In an ironic twist, Eaker relinquished command of Eighth Air Force in January 1944 and took over the parent command in Italy, the Mediterranean Allied Air Force (MAAF). MAAF's commander, Sir Arthur Tedder, along with Spaatz and most of the other members of Eisenhower's air team, were moving to the United Kingdom to continue to serve as his deputies in that theater. By then, MAAF included, in addition to the British units, the American Twelfth Air Force, with tactical assets, and Fifteenth Air Force, whose establishment Eaker had lobbied so hard to prevent. General Doolittle, who had labored for almost two years commanding the heavy bomber force in the Mediterranean, took over Eaker's post as commander of Eighth Air Force.[68]

As part of the argument for further deployment of heavy bomber groups in Italy, Arnold suggested that they could be used to cut rail lines and "starve to death all of the German Divisions that they could put in the Po Valley."[69] He acknowledged that "success in Tunisia was due in large part to the strategic use of heavy bombers at long range to disrupt the enemy supply system. Medium and short range aircraft at the same time were used with telling effect to destroy enemy aircraft, lines of communication and supplies within the theater." Arnold's views reflect the USAAF's continuing desire to separate the long-range aircraft and direct them against strategic targets while the medium bombers and fighters would be allocated within the theater. But the new interdiction campaign, eventually implemented in 1944 under the code-name Operation STRANGLE, proved to be another case of rhetoric failing to match reality, and the Axis proved much more adept at maintaining supply lines that did not stretch across open expanses of water.

Conclusion

The Army Air Forces flew its last combat missions from North African shores in late 1943. Ninth Air Force transferred most of its assets to Twelfth Air Force and moved to the United Kingdom to serve as headquarters of the tactical air force for the upcoming Normandy invasion, alongside Eighth Air Force, which retained the strategic mission. Twelfth Air Force, shorn of its heavy bombers and their escort fighters, remained in the Mediterranean for the duration of the war as the primary tactical air force and would support two more amphibious assaults: the landings at Anzio in January 1944, and again in southern France in August of that year. A portion of the Twelfth Air Force (XII Tactical Air Command [TAC]—one of the new tactical commands designated to support each numbered army) followed Seventh Army up the Rhône Valley and into Germany, while the remainder of Twelfth Air Force stayed in Italy to support Fifth Army's push across the Apennines and into the Po Valley. Meanwhile, the new Fifteenth Air Force, built up with two more B-17 groups and thirteen additional B-24 groups, waged a strategic campaign against Axis-occupied Europe from the south.

After a rapid advance across North Africa and onto the European continent, Allied ground forces in the Mediterranean were unable to duplicate that remarkable success for the remainder of the war. Despite converging on the toe of Italy from Morocco and Egypt in only ten months, it took another nine to reach Rome, and ten more to break into the Po Valley. Several factors conspired to slow Allied success in Italy. First, many assets, including the most experienced ground troops, left for the United Kingdom. With them went the most capable and experienced Allied leaders. Eisenhower, Montgomery, Bradley, Patton, Tedder, Spaatz, and Doolittle would direct the remainder of the war from Northwest Europe. Second, geography no longer favored the Allies, as it had in North Africa: Instead of a tenuous supply line stretched across the middle sea, the Germans could fall back on road and rail lines that were easier to protect and less susceptible to interdiction. Mountainous terrain offered the Allies few opportunities for the flank attacks they had employed in the desert while affording the defenders a number of strong defensive lines. While these lines could be outflanked by amphibious attacks, the shortage of landing craft gave the Allies only one chance to execute this strategy, and the January 1944 landing at Anzio was easily contained for four months by the Germans. A third factor, and one more difficult to prove, is the division of air assets into tactical and strategic air forces. Allied airmen attempted to segregate their most capable assets in a separate organization, intending to use Twelfth Air Force to support ground forces while the Fifteenth waged a strategic campaign. The result was that fewer heavy bombers and their escorts, which doubled as effective fighter-bombers, were directly available to support the Allied ground troops remaining in Italy. Despite an excellent record in North Africa, the Army Air Forces had achieved a separation that would endure for decades in the postwar United States Air Force. From 1947 until 1991, the USAF maintained two distinct air commands: Tactical Air Command (TAC) assigned to support ground forces; and the Strategic Air Command (SAC), which performed the strategic bombardment mission. The separation occurred under Spaatz's leadership as the U.S. Air Force's first Chief of Staff and, apparently, at his direction.[70] Only in 1991, with the formation of Air Combat Command, did the air force acknowledge the error of this segregation and recombine the two commands into the single, integrated command that they had employed throughout the North African campaign.

Conclusion

The operations launched on Africa's northern shores demonstrated that warfare in the third dimension had the potential to decisively influence the outcome of conflicts on the surface. In subsequent campaigns of World War II, airmen continued to accelerate the advance of ground and naval forces but at the same time insisted on testing their ideas about the strategic potential of the airplane. Firmly wedded to the recent theories of air warfare offered by Douhet, Mitchell, and de Seversky, among others, they often ignored competing ideas, including those offered by a British naval theorist but applicable to war in the air. Ironically, Sir Julian Corbett's musings on naval warfare, recorded at the conclusion of World War I, more closely approximated the way airplanes would be used in the coming conflict. The air war over the Mediterranean offered a strong case for how aircraft might be effectively employed, one that remains underappreciated by modern practitioners.

The situation facing the USAAF's senior leadership in early 1942 did not correspond with that of either the war planners during the interwar period or the authors of the service's Air War Planning Documents. Airmen wanted to conduct a strategic air campaign against Germany but lacked the forces necessary to carry out that campaign and to test their theory that air forces alone could win wars. Instead, a service equipped largely with pursuit fighters and medium bombers was stretched by calls for assistance from around the globe. The British request in the Middle East was the first the service was able to answer with anything close to what prewar planners had envisioned. In the period before the El Alamein battle, a composite wing of four groups, one each of pursuit and medium bombers and two of heavy bombers, arrived in the Levant and participated in the battle to save Egypt and the Suez Canal. After almost squandering one of these groups, the Halverson Provisional detachment, in an abortive raid on the oil refineries near Ploesti, Romania, the USAAF settled into a campaign of interdiction and close support that materially aided the British ground and naval forces in the eastern Mediterranean, pre-

Invasion Air Leaders: Air Marshal Sir Arthur Coningham, Air Chief Marshal Sir Arthur Tedder, Lieutenant General Carl Spaatz, and Major General James Doolittle. (National Archives and Records Administration, Still Pictures Division, Photo 208-PU-41-M-3, Copyright © Acme Newspictures)

serving Allied access to Middle East oil and saving the lives of Allied servicemen. In the process, these four groups joined what was, at the time, the most capable air-ground team then in existence and absorbed valuable experience that continues as the foundation of American air-ground doctrine today. While the P-40s, B-25s, and especially the B-24s did not conduct a strategic campaign, as the USAAF's leadership desired, they made a far more substantial contribution to the eventual Allied victory than they could have in any other theater or by being employed in any other manner.

While the USAAF built the fledgling Ninth Air Force in Egypt and Palestine, it also embarked on its preferred strategy for conducting air operations against Germany: the buildup of a strategic bomber force in the United Kingdom. But before this force reached critical mass, a large portion of it was diverted to support the invasion of North Africa. The new Twelfth Air Force, like the Ninth, was a composite air force built of fighters, medium bombers, and heavy bombers, as well as reconnaissance and transport aircraft. While initially under-strength, the Twelfth, as the major element of the Northwest African Air Forces, eventually wrested control of the skies over Tunisia from the Luftwaffe and Regia Aeronautica and contributed directly to the destruction of the vaunted Afrika Korps and the capture of more than 200,000 Axis prisoners. In the process, the USAAF forced the Luft-waffe to divert critical assets from other theaters, including more than 250 transport aircraft that could have been used in the aerial resup-ply campaign at Stalingrad, and inflicted serious damage on the Axis air forces in the Mediterranean.[1] As one German general later noted, "The backbone of the [German] bomber groups in the Mediterranean was broken in these months. They never recovered."[2]

Control of the skies over the middle sea allowed the Allies to build on their success by invading Sicily and Italy proper. Again Allied air-men protected invasion convoys from attack by destroying the Luft-waffe's offensive capability and provided valuable assistance to ground forces in both campaigns. But the USAAF's increase in size after a year of high production at home gave added momentum to the bomber offensive against Germany. After the landings in Italy, heavy bomber groups, which had played the most important part in the air superior-ity and interdiction campaigns, allowing other aircraft to render close support unimpeded, were drawn off and segregated in a new air force, the Fifteenth, along with the USAAF's most capable fighters. Com-mitted increasingly to a strategic campaign, these bombers were no longer immediately available to the theater commander and rendered comparatively less support during the remainder of the Mediterra-nean campaign.

Despite these accomplishments, the USAAF's efforts in the Medi-terranean suffered from several flaws. First, the effort to concentrate aircraft in the United Kingdom for a strategic bombing offensive came at the expense of sufficient long-range aircraft dedicated to anti-submarine work. While the Battle of the Atlantic was eventually won when more aircraft became available, an earlier and more substantial commitment could have saved countless merchant vessels and their cargoes and crews and possibly accelerated the end of the war.[3] Like-wise, the USAAF's preoccupation with the oil refineries at Ploesti cost not only the bulk of the Halverson detachment at the height of the battle for Egypt; a year later, a second, equally costly and ineffec-tive raid decimated a powerful heavy bomber force that could have been put to better use preparing for and supporting the invasion of the Italian boot. Finally, the loss of its heavy bombers and their fighter escorts to Fifteenth Air Force made Twelfth Air Force much less effective for the remainder of the war.

One might suggest that the air campaigns of 1944–1945 were comparatively more important than those of 1942–1943, given the much larger force available and the significant damage inflicted on the German war machine. But the operations later in the war came when the USAAF had an almost unlimited supply of bombers and, finally, the airmen to crew them. The U.S. Air Force will probably never launch another 1,000-bomber raid again. In an era of tightening defense budgets and shrinking force sizes, the questions of force procurement and allocation become much more important. Future conflicts are far more likely to be fought in conditions approximating those of 1942–1943 than those experienced later in the war.

A final point that bears emphasis is the relationship between theater commanders and air forces. A long-held tenet of air advocates states that air forces are best controlled by airmen who fully understand their capabilities and limitations. While the efforts of men like Carl Spaatz, James Doolittle, and Sir Arthur Tedder in North Africa seem to reinforce this perception, it is equally important to have theater commanders who likewise fully understand how to employ an air force and can simultaneously provide airmen with the resources they need to succeed while resisting the temptation to micromanage the operation. In North Africa, the Allies enjoyed the leadership of a gifted field commander in Dwight D. Eisenhower. Like his mentor, George C. Marshall, and his most successful subordinate on the battlefield, George Patton, Ike clearly understood how airpower could best help him achieve his campaign objectives and directed that it be employed in war winning strategies, such as destroying the Axis air forces and preventing reinforcements from reaching the battlefield. He wisely resisted the pleas of ground commanders, who urged him to shift more assets to direct support of their forces, and air leaders, who wanted more aircraft released for strategic raids against distant centers of production. In striking this balance, the future president provided critical leadership for the Allies.

Throughout the campaign along the shores of the Mediterranean, the Ninth and Twelfth Air Forces, as principal components of the Mediterranean Allied Air Force, rendered vital aid to Allied ground and naval forces in opening up the middle sea and securing valuable bases along its shores, furthering successful prosecution of the war.

By doing so, they continued a pattern that held true in virtually every theater of the war: The side that controlled the skies also enjoyed victory on the ground and at sea. This was the case in the German invasions of Poland, Norway, the Low Countries, and France, as well as the initial thrust into the Soviet Union.[4] The Japanese likewise controlled the skies over Pearl Harbor, Singapore, the Philippines, and Java. Only when Allied air forces successfully resisted Axis control of the skies did ground and naval forces have an opportunity to stall the Axis advance, first at Midway and Guadalcanal in the Pacific theater, then at Stalingrad and El Alamein in the European theater. Throughout the remainder of the war, the Allies maintained and even increased their control from local to general superiority and then supremacy, ensuring that German and Japanese forces never again regained the initiative at land and at sea. Even then, air operations often determined the pace of the ground advance, as the Western Allies made their largest gains during the summer months, when they enjoyed good flying weather, but bogged down in the winter, first in 1942–1943 in Tunisia, then in 1943–1944 along the Gustav Line in Italy, and again in 1944–1945 along the Rhine. But the USAAF's most significant contribution to World War II was undoubtedly helping Allied ground forces to cross the Channel and enter Germany proper, finally ending the war. A leading historian of the air war in Europe concluded that "the development of operational air warfare for land or sea campaigns was the most significant contribution aircraft could make to the conduct of the war."[5]

Incidentally, emphasizing the importance of air forces to success in ground campaigns also requires a reappraisal of the relative contributions of the Western Allies compared to those of the Soviet Union. Ninety percent of the German ground combat casualties occurred on the Eastern Front, making it seem that the Soviet Union made the largest contribution to Nazi Germany's defeat. But if control of the skies is a decisive factor in conventional ground combat, then the Western Allies' occupation and destruction of the Luftwaffe becomes a much more significant contribution. While the Western Allies did not destroy as many German armies as the Soviets, they did help to deprive those armies of desperately needed air cover, facilitating their destruction. Just as the joint team benefits from the contributions of air, ground, and naval forces—each leveraging one another's strengths to combat any weaknesses—so too did the Allies synergistically combine their various strengths to destroy Axis forces in the air, on land, and at sea.

In histories of the war, especially those published by airpower historians, this accomplishment has often taken a backseat to the strategic bombing efforts over Germany and Japan. The Combined Bomber Offensive appeared to have wrought overwhelming destruction across Germany, prompting U.S. and British authorities to launch a massive effort to catalog these efforts and determine their impact on the German war machine. The U.S. Strategic Bombing Survey remains a contentious subject, as evidenced by the recent scholarship on both the study itself and the biases of its authors and those who commissioned it, but the emphasis, which has carried over into recent scholarship, remains.[6] In spite of the large number of critics, few have offered an alternative vision. Even the master, Carl von Clausewitz, observed that "one can, after all, not condemn a method without being able to suggest a better alternative."[7] Only recently have scholars paused to consider an alternative use for U.S. heavy bombers in World War II. One noted airpower historian has speculated:

> A less intense bombing of German urban areas, and greater emphasis on close air support, might have yielded victory in more time but with fewer losses—for all concerned—than actually occurred. The faith of air leaders in the perceived progressive merits of strategic bombing—which they viewed as the surest path to service autonomy—led them to dismiss alternatives for using heavy bombers in an auxiliary role to surface forces.[8]

But, in reality, it is impossible to isolate the effects of the tactical and strategic campaigns because both worked toward the same objective: the end of the war and the collapse of Nazi Germany. Scholars now willingly recognize this connection. In 2009, Robert Ehlers's study of the role of intelligence in the strategic campaign found that

> bombing never became the war-winning instrument envisioned in the writings of Douhet, Trenchard and Mitchell. It helped win the war in combination with soldiers, whose role was fundamental to Allied victory. The growing Allied expertise in planning and executing combined and joint operations allowed heavy bombers to play an increasingly vital role not only at the military-strategic level, but also in operational and tactical engagements, by starving the Germans of fuel, transport, and ammunition and by providing direct support to ground forces in the opening stages of major offensives.[9]

Although this was not what the USAAF leaders envisioned at the beginning of the war, it has become one of the strongest justifications for the Combined Bomber Offensive in the years since.

If airpower has the ability to influence ground campaigns, it seems that the best, most effective, and efficient way to win wars is to focus air efforts on supporting surface forces. On 10 May 1945, Spaatz, along with the commander of the U.S. Seventh Army, General Alexander "Sandy" Patch, General Vandenberg, and the Eighth Air Force historian, Dr. Bruce Hopper, interviewed the Luftwaffe chief, Hermann Goering, in Augsburg. Spaatz expressed his belief that airpower had won the war, but Goering responded that it was the speed of the ground forces that had been decisive—much to Patch's delight.[10] But, again, the two cannot be separated. Spaatz was correct that airpower had been important, maybe even decisive, but it became so because it allowed the speedy advance of Allied ground forces.

If airpower is best used to support the ground and naval forces, the only question is how to best achieve these results. It could (and has) been argued that the Combined Bomber Offensive did great damage to the German war effort and, by destroying the Luftwaffe and denying the Wehrmacht the fuel it needed to fight, hastened the end of the war. It could also be shown that employing aircraft in both direct and indirect support of ground forces, by interdicting the enemy flow of supplies and destroying forces actually opposing the ground advance, air forces can likewise speed the end of conflict. In reality, some combination of the two is likely required, but the nature of conflicts since the end of World War II has shown that one form is often more effective than the other for several reasons.

While many historians of the Pacific War link the atomic attacks of 6 and 9 August on Hiroshima and Nagasaki with the Japanese surrender on 15 August, few emphasize the Soviet declaration of war on 8 August (three months to the day after the end of the war in Europe, as the Soviets had agreed), which not only closed down the final diplomatic channel the Japanese hoped to exploit for a less-than-unconditional surrender but also cost Japan control of half of Manchuria.[11] The incendiary attacks, launched in March, destroyed more Japanese cities and cost more lives without bringing about an end to the conflict. And none of these attacks would have been possible without the drive across the Central Pacific, in which naval and ground forces of the U.S. Army and Marines seized the bomber bases in the Marianas. Even the atomic weapons themselves were delivered to the air bases in the Marianas by U.S. Navy warships.[12]

In U.S. wars since 1945, strategic airpower has played only a limited role. In Korea, the industrial and logistic infrastructure that supported the North Koreans and, later, the Chinese remained off-limits north and west of the Yalu River. In Vietnam, the case was similar, as North Vietnamese armaments came from factories in China and the Soviet Union and entered through ports and other zones protected from bombing. But as Mark Clodfelter has demonstrated, even heavy, unrestricted attacks on these areas of North Vietnam would probably not have altered the outcome of that war, due to its special nature.[13] While conventional forces are susceptible to interdiction and strategic attack, unconventional forces can remain largely impervious, leaving an Air Force built on a strategic mission either struggling to provide tactical support or searching for another role. It is interesting to speculate on the outcome of the conflict in Vietnam had the air forces been more closely tied to the ground forces and devoted exclusively to their support instead of on a distant and often ineffective air-coercion campaign, but such a counterfactual assumes that there was even a military solution to what was largely a political problem.

In the subsequent U.S. conflicts in the Middle East, air forces have rendered valuable aid to ground forces, especially in areas such as reconnaissance, airlift and logistic support, and medical evacuation, roles honed in North Africa in 1942–1943, but they have also displayed a continuing desire to strike strategic targets, such as electrical generating facilities, communications nodes, and even civilian leadership, located in the heart of heavily populated areas such as Baghdad. In 1991, the air phase of Operation DESERT STORM concentrated on Iraqi command-and-control nodes and logistic infrastructure, which it hoped would leave the fielded forces leaderless and unable to fight. In 2003, air operations against the Iraqi capital began with a so-called decapitation strike designed to remove Saddam Hussein from power.

One of the architects of the first campaign against Iraq was Colonel John Warden. In 1988, he published his thoughts on air warfare, distilled over a long career in tactical aviation, including combat experience in Vietnam. The signal feature of his argument is a model known as the "five rings," in which he postulates that enemy states are constructed of five concentric rings labeled, from outside to center, Fielded Forces, Population, Infrastructure, Means of Production, and Leadership.[14] Warden advocates attacking these target sets from the *inside out* (or, ideally, simultaneously), with leadership first and fielded forces last. In addition to directly contradicting noted theorist Carl von Clausewitz's ideas (see below), the most distasteful aspect of Warden's theory is that it retains the population as a target set. In addition, most of the infrastructure he advocates targeting will likely be colocated with population centers and might prove valuable to the occupier in a postconflict environment. While Warden does advocate using air forces, once air superiority has been achieved—in support of the surface forces—he also clings to the idea that air forces are capable of successful, even decisive action alone in the absence of surface forces. As the most prominent critic of Warden's work, David Mets, has pointed out, many of Warden's ideas do not differ significantly from earlier theorists, including Douhet, Trenchard, and Mitchell.[15] If Warden's theory is just "old wine in new bottles," then we still lack any coherent theory of airpower developed since the interwar period.

The absence of strategic targets, or the inability to hit them due to political limitations, had led the service to concentrate more on tactical support for the ground forces. This has a number of advantages. First, it complies with noted military philosopher Carl von Clausewitz's ideas of the proper targets for military forces. In years of study of contemporary campaigns, the Prussian found that "three broad objectives, which between them cover everything: the *armed forces*, the *country*, and the *enemy's will*" (emphasis in original). Too often, air planners have focused exclusively on the third of these, hoping to influence the enemy's will through air action alone. Just as often, as Robert Pape found in *Bombing to Win: Air Power and Coercion in War*, they have been frustrated.[16] Clausewitz recognized that occupation of an enemy's country might not lead to success in every case, as in Napoleon's ill-fated 1812 invasion of Russia, but this led him to emphasize the importance of the enemy's military. He wrote, "The fighting forces must be *destroyed*: that is, they must be put in such a condition that they can no longer carry on the fight. . . . The country must be occupied; otherwise the enemy could raise fresh military forces." He returns to this point later in his work, advocating, "To sum up: of all the possible aims in war, the destruction of the enemy's armed forces always appears as the highest." This seems to make it clear that the enemy's fielded forces provide the best and most suitable targets for airpower, and since aircraft can neither take nor hold ground, they are best attacked in conjunction with ground and naval forces.[17]

Focusing on the enemy's fielded forces has a number of advantages. First, it greatly reduces the likelihood of collateral damage. Enemy factories, transportation hubs, leadership, and other targets are often located in large population centers, with large numbers of noncombatants. Even with stealth technology and precision weapons, it is almost impossible to attack these without some collateral damage and loss of innocent life, and with imperfect intelligence it is even possible to mistake a civilian air-raid shelter for an Iraqi command-and-control facility or a foreign consulate for a legitimate Serbian target. In addition, much of the vital infrastructure destroyed is likely to be necessary for any postconflict stability, or so-called Phase IV operations, when a functioning economy, utilities, and essential services will likely affect the security situation. In his study of the air phase of Operation IRAQI FREEDOM in 2003, Williamson Murray argued that "the 'Shock and Awe' campaign, while doing little substantive damage to the regime's willingness to continue the conflict, did inflict considerable damage on the civilian and bureaucratic infrastructure that would be necessary in putting Iraq back together."[18] Targeting fielded forces would instead destroy much military equipment, which would likely only be used to destabilize the postconflict environment. Rather than bypassing hardened fighters who might oppose a postconflict era of peace, air attacks on fielded forces would likely inflict heavy casualties on them, leaving the few survivors chastened.

Of course, this applies only in a conflict in which the enemy chooses to use conventional forces. But the overarching mission of support for the ground forces has an equally vital role in unconventional war. While lethal forms of airpower would play a smaller role, the ancillary missions (primarily airlift and reconnaissance) would make it easier for ground forces to accomplish their mission. Moving supplies by air makes it difficult for the enemy to plan ambushes, as the skies offer any numbers of routes, including those away from populated areas, while terrestrial forms of transport are easier to predict and far more difficult to isolate from the local population. Likewise, reconnaissance assets can reduce casualties among friendly ground forces by providing up-to-the-second information on what lies around the next corner and detailed and continuous surveillance of important installations.[19] Sadly, the recently published *The U.S. Army/Marine Corps Counterinsurgency Field Manual* devotes only four of its almost 250 pages to airpower's role in unconventional war, despite some excellent recent works on the subject.[20] While lethal forms of airpower, as Clodfelter has also argued, have the potential to further alienate a population, nonlethal forms have the potential to provide vital assistance to ground forces involved in stability and security operations.[21]

An air doctrine built around support of land and naval forces would be the U.S. Air Force's strongest possible contribution to building an effective joint team. As the campaign in North Africa demonstrated, armed forces are most effective when used synergistically, multiplying the effectiveness of each individual arm. A sustained ground campaign forces an opponent to deploy his forces, which makes them susceptible to attack, and consumes supplies at a much higher rate, which makes him vulnerable to an effective interdiction campaign. Ground and naval forces, especially airborne troops and naval infantry, are ideally suited to seizing air bases, which extends the umbrella of protection for the ground and naval forces themselves and enables them to expand their operating range. Any of these operations are more effective that an air campaign used in isolation. Air forces can neither take nor hold ground and require persistence in order to achieve an objective. Between raids, an enemy can effect repairs, move vital targets into hardened shelters that might be impervious to air attack, or shield them by burying them among the civilian population. As one air officer observed before World War II, "The air forces are now co-equal in importance with any fighting branch of the military organization and by some it is considered to be the decisive weapon, but just because a man is a star, triple-threat football player is no cause for a declaration of independence from the rest of the team."[22]

Of course, operating air forces as part of the joint team is not a new idea, and many of the early theorists cut their teeth in tactical campaigns. Tami Davis Biddle revealed Hugh Trenchard's "predilection for using air power to support ground operations whenever possible" and noted that he was roundly criticized because he "allowed the independent air force to be diverted in attacking purely military objectives of minor importance in the army zone."[23] No less a theorist that Billy Mitchell recognized air's potential as early as 1921. In *Our Air Force*, writing based on his experiences in World War I, Mitchell observed, "We need every branch of national defense to form the complete chain. . . . No navies can operate on the seas, nor armies on the land, until the air forces have first attained a decision against the opposing air forces."[24] At the time, he believed that "our doctrine of aviation, therefore, should be to find out where the hostile air force is, to concentrate on that point with our Pursuit, Attack, and Bombardment Aviation, to obtain a decision over the hostile air force, and then to attack the enemy's armies on land or navies on the water, and obtain a decision over them."[25] Mitchell considered observation aviation to form a fourth branch and advocated that it be "attached to the ground troops, to navies, and to air troops for the purpose of observing everything that is necessary for their own use; that is, to help them fight on the ground, on the water, or in the air." Considering that much of the observation mission is now conducted from satellites in orbit, and that the Army, Navy, and Air Force each maintain a separate, internal space command, Mitchell's views on observation were indeed prescient. Mitchell even foresaw the requirement for escort fighters, which retarded the Combined Bomber Offensive's effectiveness until 1944. In 1921 he argued, "Bombardment and Pursuit Aviation always act together when in the face of strong enemy opposition," that "bombardment raids have to be protected by Pursuit Aviation," and that "the heavily armored attack airplanes, no matter how well protected, will be shot down without the assistance of pursuit aviation."[26]

About the same time Mitchell published *Our Air Force*, another theorist was putting pen to paper to record his thoughts on how naval forces should be employed, based on the recent lessons of World War I. Sir Julian Corbett recognized that control of the sea, like control of the air, offered the possessors nothing in and of itself and had no value except that of being able to influence events ashore. Corbett's theory, which has been described as "Clausewitz for navies," is equally applicable to warfare in the third dimension. As an example, it is worthwhile to examine Corbett's signal work, *Some Principles of Maritime Strategy*, to see what happens when his references to "the sea" are replaced with "the air."[27] If airpower advocates would only accept Corbett's maxim ("it is almost impossible that a war can be decided by naval action alone") and apply it to their arena, his contribution as a theorist of air warfare would be immense.[28]

Corbett justifies his assertion for the interrelation of ground and naval warfare, and for the primacy of ground warfare in his observation that "since men live upon the land and not upon the sea, great issues between nations at war have always been decided—except in the rarest cases—either by what your army can do against your enemy's territory and national life, or else by the fear of what the fleet makes it possible for your army to do." The same can be said for war in the air. Men do not live in or farm the sky, and so the only way aerial warfare can be decisive is by directly influencing events on the ground. Since air forces cannot take and hold ground, most often this influence will come in the form of support for surface forces, either in protection from enemy air attack or by removing obstacles to their advance. This should be a fundamental role for airpower in war.[29]

For Corbett, it follows that "the paramount concern, then, of maritime strategy is to determine the mutual relations of your army and navy in a plan of war."[30] We could therefore include the airplane and paraphrase: the paramount concern of *military* strategy is to determine the mutual relations of your army, navy *and air force* in a plan of war. The key then becomes joint operations, or how well one can integrate all three instruments of military power. This would have served planners well in World War II. Combat ranged across all three dimensions, and the side that was best able to integrate and sustain the three was usually successful.

Douhet would likely respond that war in the air, unencumbered by any restraint, should be capable of forcing a decision on its own. In *Command of the Air*, he observed, "Either one wages war or one doesn't; but when one does, one must do it without gloves."[31] Again, Douhet's narrow vision of total war is flawed and fails to take into account Clausewitz's case of limited war. Corbett, however, recognized this possibility and accounted for it. In planning for war, military leaders "may find that certain means are barred to them for political reasons."[32] This has certainly been the case since 1945. American air planners in Korea and Vietnam chafed under what they believed were unjust restrictions placed upon them by civilian leaders. But rather than viewing the political environment as an intrusion on the capabilities of airpower, they should have recognized it as an inherent and fundamental part of war—and planned accordingly.

Another of Corbett's observations would have proved useful to operational planners in conducting World War II. In early 1942, when faced with a German monolith on the continent and lacking the strength to attack it directly, the Western Allies instead adopted a peripheral strategy in North Africa. They were, in a sense, adhering to Bacon's maxim, quoted by Corbett, that "he that commands the sea [read: air] is at great liberty to take as much or as little of the war as he will."[33] While a cross-Channel attack in 1943 would have been taking on more than the Allies were ready for, committing more forces to the campaign already under way in North Africa enabled the British and Americans to assume only as much as they were prepared for at the time. The successful conclusion of this campaign vindicated that decision.

In a corollary to the previous observation, Allied planners in World War II applied Corbett's ideas on how to regulate the ground war. He noted, "We are able by the use of our navy [read: air force] to restrict the amount of force our army will have to deal with."[34] This principle was enshrined in the phrase *isolation of the battlefield* and was successfully applied in the North African campaign. With a successful and sustained interdiction campaign, air units severed vital transportation links and prevented substantial German reinforcements and supplies from reaching the Afrika Korps.

The critical factor limiting the German response was command of the air. Had the buildup been opposed by strong units of the Luftwaffe, or had the Axis air forces successfully interfered in the Allied interdiction campaign, the result would not have been positive. Corbett identifies the means by which this can be accomplished: "The most favorable circumstances, and the only circumstances by which we ourselves can profit are such as permit the more or less complete isolation of the object by naval action, and such isolation can never be established until we have entirely overthrown the enemy's naval forces." In arriving at this conclusion, Corbett foreshadows Douhet, Mitchell, and de Seversky, among others, in their fundamental observation that command of the air is the vital prerequisite. Here is the necessity of a preliminary air battle. Corbett observes that "the only way of securing such command by naval means is to obtain a decision by battle against the enemy's fleet." This is the primary objective of an air force. Without a decision against the enemy's air force, it is impossible to support ground forces. Corbett notes that "the first business of our fleet is to seek out the enemy's fleet and destroy it." This has been, and continues to be, the primary mission of air forces. By gaining and maintaining control of the air, the Allies successfully applied this principle in the North African campaign.[35]

It is important to keep this distinction in mind. Unlike theorists who espouse command of the sea (or of the air) as an end unto itself, Corbett sees value only in what it enables one to do. "You cannot conquer the sea because it is not susceptible to ownership, at least outside territorial waters. . . . You cannot subsist your armed force upon it as you can your enemy's territory. . . . The only right we or our enemy can have on the sea is the right of passage; in other words, the only positive value which the high seas have for national life is as a means of communication."[36] The same is true for the air. Except for sovereign airspace, there is no ownership of the air. Furthermore, it is even more difficult to occupy than the sea. Besides being completely lacking in sustenance, the fuel demands to remain aloft and the speeds traveled are so much higher in the air than at sea that control is even more problematic. However, the concept of "right of passage" is equally applicable. Being able to control the sky means no more than the ability to move across it unhindered. What you choose to move across it— whether bomber aircraft destined for enemy troop concentrations or cargo aircraft full of troops or supplies—can have a significant impact on events on the ground. Corbett adds, "By winning command of the sea we remove that barrier from our path, thereby placing ourselves in a position to exert direct military pressure upon the national life of our enemy ashore, while at the same time we solidify it against him and prevent his exerting direct military pressure upon ourselves."[37] No more—and no less—is promised by gaining command of the air.

In discussing the proper mixture of ships-of-the-line, cruisers, and frigates to exercise command of the sea, Corbett's ideas are useful in composing an air force. He even uses terminology air planners would have recognized, noting that "in order to exercise that control effectively we must have a numerous class of vessels specially adapted for pursuit."[38] Command of the air had identical requirements. In order to gain control, fighter aircraft ("pursuit" in Air Corps parlance) were the most effective and were required in large numbers. In *Our Air Force*, Mitchell suggested that pursuit types should comprise 60 percent of the air arm. Observation aircraft, which fulfilled a role assigned to cruisers in Corbett's writings, would be essential to collecting and disseminating information. In the early months of World War II, the observation arm was perhaps the most deficient in terms of organization, equipment, and capabilities. Finally, the transports that threatened to land foreign invaders on Britain's shores, and therefore gained the full attention of British admirals, would approximate transport aircraft. Their importance to the outcome of a campaign was twice illustrated in World War II. First, at Stalingrad, Soviet fighters properly concentrated on Luftwaffe transport aircraft used to bring vital supplies to Friedrich von Paulus's surrounded Sixth Army.[39] In North Africa, Allied airmen focused on transport aircraft bringing supplies to Tunisia across the Sicilian Strait once the sea lines of communication had been severed. Again, Corbett's lesson is clear: Although gaining command of the sea is important, it is useless if it does not prevent the enemy from using it to his advantage.

If Corbett's work is so applicable to the aerial arena, it begs the question: Why wasn't he consulted? There are a number of possible answers. The first, as already mentioned, is the prominence of Douhet's ideas and their special attraction to an air force laboring to achieve independence. His promise of an aerial weapon employed in a manner to assure victory by itself was far too alluring to Air Corps officers in the 1920s and 1930s. Even absent a Douhet, it would have taken a concerted effort to find a fair hearing for Corbett's ideas, even among naval critics. In defining a subordinate role for the Royal Navy, Corbett had attracted the ire of his own countrymen, who lashed out against his "amateur excursions into the subject" and resented the "presumption" of a civilian barrister with no military training to lecture on matters of national defense.[40] Even after World War I, when Corbett's ideas received some vindication, the Admiralty Board felt it necessary to preface Corbett's official history of the war with the following: "Some of the principles advocated in this book, especially the tendency to minimize the importance of seeking battle and forcing it to a conclusion, are directly in conflict with their own views."[41] In competition with Alfred Thayer Mahan's vision of lines of battle fleets slugging it out barrel-to-barrel, Corbett's narrative of commerce raiding and shore support could not compete. One suspects that airpower theorists, seeking a decisive resolution in the sky, would have treated a translation of Corbett's ideas into an emphasis on close support and airlift with no less derision.

But there is another possible explanation. In searching for a shortcut over the trenches that dominated the Western Front during World War I, American airmen were tapping into rich cultural traditions of innovation in warfare and an appeal to technology to solve problems.[42] The allure of a new bomber flying higher and faster than existing fighters and antiaircraft artillery proved difficult to resist. While service interests dictated that strategic bombing would get a full test, its advocates really did believe that they could shorten the war and spare the ground forces the horrors of another Western Front. And while strategic bombing required attacking targets in densely populated areas, airmen again hoped that new technological innovations, particularly the Norden bombsight, would enable them to minimize civilian casualties. Even if some civilians were harmed, previous American wars had demonstrated an acceptance of the ideas of an entire nation in arms and that some collateral damage was inevitable. Even in 1921, Mitchell agreed with Douhet's ideas about the lack of distinction between combatants and noncombatants, noting:

> Warfare to-day between first-class powers includes all of the people of the nations so engaged—men, women and children. This inclusion of women and children is not merely a sentimental and economic one, but during the last war was an actual one from a military standpoint. Women and children actually were part of the military and naval forces at home and abroad, and this inclusion did not stop short of the actual firing line. The entire nations were combatant forces.[43]

Here Mitchell was tapping into a long American tradition of seeing entire groups as the enemy, whether they were Pequot or Filipino.[44]

Despite an American affinity for technological innovation and experimental ways of warfare, World War II demonstrated that there were still no shortcuts to victory. Ground forces still had to fight their way into an enemy's country and, as Clausewitz predicted, destroy the opposing forces before the enemy capitulated. History still lacks any clear example where air forces have been able to relieve ground forces of this burden. In his 1992 discussion of the development of airpower theory, Harold Winton found: "It is, of course, true that there are not now contemporary theories of war on land or at sea that have kept pace with modern developments. However, the fact that Clausewitz's *On War*, and Corbett's *Some Principles of Maritime Strategy* are both technologically out of date does not detract from the fact that their ideas have provided organizing frameworks that have stood the test of time." Winton concluded that "the theory of air power has not reached a similar state," and therefore "there is no comprehensive theory of air power."[45] In the absence of such, airmen could do worse than to revisit other ideas that have stood the test of time. Based on the USAAF's employment in North Africa, it seems that air forces can best hasten the end of conflict, if they are unable to deter it in the first place, when they are fully prepared to help the surface forces accomplish their tasks as fully integrated members of the joint team.

Appendix 1: USAAF Aircraft in the North African Campaign

While the USAAF placed its faith in the potential of strategic bombing and began to develop aircraft types to carry out a strategic air campaign, it also developed and procured large numbers of aircraft designed to support surface forces. The various types of aircraft employed in the United Kingdom and in North Africa had significant qualitative differences, and it is important to understand each in order to analyze the USAAF's allocation decisions. In all, the USAAF employed four types of U.S.-built fighters, three types of twin-engine bombers, two types of heavy bombers, and one type of transport aircraft during the campaign. In theory, the service preferred to retain the most capable aircraft types in the United Kingdom, where they would be used to conduct the Combined Bomber Offensive against Germany, but it also allocated sufficient numbers of all types to support the campaign in North Africa and elsewhere across the globe. In mid-1942, the most capable aircraft were B-17 and B-24 heavy bombers and the P-38 escort fighter. Almost every P-38 in the United Kingdom went to North Africa with Twelfth Air Force, leaving General Ira Eaker, commanding Eighth Air Force in the United Kingdom, to complain, "I think this is the most serious blunder we have made in a long time."[1] Eaker was assuaged with promises that he would receive the first of the new P-47 fighters to enter combat, which he did.[2] No P-47s served in the Mediterranean until *after* they have proved to be unsatisfactory in the bomber escort mission in the United Kingdom due to their short range. The P-38, by contrast, was a godsend to the bomber forces in North Africa. In letters describing the various capabilities of the aircraft then operating in his theater (and from which many of the following descriptions are taken), Spaatz wrote Arnold that "of all our aircraft, the P-38 deserves special mention" and that their efforts had been a major factor in the "excellent record established by the B-17 in this theater."[3] Another observer recorded that "North Africa has demonstrated a fighter–heavy bomber team that works. . . . The fighter's sole mission was escort. . . . In both the Ninth and Twelfth Air Forces, this mission was often accomplished by the mere presence of the fighters."[4] James H. (Jimmy) Doolittle, as commander of Twelfth Air Force's heavy bomber force, was even more emphatic and called attention to the physical as well as moral effects of escorted missions: "It has been conclusively proved in this theater that more precise bombing can be done with substantially reduced bomber losses if the bombers are escorted by fighters. . . . The psychological effect on the entire bomber crew is most valuable and shows up not only in results but in the frequency at which they can be effectively sent on missions and the number of missions they can effectively execute." Doolittle added that he had been "holding down bomber losses by seriously overworking our inadequate number of escort fighters."[5] Sadly, it would take another two months, and the costly raids of October 1943, before this lesson penetrated the Eighth Air Force in the United Kingdom.

But the four-engine B-17 *Flying Fortress* was undoubtedly the star of the North African Campaign. The four groups assigned to Twelfth Air Force did much of the heavy lifting in the air superiority and interdiction campaigns and compiled an enviable combat record. From 12 December 1942 to 16 February 1943, the first two groups deployed flew 962 separate sorties, dropped 1,778 tons of bombs.[6] They claimed 125 enemy fighters shot down (a figure later shown to be excessive) at a loss of only seven of their own.[7] The loss rate (0.7 percent) was remarkable, a testament to the plane's design as well as the skill of the aircrews and their fighter escorts.

The B-17 used precision high-altitude attacks on ports and airfields. The precision required excellent weather and was reduced when bombers were forced to bomb through overcast conditions, but the crew of ten (pilot, copilot, navigator, bombardier, engineer, radio operator, and four gunners) demonstrated that they could effectively deliver bombs on critical targets. The bomber suffered some criticism early in the war, especially in the hands of the foreign media, prompting Spaatz to write, "In spite of the *London Times*, Seversky, or anyone else, the B-17's are far superior to anything in this Theater and are fully adequate for their job."[8]

Similarly, the two groups of B-24s sent to Palestine with Ninth Air Force provided the only large heavy bomber units allocated to the Western Desert.[9] These planes played an integral role in cutting Rommel's supply lines in Egypt and supporting the advance across Libya. Like the B-17, the B-24 was an engineering marvel, a heavy, four-engine bomber with a crew of ten. Its uniquely tapered wing design gave it more lift, enabling it to carry an even larger payload over longer ranges. As such, it was ideally suited for antisubmarine work in the Battle of the Atlantic, where the Combined Chiefs of Staff decision to finally allocate sufficient numbers in early 1943 helped turn the tide against the U-boat. The force that attacked the oil refineries in Ploesti on 1 August 1943 was composed entirely of B-24s.

The USAAF employed three twin-engine bombers in North Africa. The Douglas A-20 *Havoc* was technically designated a light bomber and, along with the British *Wellington*, formed the bulk of the RAF's bomber force in the Western Desert. Designed as the USAAF's principal close support platform before the war, the A-20 was rapidly becoming obsolete, and only a single group participated in the battle in Tunisia. The new B-25 and B-26 medium bombers were designed to replace the A-20 and became superior tactical platforms for the duration of the war. As their twin-engine design prevented them from reaching the high altitudes necessary for a strategic campaign, they were most often employed against tactical targets, including airfields, rail lines, and especially shipping. In North Africa, medium bombers played an important role in the antishipping campaign, as ships at sea were not as heavily defended as static targets such as ports. According to Doolittle:

B-25's and B-26's have done a magnificent job in this theater but are not as efficient for strategic bombing as the B-17 for the following reasons:

a. inability to fly high enough to get over the worst of the flak. This is important in attacking heavily defended targets such as ports.
b. Inability to protect themselves as well as the B-17.

Doolittle noted the two medium bombers had a loss rate of 1.8 percent per effective sortie, compared to the B-17's 0.6 percent in Twelfth Air Force.[10] Both aircraft were a significant part of the support forces, and the numbers available for service and actually employed in North Africa provide further evidence that the USAAF had not neglected development and procurement of these types during the interwar period. Four groups of B-25s saw service in the theater, two each with the Twelfth and Ninth Air Forces. All three B-26 groups were assigned to the Twelfth.

The USAAF assigned four different types of U.S.-built fighters to support operations in North Africa.[11] One, the Bell P-39 *Airacobra*, was already obsolete and eventually assigned only to escorted strafing and observation missions. The USAAF realized early on that the plane could not hold its own against German fighters and therefore assigned most of the production to fulfill Lend-Lease requirements to the Soviet Union. Many of these aircraft (designated the P-400 in the export version) were already in the United Kingdom awaiting shipment to Murmansk when German aircraft in Norway threatened to close the northern sea route.[12] As a result, many of these aircraft were reallocated to Twelfth Air Force, where they played only a small part in the battle. The few fighters that did arrive could be employed only with the protection of an escort, and it was much more economical to simply equip and supply a fighter that could both perform the ground attack mission and adequately defend itself, if necessary. Even before the campaign, Spaatz wrote, "We still feel that the P-39 can be profitably used in attacking ground targets. Admittedly, this type is no 'great shakes' as a fighter." After the campaign, Spaatz's views were confirmed, and he wrote Arnold, "the P-39 . . . in spite of its speed, has not been proven in strictly fighter action."[13]

The one fighter that was capable of fulfilling both roles was the Curtiss P-40 *Warhawk*. Exported in large numbers to the RAF, where it was known as the *Kittyhawk*, the P-40 formed the bulk of the Allied fighter force in North Africa. The majority of the RAF support squadrons in the Western Desert flew *Kittyhawks*, as most of the *Spitfires* (the RAF's best fighter) were retained for the defense of the home islands or Malta.[14] USAAF squadrons flew P-40s in the Western Desert, where a total of three groups were eventually assigned, and in Tunisia, where an additional group and a French squadron provided ground support.[15] The P-40's development as a fighter-bomber, based on the British experience, was one of the most significant airpower developments of the war. It rendered obsolete both the light bomber and the dive-bomber, both of which were in the USAAF's prewar inventory, but saw limited action in North Africa. In addition to its six .50-caliber machine guns, the P-40 could carry up to three 500-pound bombs or one 1,000-pound bomb. By September 1943, the USAAF operated four full groups of P-40s in the Mediterranean, plus one additional squadron (the 99th, the initial squadron of the famed "Tuskegee Airmen").[16] By early 1943, the director of the USAAF's School of Applied Tactics in Orlando was writing, "Reports from theaters indicate that the use of fighter-bombers as attack planes, glide bombers, and medium level bombers is increasing, due to their proven effectiveness in combat."[17] The P-40 was not as capable as the front-line German fighters but, when properly handled, could provide a close match or escape without heavy losses. Even today, it remains the Allied aircraft that is most closely associated with the North African campaign. Spaatz even saw fit to include it with the P-38/B-17 team, noting after the campaign, "I believe the B-17, the P-40, and the P-38 have been the major factors in the North African battle."[18]

The Lockheed P-38 *Lightning* was the most valuable fighter sent to North Africa and was one of the engineering marvels of the war. Lockheed's unique twin-boom design provided something no other nation could match, a twin-engine fighter that was maneuverable enough to hold its own in combat with the best single-engine fighters yet had the endurance to perform long-range escort missions. Perhaps this is why Eaker felt their loss so keenly in fall 1942 and why P-38s continued to operate with front-line units until the end of the war. The two engines provided a redundant power plant that made it capable of performing the ground attack mission and returning to base on one engine, if necessary, but its true value came as an escort fighter for the B-17s assigned to Twelfth Air Force. While the Eighth Air Force in the United Kingdom was still limited by the lack of an escort fighter, or attempting to fight its way through to its targets without them, the three P-38 groups in the Twelfth were demonstrating that escorts would be essential to penetrating German air defenses. On the long missions from Tunisia and Algeria to Sicily and Italy, P-38s successfully attacked German and Italian interceptors, enabling the B-17s to enjoy low loss rates and high mission success rates. The USAAF leadership in North Africa noticed these results almost immediately. In addition to preserving the force, the escorts enabled more accurate bombing and higher sortie rates, as "the operation of heavy bombers without fighter escort results in considerable damage to heavy bombers, even though they are not being shot down. . . . They are rendered nonoperational for a considerable period of time," requiring a much larger reserve than originally planned.[19]

Photoreconnaissance versions of the P-38, designated the F-4 and F-5, also equipped the two photographic reconnaissance groups assigned in North Africa, though it was rivaled in this mission by the British *Mosquito*. Stateside tests in early 1943 confirmed that "cooling capacity of the intercooler is not sufficient to allow maximum horsepower to be extracted from the engine at [high] altitude," and at 30,000 feet the carburetor air temperatures exceeded 50 degrees Celsius. Engineers at the test center at Eglin Air Force Base in Florida recommended that a heat shield be installed between the intercooler and exhaust duct to remedy the problem. Performance tests confirmed that the P-38 was superior to the P-47, P-51 (without the Merlin engine), P-40F, and P-39D and comparable to the *Spitfire* Mark IX, then the front-line British fighter.[20] After the campaign, Spaatz praised the P-38, writing, "The P-38 has proven itself, and I consider it the most valuable fighter airplane that we have here at this time."[21] He later told Arnold, "A good way to start a fight is to suggest to a P-38 pilot that there is a better plane."[22]

The A-36 *Apache* was the final fighter employed in North Africa, not actually appearing until the battle for Sicily. The A-36 was essentially a P-51 *Mustang* equipped with dive brakes and other modifications to enable it to perform as a dive-bomber. Once free of its payload, it was an excellent dogfighter, finishing the war as perhaps the most capable fighter in the USAAF inventory, and it was still in use when the Korean War erupted the next decade. The A-36 owed its development to an engineering accident, as its initial power plant configuration left it underpowered and unappealing to the USAAF leadership, but when the American airframe was married with the British Rolls-Royce Merlin engine, the plane demonstrated the best range and performance of any fighter in the war. Once this was realized, the A-36s were pulled from the two groups in the Mediterranean, where they had performed exceptionally over Sicily and Salerno, and the two groups operating them were reequipped, initially with P-40s and, later, with the P-47s that the Eighth Air Force had found unsuitable. Arnold explained his rationale to Spaatz on 14 August 1943: "It was originally planned to re-equip the P-40 Groups with P-51B's when the Packard-powered P-40 was discontinued. However, due to the urgent need in the U.K. for a balanced fighter force including an airplane with greater range than the P-47, it was decided to send all available P-51's to England and therefore the only airplane available for re-equipping your P-40 groups is the P-47."[23]

The final aircraft type deployed to North Africa was the most important for the logistics effort. The Douglas C-47 *Skytrain* (*Dakota*) was based on the commercial DC-3, which entered airline service in the mid-1930s and revolutionized the industry. In its wartime configuration, it provided essential airlift for supplies (for both the ground and air forces) and a troop transport capability for the airborne forces. Although unarmed, the C-47 was frequently employed in hostile conditions, especially in the initial stages of amphibious landings. The C-47 had no peer in the Allied arsenal and was in great demand by Allied air forces, which had almost uniformly neglected the development of transport aircraft during the interwar period. Seven complete groups were eventually deployed in theater, augmenting strained logistics networks and making airborne operations possible. Each aircraft carried two pilots, representing a significant commitment from the USAAF's manpower and training infrastructure.

Each of these various types of aircraft were organized into squadrons, groups, occasionally wings, and finally numbered air forces. Fighter groups contained three fighter squadrons, each with twenty-five aircraft (for a total of seventy-five per group) and, by 1944, after earlier rates proved inadequate, a reserve of 50 percent, for a total of 111 planes. Bomber and Transport (also called Troop Carrier) groups contained four squadrons of twelve aircraft each (forty-eight aircraft) and, eventually, a 50 percent reserve for a total of seventy-two planes.[24] Throughout the North African campaign, the Twelfth Air Force's groups were continually and sometimes significantly understrength as a result of the high demand globally for scarce assets.[25] On 2 February 1943, General Spaatz reported that his three P-38 groups had only eighty-two aircraft in the squadrons (and only fifty-one of them serviceable) and another twenty-four in repair depots for a total of 106 and needed another 240 just to get up to strength. Replacements had initially been assigned at a rate of 15 percent per month, but this was found to be inadequate and later increased to 25 percent for

Table A1-1: Summary of Aircraft Types Employed by the USAAF in
North Africa

Ninth Air Force (Palestine, Egypt, and Libya)		Twelfth Air Force (Morocco, Algeria, and Tunisia)	
B-24 Two Groups (98th & 376th)		B-17	Four Groups (2nd, 97th, 99th, & 301st)
B-25 Two Groups (12th & 340th)		B-25	Two Groups (310th, 321st)
P-40 Three Groups (57th, 79th & 324th)		B-26	Three Groups (17th, 319th, 320th)
C-47 One Group (316th)		A-20	One Group (47th)
		P-38	Three Groups (1st, 14th, 82nd)
		P-39	Two Groups (81st, 350th)
		P-40	Two Groups (33rd, 325th)
		A-36	Two Groups (27th, 86th)
		Spitfire	Two Groups (31st, 52nd)
		C-47	Six Groups (60th, 61st, 62nd, 64th, 313th, 314th)
		F-4/F-5	Two Groups (3rd, 5th)

bombers and 30 percent for fighters.[26] The P-38 remained in short supply due to high demand in the Pacific, where pilots valued its range and
second engine on long overwater flights. Crews were ideally assigned at
a rate of 1.5 per plane (111 pilots per fighter group, 720 aircrewmen per
heavy bomber group), but squadrons sometimes found themselves with
mission-ready planes but no available crews due to losses and shortages
in the expanding training establishment at home. A rotation policy that
sent combat-weary crews back home to serve as instructors placed an additional strain on the training infrastructure, one that was not overcome
until later in the war.

Groups of similar types of aircraft were sometimes organized into
wings, but this additional administrative layer often absorbed scarce manpower and was dispensed with early in the campaign. The groups and,
when used, the wings reported to a numbered air force. In the Mediterranean, the Ninth Air Force operated initially from Egypt and Palestine while the Twelfth was based in French North Africa. Eventually,
the Twelfth absorbed the Ninth's flying units, while the Ninth's name
and headquarters personnel moved to England to support the Normandy
landings.

Of course, air forces are far more than just airplanes. The logistics requirements necessary to support these forces are extensive and represented a significant commitment of American manpower and materiel throughout the war. Front-line squadrons required massive networks of repair shops and depots to repair damaged planes or assemble new ones, tankers and pipelines of fuel to deliver the high-octane gasoline, the lifeblood of air forces, as well as a constant supply of bombs, ammunition, and spare parts for the planes. Aircrews and ground support personnel required, at a minimum, food, water, shelter, and medical supplies to keep them at their jobs of flying and fixing airplanes in a desert environment. Maintaining a communications network, including the collection and dissemination of vital intelligence, to manage this vast enterprise and coordinate the various activities proved most challenging and significantly inhibited operations during the early phases. In a static campaign, these challenges are hard enough, but when everything must be picked up and moved on a few hours' notice, the task can become overwhelming. Without a well-developed logistics network, established at great cost in terms of stateside training and manufacturing, and transported across the Atlantic at a further cost of fuel, lives, and shipping space, the USAAF could not have played any part in the campaign in North Africa.

Appendix 2: Air Orders of Battle

Air Orders of Battle are complicated because air units can be moved much more quickly than ground units, making them more susceptible to significant change over short periods of time; and because actual strength could (and frequently did) vary considerably from authorized strength. For example, serviceability on Allied units often approached 80 percent, while in Axis units it was closer to 50 percent. Nevertheless, the attached tables are included to demonstrate the initial and growing disparity in air strength in the theater, the extent to which USAAF units were integrated with those of other nations, principally the RAF, as the campaign progressed, and the increased deployment of more modern types of aircraft to the theater.[1]

1. El Alamein & TORCH, November, 1942
   A. Allied
      I. Eastern and Central Mediterranean: RAF Middle East Command
         a. H.Q., R.A.F., M.E.
            2 PRU, 24 *Spitfire, Hurricane*
            60 Squadron, SAAF, *Maryland*
            162 Squadron, 8 *Wellington*
         b. 201 Group (139 a/c)
            1 GRU, 6 *Wellington*
            14 Squadron, 16 *Boston, Marauder*
            15 Squadron, SAAF, 24 *Blenheim, Bisley*
            94 Squadron, *Spitfire*
            203 Squadron, 16 *Blenheim, Bisley, Baltimore, Wellington*
            230 Squadron, 6 *Sunderland*
            252 Squadron, 16 *Beaufighter*
            272 Squadron, 16 *Beaufighter*
            815 Squadron, Fleet Air Arm, 12 *Swordfish*
            821 Squadron, Fleet Air Arm, 12 *Albacore*
            826 Squadron, Fleet Air Arm, 12 *Albacore*

235 Wing
   13 Squadron, Hellenic, 16 *Blenheim, Bisley*
   47 Squadron, 16 *Beaufort, Wellesley*
   459 Squadron, RAAF, 16 *Hudson*
   701 Squadron, Fleet Air Arm, 12 *Walrus*
248 Wing
   38 Squadron, 16 *Wellington*
   458 Squadron, RAAF, 16 *Wellington*
   39 Squadron, 16 *Beaufort*
   221 Squadron, 16 *Wellington*
c. 205 Group (90 a/c)
  231 Wing
   37 Squadron, 16 *Wellington*
   70 Squadron, 16 *Wellington*
  236 Wing
   108 Squadron, 16 *Wellington*
   148 Squadron, 16 *Wellington*
  238 Wing
   40 Squadron, 16 *Wellington*
   104 Squadron, 16 *Wellington*
  242 Wing
   160 Squadron, 16 *Liberator*
  245 Wing
   462 Squadron, RAAF, 16 *Halifax*
d. 216 Group
  117 Squadron, 16 *Hudson*
  173 Squadron, 16 *Boston III/Lodestar*
  216 Squadron, 16 *Bombay, Hudson, Lodestar*
  267 Squadron, 16 *Hudson, Lodestar, Dakota*
e. Western Desert Air Force (596 a/c)
  3 Wing, SAAF
   12 Squadron, SAAF, 24 *Boston*
   24 Squadron, SAAF, 24 *Boston*
   21 Squadron, SAAF, 24 *Baltimore*
  232 Wing
   55 Squadron, 24 *Baltimore*
   223 Squadron, 24 *Baltimore*
   12th Medium Bomb Group, USAAF
    81st Bomb Squadron, 13 B-25
    82nd Bomb Squadron, 13 B-25
    83rd Bomb Squadron, 13 B-25
    434th Bomb Squadron, 13 B-25

285 Wing
   2 PRU (Det), *Spitfire*
   40 Squadron, SAAF, 18 *Hurricane*
   60 Squadron, SAAF, 12 *Maryland*
   208 Squadron, 18 *Hurricane*
211 Group
   6 Squadron, SAAF, 32 *Hurricane*
   57th Fighter Group, USAAF
      64th Fighter Squadron, 25 P-40
      65th Fighter Squadrons, 25 P-40
   233 Wing
      2 Squadron, SAAF, 16 *Kittyhawk*
      4 Squadron, SAAF, 16 *Kittyhawk*
      5 Squadron, SAAF, 16 *Tomahawk*
      260 Squadron, 16 *Kittyhawk*
   239 Wing
      3 Squadron, SAAF, 16 *Kittyhawk*
      112 Squadron, RAAF, 16 *Kittyhawk*
      250 Squadron, RAAF, 16 *Kittyhawk*
      450 Squadron, RAAF, 16 *Kittyhawk*
      66th Fighter Squadron, USAAF, 25 P-40
   244 Wing
      73 Squadron, 16 *Hurricane*
      92 Squadron, 16 *Spitfire*
      145 Squadron, 16 *Spitfire*
      601 Squadron, 16 *Spitfire*
212 Group
   7 Wing, SAAF
      80 Squadron, 16 *Hurricane*
      127 Squadron, 16 *Hurricane*
      335 Squadron (Hellenic), 16 *Hurricane*
      274 Squadron, 16 *Hurricane*
   243 Wing
      1 Squadron, SAAF, 16 *Hurricane*
      35 Squadron, 16 *Hurricane*
      213 Squadron, 16 *Hurricane*
      238 Squadron, 16 *Hurricane*
f. U.S. Army Middle East Air Force (42 a/c)
IX Bomber Command
   1st Provisional Bomb Group (Heavy)
      Halverson Squadron, 8 B-24
      9th Bomb Squadron, 8 B-17

98th Bomb Group (Heavy)
   343rd Bomb Squadron, 8 B-24
   344th Bomb Squadron, 8 B-24
   345th Bomb Squadron, 8 B-24
   415th Bomb Squadron, 8 B-24
g. A.H.Q. Egypt (145 a/c)
  234 Wing
    889 Squadron, Fleet Air Arm, 12 *Fulmar, Hurricane*
  250 Wing
    89 Squadron, 16 *Beaufighter*
    94 Squadron, 16 *Hurricane, Spitfire*
  252 Wing
    46 Squadron, 16 *Beaufighter*
    417 Squadron, RCAF, 16 *Hurricane, Spitfire*
h. A.H.Q. Malta
  69 Squadron, 12 *Wellington, Baltimore, Spitfire*
  89 Squadron, *Beaufighter*
  126 Squadron, 24 *Spitfire*
  185 Squadron, 24 *Spitfire*
  227 Squadron, 20 *Beaufighter*
  229 Squadron, 16 *Hurricane, Spitfire*
  249 Squadron, 16 *Spitfire*
  828 Squadron, Fleet Air Arm, 3 *Albacore*
  830 Squadron, Fleet Air Arm, 3 *Swordfish*
II. Western Mediterranean
  a. Eastern Air Command
    242 Group
     322 Wing
      81 Squadron, *Spitfire*
      154 Squadron, *Spitfire*
      242 Squadron, *Spitfire*
      225 Squadron, *Hurricane*
     323 Wing
      43 Squadron, *Hurricane*
      253 Squadron, *Hurricane*
      No. 4 PRU
     324 Wing
      72 Squadron, *Spitfire*
      93 Squadron, *Spitfire*
      111 Squadron, *Spitfire*
      152 Squadron, *Spitfire*
      255 Squadron, *Beaufighter*

325 Wing
    13 Squadron, *Bisley*
    18 Squadron, *Bisley*
    114 Squadron, *Bisley*
    614 Squadron, *Bisley*
328 Wing
    500 Squadron, *Hudson*
    608 Squadron, *Hudson*
    700 Squadron, Fleet Air Arm, *Walrus*
    813 Squadron, Fleet Air Arm, *Swordfish*
  89 Squadron, *Beaufighter*
  142 Squadron, *Wellington*
  150 Squadron, *Wellington*
  153 Squadron, *Beaufighter*
  651 Squadron, *Auster*

b. 12th Air Force
97th Bomb Group (Heavy), 35 B-17E
  340th Bomb Squadron
  341st Bomb Squadron
  342nd Bomb Squadron
  414th Bomb Squadron
301st Bomb Group (Heavy), 35 B-17F (arr. Nov.)
  32nd Bomb Squadron
  352nd Bomb Squadron
  353rd Bomb Squadron
  419th Bomb Squadron
310th Bomb Group (Medium), 57 B-25C (in U.K., arr. Dec.)
  379th Bomb Squadron
  380th Bomb Squadron
  381st Bomb Squadron
  428th Bomb Squadron
319th Bomb Group (Medium), 57 B-26B (in U.K., arr. Nov.)
  437th Bomb Squadron
  438th Bomb Squadron
  439th Bomb Squadron
  440th Bomb Squadron
320th Bomb Group (Medium), 57 B-26B (in U.S.)
  441st Bomb Squadron
  442nd Bomb Squadron
  443rd Bomb Squadron
  444th Bomb Squadron

17th Bomb Group (Medium), 57 B-26B (in U.S., arr. Dec.)
   34th Bomb Squadron
   37th Bomb Squadron
   95th Bomb Squadron
   432nd Bomb Squadron
321st Bomb Group (Medium), 57 B-25C (in U.S.)
   445th Bomb Squadron
   446th Bomb Squadron
   447th Bomb Squadron
   448th Bomb Squadron
47th Bomb Group (Light), 57 A-20B (in U.K., arr. Dec.)
   84th Bomb Squadron
   85th Bomb Squadron
   86th Bomb Squadron
   87th Bomb Squadron
15th Bomb Squadron (Light), 15 A-20
1st Fighter Group, 75 P-38F
   27th Fighter Squadron
   71st Fighter Squadron
   94th Fighter Squadron
14th Fighter Group, 75 P-38F
   37th Fighter Squadron (in Iceland)
   48th Fighter Squadron
   49th Fighter Squadron
31st Fighter Group, 80 *Spitfire V*
   307th Fighter Squadron
   308th Fighter Squadron
   309th Fighter Squadron
52nd Fighter Group, 46 *Spitfire V*
   2nd Fighter Squadron
   4th Fighter Squadron
   5th Fighter Squadron
33rd Fighter Group, P-40F
   58th Fighter Squadron
   59th Fighter Squadron
   60th Fighter Squadron
82nd Fighter Group, 75 P-38G (arr. Dec.)
   95th Fighter Squadron
   96th Fighter Squadron
   97th Fighter Squadron

81st Fighter Group, 80 P-39 (P-400, arr. Jan.)
   91st Fighter Squadron
   92nd Fighter Squadron
   93rd Fighter Squadron
350th Fighter Group, 80 P-39 (P-400, arr. Jan.)
   345th Fighter Squadron
   346th Fighter Squadron
   347th Fighter Squadron
60th Troop Carrier Group, 52 C-47
   10th Troop Carrier Squadron
   11th Troop Carrier Squadron
   12th Troop Carrier Squadron
   28th Troop Carrier Squadron
62nd Troop Carrier Group, 52 C-47
   4th Troop Carrier Squadron
   7th Troop Carrier Squadron
   8th Troop Carrier Squadron
   51st Troop Carrier Squadron
64th Troop Carrier Group, 52 C-47
   16th Troop Carrier Squadron
   17th Troop Carrier Squadron
   18th Troop Carrier Squadron
   35th Troop Carrier Squadron
3rd Photographic Reconnaissance Group
   5th Photographic Reconnaissance Squadron, 13 F-4
   12th Photographic Reconnaissance Squadron, 13 F-4
   15th Photographic Mapping Squadron, 4 B-17F
68th Observation Group, (arr. Jan.) 61 P-39L, 36 A-20B
   16th Observation Squadron
   111th Observation Squadron
   122nd Observation Squadron
   154th Observation Squadron
c. RAF Coastal Command (Gibraltar)
  10 Squadron, RAAF, *Sunderland*
  202 Squadron, *Catalina*
  210 Squadron, *Catalina*
  233 Squadron, *Hudson*
  235 Squadron, *Beaufighter*
  540 Squadron, *PR Mosquito*
  544 Squadron, *PR Spitfire*

III. Naval Units
  a. Western Naval Task Force, Morocco
    Northern Air Group, TG 34.8
      USS *Sangamon* (CVE-26)
        VGF-26, 12 F4F-4
        VGS-26, 9 TBF, 9 SBD
      USS *Chenango* (CVE-28)
        76 P-40F (33rd Fighter Group)
    Center Air Group, TG 34.9
      USS *Ranger* (CV-4)
        VF-9, 27 F4F-4
        VF-41, 27 F4F-4
        VS-41, 18 SBD
      USS *Suwannee* (CVE-27)
        VGS-27, 9 TBF
        VGF-27, 12 F4F-4
        VGF-28, 12 F4F-4
        VGS-30, 6 F4F-4
    Southern Air Group, TG 34.10
      USS *Santee* (CVE-29)
        VGS-29, 9 TBF, 9 SBD
        VGF-29, 12 F4F-4
    Port Lyautey (after capture)
      VP-73, PBY-5A
      VP-92, PBY-5A
  b. Center Task Force—Oran
    HMS Furious
      801 Squadron, 12 *Seafire*
      807 Squadron, 12 *Seafire*
      882 Squadron, 8 *Albacore*, 1 *Fulmar*
    HMS Biter
      800 Squadron, 15 *Sea Hurricane*
    HMS Dasher
      804 Squadron, 6 *Sea Hurricane*
      891 Squadron, 6 *Sea Hurricane*
  c. Eastern Task Force—Algiers
    HMS Argus
      880 Squadron, 12 *Seafire*
    HMS Avenger
      802 Squadron, 6 *Sea Hurricane*
      883 Squadron, 6 *Sea Hurricane*

    d. Force H, Carrier Covering Force
      HMS Victorious
        884 Squadron, 9 *Seafire*
        882 Squadron, 12 *Martlet* (F4F)
        809 Squadron, 6 *Fulmar*
        817 Squadron, 9 *Albacore*
        832 Squadron, 12 *Albacore*
      HMS Formidable
        885 Squadron, 6 *Seafire*
        888 Squadron, 12 *Martlet*
        893 Squadron, 12 *Martlet*
        820 Squadron, 6 *Albacore*
B. Axis
  I. German
    Luftflotte 2, Rome
      Fliegerkorps II, Messina (579 a/c)
        KG-606
        KG-806
        II, NJG-2, Ju-88 & Me-110
        II, JG-53, Me-109
        FAG-122, Ju-88
      Fliegerkorps X, Athens (266 a/c)
        2, FAG-123, Ju-88
        I-II, 1st Luftwaffe Area Command, Ju-88
        II, KG-100, He-111
        I, KG-54, Ju-88
      Fliegerfuhrer Afrika, Fuka (324 a/c)
        JG-27, Me-109
        III, JG-53, Me-109
        8, ZG-26, Me-110
        7,8, ZG-1, Me-210
        StG-3, 80 Ju-87
        12, LG-2, Ju-88
        4, NAG-12, 5 Me-109
        2, NAG-14, 6 Me-109
        1, FAG-121, 5 Ju-88
      Transportflieger, 180 a/c

  II. Vichy French[2]
    Algeria
      La Senia
        49 Dewoitine 520
        15 LEO 45
        15 Bloch 174-5

Maison Blanche
    52 Dewoitine 520
Blida
    26 DB-7
    13 Glenn Martin 167 (*Maryland*)
    6 Potez 63
Setif
    13 Potez-63
Arzeu
    12 Latecoere 298
Lartigues
    12 Glenn Martin 167
Morocco
    Marrakesh
        13 LEO 45
        13 Potez-63
    Rabat
        24 Curtiss 75a
        15 LEO 45
    Meknes
        13 LEO 45
    Casablanca
        38 Dewoitine 520
        15 DB-7
    Port Lyautey
        12 Dewoitine 520
        12 Glenn Martin 167
    Agadir
        13 DB-7
Tunisia
    El Aouina
        26 LEO 45
        13 Bloch 174–5
    Gabes
        18 Potez 631
    Bizerte-Sidi Ahmed
        25 Dewoitine 520
    Bizerte-Karouba (Marine)
        3 Briguet-Bicenta
        3 LEO 257
        17 Loire 130

2. The Battle for Tunisia, April, 1943
  A. Allied: Mediterranean Air Command
    I. Northwest African Air Forces
      a. Northwest African Tactical Air Force (NATAF)
      Western Desert Air Force
        12 Squadron, SAAF, 16 *Boston*
        21 Squadron, SAAF, 16 *Baltimore*
        24 Squadron, SAAF, 16 *Boston*
        12th Bomb Group, Medium
          83rd Bomb Squadron, 13 B-25
          434th Bomb Squadron, 13 B-25
        232 Wing
          55 Squadron, 16 *Baltimore*
          223 Squadron, 16 *Baltimore*
        249 Wing
          117 Squadron, *Hudson*
          216 Squadron, *Hudson*
        821 Squadron, FAA, *Albacore*
      XII Air Support Command
        31st Fighter Group, 75 *Spitfire V*
          307th Fighter Squadron
          308th Fighter Squadron
          309th Fighter Squadron
        33rd Fighter Group, 75 P-40F
          58th Fighter Squadron
          59th Fighter Squadron
          60th Fighter Squadron
        52nd Fighter Group, 75 *Spitfire V*
          2nd Fighter Squadron
          4th Fighter Squadron
          5th Fighter Squadron
        68th Observation Group, 18 P-39
          154th Observation Squadron,
      242 Group
        322 Wing
          81 Squadron, 16 *Spitfire*
          152 Squadron, 16 *Spitfire*
          154 Squadron, 16 *Spitfire*
          232 Squadron, 16 *Spitfire*
          242 Squadron, 16 *Spitfire*

324 Wing
  72 Squadron, 16 *Spitfire*
  93 Squadron, 16 *Spitfire*
  111 Squadron, 16 *Spitfire*
  225 Squadron, 16 *Spitfire*
  241 Squadron, 16 *Hurricane*
  243 Squadron, 16 *Spitfire*
211 Group
  7 Wing, SAAF
    2 Squadron, SAAF, 21 *Kittyhawk*
    4 Squadron, SAAF, 21 *Kittyhawk*
    5 Squadron, SAAF, 21 *Kittyhawk*
  57th Fighter Group, 80 P-40
    64th Fighter Squadron
    65th Fighter Squadron
    66th Fighter Squadron
    314th Fighter Squadron (324th Fighter Group)
  79th Fighter Group, 80 P-40
    85th Fighter Squadron
    86th Fighter Squadron
    87th Fighter Squadron
    316th Fighter Squadron (324th Fighter Group)
  239 Wing
    3 Squadron, RAAF, 21 *Kittyhawk*
    112 Squadron, 21 *Kittyhawk*
    250 Squadron, 21 *Kittyhawk*
    260 Squadron, 21 *Kittyhawk*
    450 Squadron, RAAF, 21 *Kittyhawk*
  244 Wing
    1 Squadron, SAAF, 19 *Spitfire*
    6 Squadron, 16 *Hurricane*
    92 Squadron, 21 *Spitfire*
    145 Squadron, 21 *Spitfire*
    417 Squadron, RCAF, 19 *Spitfire*
    601 Squadron, 19 *Spitfire*
  285 Wing
    40 Squadron, SAAF, 18 *Hurricane*
    60 Squadron, SAAF, 7 *Baltimore*
    73 Squadron, 21 *Hurricane*
    680 Squadron, *Spitfire*
Northwest African Tactical Bomber Force
  Huitieme Groupement, Free French Air Force, 16 LEO-45

12th Bomb Group (Medium)
   81st Bomb Squadron, 13 B-25
   82nd Bomb Squadron, 13 B-25
47th Bomb Group (Light)
   84th Bomb Squadron, 13 A-20
   85th Bomb Squadron, 13 A-20
   86th Bomb Squadron, 13 A-20
   87th Bomb Squadron, 13 A-20
326 Wing
   13 Squadron, 16 *Bisley*
   18 Squadron, 16 *Bisley*
   114 Squadron, 16 *Boston*
   614 Squadron, 16 *Bisley*

b. Northwest African Strategic Air Force (NASAF)
   142 Squadron, 16 *Wellington*
   150 Squadron, 16 *Wellington*
   5th Heavy Bombardment Wing
     2nd Bomb Group (Heavy), 32 B-17E
      20th Bomb Squadron
      49th Bomb Squadron
      96th Bomb Squadron
      429th Bomb Squadron
     97th Bomb Group (Heavy), 32 B-17E
      340th Bomb Squadron
      341st Bomb Squadron
      342nd Bomb Squadron
      414th Bomb Squadron
     99th Bomb Group (Heavy), 35 B-17F
      346th Bomb Squadron
      357th Bomb Squadron
      348th Bomb Squadron
      416th Bomb Squadron
     301st Bomb Group (Heavy), 32 B-17F
      32nd Bomb Squadron
      352nd Bomb Squadron
      353rd Bomb Squadron
      419th Bomb Squadron
     1st Fighter Group, 75 P-38F
      27th Fighter Squadron
      71st Fighter Squadron
      94th Fighter Squadron

47th Medium Bombardment Wing
  17th Bomb Group (Medium), 52 B-26B
    34th Bomb Squadron
    37th Bomb Squadron
    95th Bomb Squadron
    432nd Bomb Squadron
  310th Bomb Group (Medium), 52 B-25C
    379th Bomb Squadron
    380th Bomb Squadron
    381st Bomb Squadron
    428th Bomb Squadron
  319th Bomb Group (Medium), 52 B-26B
    437th Bomb Squadron
    438th Bomb Squadron
    439th Bomb Squadron
    440th Bomb Squadron
  320th Bomb Group (Medium), 52 B-26B
    441st Bomb Squadron
    442nd Bomb Squadron
    443rd Bomb Squadron
    444th Bomb Squadron
  321st Bomb Group (Medium), 52 B-25C
    445th Bomb Squadron
    446th Bomb Squadron
    447th Bomb Squadron
    448th Bomb Squadron
  82nd Fighter Group, 75 P-38G
    95th Fighter Squadron
    96th Fighter Squadron
    97th Fighter Squadron
  325th Fighter Group, 75 P-40
    317th Fighter Squadron
    318th Fighter Squadron
    319th Fighter Squadron
c. Northwest African Coastal Air Force (NACAF)
  323 Wing
    32 Squadron, 16 *Hurricane*
    43 Squadron, 16 *Spitfire*
    87 Squadron, 16 *Hurricane*
    253 Squadron, 16 *Hurricane*

325 Wing
   153 Squadron, 16 *Beaufighter*
   255 Squadron, 16 *Beaufighter*
   600 Squadron, 16 *Beaufighter*
328 Wing
   14 Squadron, 16 *Marauder*
   500 Squadron, 16 *Hudson*
   608 Squadron, 16 *Hudson*
813 Squadron, FAA, 12 *Swordfish*
826 Squadron, FAA, 12 *Albacore*
1st Provisional Anti-Submarine Wing
   1st Anti-Submarine Squadron, 8 B-24
   2nd Anti-Submarine Squadron, 8 B-24
2nd Air Defense Wing
   81st Fighter Group, 75 P-39
      91st Fighter Squadron
      92nd Fighter Squadron
      93rd Fighter Squadron
   350th Fighter Group, 75 P-39
      345th Fighter Squadron
      346th Fighter Squadron
      347th Fighter Squadron
d. Northwest African Troop Carrier Command (NATCC)
   51st Troop Carrier Wing
      62nd Troop Carrier Group, 52 C-47
         4th Troop Carrier Squadron
         7th Troop Carrier Squadron
         8th Troop Carrier Squadron
         51st Troop Carrier Squadron
      64th Troop Carrier Group, 52 C-47
         16th Troop Carrier Squadron
         17th Troop Carrier Squadron
         18th Troop Carrier Squadron
         35th Troop Carrier Squadron
e. Northwest African Photo Reconnaissance Wing (NAPRW)
   682 Squadron, 12 *Spitfire*
   3rd Photographic Reconnaissance Group
      5th Photographic Reconnaissance Squadron, 13 F-4/5
      12th Photographic Reconnaissance Squadron, 13 F-4/5
      15th Photographic Reconnaissance Squadron, 4 B-17
f. Northwest African Training Command (NATC)
   (Arriving replacement aircraft and crews)

g. Northwest African Air Service Command (NAASC)
  60th Troop Carrier Group, 52 C-47
    10th Troop Carrier Squadron
    11th Troop Carrier Squadron
    12th Troop Carrier Squadron
    28th Troop Carrier Squadron
II. Malta Air Command
  23 Squadron, 16 *Mosquito*
  39 Squadron, 16 *Beaufort*
  69 Squadron, 10 *Baltimore*
  126 Squadron, 16 *Spitfire*
  185 Squadron, 16 *Spitfire*
  221 Squadron, 16 *Wellington*
  229 Squadron, 16 *Spitfire*
  249 Squadron, 16 *Spitfire*
  272 Squadron, 16 *Beaufighter*
  458 Squadron, RAAF, 16 *Wellington*
  683 Squadron, 12 *Spitfire*
  821 Squadron, FAA, 12 *Albacore*
  828 Squadron, FAA, 12 *Albacore*
  830 Squadron, FAA, 12 *Swordfish*
  1435 Squadron, 16 *Spitfire*
III. Middle East Air Command (units forward in the battle area)
  Ninth Air Force
    Ninth Bomber Command
      178 Squadron, 16 *Liberator*
      98th Heavy Bombardment Group
        343rd Bomb Squadron, 9 B-24
        344th Bomb Squadron, 9 B-24
        345th Bomb Squadron, 9 B-24
        415th Bomb Squadron, 9 B-24
      376th Bomb Group
        512th Bomb Squadron, 9 B-24
        513th Bomb Squadron, 9 B-24
        514th Bomb Squadron, 9 B-24
        515th Bomb Squadron, 9 B-24
     316th Troop Carrier Group
       36th Troop Carrier Squadron, 13 C-47
       37th Troop Carrier Squadron, 13 C-47
       44th Troop Carrier Squadron, 13 C-47
       45th Troop Carrier Squadron, 13 C-47

201 Group
  1 GRU, 3 *Wellington*
  15 Squadron, SAAF, 16 *Blenheim*
  52 Squadron, 16 *Baltimore*
  227 Squadron, 16 *Beaufighter*
  454 Squadron, RAAF, 16 *Baltimore*
  701 Squadron, FAA, 7 *Walrus*
  815 Squadron, FAA, 12 *Swordfish*
  235 Wing
    13 Hellenic Squadron, 16 *Blenheim*
    459 Squadron, RAAF, 16 *Hudson*
  238 Wing
    47 Squadron, 16 *Beaufort*
    603 Squadron, 16 *Beaufighter*
  245 Wing
    458 Squadron, RAAF, *Wellington*
  247 Wing
    38 Squadron, 16 *Wellington*
    203 Squadron, 16 *Baltimore*
    252 Squadron, 16 *Beaufighter*
Air Defenses, Eastern Mediterranean
  210 Group
    89 Squadron, 16 *Beaufighter*
    213 Squadron, 16 *Hurricane*
    274 Squadron, 16 *Hurricane*
  212 Group
    7 Squadron, SAAF, 16 *Hurricane*
    33 Squadron, 16 *Hurricane*
    46 Squadron, 16 *Beaufighter*
    80 Squadron, 16 *Hurricane*
    94 Squadron, 16 *Hurricane*
    123 Squadron, 16 *Hurricane*
HQ, RAF, Middle East
  148 Squadron, 14 *Liberator*
  162 Squadron, 15 *Wellington*
  680 Squadron, 12 *Spitfire*
  205 Group
    231 Wing
      37 Squadron, 16 *Wellington*
      40 Squadron, 16 *Wellington*
      70 Squadron, 16 *Wellington*

236 Wing
  104 Squadron, 16 *Wellington*
  462 Squadron, RAAF, 16 *Halifax*
216 Group
  117 Squadron, 30 *Hudson*
  173 Squadron, 35 *Lodestar*
  216 Squadron, 30 *Hudson*
  267 Squadron, 30 *Hudson*
B. Axis
  Luftflotte 2, Rome
    Fliegerkorps II, Messina
      I-III, KG-26
      II, KG-30
      I-II, KG-54
      I-II, KG-76
      I, KG-77
      III, ZG-26
      II, JG-27
      I-II, NJG-2
      FAG-122
    Fliegerkorps X, Athens
    Fliegerkorps Tunis
      JG-53, 90 Me-109s
      JG-77, 90 Me-109s
      III, SG-1, 25 Me-109s
      III, SG-4, 25 Fw-190s
      2, 4 NAG-14, 16 Me-109s
    Lufttransportfuhrer Mittelmeer
      400 Ju-52
      20 Me-323
      15 Fw-200
      3 BV-222

Notes

Introduction

1. "United States Department of Defense, Fiscal Year 2011 Budget Request," p. 8-1; available at http://comptroller.defense.gov/budget.html (accessed on 1 February 2011).

2. Tami Davis Biddle, *Rhetoric and Reality in Air Warfare* (Princeton: Princeton University Press, 2002), p. 289.

3. Phillip S. Meilinger, "The Historiography of Airpower: Theory and Doctrine," *Journal of Military History* 64:2 (April 2000): 467.

4. Rick Atkinson, *An Army at Dawn: The War in North Africa, 1942–43* (New York: Henry Holt, 2002), and Douglas Porch, *The Path to Victory: The Mediterranean Theater in World War II* (New York, Farrar, Straus and Giroux, 2004).

5. Atkinson, *An Army at Dawn*; and Porch, *The Path to Victory*, especially pp. 87–89 (Regia Aeronautica [Italian Air Force]) and 216–218 (comparisons between Allied and Axis fighters).

6. The exceptions are Dan Mortensen, *A Pattern for Joint Operations* (Washington, DC: Office of Air Force History, 1987), and Brad Gladman, *Intelligence and Anglo-American Air Support in World War Two: The Western Desert and Tunisia, 1940–43* (London: Palgrave Macmillan, 2009).

7. On 31 August 1942, General Carl Spaatz cabled General Arnold his belief that "any application of our air forces now in United Kingdom for any other purpose jeopardizes the attainment of air superiority over Germany and ultimate victory." Arnold Papers, Box 156, Library of Congress.

8. U.S. War Department, *Field Manual 100-20, Command and Employment of Air Power* (Washington, DC: U.S. Government Printing Office, 1943), p. 1.

9. As a model for the genre, I am indebted to Joel S.A. Hayward for his excellent volume *Stopped at Stalingrad: The Luftwaffe and Hitler's Defeat in the East, 1942–1943* (Lawrence: University Press of Kansas, 1998).

10. Quoted in Adrian Lewis, *Omaha Beach: A Flawed Victory* (Chapel Hill: University of North Carolina Press, 2001), p. 148.

11. See, among many others, Biddle, *Rhetoric and Reality*; Mark Clodfelter, *The Limits of Air Power* (New York: Free Press, 1989); Robert S. Ehlers, *Targeting the Third Reich: Air Intelligence and the Allied Bombing Campaigns* (Lawrence: University Press of Kansas, 2009); Conrad Crane, *Bombs, Cities, and Civilians* (Lawrence: University Press of Kansas, 1993); Gian Gentile, *How Effective is Strategic Bomb-*

ing? (New York: New York University Press, 2001); and Michael S. Sherry, *The Rise of American Air Power: The Creation of Armageddon* (New Haven: Yale University Press, 1987).

12. See especially Sherry, *The Rise of American Air Power.* In *Bombs, Cities, and Civilians,* Conrad Crane argues strongly for the differences between the British and American approaches, but both sides did inflict large numbers of civilian casualties, whether it was through doctrinal differences or technological limitations.

13. Those who suggest that the atomic bombs alone caused the Japanese to surrender in World War II ignore the Soviet entry into the war on 8 August 1945 and the American ground and naval forces that seized the advanced bases the bombers operated from. Those who believe the North Atlantic Treaty Organization's March to June 1999 air campaign against Serbia single-handedly forced the Serbs to capitulate ignore the diplomatic efforts that isolated Slobodan Milosevic's regime, especially from Russia, and NATO's deployment of ground forces to the region that suggested a ground phase would follow the air campaign. For an extreme example, see John Keegan, "Please, Mr. Blair, Never Take Such a Risk Again," *London Daily Telegraph,* Issue 1472 (6 June 1999); available at http://www.portal.telegraph.co.uk/htmlContent.jhtml?html=%2Farchive%2F1999%2F06%2F06%2Fwkee06.html (accessed 31 August 2009). And in March 2011, Western leaders demonstrated their continuing commitment to these ideas with an air-only intervention in Libya that eventually removed Colonel Muammar Gadhafi from power, but only by cooperating closely with the ground forces of the Libyan resistance.

14. Spaatz to Arnold, 7 March 1943, Central Decimal File, Folder 312.1-B, Operations Letters, Box 193, Entry 294A, Serial 312, Record Group 18, Records of the Army Air Forces, National Records and Archives Administration (hereinafter NARA 2), College Park, MD.

15. Wesley Frank Craven and James Lea Cate, eds., *The Army Air Forces in World War II.* 7 vols. (Chicago: University Press, 1948–1958).

16. Ibid., repr. (Washington, DC: Office of Air Force History, 1983), vol. 1, pp. v–vi.

17. Alfred D. Chandler and Louis Galambos, et al., eds., *The Papers of Dwight David Eisenhower.* 21 vols. (Baltimore: Johns Hopkins University Press, 1970–2001).

18. Karl Gundelach, *Die Deutsche Luftwaffe im Mittelmeer, 1940–1945* (The German Air Force in the Mediterranean, 1940–1945) (Frankfurt: Peter Lang, 1981); Hellmuth Felmy, *The German Air Service Versus the Allies in the Mediterranean,* United States Air Force Historical Studies, No. 161 (Maxwell AFB, AL: USAF Historical Division, Research Studies Institute, Air University, 1955); Williamson Murray, *Strategy for Defeat: The Luftwaffe, 1933–1945* (Maxwell AFB, AL: Air University Press, 1983); and James Corum, *The Luftwaffe: Creating the Operational Air War, 1918–1940* (Lawrence: University Press of Kansas, 1997).

Chapter 1: Theory and Doctrine During the Interwar Period

1. Edward Warner, "Douhet, Mitchell, Seversky: Theories of Air Warfare," pp. 485–503 in Edward Mead Earle (ed.), *Makers of Modern Strategy* (Princeton: Princeton University Press, 1943).

2. See Conrad Crane, *Bombs, Cities and Civilians* (Lawrence: University Press of Kansas, 1993).

3. Alexander de Seversky, *Victory Through Airpower* (New York: Simon and Schuster, 1942).

4. Giulio Douhet, *The Command of the Air*, translated by Dino Ferrar, repr. (Washington, DC: U.S. Government Printing Office, 1998), pp. 145, 179, 191.

5. The only confirmed release was, ironically, in Douhet's Italy when an American transport loaded with mustard gas (stockpiled in case of Axis first use) was struck in an air raid on Bari in December 1943. See Rick Atkinson, *Day of Battle* (New York: Henry Holt, 2007), pp. 271–278.

6. De Seversky, *Victory Through Airpower*, pp. 246, 146.

7. De Seversky, *Victory Through Airpower*, p. 102.

8. Thomas Alexander Hughes, *Overlord: General Pete Quesada and the Triumph of Tactical Air Power in World War II* (New York: Free Press, 1995), p. 86.

9. Williamson Murray, *Strategy for Defeat: The Luftwaffe 1933–1945* (Maxwell AFB, AL: Air University Press, 1983), pp. xxiii–xxiv.

10. Robert T. Finney, *History of the Air Corps Tactical School, 1920–1940*, USAF Historical Studies No. 100 (Maxwell AFB, AL: Air University Press, 1955), p. 38, and Martha Byrd, *Chennault: Giving Wings to the Tiger* (Tuscaloosa: University of Alabama Press, 1987).

11. Letter, John Cannon to George Brett, 22 June 1931, Folder 3, Box 6, John Cannon Papers, Merrill-Cazier Memorial Library, Utah State University, Logan.

12. J. C. Slessor, *Air Power and Armies* (Oxford, UK: Oxford University Press, 1936), p. vii.

13. William Mitchell, *Our Air Force: The Keystone of National Defense* (New York: E. P. Dutton, 1921), p. xix.

14. William Mitchell, *Winged Defense: The Development and Possibilities of Modern Air Power—Economic and Military* (New York: G. P. Putnam's Sons, 1925).

15. Alfred F. Hurley, *Billy Mitchell: Crusader for Air Power* (Bloomington: University of Indiana Press, 1964), p. 148.

16. Finney, *History of the Air Corps Tactical School*, pp. 27, 28.

17. De Seversky, *Victory Through Airpower*, 48.

18. Ibid., p. 123.

19. The principal authors were Harold George, Kenneth Walker, Laurence Kuter, and Haywood Hansell, all current or former faculty members at the Air Corps Tactical School and advocates for strategic bombing. For a complete discussion of the plan and the process that created it, see Haywood Hansell, *The Air Plan That Defeated Hitler* (Atlanta: Longino and Porter, 1972).

20. See David R. Mets, *Master of Airpower: General Carl A. Spaatz* (Novato, CA: Presidio, 1988), and Richard G. Davis, *Carl A. Spaatz and the Air War in Europe* (Washington, DC: Smithsonian Institute Press, 1994).

21. See Richard G. Davis, "'Take Down That Damned Sign': Doolittle as Combat Commander," *Air Power History* 40:4 (Winter 1993): 16–21; and James H. Doolittle, *I Could Never Be So Lucky Again* (New York, Bantam, 1991).

22. See Lewis Hyde Brereton, *The Brereton Diaries* (New York: Morrow, 1946).

23. See David R. Mets, "A Glider in the Propwash of the Royal Air Force? General Carl A. Spaatz, the RAF, and the Foundations of American Tactical Air Doctrine," in Daniel Mortensen (ed.), *Airpower and Ground Armies: Essays on the Evolution of Anglo-American Air Doctrine, 1940–43* (Maxwell AFB, AL: Air University Press, 1998), pp. 45–92.

24. U.S. War Department, *Field Manual 31-35, Aviation in Support of Ground Forces* (Washington, DC: U.S. Government Printing Office, 1942), para. 1–6.

25. Kent Roberts Greenfield, *Army Air Forces and the Air-Ground Battle Team* (Washington, DC: Historical Section, Army Ground Forces, 1948), p. 45.

26. See Christopher R. Gabel, *The U.S. Army GHQ Maneuvers of 1941* (Washington, DC: Center of Military History, United States Army, 1991), pp. 39–41.

27. Greenfield, *Army Air Forces and the Air-Ground Battle Team*, p. 1.

28. In his study of the prewar training maneuvers, Christopher Gabel found that "the subordination of air to ground units continued to hold sway among ground officers even after the (1941) creation of the Army Air Forces." Gabel, *The U.S. Army GHQ Maneuvers of 1941*, p. 37.

29. Ibid., p. 47; Robert Futrell, *Ideas, Concepts, Doctrine: Basic Thinking in the United States Air Force, 1907–1960* (Maxwell AFB, AL: Air University Press, 1971 [repr. 1989]), p. 135.

30. Greenfield was a professor of modern European history and chair of the history department at Johns Hopkins University; he also served as chief historian for the Department of the Army from 1946 until 1958 and edited the first fifty-one of eighty series volumes. See http://ead.library.jhu.edu/ms022.xml, accessed on 1 May 2009.

31. George Howe, *Northwest Africa: Seizing the Initiative in the West* (Washington, DC: Center of Military History, 1991), p. 61.

32. Howe, *Northwest Africa: Seizing the Initiative in the West*, p. 493.

33. David Mets, "A Glider in the Propwash of the Royal Air Force?" in Mortensen, *Airpower and Ground Armies*, pp. 52–53.

34. Finney, *History of the Air Corps Tactical School*, p. 36.

35. See, among others, Mark Calhoun, "Defeat at Kasserine: American Armor Doctrine, Training, and Battle Command in Northwest Africa (During) World War II," Unpubl. thesis, U.S. Army Command and General Staff College, Fort Leavenworth, KS, 2003.

36. James Huston, "Tactical Use of Air Power in World War II: The Army Experience," *Military Affairs* 14:4 (Winter 1950): 167.

37. Ibid., p. 184.

38. Ibid., pp. 186–191.

39. Ibid., p. 187.

40. Ibid., p. 189.

41. Ibid., p. 190.

42. Thomas Greer, *The Development of Air Doctrine in the Army Air Arm, 1917–1941* (Washington, DC: Office of Air Force History, 1953 [repr. 1985]), p. 12.

43. Ibid., p. 67.

44. Ibid., p. 130.

45. Futrell, *Ideas, Concepts, Doctrine*, p. 83.

46. Daniel Mortensen, *A Pattern for Joint Operations: World War II Close Air Support, North Africa* (Washington, DC: U.S. Government Printing Office, 1987).

47. Ibid., p. iii.

48. Benjamin Franklin Cooling (ed.), *Case Studies in the Development of Close Air Support* (Washington, DC: Office of Air Force History, 1990).

49. Lee Kennett, "Developments to 1939," in Benjamin Franklin Cooling (ed.), *Case Studies in the Development of Close Air Support* (Washington, DC: Office of Air Force History, 1990), p. 52.

50. Ibid., p. 53.

51. Ibid., p. 60.

52. David Syrett, "The Tunisian Campaign, 1942–1943," in Benjamin Franklin Cooling (ed.), *Case Studies in the Development of Close Air Support* (Washington, DC: Office of Air Force History, 1990), p. 157.

53. Ibid., pp. 165–167.

54. Ibid., p. 169.

55. Ibid., p. 184.

56. Joe Gray Taylor, "American Experience in the Southwest Pacific" in Benjamin Franklin Cooling (ed.), *Case Studies in the Development of Close Air Support* (Washington, DC: Office of Air Force History, 1990), p. 297.

57. Ibid., p. 298.

58. Ibid., p. 311.

59. Richard Muller, "Close Air Support: The German, British, and American Experiences, 1918–1941," in Williamson Murray and Allan Millett (eds.), *Military Innovation in the Interwar Period* (Cambridge, UK: Cambridge University Press, 1996), p. 173.

60. Ibid., p. 173.

61. Ibid., p. 175.

62. Hughes, *Overlord*, p. 57.

63. Hughes, *Overlord*, p. 60.

64. Gary Cox, "Beyond the Battle Line: U.S. Air Attack Theory and Doctrine, 1919–1941," unpubl. thesis (Maxwell AFB, AL: School of Advanced Air and Space Studies, 1995), p. 5.

65. David E. Johnson, *Fast Tanks and Heavy Bombers: Innovation in the U.S. Army, 1917–1945* (Ithaca: Cornell University Press, 1998), pp. 167, 215, 226.

66. Jonathan House, *Combined Arms Warfare in the Twentieth Century* (Lawrence: University Press of Kansas, 2001).

67. Ibid., p. 67.

68. Ibid., p. 103.

69. Brad Gladman, "The Development of Tactical Air Doctrine in North Africa, 1940–43," in Sebastian Cox and Peter Gray, eds., *Air Power History: Turning Points from Kitty Hawk to Kosovo* (London: Frank Cass, 2002), p. 188.

70. B. Michael Bechthold, "A Question of Success: Tactical Air Doctrine and Practice in North Africa, 1942–43," *Journal of Military History* 68:3 (July 2004), p. 821.

71. Ibid., p. 822.

72. Ibid., pp. 824, 841, 846.

73. Phillip Meilinger, *Airpower: Myths and Facts* (Maxwell AFB, AL: Air University Press, 2003).

74. Ibid., p. 18. In defense of this comparison, "equitation" did not involve training in the use of the horse on the battlefield but, rather, was widely considered to be a form of recreation or physical training. Similar studies of service schools today would likely find that the time officers spend in physical or recreational activities (such as golf) still consume disproportionate amounts of students' time.

75. Ibid., p. 20.

76. Adrian Lewis, *The American Culture of War: The History of U.S. Military Force from World War II to Operation Iraqi Freedom* (New York: Routledge, 2007), p. 38.

77. For a thorough discussion of the USAAF's early intelligence difficulties, especially in the strategic campaign, see Robert S. Ehlers Jr., *Targeting the Reich: Air Intelligence and the Allied Bombing Campaigns* (Lawrence: University Press of Kansas, 2009).

Chapter 2: The Western Desert

1. David R. Mets, "A Glider in the Propwash of the Royal Air Force? General Carl A. Spaatz, the RAF, and the Foundations of American Tactical Air Doctrine," in Daniel Mortensen, ed., *Airpower and Ground Armies: Essays on the Evolution of Anglo-American Air Doctrine 1940–43* (Maxwell AFB, AL: Air University Press, 1998), pp. 45–92.

2. See Vincent Orange, "Getting Together: Tedder, Coningham and Americans in the Desert and Tunisia, 1940–43," in Daniel Mortensen, ed., *Airpower and Ground Armies: Essays on the Evolution of Anglo-American Air Doctrine 1940–43* (Maxwell AFB, AL: Air University Press, 1998), pp. 1–44.

3. Brett to Arnold, 17 September 1941, in Elmer Adlers Papers, AFHRA 168.605–1, v. 2. Hereafter Adler Papers, AFHRA.

4. Wesley Frank Craven and James Lea Cate, eds., *The Army Air Forces in World War II*, 7 vols. (Chicago: University of Chicago Press, 1948–1958), vol. 2, p. 6.

5. Memorandum, Roosevelt to Henry L. Stimson, 13 September 1941, Adler Papers, AFHRA.

6. Craven and Cate, *Army Air Forces in World War II*, vol. 2, p. 6.

7. Stimson to Maxwell, 27 October 1941, Arnold Papers, Box 212, Library of Congress.

8. "Memorandum Reference Activities in Philippine Islands," 18 December 1941, Arnold Papers, Box 201, Library of Congress.

9. "Interview with Colonel Demas T. Craw," 3 July 1942, AFHRA 142.052, Maxwell AFB, Alabama (unpublished). Craw was apparently unaware that four B-17s were sent to North Africa but that the British "found them a failure. We couldn't make the height." Interview with Group Captain J. W. Merer, 5 May 1942, AFHRA MF 28142. The British were likewise unimpressed with a shipment of twenty B-17Cs they received in 1941 and employed over northern Europe. See Craven and Cate, *Army Air Forces in World War II*, vol. 1, pp. 600–601.

10. Roosevelt to Churchill, 12 May 42, Arnold Papers, Box 180, Library of Congress.

11. Portal to Arnold, 31 May 1942, Arnold Papers, Box 212, Library of Congress.

12. Arnold to Portal, 30 May 1942, Arnold Papers, Box 212, Library of Congress.

13. Arthur Tedder, *With Prejudice: The War Memoirs of Marshal of the Royal Air Force Lord Tedder G.C.B.* (Boston: Little, Brown, 1966), pp. 294, 342.

14. Craven and Cate, *Army Air Forces in World War II*, vol. 1, p. 561.

15. Annex "A" to UNAF 42 (12), Proposed British Employment of Heavy Bombers, Arnold Papers, Box 212, Library of Congress. The RAF planned to send 32 *Halifaxes* by 5 July 1942, to be followed by 22 *Liberators*, but by the time of El Alamein, only No. 160 Squadron, with 16 *Liberators*, and No. 462 Squadron, with 16 *Halifaxes*, were operational in the Middle East (see Appendix 2). Data from I. S. O. Playfair, *The Mediterranean and the Middle East*, 6 vols. (London: Her Majesty's Stationery Office, 1966), vol. 3, pp. 282, 347, 458; and vol. 4, p. 490.

16. James Walker, *The Liberandos: A World War II History of the 376th Bomb Group* (Waco, TX: 376th Bomb Group Veteran's Association, 1994), p. 17.

17. John Herrington, *Air War Against Germany and Italy, 1939–1943*, volume 3 in Series 3 (Air) of *Australia in the War of 1939–1945* (Canberra: Australian War Memorial, 1954), pp. 249–250.

18. Walker, *The Liberandos*, pp. 472–477.

19. Mission Reports, First Provision Bomb Group, AFHRA "GP-1-SU-OPS (9th AF)."

20. Herrington, *Air War Against Germany and Italy, 1939–1943*, p. 239.

21. Playfair, *The Mediterranean and Middle East*, vol. 3, p. 311.

22. Chronology, Operational and Historic, Middle East, 9th Air Force, AFHRA 533.3069–3; Craven and Cate, *Army Air Forces in World War II*, vol. 2, p. 17.

23. Air Ministry, Air Historical Branch, *The Middle East Campaigns*, 10 vols., vol. 4, *Operations in Libya and the Western Desert: – July 1942–May 1943*, pp. 185, 198. AFHRA 512.041–12.

24. Recorded in Playfair, *The Mediterranean and Middle East*, vol. 3, p. 335.

25. Alan J. Levine, *The War Against Rommel's Supply Lines, 1942–43* (Westport, CT: Praeger, 1999), p. 31.

26. *Desert Campaign: The Story of the Ninth U.S. Army Air Force in Support of the British in Africa* (Unknown: 9th Air Force, 1943) 3; available at http://home.comcast .net/~dhsetzer/paper_index.htm (accessed 20 May 2009).

27. Levine, *The War Against Rommel's Supply Lines*, 27.

28. Craven and Cate, *Army Air Forces in World War II*, vol. 2, p. 25.

29. Lewis H. Brereton, *The Brereton Diaries* (New York: Morrow, 1946), p. 142.

30. Ibid., p. 26.

31. Playfair, *The Mediterranean and Middle East*, vol. 3, p. 375.

32. For a complete discussion of these developments, see Ian Gooderson, *Air Power at the Battlefront: Allied Close Support in Europe, 1043–1945* (London: Frank Cass, 1998), pp. 24–27; and Brad Gladman, *Intelligence and Anglo-American Air Support in World War Two: The Western Desert and Tunisia, 1940–43* (London: Palgrave Macmillan, 2009), esp. chap. 3.

33. Gladman, *Intelligence and Anglo-American Air Support*, p. 82.

34. "Direct Air Support in the Libyan Desert," AFHRA 533.04.

35. Brereton to Arnold, 22 August 1943, in "Ninth U. S. Air Force, Middle East," AFHRA 533.04.

36. "Direct Air Support in the Libyan Desert," AFHRA 533.04.

37. "Interview with Major P. R. Chandler" by Assistant Chief of Air Staff, Intelligence, 17 June 1943, AFHRA 142.052.

38. Ibid.

39. Memo, Brereton to Maxwell, 9 August 1942, Adler Papers, AFHRA 168.605–2.

40. 12th Bomb Group Post-Mission Reports, AFHRA, GP-12-SU-OP (BOMB); Craven and Cate, *Army Air Forces in World War II*, vol. 2, p. 27.

41. 12th Bomb Group Post-Mission Reports, AFHRA, GP-12-SU-OP (BOMB); Richard Thruel and Eliott Arnold, *Mediterranean Sweep* (New York: Duell, Sloan and Pearce, 1944), pp. 11–16.

42. Gooderson, *Air Power at the Battlefront*, pp. 58–59.

43. Brereton, *The Brereton Diaries*, p. 143.

44. Gooderson, *Air Power at the Battlefront*, p. 51.

45. For a detailed account of this campaign, including the strain it placed on Luftwaffe ground support assets, see Joel S.A. Hayward, *Stopped at Stalingrad* (Lawrence: University Press of Kansas, 1998).

46. Air Ministry, Air Historical Branch, *The Middle East Campaign*, vol. 3, p. 221, AFHRA 512.041.

47. Bernard Montgomery, *Eighth Army: El Alamein to the River Sangro* (Germany: Printing and Stationery Services, British Army of the Rhine, 1946), 7–10.

48. Air Ministry, Air Historical Branch, *The Middle East Campaign*, vol. 3, pp. 202–203; Erwin Rommel, *The Rommel Papers*, edited by B. H. Liddell Hart (New York: Harcourt, Brace, 1953), pp. 283–285.

49. Levine, *The War Against Rommel's Supply Lines*, p. 30.

50. Martin van Creveld, *Supplying War: Logistics from Wallenstein to Patton*, 2d ed. (Cambridge, UK: Cambridge University Press, 2004), p. 200.

51. Levine, *The War Against Rommel's Supply Lines*, p. 27; James Gannon, *Stealing Secrets, Telling Lies: How Codebreakers Helped Shape the Twentieth Century* (Dulles, VA: Brassey's, 2001), p. 81; Craven and Cate, *Army Air Forces in World War II*, vol. 3, p. 2; "Chronology, Operational and Historic, Middle East, 9th Air Force, 12 June 1942 to 10 August 1943," 533.3069-3, AFHRA .

52. Niall Barr, *Pendulum of War: The Three Battles of El Alamein* (New York: Overlook, 2004), p. 302; 57th Fighter Group History, GP-57-HI (January 1941–May 1943), AFHRA.

53. 12th Bomb Group Post-Mission Reports, AFHRA, GP-12-SU-OP (BOMB), AFHRA; Air Ministry, Air Historical Branch, *The Middle East Campaign*, vol. 4, p. 226.

54. Air Ministry, Air Historical Branch, *The Middle East Campaign*, vol. 4, pp. 262–265.

55. "Supply and Maintenance of U.S. Army Air Force Units in the Middle East Theater of Operations," Adler Papers, 168.605-7, AFHRA.

56. Quoted in Karl Gundelach, *Die Deutsche Luftwaffe im Mittelmeer, 1940–1945* (Frankfurt: Peter Lang, 1981), p. 442.

57. Air Ministry, Air Historical Branch, *The Middle East Campaign*, vol. 4, p. 410; Montgomery, *Eighth Army: El Alamein to the River Sangro*, p. 29; Playfair, *The Mediterranean and Middle East*, vol. 4, p. 91.

58. Air Ministry, Air Historical Branch, *The Middle East Campaign*, vol. 4, p. 339.

59. Arnold to Brereton, 8 November 1942, Arnold Papers, Box 153, Library of Congress.

60. Mark Clodfelter, "A Strategy Based on Faith: The Enduring Appeal of Progressive American Airpower," *Joint Forces Quarterly* 49:2 (May 2008): 157.

61. While the British tactical intelligence and air-ground support system was well developed by summer 1942, the TORCH operation was not finally approved until late July, and the units assigned to it were still being identified and trained as late as September. There were some efforts to imbue the TORCH units with the experiences of the Western Desert, but the hasty nature of the operation, combined with the geographic separation (the main American ground-support command sailed directly from the United States), left too few opportunities to completely train the units in the new techniques.

62. Adler Papers, AFHRA 168.602-2; Arnold to Brereton, 21 October 1942, Arnold Papers, Box 156, Library of Congress.

63. For one prominent example of this argument, see David Johnson, *Fast Tanks and Heavy Bombers: Innovation in the U.S. Army, 1917–1945* (Ithaca: Cornell University Press, 2003).

Chapter 3: TORCH and Twelfth Air Force

1. Elmer Adler to Clements MacMullen, 21 September 1942, Adler Papers, AF-HRA 168.605–4; Lewis Brereton, *The Brereton Diaries* (New York: Morrow, 1946), p. 140.

2. See John Abbatiello, *Anti-Submarine Warfare in World War I* (New York: Routledge, 2006).

3. Clay Blair, *Hitler's U-Boat War, Volume 2: The Hunted, 1942–1945* (New York: Random House, 1998), p. 377.

4. Ibid., p. 402.

5. Wesley Frank Craven and James Lea Cate, eds., *The Army Air Forces in World War II*, 7 vols. (Chicago: University Press, 1948–1958), vol. 2, p. 254.

6. The thirty-seven total missions devoted to U-boat yards and bases represent exactly one-half of the seventy-four effective missions flown by Eighth Air Force from August 1942 to July 1943. The totals by month are: August 1942: 0/8, September: 0/3, October: 1/3, November: 7/8, December: 2/4, January 1943: 3/4, February: 4/5, March: 3/9, April: 2/4, May: 7/9, June: 3/7, July: 5/10. "Statistical Summary of Eighth Air Force Operations, August 1942-December, 1943," Box 17, Entry 10, Record Group 18, Records of the Army Air Forces, NARA 2, College Park, MD.

7. King to Arnold, 20 February 1942, Box 178, Arnold Papers, Library of Congress.

8. Towers to Arnold, 14 February 1942, Box 178, Arnold Papers, Library of Congress.

9. Arnold to King, 25 February 1942, Box 178, Arnold Papers, Library of Congress; Arnold to Marshall, 25 February 1942, Box 178, Arnold Papers, Library of Congress.

10. Minutes of the 14th Meeting of the Combined Chiefs of Staff, Record Group 218, Records of the U.S. Joint Chiefs of Staff, Central Decimal File, 1942–1944, Box 169, Folder 1, NARA 2, College Park, MD.

11. Minutes of the 26th Meeting of the Combined Chiefs of Staff (CCS), 19 May 1942, Record Group 218, Records of the U.S. Joint Chiefs of Staff, Central Decimal File, 1942–1944, Box 169, Folder 1, NARA 2, College Park, MD. The document referred to was CCS 73: "Air Offensive Against Enemy Submarine Bases, Building Yards and Heavy Ships."

12. Arnold to Stark, 23 April 1942, Arnold Papers, Box 199, Library of Congress.

13. Report, U.S. Strategic Committee, 28 August 1942, Folder 4, Box 435, Record Group 218, Records of the U.S. Joint Chiefs of Staff, NARA 2, College Park, MD.

14. Craven and Cate, *The Army Air Forces in World War* II, vol. 1, 540.

15. Ibid., Craven and Cate, vol. 1, p. 542.

16. Ibid., Craven and Cate, vol. 1, p. 537.

17. Marshall to Eisenhower, Cable R-2096, 18 October 1942, Arnold Papers, Box 157, Library of Congress.

18. Eisenhower to Marshall, Cable 2692, 21 December 1942, Arnold Papers, Box 157, Library of Congress.

19. Minutes of the 55th Meeting of the Combined Chiefs of Staff, Central Decimal File, 1942–1944, 14 January 1943, Box 169, Folder 3, Record Group 218, Records of the U.S. Joint Chiefs of Staff, NARA 2, College Park, MD.

20. Minutes of the 65th Meeting of the Combined Chiefs of Staff, 21 January 1943, Central Decimal File, 1942–1944, Box 169, Folder 3, Record Group 218, Records of the U.S. Joint Chiefs of Staff, NARA 2, College Park, MD.

21. Minutes of the 76th Meeting of the Combined Chiefs of Staff, 19 March 1943, and Minutes of the 77th Meeting of the Combined Chiefs of Staff, 26 March 1943, Central Decimal File, 1942–1944, Box 170, Record Group 218, Records of the U.S. Joint Chiefs of Staff, NARA 2, College Park, MD.

22. CCS 189/2, Box 170, Record Group 218, Records of the U.S. Joint Chiefs of Staff, NARA 2, College Park, MD.

23. Minutes of the 81st Meeting of the Combined Chiefs of Staff, 23 April 1943, Box 170; Memo, "VLR Aircraft for Anti-Submarine Duty," 30 April 1943, Box 434, Record Group 218, Records of the U.S. Joint Chiefs of Staff, NARA 2, College Park, MD.

24. Cable, Andrews to Marshall (USFOR 8194), 26 March 1943; Cable, Andrews to Marshall (USFOR 8319), 30 March 1943. Both located in Box 434, Record Group 218, Records of the U.S. Joint Chiefs of Staff. NARA 2, College Park, MD.

25. USAAF OPD to ETO (OPD 384), 14 April 1943, Box 434, Record Group 218, Records of the U.S. Joint Chiefs of Staff, NARA 2, College Park, MD.

26. Annex C to CCS 189/2, 28 March 1943, Box 434, Record Group 218, Records of the U.S. Joint Chiefs of Staff, NARA 2, College Park, MD.

27. Minutes of the 99th Meeting of the Combined Chiefs of Staff, 25 June 1943, Box 170, Record Group 218, Records of the U.S. Joint Chiefs of Staff, NARA 2, College Park, MD.

28. Axel Niestle, *German U-Boat Losses During World War II* (Annapolis: Naval Institute Press, 1998), 202.

29. Enclosures "A" and "B," CCS 189/6, Box 434, Record Group 218, Records of the U.S. Joint Chiefs of Staff, NARA 2, College Park, MD.

30. Richard J. Overy, *The Air War, 1939–1945* (Washington, DC: Potomac, 1980), p. 65.

31. Murray, Williamson, and Allan Millett. *A War to Be Won: Fighting the Second World War* (Cambridge, MA: Belknap, 2000), p. 260.

32. Blair, *Hitler's U-Boat War*, vol. 2, p. 152.

33. Spaatz to Eaker, 6 June 1942, Spaatz Papers, Box 8, Library of Congress.

34. Office, Secretary of the Air Staff, Statistical Control Division, Statistical Summaries, World War II, 1942–1945, Box 10, Record Group 18, Records of the Army Air Forces, NARA 2, College Park, MD.

35. "Army Fliers Blast Two Jap Fleets at Midway," *The New York Times*, 9 June 1942 (clipping included with the letter); Laurence Kuter to Haywood Hansell, 30 September 1942, Box 8, Spaatz Papers, Library of Congress.

36. Undated clipping in letter, Kuter to Hansell, 30 September 1942, Box 8, Spaatz Papers, Library of Congress.

37. Spaatz Diary, 7 June 1942, Spaatz Papers, Box 8, Library of Congress.

38. Dwight D. Eisenhower, *Crusade in Europe* (Garden City: NY: Doubleday, 1948), p. 56.

39. Spaatz Diary, 6 July 1942; and Spaatz to Arnold, 6 July 1942. Both located in Box 8, Spaatz Papers, Library of Congress. Spaatz later admitted that the P-39 was "no 'great shakes' as a fighter" but "can be profitably used in attacking ground targets." Spaatz to E.P. Curtis, 15 July 1942, Box 8, Spaatz Papers, Library of Congress.

40. Arnold to Spaatz, 4 July 1942, Box 8, Spaatz Papers, Library of Congress.

41. Entry, Spaatz Diary, 26 June 1942, Box 8, Spaatz papers, Library of Congress.

42. Spaatz to Marshall, 22 July 1942, Spaatz Papers, Box 8, Library of Congress.

43. Craven and Cate, *The Army Air Forces in World War* II, vol. 1, pp. 658–659,

44. Paul Tibbets Jr., with Clair Stebbins and Harry Franken, *The Tibbets Story* (New York: Stein and Day, 1978), p. 82.

45. Craven and Cate, *The Army Air Forces in World War* II, vol. 2, pp. 655–668; 97th Bomb Group History, "Raid on Rouen," GP-97-HI (BOMB), 8 February–8 November 1942, vol. 2, AFHRA, Maxwell AFB, AL.

46. Tibbets, *The Tibbets Story*, p. 90.

47. Spaatz to Stratemeyer, 21 August 1942, Box 8, Spaatz Papers, Library of Congress.

48. Statistical Summary of 8th Air Force Operations, August 1942–December 1943, Entry 10, Box 13, Record Group 18, Records of the Army Air Forces, NARA 2, College Park, MD.

49. Eisenhower to Spaatz, 13 October 1942, Spaatz Papers, Box 9, Library of Congress.

50. Eaker to Spaatz, 14 October 1942, Spaatz Papers, Box 9, Library of Congress.

51. Spaatz to Arnold, 31 October 1942, Spaatz Papers, Box 9, Library of Congress.

52. Translated memo from Colonel Couslet, 30 October 1942, Spaatz Papers, Box 9, Library of Congress.

53. Eaker to Spaatz, 19 November 1942, Spaatz Papers, Box 9, Library of Congress.

54. Blair, *Hitler's U-Boat War*, vol. 2, pp. 151, 164.

55. Tibbets, *The Tibbets Story*, p. 109.

56. Eaker Diary Entry, 4 August 1942, Parton Papers, MS 10, Clark Special Collections, McDermott Library, U.S. Air Force Academy, Colorado Springs, CO.

57. History of the 51st Troop Carrier Wing, Arnold Papers, Library of Congress; George Howe, *The United States Army in World War II—The Mediterranean Theater of Operations: Northwest Africa: Seizing the Initiative in the West* (Washington, DC: Center for Military History, 1957 [repr. 1957]), p. 212.

58. Letter, Bentley to "Paratroop Force," 18 November 1942, Central Decimal Files, October 1942–May 1944, Box 561, Record Group 18, Records of the Army Air Force, NARA 2, College Park, MD. This letter includes reports from each of the twenty-eight pilots whose aircraft arrived in the vicinity of Oran.

59. Raymond Report, History, 51st Troop Carrier Wing, Arnold Papers, Library of Congress.

60. History, 51st Troops Carrier Wing, Arnold Papers, Library of Congress.

61. I. S. O. Playfair, *The Mediterranean and the Middle East*, 6 vols. (London: Her Majesty's Stationery Office, 1966), vol. 4, p. 148.

62. Appendices H and J, History of the 51st Troop Carrier Wing, Arnold Papers, Library of Congress.

63. History, 51st Troop Carrier Wing, Arnold Papers, Library of Congress.

64. Doolittle to Arnold, 19 November 1942, Arnold Papers, Box 13, Library of Congress.

65. Doolittle to Arnold, 19 November 1942, Arnold Papers, Box 13, Library of Congress.

66. Doolittle to Arnold, 19 November 1942, Arnold Papers, Box 13, Library of Congress.

67. "The 12th Air Force in North Africa," Reel 1, Box 3, Parton Papers, MS 10, Clark Special Collections Branch, McDermott Library, U.S. Air Force Academy, Colorado Springs, CO.

68. Doolittle to Arnold, 19 November 1942, Arnold Papers, Box 13, Library of Congress.

69. Doolittle to Arnold, 21 October 1942, Arnold Papers, Box 13, Library of Congress.

70. Doolittle to Arnold, 19 November 1942, Arnold Papers, Box 13, Library of Congress.

71. 52nd Fighter Group, Folders 1 and 2, NM-6, Entry 7, Box 3261, Record Group 18, Records of the Army Air Forces, NARA 2, College Park, MD.

72. Marshall to Eisenhower (AGWAR to ETO), Cable R-918, 18 September 1942, Dwight D. Eisenhower Pre-Presidential Papers, Box 131, Eisenhower Library, Abilene, KS.

73. Eisenhower to Marshall (London to AGWAR, 2396), 19 September 1942, Arnold Papers, Box 156, Library of Congress; Marshall to Eisenhower (AGWAR R757), 14 September 1942, Arnold Papers, Box 157, Library of Congress.

74. Annex 1e to Outline Air Plan, Operation TORCH, Allied Force Headquarters, 20 September 1942, Eisenhower Pre-Presidential Papers, Box 152, Eisenhower Library.

75. Henry H. Arnold, *Global Mission* (New York: Harper Brothers, 1949), p. 327.

76. Howe, *U.S. Army in World War II*, pp. 147–150.

77. Lucien K. Truscott Jr., *Command Decisions: A Personal Story* (New York: E. P. Dutton, 1954), p. 119.

78. Cannon to John M. Grimsley, 14 January 1954, Cannon Papers, Merrill-Cazier Memorial Library, Utah State University, Logan.

79. John K. Cannon to Lavon B. Cannon, 23 November 1942, Cannon Papers; http://www.army.mil/cmh-pg/mohiia1.htm; accessed on 9 July 2007.

80. Arnold, *Global Mission*, p. 352.

81. Spaatz to Arnold, 23 November 1942, James Parton Papers, Clark Special Collections Branch, McDermott Library, U.S. Air Force Academy, Colorado Springs, CO.

82. Samuel Eliot Morison, *History of United States Naval Operations in World War II*, 15 vols. *Volume 2: Operations in North African Waters* (Boston: Little, Brown, 1947), pp. 79, 131.

83. Max Schoenfeld, *Stalking the U-Boat* (Washington, DC: Smithsonian Institute Press, 1995), pp. 83–84.

Chapter 4: The Tunisian Campaign

1. An interrogation of a German bomber crew shot down on 15 November 1942 near Algiers found that a week earlier they had been in Norway, where during the previous summer they had participated in the costly attacks on Murmansk-bound convoys. Box 14, Norstad Papers, Eisenhower Library.

2. Douglas Porch, *The Path to Victory: The Mediterranean Theater in World War II* (New York: Farrar, Straus and Giroux, 2004), p. 412.

3. Williamson Murray, *Strategy for Defeat: The Luftwaffe 1933–1945* (Maxwell AFB, AL: Air University Press, 1983), pp. 163, 148–149.

4. Johannes Steinhoff, *Messerschmitts Over Sicily*, repr. (Mechanicsburg, PA: Stackpole, 2004), p. 11.

5. Alfred Chandler and Louis Galambos, et al., eds., *The Papers of Dwight David Eisenhower*, 21 vols. (Baltimore: Johns Hopkins University Press, 1970–2001), vol. 2, p. 788.

6. Wesley Frank Craven and James Lea Cate, eds., *The Army Air Forces in World War II*, 7 vols. (Chicago: University Press, 1948–1958), vol. 2, p. 85.

7. Ibid., vol. 2, p. 87.

8. This and the previous quotation in Chandler, et al., *The Papers of Dwight David Eisenhower*, vol. 2, pp. 791–793.

9. Ibid., vol. 2, p. 811.

10. AFHQ No. 1098, 2 December 42, Spaatz Papers, Box 10, Library of Congress.

11. Tedder to Algiers, No. 2974, 6 December 1942, Spaatz Papers, Box 10, Library of Congress; also summarized in Sir Arthur Tedder, *With Prejudice* (Boston: Little, Brown, 1966), pp. 374–375.

12. I. S. O. Playfair, *The Mediterranean and the Middle East*, 6 vols. (London: Her Majesty's Stationery Office, 1966), vol. 4, p. 211.

13. Eisenhower to Eaker, 6 December 42, Spaatz Papers, Box 322, Library of Congress.

14. Tedder, *With Prejudice*, 380.

15. Stratemeyer to Spaatz, 2 December 1942, Spaatz Papers, Box 10, Library of Congress.

16. Stratemeyer to Spaatz, 13 November 1942, Spaatz Papers, Box 9, Library of Congress.

17. Chandler, et al., *The Papers of Dwight David Eisenhower*, vol. 2, pp. 811, 704.

18. Arnold to Spaatz, 15 November 1942, Spaatz Papers, Box 8, Library of Congress.

19. Chandler, et al., *The Papers of Dwight David Eisenhower*, vol. 2, p. 811, 790; Craven and Cate, *The Army Air Forces in World War II*, vol. 2, p. 107.

20. Spaatz Diary, 23 December 1942, Spaatz Papers, Box 9, Library of Congress.

21. Spaatz to Arnold, 9 December 1942, Spaatz Papers, Box 9, Library of Congress.

22. Chandler, et al., *The Papers of Dwight David Eisenhower*, vol. 2, pp. 779–780.

23. Doolittle to Spaatz, 25 December 42, Doolittle Papers, Box 19, Library of Congress.

24. Robinett to Marshall, 8 December 1942, AFHRA Microfilm 28142, Maxwell AFB, AL.

25. See Thomas Hughes, *Overlord: General Pete Quesada and the Triumph of Tactical Air Power in World War II* (New York: Free Press, 1995), and David N. Spires, *Patton's Air Force* (Washington, DC: Smithsonian Institute Press, 2002).

26. Stratemeyer to Assistant Chief of Staff, Operations, 31 January 1943, AFHRA Microfilm 28142, Maxwell AFB, AL.

27. Eisenhower to Marshall, 3 March 1943, George C. Marshall Papers, Folder 49, Box 66, Marshall Library, Virginia Military Institute, Lexington, VA.

28. "Combat Aviation in Direct Support of Ground Units," Allied Force Headquarters, Operation Memorandum 17, 13 October 1942, AFHRA 533.327, Maxwell AFB, AL.

29. See Harry Coles, *Ninth Air Force in the Western Desert Campaign to 23 January 1943* (Washington, DC: USAAF Historical Division, 1945), p. 80.

30. Coles, *Ninth Air Force*, p. 77.

31. See Playfair, *The Mediterranean and the Middle East*, vol. 4, p. 342.

32. General Orders No. 26, 7 December 1942, and No. 10, 6 February 1943, Folder 96, Box 185, Record Group 407, Records of the Adjutant General's Office, NARA 2, College Park, MD.

33. Edith Rogers, *The AAF in the Middle East: A Study of the Origins of the Ninth Air Force*, Historical Study No. 108 (Washington, DC: USAAF Historical Division, 1945), p. 115; and Playfair, *The Mediterranean and Middle East*, vol. 4, p. 216.

34. Coles, *Ninth Air Force*, p. 83.

35. Coles, *Ninth Air Force*, pp. 90, 123–124.

36. One of these was the 8,329-ton *Agostino Bertani* on 15 January; see Playfair, vol. 4, p. 243. Chronology, Operational and Historic, Middle East, 9th Air Force, 12 June 1942–10 August 1943, 533.3069–3; 98th Bomb Group Mission Logs, GP-98-SU-OPS, AFHRA Maxwell AFB, AL; Solly Zuckerman, *From Apes to Warlords* (London: Collins, 1988), p. 178.

37. Coles, *Ninth Air Force*, p. 120; Playfair, *The Mediterranean and Middle East*, vol. 4, p. 235.

38. Minutes of the 55th and 56th Meetings, 14 January 1943, Combined Chiefs of Staff, Central Decimal File, 1942–1944, Folder 3, Box 169, Record Group 218, Records of the Joint Chiefs of Staff, NARA 2, College Park, MD.

39. Minutes of the 58th Meeting, 16 January 1943, Combined Chiefs of Staff, Central Decimal File, 1942–44, Folder 3, Box 169, Record Group 218, Records of the Joint Chiefs of Staff, NARA 2, College Park, MD.

40. Murray, *Strategy for Defeat*, p. 151.

41. The Luftwaffe would eventually lose almost 500 aircraft and many crews, including irreplaceable instructors from the training establishment at home, in the attempt to keep Stalingrad supplied from the air. Ibid., p. 155.

42. Minutes of the 57th Meeting, Combined Chiefs of Staff, 15 January 1943, Central Decimal File, 1942–1944, Folder 3, Box 169, Record Group 218, Records of the U.S. Joint Chiefs of Staff, NARA 2, College Park, MD.

43. Robinett to Marshall, 11 December 1942, Arnold Papers, Box 199, Library of Congress.

44. Chandler, et al., *The Papers of Dwight David Eisenhower*, vol. 2, p. 952. There were two airfields at Thelepte.

45. Craven and Cate, *The Army Air Forces in World War II*, vol. 2, p. 156.

46. Ibid., vol. 2, pp. 157–158.

47. Report, 52nd Fighter Group, Office of the Intelligence Officer, 21 February 1943, GP-52-SU-OP, AFHRA, Maxwell AFB, AL.

48. Playfair, *The Mediterranean and Middle East*, vol. 4, p. 311.

49. Albert Kesselring, *The Memoirs of Field-Marshal Kesselring*, repr. (Novato, CA: Presidio, 1988 [1953]), p. 154.

50. History, 51 Troop Carrier Wing, Arnold Papers, Library of Congress.

51. Ibid.

52. "XII Air Support Command in the Tunisian Campaign, January—May 1943," AFHRA 655.01–2, Maxwell AFB, AL, p. 7.

53. Letter, Patton to XII Air Support Command, 24 March 1943, AFHRA GP-52-SU-CO, Maxwell AFB, AL.

54. Vincent Orange, *Coningham: A Biography of Air Marshal Sir Arthur Coningham* (London: Methuen, 1990; repr. Washington, DC: Office of Air Force History, 1992), pp. 146–149.

55. Spaatz to Eisenhower, 2 April 1943, Folder "April 1943, Personal," Box 11, Spaatz Papers, Library of Congress.

56. Eisenhower to Marshall, 5 April 1943, in Chandler, et al., *The Papers of Dwight David Eisenhower*, vol. 2, p. 1071.

57. Eisenhower to Patton, 5 April 1943 in ibid., p. 1073.

58. Zuckerman, *From Apes to Warlords*, p. 204.

59. Dwight D. Eisenhower, *Crusade in Europe* (Garden City: NY: Doubleday, 1948), p. 145.

60. Thomas Maycock, *The Twelfth Air Force in the North African Winter Campaign* (Washington, DC: USAAF Historical Office, 1946), p. 50.

61. Eaker to Arnold, 15 February 1943, Folder 312.1-B, "Operations Letters," Box 193, Entry 294, Record Group 18, Records of the Army Air Forces, NARA 2, College Park, MD.

62. Stratemeyer to Eaker, 8 March 1943, Folder 322-C, Box 357, Entry 294, Record Group 18, Records of the Army Air Force, NARA 2, College Park, MD.

63. Combat Operations Report, 301st Bomb Group, 1941–1946, Box 753, NM-6, Entry 7, Record Group 18, Records of the Army Air Force, NARA 2, College Park, MD.

64. "CBO Progress Report, 4 Feb–1 Nov 1943," Box 15, Norstad Papers, Eisenhower Library, Abilene, KS.

65. Craven and Cate, *The Army Air Forces in World War II*, vol. 2, p. 184; Alan J. Levine, *The War Against Rommel's Supply Lines, 1942–43* (Westport, CT: Praeger, 1999), p. 171. A source claims the blast sank seven ships, totaling 11,500 tons; see Playfair, *The Mediterranean and Middle East*, vol. 4, p. 412.

66. Levine, *The War Against Rommel's Supply Lines*, p. 182.

67. See Craven and Cate, *The Army Air Forces in World War II*, vol. 2, facing p. 185.

68. Combat Operations Report, 301st Bomb Group, 1941–1946, Box 753, NM-6, Entry 7, Record Group 18, Records of the Army Air Force, NARA 2, College Park, MD; Levine, *The War Against Rommel's Supply Lines*, p. 182.

69. Playfair, *The Mediterranean and Middle East*, vol. 4, p. 414.

70. Ibid., vol. 4, p. 284.

71. Maycock, *The Twelfth Air Force in the North African Winter Campaign*, pp. 63–65.

72. See Matt Rodman, *A War of Their Own: Bombers Over the Southwest Pacific* (Maxwell AFB, AL: Air University Press, 2005), pp. 31–32. In many cases "bombs were dropped from less than 200 feet by aircraft moving at high speed." Playfair, *The Mediterranean and Middle East*, vol. 4, p. 241.

73. Playfair, *The Mediterranean and Middle East*, vol. 4, pp. 241–242.

74. Levine, *War Against Rommel's Supply Lines*, p. 165.

75. Playfair, *The Mediterranean and Middle East*, vol. 4, pp. 411–412, 417.

76. Tedder, *With Prejudice*, pp. 411–413.

77. Combat Operations Report, 301st Bomb Group, 1941–1946, Box 753, NM-6, Entry 7, Record Group 18, Records of the Army Air Forces, NARA 2, College Park, MD. Playfair (*The Mediterranean and Middle East*, vol. 4, p. 358) reports that only four Ju-52s were destroyed in this raid, highlighting the often extreme differences between claimed and actual losses.

78. "The Battle Story of FLAX," Folder "Operations Bulletins, 1–30 April 1943," Box 12, Norstad Papers, Eisenhower Library, Abilene, KS. Playfair (*The Mediterranean and Middle East*, vol. 4, p. 392) reports that the bombers enjoyed better success at Trapani, where twenty-one were destroyed and forty-one damaged.

79. Major P. R. Chandler of the 66th Fighter Squadron, 57th Fighter Group, reported the following: "In all the excitement—the screaming in the operations tent—when the boys came back to report on that, it is interesting that four or five of them found time to say to me: 'Be sure to include in your report congratulations to the *Spitfires* for what they did as top cover.' We had 48 P-40's and 18 *Spitfires* above. The 18 *Spitfires* kept off forty plus Messerschmitts while our boys went in against the transports and more Messerschmitts below. If we hadn't had that Spitfire top cover we couldn't have done anything." Interview with Major P. R. Chandler, 57th Fighter Group, 17 June 1943, AFHRA 142.052, Maxwell AFB, AL; Playfair, *The Mediterranean and Middle East*, vol. 4, p. 416.

80. "The Battle Story of FLAX," supra; "The Air Victory in North Africa," Folder "Air Force General Information Bulletin # 12, June 1943" Box 8, Norstad Papers, Eisenhower Library, Abilene, KS; also Playfair, *The Mediterranean and Middle East*, vol. 4, p. 416.

81. Murray, *Strategy for Defeat*, p. 163.

82. See especially Eduard Mark, *Aerial Interdiction in Three Wars* (Washington, DC: Center for Air Force History, 1994).

83. Daniel Mortensen, *A Pattern For Joint Operations: World War II Close Air Support, North Africa* (Washington, DC: U.S. Government Printing Office, 1987).

84. "Enemy Shipping Losses in the Tunisian Campaign, 1 July 1942–11 April 1943," 17 April 1943, Box 185, Record Group 407, Records of the Adjutant General's Office, NARA 2, College Park, MD.

85. Brad Gladman, *Intelligence and Anglo-American Air Support in World War Two: The Western Desert and Tunisia, 1940–43* (London, UK: Palgrave Macmillan, 2009), p. 146.

86. Elwood Quesada Oral History Interview, Reel 3, K239.0512–1813, AFHRA, Maxwell AFB, AL.

87. "Intelligence in the Lower Echelons, North African Air Forces," Office of the Assistant Chief of Air Staff, Intelligence (A-2), Washington, DC, 30 October 1943, AFHRA 142.034–3, Maxwell AFB, AL.

88. Spaatz to Arnold, 25 February 1943, Box 357, Entry 294, Record Group 18, Records of the Army Air Force, NARA 2, College Park, MD.

89. Craven & Cate, vol. 2, p. 163.

90. Letter, Major Boyle to "Folks at Home," 21 March 1943, AFHRA 650.309–2, Maxwell AFB, AL.

91. Arnold to Spaatz, 4 January 1944, Arnold Papers, Box 173, Library of Congress.

92. "Interview with Lt. Richard Kremer," AFHRA 650.03–4, Maxwell AFB, AL.

93. Supra, "Intelligence in the Lower Echelons, North African Air Forces."

94. *Sorties per plane* is the number of sorties *divided by* number of plane-months. A *plane-month* is the equivalent of one plane assigned for one month. During this period Eighth Air Force had 6,114 plane-months and Twelfth Air Force had 2,396 plane-months. All figures are from Office of the Secretary of the Air Staff, Statis-

tical Control Division, Statistical Summaries, World War II, 1942–1945, Box 12, Record Group 18, Records of the Army Air Force, NARA 2, College Park, MD.

95. *Ineffective sorties* were those that returned without completing the assigned mission, most often due to weather obscuring the target.

96. Eighth Air Force had seven groups of heavy bombers assigned until March 1943, when five more arrived; it built steadily, to eighteen groups, by the end of August. Twelfth Air Force remained at four groups throughout the entire period.

97. The Luftwaffe was somewhat spared, as it was able to fly out operational aircraft, even squeezing ground personnel into stowage compartments for the short flight to Sicily. See Johannes Steinhoff, *Messerschmitts Over Sicily*, repr. (Mechanicsburg, PA: Stackpole, 2004).

98. Murray, *Strategy for Defeat*, p. 163.

Chapter 5: The Sicilian Campaign

1. Eisenhower to Marshall, 13 May 1943, in Alfred Chandler and Louis Galambos, et al., eds., *The Papers of Dwight David Eisenhower*, 21 vols. (Baltimore: Johns Hopkins University Press, 1970–2001), vol. 2, p. 1130.

2. "Supreme Commander's Dispatch," Box 68, Spaatz Papers, Library of Congress, Washington, DC.

3. "The Air Effort Against Pantelleria," 3 June 1943, Folder "Field Operations Bulletins," Box 12, Norstad Papers, Eisenhower Library, Abilene, KS.

4. "The Hand That Held the Dagger," *Time Magazine*, 21 June 1943; available at http://www.time.com/time/magazine/article/0,9171,766739,00.html (accessed 28 January 2012).

5. "The Surrender of Pantelleria," Report of LCDR G. A. Martelli, R.N., 14 June 1943, Norstad Papers, Box 12, Eisenhower Library, Abilene, KS.

6. Solly Zuckerman to Spaatz, 20 July 1943, Spaatz Papers, Box 170, Library of Congress.

7. Spaatz Diary, 12 June, Spaatz Papers, Box 11, Library of Congress.

8. Chandler, et al., *The Papers of Dwight David Eisenhower*, vol. 2, pp. 1190–1191.

9. "The Hand That Held The Dagger," *Time Magazine*, 21 June 1943.

10. James H. Doolittle, *I Could Never Be So Lucky Again* (New York: Bantam, 1991), pp. 327–329.

11. Statement of Commander Martelli, Spaatz Diary, 15 June 1943, Spaatz Papers, Box 11, Library of Congress.

12. Richard G. Davis, *Carl A. Spaatz and the Air War in Europe* (Washington, DC: Office of Air Force History, 1993), p. 238; Solly Zuckerman, *From Apes to Warlords* (London: Collins, 1988), p. 195.

13. Davis, *Carl A. Spaatz and the Air War in Europe*, p. 236.

14. "Air Power in the Mediterranean, November 1942- February 1945," p. 9, Box 14, Norstad Papers, Eisenhower Library, Abilene, KS.

15. In his magisterial survey of the war, Gerhard Weinberg devotes a single

sentence to the fall of Pantelleria. Weinberg, *A World At Arms*, 2d ed. (Cambridge, UK: Cambridge University Press, 2005), p. 596. Williamson Murray and Allan Millett omit the campaign entirely in *A War to be Won* (Cambridge, MA: Belknap, 2001).

16. Edith Rogers, *The Reduction of Pantelleria and Adjacent Islands, 8 May to 14 June 1943*, USAAF Historical Study No. 52 (Washington, DC: Air Historical Office, 1947), available at http://www.afhra.af.mil/shared/media/document/AFD-090529–104.pdf (accessed 2 November 2010); Wesley Frank Craven and James Lea Cate, eds., *The Army Air Forces in World War II*, 7 vols. (Chicago: University of Chicago Press, 1948–1958) vol. 2, chap. 13 ("Pantelleria," pp. 415–445), and chap. 14 ("Conquest of Sicily," pp. 446–487); see pp. 477–484 for a discussion of Ploesti.

17. Samuel Eliot Morison, *History of United States Naval Operations in World War II*, 15 vols. (Boston: Little, Brown, 1947–1962), vol. 9, pp. 279–280.

18. See Mark Clodfelter, *The Limits of Air Power*, repr. (Lincoln: University of Nebraska Press, 2006 [1989]).

19. Richard G. Davis titles his chapter on the period "Pantelleria and Sicily," in *Carl A. Spaatz and the Air War in Europe* (Washington, DC: Center for Air Force History, 1993), pp. 225–253. Half the text in this chapter (pp. 225–239) covers Pantelleria. Geoffrey Perret likewise emphasizes the campaign in *Winged Victory* (New York: Random House, 1993).

20. Herman S. Wolk, "Pantelleria, 1943," *Air Force* 85:6 (June 2002): 65.

21. John Keegan, "Please, Mr. Blair, Never Take Such a Risk Again," *London Daily Telegraph*, 6 June 1999, p. 1.

22. For a full and complete rebuttal online, see Anthony Hinen, "Kosovo: 'The Limits of Air Power II,'" *Chronicles Online Journal* (16 May 2002); available at http://www.airpower.au.af.mil/airchronicles/cc/hinen.html (accessed 4 November 2010).

23. Entry, Spaatz Diary, 19 May 1943, Spaatz Papers, Box 11, Library of Congress.

24. A definitive source estimates the Allied strength at 3,642 aircraft (2,510 serviceable) and the Axis at 1,750, with about 775 operational and within range of Sicily; Fliegerfuhrer Sicily controlled only 289 (143 serviceable). I. S. O. Playfair, *The Mediterranean and the Middle East*, 6 vols. (London: Her Majesty's Stationery Office, 1966), vol. 5, p. 46.

25. Chandler, et al., *The Papers of Dwight David Eisenhower*, vol. 4, p. 1106.

26. Arnold to Andrews, 2 May 1943, Box 173, Arnold Papers, Library of Congress.

27. "Aircraft Status Report for Units as of 1800 31 May 43," Norstad Papers, Box 12, Eisenhower Library, Abilene, KS; Arnold to Andrews, 6 April 1943, Box 214, Arnold Papers, Library of Congress.

28. The first two groups, the 44th and 93rd, were to arrive by 25 June, with the 389th to follow ten days later. All three were designated for the "exclusive use" of the attack on Ploesti and were to be "returned immediately" afterward. USFOR

W757 to WAR-OPD (Devers to Marshall) 15 June 43, Arnold Message File, Box 163, Arnold Papers, Library of Congress.

29. Spaatz to Arnold, 14 July 1943, Box 172, Arnold Papers, Library of Congress.

30. This was the purpose of the British deception plan Operation MINCE-MEAT, in which "The Man Who Never Was," a cadaver from a London morgue, was dropped off the Spanish coast with a briefcase full of plans for fictional invasions of Sardinia and Greece. There is some evidence that the higher echelons of the Axis command took the bait and stationed additional assets in those locations, but it is also clear that Sicily's defenders expected and were largely prepared for an invasion.

31. Spaatz to Arnold, 14 July 1943, Box 172, Arnold Papers, Library of Congress.

32. "Summary of Operations Against Sicily and Italy," Office of the Secretary of the Air Staff, Statistical Control Division, Statistical Summaries, World War II, 1942–45, Folder 2, Box 9, Entry 10, Record Group 18, Records of the Army Air Force, NARA 2, College Park, MD.

33. For a graphic description, see Johannes Steinhoff, *Messerschmitts Over Sicily* (Mechanicsburg, PA: Stackpole, 2004).

34. Ibid., p. 118.

35. Supra, "Summary of Operations Against Sicily and Italy."

36. "Interrogation and Documents: 7/KG.30," Folder "Weekly Air Intelligence Summary, 10–16 July 1943," Box 8, Norstad Papers, Eisenhower Library.

37. "Summary of Operations Against Sicily and Italy."

38. "The Sicilian Campaign: Western Naval Task Force Action Report," p. 78, Box 19, Norstad Papers, Eisenhower Library.

39. Morison, *History of United States Naval Operations in World War II*, vol. 9, p. x.

40. "The Sicilian Campaign: Western Naval Task Force Action Report," pp. 90 and 119, Box 19, Norstad Papers, Eisenhower Library.

41. Morison, *History of United States Naval Operations in World War II*, vol. 9, p. 55.

42. Albert N. Garland and Howard McGaw Smyth, *Sicily and the Surrender of Italy*, Volume 2 of *The United States Army in World War II: The Mediterranean Theater of Operations* (Washington, DC: U.S. Army Chief of Military History, 1965), p. 147.

43. Dwight D. Eisenhower, *Crusade in Europe* (Garden City, NY: Doubleday, 1948), p. 179.

44. Craven & Cate, vol. 2, p. 441.

45. Morison, *History of United States Naval Operations in World War II*, vol. 9, pp. 59, 23.

46. Spaatz to Arnold, 14 July 1943, Arnold Papers, Box 172, Library of Congress.

47. Playfair, et al., *The Mediterranean and the Middle East*, vol. 5, p. 79.

48. "Report of Airborne Operations, HUSKY," Box 5, Howard A. Craig Papers, Special Collections Research Center, Syracuse University Library, Syracuse, NY.

49. Ibid.

50. "Supreme Commander's Dispatch," Spaatz Papers, Box 68, Library of Congress.

51. "Report of Airborne Operations, HUSKY," Box 5, Howard A. Craig Papers, Special Collections Research Center, Syracuse University Library, Syracuse, NY.

52. Ibid.; also Garland and Smyth, *Sicily and the Surrender of Italy*, pp. 150, 156.

53. The additional units included HQ/504 PIR, Batteries A & B of the 376th Field Artillery Battalion, carried by the 314th Troops Carrier Group, and HQ, C & D/376 FA, and C/307 Airborne Engineers, carried by the 316th TCG.

54. Harry L. Coles Jr., *Participation of the Ninth and Twelfth Air Forces in the Sicilian Campaign*, USAAF Historical Study No. 37 (Maxwell AFB, AL: USAAF Historical Office, 1945), p. 89.

55. "Reported Loss of Transport Planes and Personnel due to Friendly Fire," Headquarters, 82nd Airborne Division, 2 August, 1943, Box 168, Arnold Papers, Library of Congress.

56. Supra, "Report on Airborne Operations, HUSKY."

57. McNair to Arnold, 15 June 1943, Box 168, Arnold Papers, Library of Congress.

58. Arnold to Spaatz, 1 July 1943, Army Air Forces Central Decimal Files, Serial 312.1D, Box 194, Record Group 18, Records of the Army Air Forces, NARA 2, College Park, MD.

59. Robert F. Dorr and Thomas D. Jones, *Hell Hawks: The Untold Story of the American Fliers Who Savaged Hitler's Wehrmacht* (Minneapolis: Zenith, 2008), p. 12.

60. Supra, "Reported Loss of Transport Planes and Personnel due to Friendly Fire."

61. "Supreme Commander's Dispatch," Box 68, Spaatz Papers, Box 68, Library of Congress.

62. Sixteen Allied fighter squadrons were operating from Sicilian airdromes within a week. Arthur Tedder, *With Prejudice: The War Memoirs of Marshal of the Royal Air Force Lord Tedder G.C.B.* (Boston: Little, Brown, 1966), p. 452. For a complete schedule of NAAF's deployment to Sicily, see Coles, *Participation of the Ninth and Twelfth Air Forces in the Sicilian Campaign*, pp. 234–235.

63. Omar N. Bradley and Clair Blair, *A General's Life* (New York: Simon and Schuster, 1983). For a brief discussion of these supposedly autobiographical comments, and their disagreement with Bradley's earlier recollections, see David R. Mets, *Master of Airpower: General Carl A. Spaatz* (Novato, CA: Presidio, 1988), n. 72, pp. 377–378.

64. Garland and Smyth, *Sicily and the Surrender of Italy*, pp. 250, 256.

65. Tedder, *With Prejudice*, p. 451.

66. "The A-36 in Sicily," Folder "Operations Bulletin 5, August 1943," Box 12, Norstad Papers, Eisenhower Library.

67. Arnold to Spaatz, 20 August 1943, Box 11, Spaatz Papers, Library of Congress.

68. Supra, "The A-36 in Sicily"; Garland and Smyth, *Sicily and the Surrender of Italy*, pp. 342, 344.

69. Ian Gooderson, *Air Power at the Battlefront: Allied Close Support in Europe, 1943–1945* (London: Frank Cass, 1998), pp. 48–49.

70. Spaatz to Arnold, 14 July 1943, Box 172, Arnold Papers, Library of Congress.

71. Arnold to Spaatz, 20 August 1943, Folder 312.E, Box 194, Record Group 18, Records of the Army Air Forces, NARA 2, College Park, MD.

72. Spaatz to Arnold, 30 July 1943, Folder 312.E, Box 194, Record Group 18, Records of the Army Air Forces, NARA 2, College Park, MD.

73. Spaatz to Major General Edwin House, 3 August 1943, and Spaatz Diary, 5 August 1943, Box 11, Spaatz Papers, Library of Congress.

74. An estimated 120 "heavy" and 112 "light" anti-aircraft guns were guarding both sides of the passage. Playfair, *The Mediterranean and Middle East*, vol. 5, p. 168.

75. Garland and Smyth, *Sicily and the Surrender of Italy*, p. 376.

76. Eduard Mark, *Aerial Interdiction in Three Wars* (Washington, DC: Center for Air Force History, 1994), p. 64.

77. Ibid., pp. 67–68.

78. Ibid., p. 76. For a detailed discussion of these issues, see Garland and Smyth, *Sicily and the Surrender of Italy*, pp. 379–380 and 411–412. This is in addition to the 12,000 men, 4,500 vehicles, and 5,000 tons of equipment evacuated between 1 August and 10 August. In total, 60,000 German and 75,000 Italian troops escaped; Playfair, et al., *The Mediterranean and Middle East*, vol. 5, pp. 166, 182.

79. Spaatz to Arnold, 27 July 1943, Folder 312.E, Box 194, Record Group 18, Records of the Army Air Forces, NARA 2, College Park, MD.

80. Arnold to Spaatz, 11 August 1943, Box 11, Spaatz Papers, Library of Congress.

81. Harry Coles, *Participation of the Ninth and Twelfth Air Forces in the Sicilian Campaign*, p. 170.

82. Minutes of the CCS 62nd Meeting, 19 January 1943, Box 169, Record Group 218, Records of the Joint Chiefs of Staff, NARA 2, College Park, MD.

83. Minutes of the CCS 77th Meeting, 26 March 1943, Box 170, Record Group 218, Records of the Joint Chiefs of Staff, NARA 2, College Park, MD.

84. Minutes of the CCS 87th Meeting, 18 May 1943, Box 170, Record Group 218, Records of the Joint Chiefs of Staff, NARA 2, College Park, MD.

85. Eisenhower to CCS, 5 June 1944, in Chandler, et al., *The Papers of Dwight David Eisenhower*, vol. 2, p. 1176.

86. Eisenhower to CCS, 5 June 1944, in Chandler, et al., *The Papers of Dwight David Eisenhower*, vol. 2, p. 1176.

87. See Eisenhower to Marshall, 20 July 1943, in Chandler, et al., *The Papers of Dwight David Eisenhower*, vol. 2, pp. 1269–1270.

88. Eisenhower to CCS (Combined Chiefs of Staff), 30 April 1943, in Chandler, *The Papers of Dwight David Eisenhower*, vol. 2, p. 1106.

89. Eisenhower to CCS, 28 July 1943, in Chandler, *The Papers of Dwight David Eisenhower*, vol. 2, pp. 1296–1297.

90. Eisenhower to CCS, 12 August 1943, in Chandler, *The Papers of Dwight David Eisenhower*, vol. 2, p. 1330.

91. Spaatz Diary, 26 July 1943, Box 11, Spaatz Papers, Library of Congress.

92. Spaatz to Arnold, 30 July 1943, Box 11, Spaatz Papers, Library of Congress.

93. Doolittle to Arnold, 31 July 1943, Box 11, Spaatz Papers, Library of Congress.

94. Mission Summaries, 2nd Bomb Group, Box 54, Entry 7, Record Group 18, Records of the Army Air Forces, NARA 2, College Park, MD.

95. Craven & Cate, *The Army Air Forces in World War II*, vol. 2, pp. 474–476; Harry Coles, *Participation of the Ninth and Twelfth Air Forces in the Sicilian Campaign*, p. 175.

96. The unescorted raid was also very costly, as sixty of the 376 bombers dispatched against the two targets were lost. Craven & Cate, *The Army Air Forces in World War II*, vol. 2, p. 683; Zuckerman, *From Apes to Warlords*, p. 205.

97. Coles, *Participation of the Ninth and Twelfth Air Forces in the Sicilian Campaign*, p. 157; Mark, *Aerial Interdiction in Three Wars*, p. 70.

98. Tedder, *With Prejudice*, pp. 460–462.

99. Garland and Smyth, *Sicily and the Surrender of Italy*, p. 411.

100. Spaatz Diary, 17 August 1943, Box 11, Spaatz Papers, Library of Congress.

101. Spaatz to Lovett, 20 August 1943, Box 11, Spaatz Papers, Library of Congress.

Chapter 6: Ploesti and Salerno

1. Duane Schultz, *Into the Fire* (Yardley, PA: Westholme, 2007), p. xii.

2. Air War Planning Document 1942, Appendix G VII, Oil, Box 66, Spaatz Papers, Library of Congress, Washington, DC. The numbers in AWPD-42 are similar to those found in Air Ministry, United Kingdom, "The Oil Supply Position in Axis-Occupied Europe," 1 July 1942, in Folder "Ministry of Economic Warfare," Box 59, Spaatz Papers, Library of Congress.

3. Minutes of the 62nd Meeting of the Combined Chiefs of Staff, 19 January 1943, Central Decimal File 1942–1944, Box 169, Record Group 218, Records of the U.S. Joint Chiefs of Staff, NARA 2, College Park, MD.

4. Minutes of the 62nd Meeting of the Combined Chiefs of Staff, 19 January 1943, Central Decimal File 1942–1944, Box 169, Record Group 218, Records of the U.S. Joint Chiefs of Staff, NARA 2, College Park, MD.

5. Jeffrey T. Haynes, "General Jacob E. Smart: Premier Staff Officer and Combat Planner," unpubl. thesis, School of Advanced Airpower Studies, Maxwell AFB, AL, 2008, p. 11.

6. Ibid., p. 15.

7. Kuter to Spaatz, 16 September 1942, Box 8, Spaatz Papers, Library of Congress.

8. The B-24 *Liberator* heavy bomber had proved susceptible to attacks from below, and new bombers were being equipped with a bottom ball turret to protect this vulnerable area. The 389th Bomb Group, which had aircraft equipped with bottom ball turrets, actually had to remove them prior to the raid to save weight,

in Brereton's words, "so everyone starts even." Brereton to Arnold, 22 July 1943, Operations Letters, Folder 312.1-E, Box 194, Central Decimal Files, Serial 312, Record Group 18, Records of the Army Air Forces, NARA 2, College Park, MD.

9. In May 1943 Eighth Air Force had sent a force of eleven more-maneuverable B-26 *Invaders* on a low-level raid against Ijmuiden in the Netherlands. The one aircraft that left the formation and returned early was the only survivor, prompting Eaker to comment, "We must discontinue low-level attack." Eaker to Barney Giles, 28 May 1943, Operations Letters, Folder 312.1-B, Central Decimal Files, Box 193, Record Group 18, Records of the Army Air Forces, NARA 2, College Park, MD.

10. Schulz, *Into the Fire*, pp. 29–30.

11. Minutes of the 83rd Meeting of the Combined Chiefs of Staff, 13 May 1943, Central Decimal File 1942–1944, Box 169, Record Group 218, Records of the U.S. Joint Chiefs of Staff, NARA 2, College Park, MD.

12. Minutes of the 87th Meeting of the Combined Chiefs of Staff, 18 May 1943, Central Decimal File 1942–1944, Box 169, Record Group 218, Records of the U.S. Joint Chiefs of Staff, NARA 2, College Park, MD. The Liberator B-24C type could carry only 3,000 pounds of bombs over that distance; the improved B-24D could make the trip with 6,000 pounds of ordnance.

13. See David Glantz and Jonathan House, *The Battle of Kursk* (Lawrence: University Press of Kansas, 2004).

14. Supra, Minutes of the 87th Meeting of the Combined Chiefs of Staff.

15. Eaker to Arnold, 8 June 1942, Operations Letters, Folder 312.1-D, Box 194, Central Decimal Files, Serial 312, Record Group 18, Records of the Army Air Forces, NARA 2, College Park, MD.

16. Lewis H. Brereton, *The Brereton Diaries* (New York: Morrow, 1946), p. 199.

17. Ent to Arnold, 3 August 1943, Operations Letters, Folder 312.1-E, Central Decimal Files, Box 194, Serial 312, Record Group 18, Records of the Army Air Forces, NARA 2, College Park, MD.

18. Marshall to Brereton, 14 September 1942, Marshall Papers, Box 58, Marshall Library, Lexington, VA.

19. James Dugan and Carroll Stewart, *Ploesti: The Great Ground-Air Battle of 1 August 1943* (New York: Random House, 1962), p. 87.

20. Leroy Newby, *Into the Guns of Ploesti* (Osceola, WI: Motorbooks, 1991), p. 100.

21. The "one" was Flight Lieutenant (later Squadron Leader) George Barwell, RAF, an air gunnery expert assigned as a liaison to Ninth Air Force and the only non-American to take part in the mission. Barwell had participated as a gunner against his superior's orders, who refused to honor him for his insubordination. Dugan and Stewart, *Ploesti*, pp. 84, 217.

22. Ibid., p. 222.

23. Michael Hill, *The Desert Rats: The 98th Bomb Group and the August 1943 Ploesti Raid* (Missoula, MT: Pictorial Histories, 1990), p. vi.

24. George Baroni, ed., *The Story of the 98th: From Palestine Through Italy*, (n.l., Inter-Collegiate Press, 1978[?]) p. 96; GP-98-SU-PH; GP-98-SU-OP-BOMB, December 1942–August 1943, AFHRA, Maxwell AFB, AL.

25. Dugan and Stewart, *Ploesti*, p. 222.

26. "Northwest African Air Force Heavy Bomber Losses, 4 July–25 September 1943," Office, Secretary of the Air Staff, Statistical Control Division, Statistical Summaries, World War II, 1942–1945, Box 9, Series o–180, Entry 10, Record Group 18, Records of the Army Air Forces, NARA 2, College Park, MD.

27. Joint Chiefs of Staff 105th Meeting, 16 August 1943, Box 214, Arnold Papers, Library of Congress.

28. Brereton, *The Brereton Diaries*, p. 206.

29. "Raid on Ploesti," Office, Secretary of the Air Staff, Statistical Control Division, Statistical Summaries, World War II, 1942–1945, Box 14, Series o–180, Entry 10, Record Group 18, Records of the Army Air Forces, NARA 2, College Park, MD; also Newby, *Into the Guns of Ploesti*, p. 101.

30. Eaker to Spaatz, 3 August 1943, Box 11, Spaatz Papers, Library of Congress.

31. "Report on Detached Service of B-24s," Box 85, Spaatz Papers, Library of Congress.

32. Office of Strategic Services Reports of 4 September 1943, 9 September 1943 (Report C-5745), and 29 September 1943 (AR-407), Folder "OSS Reports," Box 187, Spaatz Papers, Library of Congress.

33. Both previous quotations in Memorandum, Assistant Chief of the Air Staff, Plans, 12 January 1944, Comment on JIC 106/2, Box 67, Spaatz Papers, Library of Congress.

34. Air Ministry Weekly Intelligence Summary Number 240, 8 April 1944, Box 187, Spaatz Papers, Library of Congress.

35. Schulz, *Into the Fire*, p. 239.

36. Caption, Photo 21, Folder 2, Box 2, Parton Papers, Special Collections, McDermott Library, U.S. Air Force Academy, Colorado Springs, CO; also Newby, *Into the Guns of Ploesti*, p. 180.

37. Newby, *Into the Guns of Ploesti*, p. 38.

38. USFOR London to AGWAR, W3955, 3 September 1943, Box 157, Arnold Papers, Library of Congress.

39. USFOR London to AGWAR, W3957, 3 September 1943, Box 157, Arnold Papers, Library of Congress.

40. Arnold to Eaker, 1 August 1943, Box 173, Arnold Papers, Library of Congress.

41. German defenders had employed their own fighters and bombers to fire large-caliber guns upon and drop bombs into the densely packed Allied bomber formations.

42. Salerno Plan, Task of the Air Forces, Box 140, Spaatz Papers, Library of Congress.

43. AFHQ to Combined Chiefs of Staff (Cable W 7138), 12 August 1943, in Alfred Chandler and Louis Galambos, et al., eds., *The Papers of Dwight David Eisen-*

hower, 21 vols. (Baltimore: Johns Hopkins University Press, 1970–2001), vol. 2, p. 1330.

44. Wesley Frank Craven and James Lea Cate, eds., *The Army Air Forces in World War II*, 7 vols. (Chicago: University of Chicago Press, 1948–1958), vol. 2, p. 717.

45. Craven & Cate, *The Army Air Forces in World War II*, vol. 2, p. 523.

46. Dwight D. Eisenhower, *Crusade in Europe* (Garden City, NY: Doubleday, 1948), p. 188.

47. Martin Blumenson, *Salerno to Cassino*, vol. 3 of *The United States Army in World War II: The Mediterranean Theater of Operations* (Washington, DC: Center for Military History, 1969), pp. 107, 120, 122, and 130.

48. "Summary of Operations Against Sicily and Italy," Office of the Secretary of the Air Staff, Statistical Control Division, Statistical Summaries, World War II, 1942–1945, Folder 2, Box 9, O-180, Entry 10, Record Group 18, Records of the Army Air Forces, NARA 2, College Park, MD.

49. Craven & Cate, *The Army Air Forces in World War II*, vol. 2, pp. 535–536.

50. Blumenson, *Salerno to Cassino*, pp. 110, 122. The original plan for Salerno incorporated airborne troops to protect the beachhead and seize exits, but this was cancelled when the airborne troops were reallocated to a mission to drop directly into Rome in order to protect the Italian government and hasten surrender. When that mission was judged to be too risky, the airborne troops were again available for Salerno. See Craven & Cate, *The Army Air Forces in World War II*, vol. 2, pp. 519–520.

51. John Warren, *Airborne Missions in the Mediterranean, 1942–1945: USAF Historical Study No. 74* (Maxwell AFB, AL: USAF Historical Division, 1953), pp. 60, 65; Spaatz to Arnold, 18 September 1943, Box 12, Spaatz Papers, Library of Congress.

52. Office, Secretary of the Air Staff, Statistical Control Division, Statistical Summaries, World War II, 1942–1945, Box 13, Series 0–180, Entry 10, Record Group 18, Records of the Army Air Forces, NARA 2, College Park, MD; Craven & Cate, *The Army Air Forces in World War II*, vol. 2, p. 551.

53. Craven & Cate, *The Army Air Forces in World War II*, vol. 2, p. 595n.

54. The first Allied squadrons began arriving on the continent even as the landings were still being contested: 33rd Fighter Group on 13 September and the lead elements of 31st and 86th Groups a few days later. I. S. O. Playfair, et al., *The Mediterranean and the Middle East*, 6 vols. (London: Her Majesty's Stationery Office, 1966), vol. 5, p. 323.

55. Craven & Cate, *The Army Air Forces in World War II*, vol. 2, pp. 561–562.

56. *Despatches*, 27 February 1945, p. 37, Box 103, Spaatz Papers, Library of Congress.

57. Eisenhower to Marshall, 29 October 1942, Box 66, Marshall Papers, Marshall Library, Lexington, VA.

58. Tedder to Eisenhower, 8 May 1943, Dwight David Eisenhower Pre-Presidential Papers, Principal File, Box 115, Eisenhower Library, Abilene, KS.

59. Spaatz Diary, 1 June 1943, Box 11, Spaatz Papers, Library of Congress.

60. Spaatz to Arnold, 30 July 1943, Operations Letters, Folder 312.1-E, Box 194, Central Decimal Files, Serial 312, Record Group 18, Records of the Army Air Forces, NARA 2, College Park, MD.

61. Arnold to Spaatz, 14 August 1943, and Arnold to Spaatz, 10 August 1943, Operations Letters, Folder 312.1-E, Box 194, Central Decimal Files, Serial 312, Record Group 18, Records of the Army Air Forces, NARA 2, College Park, MD.

62. Spaatz to Arnold, 30 August 1943, Box 11, Spaatz Papers, Library of Congress.

63. Extract, Page 3, CCS 106th Meeting Minutes, 14 August 1943, Box 214, Arnold Papers, Library of Congress.

64. Eaker to Hansell, 25 August 1943, Box 323, Spaatz Papers, Library of Congress.

65. Eaker to Hansell, 25 August 1943, Box 323, Spaatz Papers, Library of Congress.

66. Spaatz to Arnold, 30 July 1943, Box 11, Spaatz Papers, Library of Congress.

67. Craven and Cate, *The Army Air Forces in World War II*, vol. 2, p. 724.

68. Eaker to Hansell, 25 August 1943, Box 323, Spaatz Papers, Library of Congress.

69. Arnold to Hopkins, 31 October 1943, Box 167, Arnold Papers, Library of Congress.

70. David Mets, *The Air Campaign: John Warden and the Classical Airpower Theorists* (Maxwell AFB, AL: Air University Press, 1999), p. 44.

Conclusion

1. Joel S.A. Hayward. *Stopped at Stalingrad: The Luftwaffe and Hitler's Defeat in the East, 1942–1943* (Lawrence: University Press of Kansas, 1998), pp. 219, 245.

2. Herhodt von Rohden, "The German Air Force in the Mediterranean, 1941–45," Box 289, Spaatz Papers, Library of Congress.

3. Richard Overy found that the Battle of the Atlantic "could have been won sooner and at lower cost if the air effort had been properly appreciated and the resources made available." In John Andreas Olsen, ed., *A History of Air Warfare* (Washington, DC: Potomac, 2010) ("The Air War in Europe, 1939–1945"), pp. 27–52, at p. 37.

4. In ibid., p. 29. Overy concluded that "the rapid success of German armies in the campaigns against the Netherlands, Belgium and France was achieved largely thanks to German air superiority."

5. Ibid., p. 50.

6. See especially Gian Gentile, *How Effective Is Strategic Bombing? Lessons Learned from World War II to Kosovo* (New York: New York University Press, 2000).

7. Carl von Clausewitz, *On War*, translated by Michael Howard and Peter Paret (Oxford: University Press, 2007), p. 113.

8. Mark Clodfelter, *Beneficial Bombing: The Progressive Foundations of American Air Power, 1917–1945* (Lincoln: University of Nebraska Press, 2010), p. 238.

9. Robert S. Ehlers Jr., *Targeting the Third Reich: Air Intelligence and the Allied Bombing Campaigns* (Lawrence: University Press of Kansas, 2009), p. 7.

10. Interrogation of Reichsmarschall Hermann Goering in Augsburg, 10 May 1945, Folder "Goering," Box 134, Spaatz Papers, Library of Congress. The account appears in a clipping from the 23 June 1945 edition of the *London Times*.

11. See Tsuyoshi Hasegawa, *Racing the Enemy: Stalin, Truman, and the Surrender of Japan* (Cambridge, MA: Belknap, 2005).

12. For a full discussion see Clodfelter, *Beneficial Bombing*, pp. 238–241.

13. See Clodfelter, *The Limits of Airpower* (New York: Free Press, 1989).

14. John A. Warden, III, *The Air Campaign: Planning for Combat* (Washington, DC: National Defense University Press, 1988).

15. David Mets, *The Air Campaign: John Warden and the Classical Airpower Theorists* (Maxwell AFB, AL: Air University Press, 1999), pp. 62, 66, and 69.

16. Robert Pape, *Bombing to Win: Air Power and Coercion in War* (Ithaca: Cornell University Press, 2006).

17. Von Clausewitz, *On War*, 32, 43.

18. Williamson Murray, "Operation Iraqi Freedom, 2003," pp. 279–296 in John Andreas Olsen, ed., *A History of Air Warfare* (Washington, DC: Potomac, 2010), p. 289.

19. Incidentally, refocusing could require a reassessment of weapons system procurement priorities. For example, instead of purchasing a new fighter/attack aircraft, it might be advisable to acquire more unmanned reconnaissance assets, as well as sufficient transport aircraft to carry all of the U.S. Army's airborne troops, and to move the USAF's three manned reconnaissance platforms (E-3 AWACS, E-8 Joint STARS, and RC-135 Rivet Joint) and tanker fleet off of the fifty-year-old airframe design they currently operate (and which the commercial airlines abandoned long ago).

20. *U.S. Army/Marine Corps Counterinsurgency Manual* (Chicago: University of Chicago Press, 2007). See, e.g., James Corum and Wray Johnson, *Airpower in Small Wars: Fighting Insurgents and Terrorists* (Lawrence: University Press of Kansas, 2003).

21. See Mark Clodfelter, "A Strategy Based on Faith: The Enduring Appeal of Progressive American Airpower," *Joint Force Quarterly* 49:2 (May 2008): 24–31, 150–160.

22. George H. Brett to George Marshall, 21 September 1941, Box 58, Marshall Papers, Marshall Library, Lexington, VA.

23. Tami Davis Biddle, *Rhetoric and Reality in Air Warfare: The Evolution of British and American Ideas About Strategic Bombing, 1914–1945* (Princeton: Princeton University Press, 2002), pp. 42–43.

24. William Mitchell, *Our Air Force* (New York: E. P. Dutton, 1921), pp. 179, xix.

25. Ibid., p. 15.

26. Ibid., pp. 36, 41, and 53.

27. Sir Julian Corbett, *Some Principles of Maritime Strategy*, repr. (New York: AMS Press, 1972 [1911]).

28. Ibid., p. 13.

29. Ibid., p. 16.

30. Corbett, *Some Principles of Maritime Strategy*, p. 14.

31. Giulio Douhet, *The Command of the Air*, translated by Dino Ferrar, repr. (Washington, DC: U.S. Government Printing Office, 1998), p. 196.

32. Corbett, *Some Principles of Maritime Strategy*, p. 27.

33. Ibid., p. 55.

34. Ibid., p. 68.

35. Ibid., p. 169.

36. Ibid., p. 89.

37. Ibid., p. 90.

38. Ibid., p. 111.

39. See Hayward, *Stopped at Stalingrad*.

40. Azar Gat, *A History of Military Thought from the Enlightenment to the Cold War* (Oxford, UK: Oxford University Press, 2001), p. 490.

41. Ibid., p. 493.

42. See Adrian Lewis, *The American Culture of War: The History of U.S. Military Force from World War II to Operation Iraqi Freedom* (New York: Routledge, 2007).

43. Mitchell, *Our Air Force*, pp. xxi–xxii.

44. See John Grenier, *The First Way of War* (Cambridge, UK: Cambridge University Press, 2005); and Brian Linn, *The Philippine War* (Lawrence: University Press of Kansas, 2000).

45. Harold R. Winton, "A Black Hole in the Wild Blue Yonder: The Need for a Comprehensive Theory of Air Power," *Air Power History* 39:4 (Winter 1992): 42.

Appendix 1

1. Eaker to Spaatz, 29 January 1943, Box 10, Spaatz Papers, Library of Congress.

2. By 2 January Eaker reported that "90 P-47's have arrived" and that he planned to use them to reequip 4th Fighter Group (the former "Eagle squadrons") then operating with shorter-range Spitfires. These fighters were more than enough to equip an additional fighter group in North Africa, which was then suffering severe shortages (see note 25). By 13 May, three groups were operational. Eaker to Stratemeyer, 2 January 1943, Central Decimal Files, 1942–44, Folder 312.1-A, Box 193, Record Group 18, Records of the Army Air Forces, NARA 2, College Park, MD.

3. Spaatz to Arnold 17 February 1943 and 24 May 1943, Central Decimal Files, 1942–44, Folder 312.1-B, Box 193, Record Group 18, Records of the Army Air Forces, NARA 2, College Park, MD.

4. Colonel Alfred Maxwell to General Fred Anderson, 20 Aug 1943, Central

Decimal Files, Folder 312.1-E, Operations Letters, Box 194, Record Group 18, Records of the Army Air Forces, NARA 2, College Park, MD.

5. Doolittle to Arnold, 22 May 1943, Box 19, James H. Doolittle Papers, Library of Congress.

6. I use the tonnage figure not as an end unto itself but as an indication of the level of effort. I do not wish to make a direct association between tonnage dropped and effective missions. Obviously, it matters a great deal when and where those tonnages were dropped, what they hit, and what effect that had on the Axis war effort. Chapter 5 makes the case, however, that they were employed effectively.

7. Spaatz to Arnold 17 February 1943, Central Decimal Files, 1942–44, Folder 312.1-B, Box 193, Record Group 18, Records of the Army Air Forces, NARA2, College Park, MD.

8. Spaatz to Arnold, 21 August 1942, Box 8, Spaatz Papers, Library of Congress.

9. The RAF later sent over a token force but kept the vast majority of their heavy bombers in the United Kingdom.

10. Doolittle to Spaatz, 27 June 1943, Box 19, Doolittle Papers, Library of Congress.

11. Two fighter groups (31st and 52nd) operated British-made Spitfires, which were excellent dogfighters but lacked the range to escort bombers. They were employed primarily as escorts on close-support missions and in the coastal air force protecting convoys.

12. For a full discussion of this important air campaign, see Adam R. A. Claasen, *Hitler's Northern War: The Luftwaffe's Ill-Fated Campaign* (Lawrence: University Press of Kansas, 2001).

13. Spaatz to Lieutenant Colonel E.P. Curtis, 15 July 1942, Box 8, Spaatz Papers, Library of Congress; Spaatz to Arnold, 24 May 1943, Central Decimal Files, 1942–44, Folder 312.1-B, Box 193, Record Group 18, Records of the Army Air Forces, NARA 2, College Park, MD.

14. The RAF finally began to send Spitfires to Egypt after the collapse at Gazala, and they had an immediate impact in challenging the *Luftwaffe* for air superiority. See Playfair, et al., *The Mediterranean and Middle East*, vol. 3, p. 337. Most of the Spitfires sent from the United Kingdom were assigned to Malta, with only a handful reaching Egypt by the end of September 1942. Ibid., p. 458.

15. The Lafayette Escadrille was created from former Vichy pilots in North Africa and surplus P-40s during the period immediately following the invasion. Spaatz assigned twelve P-40s on 17 December 1943, and they began operations on 9 January 1943. High attrition limited the squadron's performance, but the unit formed the backbone of the later, more formidable Free French Air Force. Spaatz Diary, 9 Jan 1943, Box 10, Spaatz Papers, Library of Congress.

16. Ian Gooderson, *Air Power at the Battlefront: Allied Close Support in Europe, 1943–1945* (London: Frank Cass, 1998), p. 60.

17. Letter, Major General Barney Giles to CG, USAAF, 14 April 1943, Central Decimal Files, 1942–44, Folder 373.1-A, Box 560, Record Group 18, Records of the Army Air Forces, NARA 2, College Park, MD.

18. Spaatz to Arnold, 24 May 1943, Central Decimal Files, 1942–44, Folder 312.1-B, Box 193, Record Group 18, Records of the Army Air Forces, NARA 2, College Park, MD.

19. Spaatz to Arnold, 8 Dec 1942, Central Decimal Files, 1942–44, Folder 322-A, Box 344, Record Group 18, Records of the Army Air Forces, NARA 2, College Park, MD.

20. "Report of Tactical Suitability of P-38," 6 March 1943, Folder "P-38," Box 48, Spaatz Papers, Library of Congress.

21. Spaatz to John Winant, 1 May 1943, Box 11, Spaatz Papers, Library of Congress.

22. Spaatz to Arnold, 14 July 1943, Box 11, Spaatz Papers, Library of Congress.

23. Arnold to Spaatz, 14 August 1943, Central Decimal File, Folder 312.1-E, Operations Letters, Box 194, Record Group 18, Records of the Army Air Forces, NARA 2, College Park, MD.

24. USAAF Letter 150–1, 12 January 1944, Box 191, Entry 294A, Serial 312, Record Group 18, Records of the Army Air Forces, NARA 2, College Park, MD.

25. On 31 January 1943, General Doolittle reported that the Twelfth Air Force was "only up to half our T.O. [Table of Organization] strength in aircraft for the groups on hand and at the moment need replacement airplanes and combat crews rather than new groups complete." He had then 790 aircraft in 22 groups when his TO strength was for 1,415 and, with only a 20 percent reserve, would be 1,698. The shortages were largely a result of "the fact that we were not up to strength nor did we have any reserve of aircraft or crews when we started." Doolittle reported his greatest shortage was in P-38s. Doolittle to Stratemeyer, 31 January 1943, Central Decimal File, Folder 312.1-B, Operations Letters, Box 193, Record Group 18, Records of the Army Air Forces, NARA 2, College Park, MD.

26. Doolittle to Arnold, 31 July 1943, Box 11, Spaatz Papers, LOC. In a single week of combat in January, Twelfth Air Force lost 80 P-38s. Mediterranean Allied Air Force Weekly Intelligence Summary, 23–29 January 1943, Box 129, Spaatz Papers, Library of Congress.

Appendix 2

1. Compiled from various sources, but especially I. S. O. Playfair and C. J. C. Molony, *The Mediterranean and the Middle East*, 5 vols. (London: HMSO, 1954–1973); Karl Gundelach, *Die Deutsche Luftwaffe im Mittelmeer 1940-1945* (Frankfurt: Peter Lang, 1981); "Einsatz der Luftwaffe gegen Hafen und Seeziele," at http://www.wlb-stuttgart.de/seekrieg/lw/luft.htm, accessed on 5 January 2012; General der Flieger Hellmuth Felmy, "The German Air Force in the Mediterranean Theater of War," Study 161 (Maxwell AFB, AL: Publisher unknown); and Lexicon der Wehrmacht, http://www.lexikon-der-wehrmacht.de, accessed on 5 January 2012.

2. From Folder "Naval Operations Orders," Box 6, Norstad Papers, Eisenhower Library, Abilene, KS.

Bibliography

Primary

Dwight D. Eisenhower Library, Abilene, KS
Lewis Brereton Papers
Dwight D. Eisenhower Pre-Presidential Papers
Lauris Norstad Papers

Library of Congress
Henry Arnold Papers
James Doolittle Papers
Ira Eaker Papers
Carl Spaatz Papers

Marshall Library, Lexington, VA
George C. Marshall Papers
Paul Robinett Papers

National Archives II, College Park, MD
Record Group 18: Records of the Army Air Forces
    Central Decimal Files
        Directives
        Groups
        Monthly Letters
        Numbered Air Forces
        Operations Letters
    33rd Fighter Group, Mission Summaries
    2nd Bomb Group, Mission Summaries
    99th Bomb Group, Mission Summaries
    Statistical Summary of Eight Air Force operations, Aug 42-Dec 43
    Office of the Secretary of the Air Staff, Statistical Control Division
    9th Air Force, Operations Reports
    12th Air Force Operations Reports
Record Group 218, Records of the U.S. Joint Chiefs of Staff
    Minutes of the Meeting of the Combined Chiefs of Staff
    Combined Chiefs of Staff, Numbered Papers
Record Group 332: Records of the United States Theaters of War, World War II

Record Group 407: Record of the Army Adjutant General's Office
    World War II Operations Reports, Africa-Middle East Theater
    Enemy Shipping Losses in the Tunisian Campaign, 1 Jul 42–11 Apr 43
Record Group 492: Records of the Mediterranean Theater of Operations

SYRACUSE UNIVERSITY, SYRACUSE, NY
Howard A. Craig Papers

U. S. AIR FORCE ACADEMY, USAF ACADEMY, CO
Laurence Kuter Papers
James Parton Papers

U.S. AIR FORCE HISTORICAL RESEARCH AGENCY, MAXWELL AFB, AL
142.034–3 Assistance Chief of Staff, Intelligence, Intelligence Summaries
142.052 P.D. Chandler Papers, A-2 intelligence Reports
168.605–1 through 16, Elmer Adler Papers
168.7365–5 through 9, Bernard Haffey Memoirs
248.211–11 ACTS Memo, Direct Air Support in the Libyan Desert
248.222–83 Operational Notes for Light Bombers in the Western Desert
512.041–13, 32 Royal Air Force, Official History
512.430C The German Air Force in the Mediterranean
512.547E Air Ministry, Great Britain, Tactical Operations Notes, Light Bombers
512.547K Air Ministry, Great Britain, Tactics and Operational Notes of Heavy
Day Bombers in the Western Desert
512.5496 Great Britain, Royal Air Force Fighter and Bomber Tactics
512.607 Air Ministry, Great Britain, Weekly Intelligence Summaries
512.674 Axis Air Operations in the Mediterranean
520.056–267 376th Bomb Group
524.01 Eighth Fighter Command
533.308–4 Statistical Report on 9th Air Force Operations, 12-26-42 to 7-31-43
533.3069–3 9th Air Force Chronology
533.327 Orders, 9th Air Force
612.277–1 Northwest African Air Forces
616.101–1 Desert Air Force
622.424–1 Mediterranean Allied Air Forces
650.01–1 12th Air Force Administrative History
650.057–3 12th Air Force History
650.309–1 12th Air Force—Interviews
650.430–1 12th Air Force, Air Support for Operation TORCH
651.816 12th Air Support Command Records
654.01 12th Fighter Command records
655.01–2 12th Tactical Air Command
Curtis Low, Oral History interview
GP-1-SU-OP-S 1st Provisional Bomb Group Mission Reports

GP-12-SU-OP-S 12th Bomb Group Mission Reports
GP-52-SU-RE-D 52nd Fighter Group History
GP-57-HI 57th Fighter Group History
GP-57-SU-OP-s 57th Fighter Group Mission Summaries, 9-1-42 to 12-31-42
GP-98-SU-OP-S 98th Bomb Group Sortie Reports, 8-23-42 to 4-15-43
GP-301-H (BOMB) 301st Bomb Group History
K239.0512–1813 Reel 3, Elwood Quesada Oral History Interview
MICFILM 23111 Baldwin Papers
MICFILM 23341 Interview with Gen. Auby Strickland
MICFILM 25076 Mediterranean Allied Air Forces, Daily Intelligence Summaries
MICFILM 34133 Parton Papers
SQ-BOMB-82-SU-RE-D 82nd Bomb Squadron War Diary
WG-1-HI 1st Bombardment Wing

U.S. ARMY MILITARY HISTORY INSTITUTE, CARLISLE BARRACKS, PA
Gordon Saville Papers

UTAH STATE UNIVERSITY, LOGAN, UT
John Cannon Papers

Published Primary

Arnold, Henry. *Global Mission.* New York: Harper Brothers, 1949.
Bland, Larry I., et al., eds. *The Papers of George Catlett Marshall.* 5 vols. Baltimore: Johns Hopkins University Press, 1991.
Bradley, Omar. *The Effects of Strategic and Tactical Air Power on Military Operations, ETO.* Washington, DC: Government Printing Office, 1945.
———. *A Soldier's Story.* New York: Henry Holt, 1951.
Bradley, Omar, and Clair Blair. *A General's Life.* New York: Simon and Schuster, 1983.
Brereton, Lewis H. *The Brereton Diaries.* New York: Morrow, 1946.
Chennault, Claire, *The Way of a Fighter: The Memoirs of Claire Lee Chennault.* New York: Putnam, 1949.
Clark, Mark W., *Calculated Risk.* New York: Harper and Brothers, 1950.
von Clausewitz, Carl. *On War.* Trans. by Michael Howard and Peter Paret. Princeton: Princeton University Press, 1976.
Corbett, Julian. *Some Principles of Maritime Strategy.* Repr. New York: AMS Press, 1972.
Craig, Howard A. *Sunward I've Climbed.* El Paso: Texas Western Press, 1975.
de Seversky, Alexander. *Victory Through Airpower.* New York: Simon and Schuster, 1942.
Douhet, Giulio. *The Command of the Air.* Trans. Dino Ferrar. Repr. Washington, DC: Government Printing Office, 1998.

Doolittle, James. *I Could Never Be So Lucky Again*. New York: Bantam, 1991.

Eisenhower, Dwight D. *Crusade in Europe*. New York: Da Capo, 1948.

Eisenhower, Dwight D., Alfred D. Chandler, Louis Galambos, and Daun Van Ee. *The Papers of Dwight David Eisenhower*. Baltimore: Johns Hopkins University Press, 1970–2001.

Galland, Adolf. *The First and the Last: The Rise and Fall of the Luftwaffe*. New York: Ballantine, 1954.

Hansell, Haywood. *The Air Plan that Defeated Hitler*. Atlanta: Longino and Porter, 1972.

Kesselring, Albert. *The Memoirs of Field Marshall Kesselring*. Novato, CA: Presidio, 1989.

Mitchell, William (Billy). *Our Air Force: Keystone of National Defense*. New York: E. P. Dutton, 1921.

Momyer, William. *Airpower in Three Wars*. Washington, DC: Office of Air Force History, 1978.

Montgomery, Bernard. *Eighth Army: El Alamein to the River Sangro*. Germany (location unknown): Printing and Stationery Services, British Army of the Rhine, 1946.

Patton, George S. *War as I Knew It*. Boston: Houghton Mifflin, 1947.

Erwin Rommel, *The Rommel Papers*. Ed. B. H. Liddell Hart. New York: Harcourt, Brace, 1953.

Slessor, John. *Air Power and Armies*. London: Oxford University Press, 1936.

Steinhoff, Johannes. *Messerschmitts Over Sicily*. Repr. Mechanicsburg, PA: Stackpole, 2004.

Tedder, Sir Arthur. *With Prejudice*. Boston: Little, Brown, 1966.

Tibbets, Paul W. Jr. *The Tibbets Story*. New York: Stein and Day, 1978.

Truscott, Lucien K. *Command Decisions*. New York: E. P. Dutton, 1959.

Zuckerman, Sally. *From Apes to Warlords*. London: Collins, 1988.

Secondary

Abbatiello, John. *Anti-Submarine Warfare in World War I*. New York: Routledge, 2006.

Ackerman, Robert. *The Employment of Strategic Bombers in a Tactical Role, 1941–1951*. Washington, DC: Office of Air Force History, 1953.

Atkinson, Rick. *An Army at Dawn*. New York: Henry Holt, 2002.

———. *Day of Battle*. New York: Henry Holt, 2007.

Barr, Niall. *Pendulum of War*. London: Overlook, 2006.

Bechthold, B. Michael. "A Question of Success: Tactical Air Doctrine and Practice in North Africa, 1942–43." *Journal of Military History* 68:3 (July 2004): 821–851.

Biddle, Tami Davis. *Rhetoric and Reality in Air Warfare*. Princeton: Princeton University Press, 2002.

Blair, Clay. *Hitler's U-Boat War*. 2 vols. New York: Random House, 1996.

Blumenson, Martin. *Salerno to Cassino*. Washington, DC: Office of the Chief of Military History, 1969.

———. *Kasserine Pass*. Boston: Houghton Mifflin, 1966.

Boog, Horst, ed. *The Conduct of the Air War in the Second World War*. New York: Berg, 1992.

Byrd, Martha. *Chennault: Giving Wings to the Tiger*. Birmingham: University of Alabama Press, 1987.

Citino, Robert M. *Death of the Wehrmacht*. Lawrence: University Press of Kansas, 2007.

Clodfelter, Mark. *The Limits of Airpower*. New York: Free Press, 1989.

———. *Beneficial Bombing: The Progressive Foundations of American Air Power, 1917–1945*. Lincoln: University of Nebraska Press, 2010.

———. "A Strategy Based on Faith: The Enduring Appeal of Progressive American Airpower." *Joint Forces Quarterly* 49:2 (May 2008): 24–31, 150–160.

Coleman, John M. *The Development of Tactical Services in the Army Air Forces*. Morningside Heights, NY: Columbia University Press, 1950.

Coles, Harry. *The Army Air Forces in Amphibious Landings in World War II*. Washington, DC: Office of Air Force History, 1953.

———. *Ninth Air Force in the Western Desert Campaign to 23 January 1943*. Washington, DC: Army Air Forces Historical Division, 1945.

———. *Participation of the Ninth and Twelfth Air Forces in the Sicilian Campaign*. Army Air Forces Historical Study No. 37. Washington, DC: Army Air Forces Historical Office, 1945.

Cooling, Benjamin, ed. *Case Studies in the Development of Close Air Support*. Washington, DC: Office of Air Force History, 1990.

Corum, James S. *The Luftwaffe: Creating the Operational Air War, 1919–1940*. Lawrence: University Press of Kansas, 1997.

Corum, James S., and Wray Johnson. *Airpower in Small Wars: Fighting Insurgents and Terrorists*. Lawrence: University Press of Kansas, 2003.

Cox, Sebastian, and Peter Gray, eds. *Air Power History: Turning Points from Kitty Hawk to Kosovo*. London: Frank Cass, 2002.

Crane, Conrad. *Bombs, Cities, and Civilians: Airpower Strategy in World War II*. Lawrence: University Press of Kansas, 1993.

Craven, Wesley, and James Cate, eds. *The Army Air Forces in World War II*. Vols. 1–7. Chicago: University of Chicago Press, 1948–1951.

Davis, Richard G. *Carl A. Spaatz and the Air War in Europe*. Washington, DC: Center for Air Force History, 1993.

———. *Tempering the Blade: General Carl Spaatz and American Tactical Air Power in North Africa, November 8, 1942–May 14, 1943*. Washington, DC: Office of Air Force History, 1989.

———. "'Take Down That Damned Sign': Doolittle as Combat Commander." *Air Power History* 40:4 (Winter 1993): 16–21.

Deichmann, P. *German Air Force Operations in Support of the Army.* United States Air Force Historical Study No. 163. Maxwell AFB, AL: Air University Press, 1962.

Desert Campaign: The Story of the Ninth U.S. Army Air Force in Support of the British in Africa. Location Unknown: 9th Air Force, 1943. Available at http://home .comcast.net/~dhsetzer/paper_index.htm, accessed on 8 May 2012.

D'Este, Carlo. *World War II in the Mediterranean, 1942–45.* Chapel Hill, NC: Algonquin, 1990.

———. *Patton: A Genius for War.* New York: Harper Collins, 1995.

Dorr, Robert F., and Thomas D. Jones. *Hell Hawks: The Untold Story of the American Fliers Who Savaged Hitler's Wehrmacht.* Minneapolis: Zenith, 2008.

Dugan, James, and Carroll Stewart. *Ploesti: The Great Ground-Air Battle of 1 August 1943.* New York: Random House, 1962.

Earle, Edward Mead, ed. *Makers of Modern Strategy.* Princeton: Princeton University Press, 1943.

Ehlers, Robert S. Jr. *Targeting the Third Reich: Air Intelligence and the Allied Bombing Campaigns.* Lawrence: University Press of Kansas, 2009.

Finney, Robert. *History of the Air Corps Tactical School, 1920–1940.* Maxwell AFB, AL: USAF Historical Division, Air University, 1955. Available at http://www .afhso.af.mil/shared/media/document/AFD-100927-026.pdf, accessed on 8 May 2012.

Futrell, Robert. *Ideas, Concepts, Doctrine: Basic Thinking in the United States Air Force, 1907–1960.* Vol. 1. Maxwell AFB, AL: Air University Press, 1989.

Gabel, Christopher R. *The U.S. Army GHQ Maneuvers of 1991.* Washington, DC: Center of Military History, United States Army, 1991.

Gannon, James. *Stealing Secrets, Telling Lies: How Codebreakers Helped Shape the Twentieth Century.* Dulles, VA: Brassey's, 2001.

Garland, Albert. *Sicily and the Surrender of Italy.* Washington, DC: Department of the Army, 1965.

Gat, Azar. *A History of Military Thought from the Enlightenment to the Cold War.* Oxford, UK: Oxford University Press, 2001.

Gentile, Gian. *How Effective Is Strategic Bombing?* New York: New York University Press, 2001.

Gladman, Brad W. *Intelligence and Anglo-American Air Support in World War II.* London: Palgrave Macmillan, 2009.

Glantz, David M. *Red Storm over the Balkans: The Failed Soviet Invasion of Romania, Spring 1944.* Lawrence: University Press of Kansas, 2007.

Glantz, David M., and Jonathan House. *The Battle of Kursk.* Lawrence: University Press of Kansas, 2004.

Glenny, A.W.F. *Mediterranean Air Power and the Second Front.* London: Conrad, 1944.

Gooderson, Ian. *Air Power at the Battlefront.* London: Frank Cass, 1997.

Greenfield, Kent. *Army Ground Forces and the Air-Ground Battle Team.* Washington, DC: Office of the Chief of Military History, 1948.

Greer, Thomas. *The Development of Air Doctrine in the Army Air Arm, 1917–1941.* Maxwell AFB, AL: USAF Historical Division, Air University, 1953.

Grenier, John. *The First Way of War.* Cambridge, UK: Cambridge University Press, 2005.

Gundelach, Karl. *Die Deutsche Luftwaffe im Mittelmeer, 1940–1945* (The German Air Force in the Mediterranean, 1940–1945). Frankfurt: Lang, 1981.

Hallion, Richard. *Strike from the Sky: The History of Battlefield Air Attack, 1911–1945.* Washington, DC: Smithsonian Institution Press, 1989.

Hasegawa, Tsuyoshi. *Racing the Enemy: Stalin, Truman, and the Surrender of Japan.* Cambridge, MA: Belknap, 2005.

Hayward, Joel S.A. *Stopped at Stalingrad: The Luftwaffe and Hitler's Defeat in the East, 1942–43.* Lawrence: University Press of Kansas, 1998.

Herrington, John. *Australia in the War of 1939–1945.* 22 vols. Canberra: Australian War Memorial, 1952–1977.

Hill, Michael. *The Desert Rats: The 98th Bomb Group and the August 1943 Ploesti Raid.* Missoula, MT: Pictorial Histories, 1990.

Hinen, Anthony. "Kosovo: 'The Limits of Air Power II.'" *Chronicles Online Journal,* 16 May 2002. http://www.airpower.maxwell.af.mil/airchronicles/cc/hinen.html.

House, Jonathan. *Combined Arms Warfare in the Twentieth Century.* Lawrence: University Press of Kansas, 2001.

Howe, George. *Northwest Africa: Seizing the Initiative in the West.* Washington, DC: Center for Military History, 1956.

Hughes, Thomas Alexander. *Overlord: General Pete Quesada and the Triumph of Tactical Air Power in World War II.* New York: Free Press, 1995.

Hurley, Alfred. *Billy Mitchell: Crusader for Air Power.* Bloomington: University of Indiana Press, 1964.

Huston, James. "Tactical Use of Air Power in World War II: The Army Experience." *Military Affairs* 14:4 (Winter 1950): 166–185.

Jablonski, Edward. *Doolittle: A Biography.* New York: Doubleday, 1968.

Johnson, David E. *Fast Tanks and Heavy Bombers: Innovation in the U.S. Army, 1919–1945.* Ithaca: Cornell University Press, 1998.

Kennett, Lee. *A History of Strategic Bombing.* New York: Scribner, 1982.

Levine, Alan J. *The War Against Rommel's Supply Lines, 1942–43.* Westport, CT: Praeger, 1999.

Lewis, Adrian. *Omaha Beach: A Flawed Victory.* Chapel Hill: University of North Carolina Press, 2001.

———. *The American Culture of War: The History of U.S. Military Force from World War II to Operation Iraqi Freedom.* New York: Routledge, 2007.

Linn, Brian. *The Philippine War, 1899–1902.* Lawrence: University Press of Kansas, 2000.

MacCloskey, Monro. *Torch and the Twelfth Air Force.* New York: Richard Rosen, 1971.

Mark, Eduard. *Aerial Interdiction in Three Wars*. Washington, DC: Center for Air
Force History, 1994.

Maycock, Thomas J. "Notes on the Development of AAF Tactical Air Doctrine."
Military Affairs 14:4 (Winter 1950): 186–191.

———. *The Twelfth Air Force in the North African Winter Campaign*. Washington,
DC: Army Air Forces Historical Office, 1946.

McFarland, Stephen, and Newton Wesley. *To Command the Sky: The Battle for Air
Superiority over Germany, 1942–44*. Washington, DC: Smithsonian Institution
Press, 1991.

Meilinger, Philip S., ed. *The Paths of Heaven: The Evolution of Airpower Theory*.
Maxwell AFB, AL: Air University Press, 1997.

———. *Air Power: Myths and Facts*. Maxwell AFB, AL: Air University Press, 2003.

———. "The Historiography of Airpower: Theory and Doctrine." *Journal of Military History* 64:2 (April 2000): 467–501.

Messenger, Charles. *The Tunisian Campaign*. London: Ian Allan, 1992.

Mets, David. *Master of Airpower: General Carl A. Spaatz*. Novoto, CA: Presidio,
1988.

———. *The Air Campaign: John Warden and the Classical Airpower Theorists*. Maxwell AFB, AL: Air University Press, 1999.

Molony, C. J. C. *The Mediterranean and the Middle East*. 6 vols. *Volume 5: The Campaign in Sicily 1943 and the Campaign in Italy, 3rd September 1943 to 31st March
1944*. London: Her Majesty's Stationery Office, 1973.

Moorehead, Alan. *The March to Tunis: The North African War, 1940–1943*. New
York: Harper, 1943.

Morison, Samuel Eliot. *History of United States Naval Operations in World War II*. 15
vols. Boston: Little, Brown, 1947–1962.

Mortenson, Daniel. *Airpower and Ground Armies: Essays on the Evolution of Anglo-
American Air Doctrine, 1940–1943*. Maxwell AFB, AL: Air University Press, 1998.

———. *A Pattern for Joint Operations: World War II Close Air Support, North Africa*.
Washington, DC: Office of Air Force History, 1987.

Murray, Williamson. *Strategy for Defeat: The Luftwaffe, 1933–1945*. Maxwell AFB,
AL: Air University Press, 1983.

———. *Military Innovation in the Interwar Period*. Cambridge, UK: University
Press, 1996.

Murray, Williamson, and Allan Millett. *A War to be Won: Fighting the Second World
War*. Cambridge, MA: Belknap, 2000.

Nalty, Bernard C., *With Courage: The U.S. Army Air Forces in World War II*. Washington, DC: Air Force History and Museums Program, 1994.

Niestle, Axel. *German U-Boat Losses During World War II*. Annapolis: Naval Institute Press, 1998.

Newby, Leroy. *Into the Guns of Ploesti*. Osceola, WI: Motorbooks, 1991.

Olsen, John Andreas, ed. *A History of Air Warfare*. Washington, DC: Potomac,
2010.

Orange, Vincent. *Coningham*. Washington, DC: Center for Air Force History, 1992.

Overy, Richard J. *The Air War, 1939–1945*. Washington, DC: Potomac, 1980.

———. *Why the Allies Won*. New York: Norton, 1997.

Owen, Roderic. *The Desert Air Force*. London: Hutchinson, 1948.

Paret, Peter, ed. *Makers of Modern Strategy: From Machiavelli to the Nuclear Age*. Princeton: Princeton University Press, 1986.

Parton, James. *"Air Force Spoken Here": General Ira Eaker and the Command of the Air*. Bethesda, MD: Adler and Adler, 1986.

Perret, Geoffrey. *Winged Victory*. New York: Random House, 1993.

Playfair, I. S. O. *The Mediterranean and the Middle East*. 6 vols. *Volume 6: The Destruction of the Axis Forces in Africa*. London: Her Majesty's Stationery Office, 1966.

Porch, Douglas. *The Path to Victory: The Mediterranean Theater in World War II*. New York: Farrar, Straus and Giroux, 2004.

Pyle, Ernie. *Brave Men*. Repr. Lincoln: University Press of Nebraska, 2001.

———. *Here Is Your War*. New York: Tess, 2004.

Rodman, Matt. *A War of Their Own: Bombers over the Southwest Pacific*. Maxwell AFB, AL: Air University Press, 2005.

Rogers, Edith. *The AAF in the Middle East: A Study of the Origins of the Ninth Air Force*. Army Air Forces Historical Study No. 108. Washington, DC: Army Air Forces Historical Division, 1945.

———. *The Reduction of Pantelleria and Adjacent Islands, 8 May to 14 June 1943*. Army Air Forces Historical Study No. 52. Washington, DC: Army Air Forces Historical Division, 1947.

Rolf, David. *The Bloody Road to Tunis: Destruction of the Axis Forces in North Africa, November 1942–May 1943*. London: Greenhill, 2001.

Rust, Kenn C. *Fifteenth Air Force Story*. Terre Haute, IN: Sunshine House, 1976.

———. *Twelfth Air Force Story*. Temple City, CA: Historical Aviation, 1975.

Schoenfeld, Max. *Stalking the U-Boat*. Washington, DC: Smithsonian Institution Press, 1995.

Schultz, Duane. *Into the Fire: Ploesti, the Most Fateful Mission of World War II*. Yardley, PA: Westholme, 2007.

Sherry, Michael. *The Rise of American Air Power: The Creation of Armageddon*. New Haven: Yale University Press, 1987.

Showell, Jak P. Mallman. *Hitler's U-Boat Bases*. Annapolis: Naval Institute Press, 2002.

Spires, David N. *Patton's Air Force*. Washington DC: Smithsonian Institution Press, 2002.

Thruel, Richard, and Elliott Arnold. *Mediterranean Sweep*. New York: Duell, Sloan and Pearce, 1944.

Tibbets, Paul, Jr., with Clair Slebbins and Harry Franken. *The Tibbets Story*. New York: Stein and Day, 1978.

United States. *U.S. Army/Marine Corps Counterinsurgency Field Manual.* Chicago: University of Chicago Press, 2007.

Walker, James. *The Liberandos: A World War II History of the 376th Bomb Group.* Waco, TX: 376th Bomb Group Veteran's Association, 1994.

Warden, John A. *The Air Campaign: Planning for Combat.* Washington, DC: National Defense University Press, 1988.

Weinberg, Gerhard. *A World at Arms: A Global History of World War II.* Cambridge, UK: Cambridge University Press, 1994.

Wells, Mark. *Courage in Air Warfare.* New York: Routledge, 1995.

Westermann, Edward B. *Flak.* Lawrence: University Press of Kansas, 2001.

Winton, Harold R. "A Black Hole in the Wild Blue Yonder: The Need for a Comprehensive Theory of Air Power." *Air Power History* 39:4 (Winter 1992): 32–42.

Wolk, Herman S. "Pantelleria, 1943." *Air Force* 85:6 (June 2002): 64–68.

Theses and Dissertations

Cox, Gary. "Beyond the Battle Line: U.S. Air Attack Theory and Doctrine, 1919–1941." Thesis, School of Advanced Air and Space Studies, Maxwell AFB, AL, 1995.

Flugel, Raymond R. "United States Air Power Doctrine: A Study of the Influence of William Mitchell and Giulio Douhet at the Air Corps Tactical School, 1921–1935." Ph.D. diss., University of Oklahoma, 1965.

Haynes, Jeffrey T. "General Jacob E. Smart: Premier Staff Officer and Combat Planner." Thesis, School of Advanced Airpower Studies, Maxwell AFB, AL, 2008.

Weller, Grant. "'Come Hell, High Water, or Nazis': The U.S. Army Quartermaster Corps Develops and Implements the First Motorized Logistics System, 1919–1945." Ph.D. diss., Temple University, 2007.

Index

Adler, Elmer, 42, 65
Air Corps Tactical School, 10, 13–14, 16, 20, 26, 28, 32, 35–36, 241n19
aircraft
A-8 *Shrike*, 24
A-17 *Nomad*, 24
A-20 *Havoc/Boston*, 24, 29, 56–57, 81–82, 98 (photo), 119, 215, 219 (table), 221–222, 226–227, 231–233
A-36 *Apache*, 135, 155–157, 184, 217–218, 219 (table)
Albacore, 49, 56, 221, 224, 228–229, 231, 235–236
B-17 *Flying Fortress*, 37, 42–44, 48, 50–51, 63, 66, 68, 77–78, 80, 82, 97, 102, 104–107, 115, 124–126, 131, 136, 139, 144, 160, 163–164, 175, 183, 186, 188, 193, 213–217, 219 (table), 223, 225, 227, 233, 235
B-24 *Liberator*, 24, 28 (photo), 45–46, 48–51, 60, 63, 66, 68, 71–72, 74–75, 95, 97, 105, 113–114, 136, 144, 160–161, 163, 168, 173–175, 178, 187–188, 193, 196, 213–214, 219 (table), 222–224, 235–237, 262n8
B-25 *Mitchell*, 29, 44–45, 52, 56–57, 63, 111, 112 (photo), 126, 156, 196, 215, 219 (table), 222, 225–226, 231, 233–234
B-26 *Marauder*, 29, 78, 126, 215, 219 (table), 221, 225–226, 234–235
B-29 *Superfortress*, 40

B-52 *Stratofortress*, 27
Baltimore, 56, 63, 222, 224, 231–232, 236–237
Beaufighter, 56, 221, 224–225, 227, 235–237
Beaufort, 47–48, 222, 236–237
Bisley, 221–222, 225, 233
Blenheim, 221–222, 237
Bombay, 222
C-47 *Skytrain/Dakota*, 64, 77, 80, 86–90, 102, 112, 113 (photo), 119, 124, 149, 150, 153, 187, 218, 219 (table), 222, 227, 235–236
CG-4A *Hadrian* (glider), 153
Dewoitine De-520, 90, 229–230
E-3A AWACS, 267n19
E-8C Joint STARS, 267n19
F4F *Wildcat/Martlet*, 228–229
Fulmar, 224, 228–229
Halifax, 45, 56, 222, 238
Hudson, 112, 222, 225, 227, 231, 235, 237–238
Hurricane/Sea Hurricane, 41, 57, 62, 90, 221, 223–224, 228, 232, 234, 237
Lodestar, 222, 238
Maryland, 221, 223
Mosquito, 131, 178, 217, 227, 236
P-38 *Lightning*, 66, 77, 80, 102, 115, 117, 124–127, 131, 155, 157, 184, 213, 216–219, 226, 233–234
P-39 *Airacobra*, 17, 77, 79–80, 101, 117, 119, 131, 215–217, 219 (table), 227, 231, 235

aircraft, *continued*
   P-40 *Warhawk/Kittyhawk*, 17, 44, 52,
      57, 58, 61, 77, 92, 94, 111, 117,
      128, 155, 157, 196, 216–218, 219
      (table), 223, 226, 228, 231–232,
      234
   P-47 *Thunderbolt*, 17, 58, 155, 213,
      217–218
   P-51 *Mustang*, 76, 79, 155, 217–218
   PBY *Catalina*, 95, 227–228
   RC-135 *Rivet Joint*, 267n19
   SBD *Dauntless*, 228
   Spitfire/Seafire, 41, 62, 77, 79, 83,
      88–91, 117, 119, 128, 184, 216–
      217, 219 (table), 221, 223–224,
      226–229, 231–232, 234–237
   Sunderland, 221, 227
   Swordfish, 221, 224–225, 235–236
   TBF *Avenger*, 228
   Typhoon, 58
   Walrus, 222, 225, 237
   Wellesley, 222
   Wellington, 43, 46, 48, 56, 62, 137,
      145, 160, 165, 215, 221–222, 225,
      233, 236–238
Air Force, U.S. (USAF), including
   U.S. Army Air Force
   (USAAF), 37–38
Air Combat Command (ACC),
   194
Air War Planning Document 1
   (AWPD-1), 18, 40, 69, 172, 191
Air War Planning Document 42
   (AWPD-42), 169, 172
Antisubmarine Command, 71
antisubmarine warfare, 68, 75,
   84–85
asset allocation, 3–5, 11, 67, 70–72,
   77, 81, 96, 115, 124–125, 144–145,
   149, 155, 157, 161, 168, 183, 191,
   197, 213
attrition/losses, 91, 101–102, 132,
   163, 168, 177, 179, 183, 197, 215,
   270n25

Commands
   I Bomber, 71
   IX Fighter, 32
   XII Air Support (ASC), 26,
      117–118, 120, 121, 147
   XII Tactical Air (TAC), 193
   XIX Tactical Air (TAC), 23
   Strategic Air (SAC), 194
   Tactical Air (TAC), 194
   doctrinal development, 10, 20–23,
      25–26, 33, 35–36, 40
   duplication of mission with U.S.
      Navy, 70–71
   effective sortie rates, comparison
      between Eighth and Twelfth
      Air Forces, 132, 191–192
   Field Manual 100-20, 3, 23, 31, 33, 35
Groups
   1st Fighter/Pursuit, 77–78, 102,
      219 (table), 226, 233
   1st Provisional Bombardment,
      Heavy, 50, 55, 60, 62, 223
      (*see also* 376th Bombardment
      Group)
   2nd Bombardment, Heavy, 125,
      144, 219 (table), 233
   3rd Photographic
      Reconnaissance, 131, 219 (table),
      227, 235
   5th Photographic
      Reconnaissance, 219 (table)
   7th Bombardment, Heavy, 50
   12th Bombardment, Medium, 44,
      52, 55, 56, 61, 63, 111, 117, 219
      (table), 222, 231, 233
   14th Fighter/Pursuit, 77, 102,
      219 (table), 226
   17th Bombardment, Medium, 126,
      219 (table), 226, 234
   27th Bombardment, Light, 155–
      156, 219 (table)
   31st Fighter/Pursuit, 77–79, 83,
      90–91, 117, 219 (table), 226,
      231

33rd Fighter/Pursuit, 92, 94–95, 117, 142–143, 219 (table), 226, 231

44th Bombardment, Heavy, 176–177, 188

47th Bombardment, Light, 219 (table), 226, 233

52nd Fighter/Pursuit, 77, 79, 88–91, 119, 219 (table), 226, 231

57th Fighter/Pursuit, 44, 52–53, 55, 57–58, 61, 63–64, 111, 128, 219 (table), 223, 232

60th Troop Carrier, 77–78, 86–88, 149, 219 (table), 227, 236

61st Troop Carrier, 149, 219 (table)

62nd Troop Carrier, 102, 149, 219 (table), 227, 235

64th Troop Carrier, 90, 102, 149, 219 (table), 227, 235

68th Observation, 117, 227, 231

79th Fighter/Pursuit, 64, 111, 128, 219 (table), 232

81st Fighter/Pursuit, 117, 219 (table), 227, 235

82nd Fighter/Pursuit, 219 (table), 226, 234

86th Bombardment, Light, 155, 219 (table)

91st Bombardment, Heavy, 124–125

93rd Bombardment, Heavy, 75, 105, 114–115, 176, 188

97th Bombardment, Heavy, 77–79, 82–83, 102, 106–107, 124, 144, 219 (table), 225, 233

98th Bombardment, Heavy, 45, 45–46, 51, 55, 60, 62, 64, 113, 115, 144, 176–177, 188, 219 (table), 224, 236

99th Bombardment, Heavy, 125, 144, 219 (table), 233

301st Bombardment, Heavy, 77, 102, 106–107, 124–125, 127, 144, 219 (table), 225, 233

306th Bombardment, Heavy, 124

310th Bombardment, Medium, 126, 219 (table), 225, 234

313th Troop Carrier, 149, 219 (table)

314th Troop Carrier, 149, 219 (table)

316th Troop Carrier, 64, 111, 113, 219 (table), 236

319th Bombardment, Medium, 126, 219 (table), 225, 234

320th Bombardment, Medium, 126, 219 (table), 225, 234

321st Bombardment, Medium, 126, 219 (table), 226, 234

323rd Service, 55

324th Fighter/Pursuit, 111, 219 (table), 232

325th Fighter/Pursuit, 132, 219 (table), 234

340th Bombardment, Medium, 111, 156, 219 (table)

350th Fighter/Pursuit, 219 (table), 227, 235

376th Bombardment, Heavy, 45, 62, 105, 113, 115, 144, 176, 188, 219 (table), 236 (see also 1st Provisional Bombardment Group)

389th Bombardment, Heavy, 175–176, 188

480th Antisubmarine Group, 95

Halverson Provisional Detachment (HALPRO), 4, 45–47, 48–50, 171, 195

insignia, 153

interdiction, 30, 31, 39, 60, 62–63, 85, 108, 113–114, 118, 121, 123–127, 128–129, 135, 158–167, 193, 207

Air Force, U.S., *continued*
  Middle East Air Force (MEAF), 39, 44
  mission, 1–2
  organization, 79, 120, 131, 192–194, 218–219, 221–238
  School of Advanced Air and Space Studies (SAASS), 33
  Squadrons
    15th Bombardment, Light, 226
    99th Pursuit/Fighter (Tuskegee Airmen), 143, 216
  strategic bombing, 5–7, 20, 23, 26, 31, 33, 36, 39–40, 71, 84, 96, 115, 123, 132, 144, 157, 165, 168–182, 189–192, 195–196, 200, 202, 210, 213
  strength, 99, 144, 183–184, 218
  support for ground forces, 5, 10, 11, 54–55, 57, 85, 91, 109–110, 121–123, 154–158, 166–167, 186–187, 193, 198, 200, 202, 204, 213, 247n61
  support for naval forces, 146–148, 166–167, 198, 204
  tactics
    escorted bomber, 114–115, 184, 214, 217
    fighter-bomber, development of, 57–58, 216
    low-level, 172–173, 263n9
    skip-bombing, 126
Alamein, El. *See* El Alamein
Alam Halfa, Battle of, 56–59
Alexander, Sir Harold, 19 (photo), 187
Alexandra, Katherine, 8, 40
Algeria, 2, 4
  Biskra airfield, 102, 124
  Bône, 102, 146
  La Senia and Tafaraoui airfields, near Oran, 87, 88–91, 102, 229
  Maison Blanche airfield, near Algiers, 90–91, 102, 230

Tebessa airfield, 118
Youks les Bains airfield, 102, 119
Anderson, Sir Kenneth, 109, 118
Andrews, Frank, 74, 144
ARCADIA Conference (Washington, DC, January 1941–1942), 45
Army, British
  Eighth Army, 2, 35, 43, 49, 59, 111, 118, 122, 131, 152, 158, 160
  Fifth Infantry Division, 150
  First Airborne Division, 152
  First Airlanding Brigade, 150
  First Army, 102, 109
  First Infantry Division, 138
Army, U.S., 23
  18th Infantry Regiment, 147
  82nd Airborne Division, 152, 153, 187
  503rd Parachute Infantry Regiment (PIR), 87, 102
  504th Parachute Infantry Regiment (PIR), 150–151, 187
  505th Parachute Infantry Regiment (PIR), 150, 187
  AirLand Battle doctrine, 27
  Command and General Staff College (CGSC), 34
  Field Manual 31-35, 10, 21–22, 25, 27, 29, 31, 35, 53, 110
  Fifth Army, 188
  First Armored Division, 29–30, 108
  Seventh Army, 152, 154, 158–160
Arnim, Hans-Jurgen von, 116
Arnold, Henry H. "Hap"
  and asset allocation/employment decisions, 44, 70, 73–74, 81, 106, 144, 218
  attacks on Rome, 161
  and Elliott Roosevelt, 131–132
  papers, 8
  Ploesti raid, 169, 172
  on strategic bombing, 183, 190, 192
  and support for ground forces, 29, 64, 109–110, 152

Arnold-Portal-Towers Agreement, 44, 52
Auchinleck, Claude, 49

Barwell, George, 263n21
Battle of the Atlantic, 68–77, 197
BAYTOWN, Operation (British amphibious assault of Italy, September 1943), 184
Bentley, Charles, 87–88
BOLERO, Operation (buildup of forces in the United Kingdom, 1942) 44
Bradley, Omar, 5, 22, 154, 193
Brereton, Lewis Hyde,
    background, 19–20
    in the Middle East, 50, 52–53, 55
    and Philippine Islands, 42
    and Ploesti raid, 182
    questionable decisions, 175
Brett, George H., 40
Brooke, Sir Alan, 116, 117, 174, 189

Cannon, John, 14, 32, 94–95
Carolina maneuvers, 22
Casablanca Conference, 2, 72, 115, 136, 161, 169
Chandler, P. R., 54–55
Chennault, Claire, 14, 32
Churchill, Sir Winston, 2, 189
Clark, Mark, 80
Clausewitz, Carl von, 2, 9, 200, 202–203, 207, 211
Combined Bomber Offensive
    competition with North African campaign for assets, 165, 169, 174, 180
    early failures and limitations, 100, 189, 206
    origins, 115
    results and costs, 5, 200–201
    See also Air Force, U.S., strategic bombing

Combined Chiefs of Staff (CCS)
    and antisubmarine campaign, 70, 72–73, 214
    asset allocation decisions, 4–5, 144, 180, 186, 190
    and Ploesti raid, 162–163, 169, 173–174
Coningham, Sir Arthur, 19 (photo), 61, 111, 120, 196 (photo)
    and cooperation with Eighth Army, 24, 34, 49, 63
    doctrinal development, 36
    incident with George Patton, 122–123
Corbett, Sir Julian, 195, 206–211
CORKSCREW, Operation (reduction of Pantelleria, 1943), 136–143
Corsica, 2, 136
Craig, Howard, 81
Craw, Demas T., 43–44, 94–95
Cunningham, Sir Andrew, 19 (photo), 160–161
Cyprus, 52, 177

Davis, Benjamin, 143
DESERT STORM, Operation (liberation of Kuwait, 1991), 31, 202
de Seversky, Alexander, 9, 11, 13, 16–17
Devers, Jacob, 163
Dill, Sir John, 70, 73, 75
Doolittle, James H. "Jimmy," 196 (photo)
    background, 18–19
    command of Eighth Air Force, 192–193
    criticism of Pantelleria, 139–140
    employment of aircraft types, 213–215
    in North Africa, 90–91, 95, 108, 120
    papers, 8
    raid on Tokyo, 45
    and replacements, 164

Douhet, Giulio, 9, 11–13, 16, 34, 141, 207, 209–210
    and chemical attack, 12
Drummond, Sir Peter, 65
Duncan, Asa, 80

Eaker, Ira
    and diversion of assets from Eighth Air Force, 77, 84–85, 96, 124–125, 163, 174–175, 178, 180, 188, 191–192, 213
    and Eighth Air Force, 82, 107
    papers, 8
Eisenhower, Dwight D., 19 (photo)
    Allied cooperation, 122–123
    at Casablanca Conference, 116
    knowledge of air operations, 85, 147–148, 166, 198
    and Operation OVERLORD, 193
    and Operation TORCH, 72, 82–83, 104–107
    and Pantelleria, 136–137, 139
    papers, 8
    and Ploesti, 161–163
    requests for heavy bombers, 4, 124, 144, 178, 184, 186
    and Robinett, Paul, 110
    and Sicily, 150
    and Spaatz, Carl, 79–80
    and strategic bombing, 189–190
    and Tunisian campaign, 117–118
El Alamein, 4, 49, 51, 199, 221
Ent, Uzal B., 175–176
ethnic cleansing, 6

ferry routes, air, 41, 46, 52, 101
FLAX, Operation (intercept of Axis transport aircraft, April, 1943), 127–128

genocide, 6
George, Harold, 32, 241n19
Gibraltar, 2
Goering, Hermann, 201

GOMORRAH, Operation (fire-bombing of Hamburg, 1943), 69, 142
Goodrich, Charles, 56, 62
Greece, 43, 60, 136, 145, 177
GYMNAST, Operation (original name for invasion of Northwest Africa), 77, 80. See also TORCH, Operation

Halverson, Harry A., 45, 47, 50–51, 168–169
Hamilton, Pierpont M., 94
Handy, Thomas T., 104
Hansell, Haywood, 191, 241n19
Harris, Sir Arthur "Bomber," 165
Hewitt, Kent, 147, 154
Hopkins, Harry, 81
Hopper, Bruce, 201
Hube, Hans, 160
HUSKY, Operation (invasion of Sicily, July 1943), 73, 115, 134, 136, 161, 171, 174

intelligence
    bomb damage assessment, 84, 178, 180–181
    code-breaking, 60, 129, 176
    collection and dissemination, 53–55, 129–132, 148
    deception, 259n30
    and Operation FLAX, 127
Iraq
    air base at Habbaniyah, 46–47
IRAQI FREEDOM, Operation (invasion of Iraq, 2003), 204
Italy, 184
    Anzio, 193
    Bari, 241n5
    Foggia, 166, 188
    Naples, 105, 114, 166
    Regia Aeronautica (Air Force), 197
    Regia Marina (Navy), 47, 105, 126, 148
    Salerno, 166, 168, 183–194

Viterbo, 146
See also Sicily

Japan, 201, 240n13
Jocelyn, Bridget, 6, 29
Johnson, Leon, 177
Joint Chiefs of Staff (U.S.), 178, 184
joint operations, 6, 13, 128–129, 160,
        186–187, 199–201, 204–205, 211
    studies of, 27, 36–37, 129
JUGGLER, Operation (raids on strategic
        targets in Austria, 1943), 184

Kane, John R., 176–177
Kasserine Pass, Battle of, 117–119, 121
Kegelman, Charles, 82
Kenney, George, 31–32, 36
Kesselring, Albert, 121
King, Ernest J., 69, 73–74, 81
Kosovo, 143, 240n13
Kremer, Richard, 132
Krista, Marie, 9, 23
Kuter, Laurence, 172, 241n19

Leahy, William D., 73
LeMay, Curtis, 165
Libya, 2, 240n13
    Benghazi, 4, 43, 48–51, 60, 63, 105,
        114, 162, 169, 174, 176–177
    Tobruk, 4, 43, 49–51, 56, 62–63
    Tripoli, 114–115
logistics, 188, 204, 220
    airlift, 86, 111–112, 124, 218
    in Egypt and the Western Desert,
        41, 58–60
    Gura, Eritrea, air depot at, 42
    Rayak, Syria, air depot at, 42, 55
    and Sicilian campaign, 136
    and Tunisian campaign, 100, 104,
        107–108
Louisiana maneuvers, 22
Lovett, Robert, 166

MacArthur, Douglas, 31, 42, 147, 175

Madeleine, Elise, 9, 18
Mahan, Alfred Thayer, 210
Malta, 2, 136, 139
    air garrison, 224, 236
    Axis attacks on, 43, 47–48, 98, 134
    interdiction of Axis supply lines, 4,
        60, 128
Marseilles, Istres-Le Tube and Salon
        airfields, 164
Marshall, George C.
    and air warfare, 18, 92, 198
    allocation decisions, 73
    and Ploesti raid, 171, 173–175
    strategic views, 81
    support for ground forces, 109–110
Martelli, G. A., 141
Massachusetts Institute of Technology
        (MIT), 18
Maxwell, Russell L., 42
McGuire, George, 51
McNair, Leslie, 22, 152–153
McNarney, Joseph, 173–174
medical evacuation (medevac), 121
Mersa Matruh, 50, 56
Midway, Battle of, 48, 78
Milosevic, Slobodan, 143
Mitchell, William "Billy," 9, 11, 23, 34,
        205–206, 209–210
    Ostfriesland trial, 17
    publications, 15
Momyer, William, 92, 142–143
Montgomery, Sir Bernard Law, 23, 35,
        59, 63, 152, 160, 193
Morocco, French, 2, 4, 101
    Port Lyautey airfield, 92, 94, 230
Morocco, Spanish, 87–88, 101
Murray, Williamson, 13, 31, 134, 204
Mussolini, Benito, 2, 161

Navy, U.S., 86, 90, 95, 142, 147, 151–
        154, 160, 201, 228
    aircraft allocation for antisubmarine
        warfare, 73–74
    at Battle of Midway, 78

Navy, U.S., *continued*
    USS *Chenango* ferries 33rd Fighter
        Group, 92
    USS *Ranger, 228*
        ferries 57th Pursuit Group, 52
        and Operation TORCH, 92, 94
    VLR aircraft, 69

Newton, Dorr, 155–156
Nimitz, Chester, 147
Noble, Sir Percy, 74
Norstad, Lauris, papers, 8
North Atlantic Treaty Organization
        (NATO), 142, 240n13

Office of Strategic Services (OSS),
        180
OVERLORD, Operation (invasion of
        France, 6 June 1944), 77, 137,
        140, 149

Pantelleria, 136. *See also* CORKSCREW,
        Operation
Patch, Alexander "Sandy," 201
Patton, George, 23, 94–95, 122–123, 158,
        160, 193, 198
Pavesi, Gino, 138, 141
Philippines, 19
Ploesti, 4–5
    first raid (June 1942), 46–47
    second raid (August 1943), 136, 161,
        163, 168–184, 186, 197, 214 (*see
        also* TIDALWAVE, Operation)
Portal, Sir Charles
    and allocation of RAF aircraft, 44,
        45, 115, 165
    and the antisubmarine campaign, 72
    cooperation with the U.S. Army
        Air Force, 81
    and P-51 development, 79
    and Ploesti raid, 169, 171, 174
    and strategic bombing, 190
Portugal, 101

QUADRANT Conference (Quebec,
        August, 1943), 178
Quesada, Elwood "Pete," 32, 36

Raff, Edson, 87
Raymond, William, 87
Republic Aviation, 17
Ridgway, Matthew, 152–154
Robinett, Paul M., 29–30, 108–110, 118
ROLLING THUNDER, Operation, 142
Rommel, Erwin, 2, 56, 58–59
Roosevelt, Elliott, 131–132, 148–149
Roosevelt, Franklin D., 2, 41, 44
ROUNDUP, Operation, 77, 80, 86. *See
        also* OVERLORD, Operation
Royal Air Force (RAF), 137, 146, 215–
        216, 221–238, 263n21
    aid to USAAF groups, 37–38, 52–53
    Bomber Command, 70, 76, 115
    close support, 20, 29, 53–54, 57, 110,
        247n61
    Coastal Command, 71, 76, 227
    doctrine, 14–15, 23–24, 34–35
    Eastern Air Command, 102, 107,
        224
    heavy bombers in Middle East, 43,
        45, 49–51, 62, 113–114, 245n15
    interdiction, 96–97, 128–129, 160,
        256n79
    losses, El Alamein, 63–64
    strength, 62, 99
    Western Desert Air Force (WDAF),
        35, 41, 48–50, 111–112, 120, 127,
        131, 222–223, 231
Royal Australian Air Force (RAAF),
        46, 222, 223, 232, 237–238
Royal Canadian Air Force (RCAF), 73,
        75, 165, 224, 232
Royal Navy, 48, 60, 96–97, 140–141,
        160, 209–210, 228–229
    Fleet Air Arm, 49, 86, 88–90,
        221–222, 224–225, 228–229, 231,
        235–237

Sardinia, 2, 98, 100, 102, 125, 136, 143–144
    La Maddalena, raid on, 126
Seversky, Alexander de. *See* de Seversky, Alexander
Sicily, 2, 4, 98, 100, 114, 135–167, 177, 184, 186
    Adrano, 158
    Bocca di Falco airfield, 127
    Bo Rizzo airfield, 127
    Gela, 151
    Gerbini, 145–146
    Palermo, 125, 154–155
    Trapani airfield, 127
    Troina, 156
    See also HUSKY, Operation
SLEDGEHAMMER, Operation (plan for emergency invasion of France, 1942–1943), 77, 80–81, 86
Slessor, J. C., 15
Smart, Jacob, 172–175, 177
SOAPSUDS, Operation, 174. *See also* Ploesti; TIDALWAVE, Operation
South African Air Force (SAAF), 57, 223, 232, 237
Soviet Union, 40–41, 65, 115, 174, 181, 199, 201, 215, 240n13
Spaatz, Carl, 19 (photo), 196 (photo)
    and aircraft allocation decision, 157
    on aircraft types, 213–214, 216–217
    and antisubmarine campaign, 84
    and attacks on Rome, 161
    on attrition and replacement rates, 164, 192, 218
    background, 18, 24
    as commander, Eighth Air Force, 78–81
    as commander, Northwest African Air Forces, 120
    and Coningham-Patton incident, 123
    on Elliott Roosevelt, 148–149
    on 99th Pursuit Squadron (Tuskegee Airmen), 143
    on observation aircraft, 130–131
    and Pantelleria, 141
    papers, 8
    and postwar organization of the USAF, 194
    and Salerno landings, 184
    and Sicilian campaign, 145
    on strategic bombing, 157, 166, 189, 191, 201
    and support of ground forces, 6, 30
    and Tunisian campaign, 95–96, 106–108
Stalin, Josef, 65
Stalingrad, 4, 199, 209, 254n41
    German losses at, 128
    impact on air operations in North Africa, 58, 65, 116, 134, 197
Stark, Harold, 70
Steinhoff, Johannes, 145–146
STRANGLE, Operation, 192
Stratemeyer, George, 73, 106, 125
Suez Canal, 2, 38
Sutherland, Richard K., 42

Tedder, Sir Arthur, 19 (photo), 196 (photo)
    aircraft allocation, 165
    British-American cooperation, 65, 105
    building the Western Desert Air Force, 41, 45, 62
    and Operation FLAX, 127
    and P-51, 155
    Ploesti raid, 178
    role and responsibilities, 18, 120, 192–193
    and Sicilian campaign, 160–161
    on strategic bombing, 189
Thach, John S., 78
Tibbets, Paul, 82, 85
TIDALWAVE, Operation, 161–162, 177, 184. *See also* Ploesti

TORCH, Operation, 4, 44, 65–68, 83,
    85–97, 221
Towers, John, 44, 69
Trenchard, Sir Hugh, 11, 205
TRIDENT Conference (Washington,
    DC, 1943), 162, 173
Truman, Harry, 166
Truscott, Lucien, 94
Tunisia, 2, 4, 28, 97–134
    Bizerte, 114, 146
    Depienne airfield, 102–103
    El Aouina airfield, Tunis, 102, 126–
        127, 230
    Oudna airfield, 104
    Sfax, 114, 116
    Sidi Ahmed airfield, near Bizerte,
        127, 230
    Sousse, 114, 125
    Thelepte airfield, 118–119

Turkey, 46, 106, 169, 171, 177

Vandenberg, Hoyt, 32, 36, 81, 190, 201
Vietnam, 202
von Arnim, Hans-Jurgen, 116
von Clausewitz, Carl. See Clausewitz,
    Carl von
von Waldau, Otto, 63

Waldau, Otto von, 63
Warden, John, 202–203
Warner, Edward, 11, 34
Weyland, Otto, 32
Williams, Paul, 153
Winton, Harold, 211

ZITADELLE, Operation, 174
Zuckerman, Dr. Solly, 114, 123, 141